**GERMAN COURAGE instead of GERMAN ANGST**
44 IDEAS FOR A BRIGHTER FUTURE

Die Deutsche Bibliothek – CIP Einheitsaufnahme:

German courage instead of German angst
44 ideas for a brighter future

Deutscher Wirtschaftsbuch Verlag, Tegernsee 2023
ISBN 978-3-949981-01-2

Editor: Prof. Dr. Ulrich Reinhardt,
Foundation for Future Studies – an Initiative of BAT,
in cooperation with the WEIMER MEDIA GROUP GmbH

Layout: Ulrike Mieth
Portrait illustration: Andrea Rexhausen
Print and binding: Westermann Druck Zwickau GmbH

Printed in Germany

ULRICH REINHARDT

# GERMAN COURAGE
## instead of GERMAN ANGST

### 44 IDEAS FOR A BRIGHTER FUTURE

DEUTSCHER
WIRTSCHAFTSBUCH
VERLAG

# CONTENT

# 01

## ABOUT COURAGE

Ulrich Reinhardt

# 02
## MORE COURAGE

# 03
## 44 INTERVIEWS

# ABOUT COURAGE

Ulrich Reinhardt

# ULRICH REINHARDT

Scientific Head of the "Foundation for Future Studies –
an Initiative of BAT"

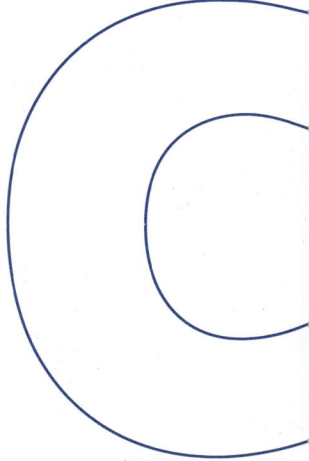

*German courage* instead of *German angst*. The central focus of this book is on this vision. Based on 24 qualitative interviews with individuals, four focus groups as well as a representative survey of more than 3,000 participants, we will gain insights into the current emotional stance of the German nation. Is the majority of German citizens in fact caught in a trap of concerns and safety needs that prevent an optimistic future outlook as so many in the media and members of the public would have you believe?

Or does this assessment merely conceal the unused potential of courage and confidence that would allow us to embrace future challenges with optimism?

To gain a closer connection to the sources and opportunities inherent in courage, as well as to understand the hindrances and reasons affiliated with boldness, it is important to also understand the opposite – fear. What role does fear play in the lives of German citizens, how does it affect their behaviour and how can it be overcome? Looking back, it is evident that the characteristics of fear have evolved throughout the course of history. The term "angst" has its roots in ancient High German and is derived from the words "angust" or "angustia", which are equivalent to being in a predicament or in distress. In antique mythology, these terms were primarily used in the context of concrete threats, such as earthquakes, hurricanes, thunderstorms or volcanic eruptions. Heroes, who were much admired in all antique cultures, were role models who were able to defeat and overcome fears caused by demons, sea

OUR

about
**COURAGE**

monsters or dragons thanks to their heroic courage. The descriptions of angst used back in those days with regard to physical symptoms are still commonly used in colloquial language today, for instance when we say that fear makes the hair stand up on the backs of our necks, that our eyes bulge out and our pupils expand, our ears start ringing and we stop breathing or cannot talk, or our heart beats loudly, our pulse races and our knees are buckling whenever we are afraid of something. Greek philosophers recommended rationality and inner reflection on emotions as tools to combat fears. However, they also regarded angst as a helpful response to take reasonable precautions in the event of dangers. The Bible often cites fear as a sign of being amazed by the wonders and appearances as well as an expression of respect and reverence for God. Psalms 34.9 says it all: "Fear the LORD, you His saints, for those who fear Him lack nothing."

During the era of Enlightenment, angst was considered a strictly negative term and was associated with irrationality and superstition. Instead of fearfully submitting to it, people were told to put their brains to use and to demonstrate intellectual reason along with free will. "Have the courage to use your own intelligence", Kant wrote in 1784. By the end of the 19th century, during the transition period to modern times, the emerging discipline of psychology interpreted angst as a complex emotional state that could be both, a response to external threats and an indication of internal conflicts. According to Freud, the psycho analyst, it springs from unprocessed conflicts still present in the subconscious and is an important reference point in being able to understand human behaviours.

These days, the meaning of angst is strongly affected by values, convictions and cultural peculiarities. Although direct external threats have declined – at least in the industrial nations – a number of fears are frequently evident on the personal level. As a result of the increased global challenges paired with a decrease in actual social relationships, growing digitization and within a multi-options society, many individuals are overwhelmed by a sense of having no direction and control over their own living scenarios, which leads to a sense of being the victims of excessive demands and powerlessness. Angst is not always tangible but is perceived as a diffuse feeling of uncertainty and instability.

In this context, it also appears that *German angst* is not solely a phenomenon in Germany but is part of the general sensitivity of the western world. Yet, some typical German oddities are in evidence.

**The term *German angst*, which today is also used in the English language, refers to a generally negative and hesitant stance among German citizens as far as the future is concerned.**

As a result, changes are accepted very slowly, and the actions of people are characterized by concerns and a strong need for certainty. The reasons for this can be primarily attributed to history and the different fear cycles anchored in the former. These anxieties range from fear of retribution in the years just after the war to the fear of communism related to the Cold War (which was dominant in the western parts of Germany in the 1950s), the fear of revolution in the 1960s and 1970s to the fear of forest devastation and nuclear warfare in the 1980s. After the reunification of Germany, worries about, among other things, the gulf war, the September 11, 2001 terrorist attacks, the reactor disaster in Fukushima, the bird flu, the challenges of the refuge migration, the Covid-19 pandemic and the war in Ukraine fuelled the fears, concerns, and worries of the German nation. Every one of these periods amplified the subsequent one and thus, over time, created a climate of general uncertainty. However, in conjunction with this we often underestimate the positive impact the historic and latest events as well as the developments had on German sensitivities and still have today. Among these drivers are the introduction of the social market economy, the expansion of the social services and benefits system, innovation in the fields of renewable energy, the automotive industry or biotechnology, the reconciliation with the nation's eastern European neighbours, the reunification as well as the European integration or the fostering of equal rights and cultural diversity. All of these developments have an impact on both, the individual citizen and society as a whole. They speak to determination, courage and confidence. An annual comparison of the German population's concerns for the future confirms this.

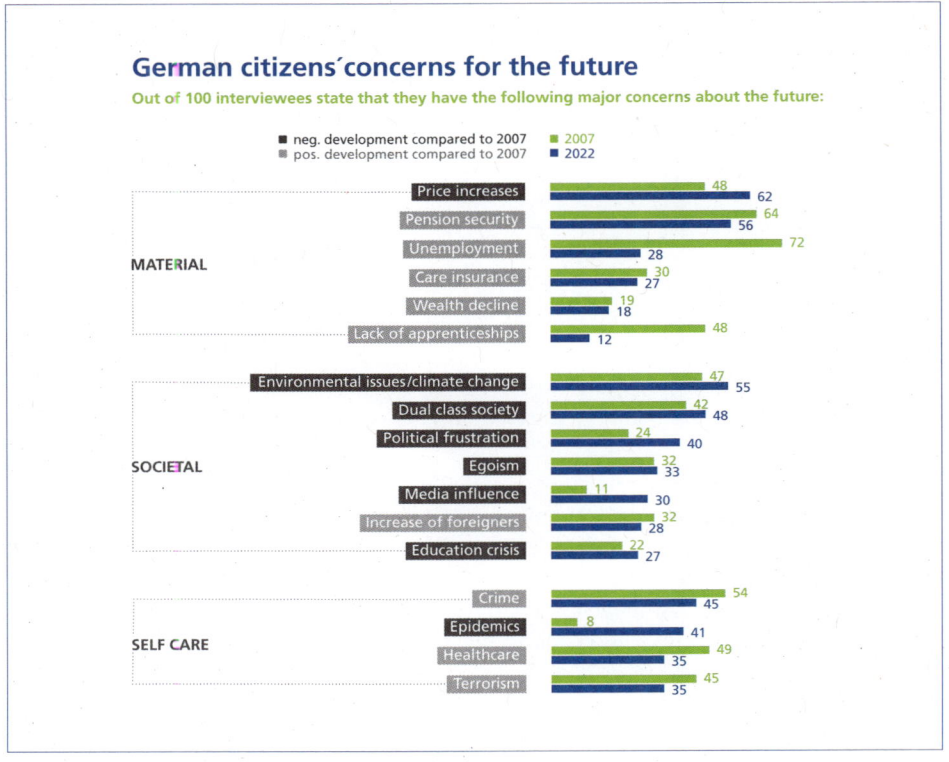

### German citizens´concerns for the future

Out of 100 interviewees state that they have the following major concerns about the future:

■ neg. development compared to 2007
■ pos. development compared to 2007

■ 2007
■ 2022

**MATERIAL**

| | 2007 | 2022 |
|---|---|---|
| Price increases | 48 | 62 |
| Pension security | 64 | 56 |
| Unemployment | 72 | 28 |
| Care insurance | 30 | 27 |
| Wealth decline | 19 | 18 |
| Lack of apprenticeships | 48 | 12 |

**SOCIETAL**

| | 2007 | 2022 |
|---|---|---|
| Environmental issues/climate change | 47 | 55 |
| Dual class society | 42 | 48 |
| Political frustration | 24 | 40 |
| Egoism | 32 | 33 |
| Media influence | 11 | 30 |
| Increase of foreigners | 32 | 28 |
| Education crisis | 22 | 27 |

**SELF CARE**

| | 2007 | 2022 |
|---|---|---|
| Crime | 54 | 45 |
| Epidemics | 8 | 41 |
| Healthcare | 49 | 35 |
| Terrorism | 45 | 35 |

Hence, in numerous material segments, the concerns for their own welfare, and the fears of the population have decreased. In 2007, for example, almost two-thirds were still sceptical about the future pension pay outs, while almost three-quarters were worried about job security or feared unemployment. The lack of apprenticeship programmes was also perceived as a serious problem for the future. In 2022, developments on the labour market were assessed much less critically. Only half as many people saw unemployment and a lack of apprenticeship programmes as urgent problems for the future. Concerns about healthcare and long-term care insurance as well as fear of terrorism and crime were reduced to the same extent.

By contrast, there was a sharp increase in concerns about rising prices and epidemics, which can be attributed to the current challenges posed by advancing inflation as a result of the war in Ukraine and the Covid-19 pandemic. Unlike material and personal concerns, however, social fears increased noticeably. Particularly clear here is the extreme increase of concerns about the influence of the media and disenchantment with politics. The discussions about fake news and the increasing influence of social media on public opinion have left their mark. More and more citizens are concerned about the impact of the media on arriving at their own conclusions and opinions, as well as the influence of social networks on the younger generation. On the one hand, concerns about the rise of disenfranchisement from politics reveal existing doubts about the performance and leadership ability of the relevant players - including in the areas of the future viability of social systems, current challenges posed by globalization, climate change, wars, pandemics and the integrity of individuals (real and perceived lobbying and corruption scandals). On the other hand, it is also clear that civil society is highly sensitive and reflective, viewing trust in political decision-makers as an indispensable foundation of a democratic society.

**Overall, it is clear that a distinction between fears must be made. A generalization that _German angst_ is the dominating factor cannot be applied.**

However, what exactly is the concise status of courage in Germany? And how did its meaning evolve over the course of history? The term "courage" can be traced back to different roots. In Indo-Germanic it comes from the word „mo", while in ancient High German it was called „mout". Both terms have the meaning of strong will, effort and sense, as well as the power of will. The Latin noun "virtus" refers to integrity, determination and risk taking capabilities.

The Greek term "andreia", on the other hand, referred to taking bold action in wars. The French word „courage", derives from the Latin „cor", which means heart and thus emphasizes the emotional ability to overcome fears. Over the course of history, the symbolic terminology changed. Whereas in Antiquity and the Middle Ages courage was considered an important part of the art of war and was associated with heroism and honour as values of boldness and bravery. In the Renaissance, for example in Shakespeare, it stood for an indispensable virtue for the formation of a complete character. In the Enlightenment, on the other hand, with its emphasis on reason, courage symbolized the will and ability to stand up against prejudice and oppression and to stand up for freedom and reason. In the transition to the 20th century, this change in meaning from physical daring to an emotional or moral level intensified.

Currently, courage is associated with a wide range of behaviours, such as determination and motivation, the willingness to stand up for one's beliefs, ideals or other people, or even the inclination to take risks and make decisions that involve uncertainty and possible consequences. These characteristics vary greatly from one individual to another and from one culture to another, but they all share the motive of overcoming fears. It does not always have to be the big challenges that make us appear courageous. Courage often shows itself in the small things of everyday life. These small things all strengthen one's own will, help us to overcome resistance and fortify an individual's confidence - after all, the world belongs to the brave. In this sense, it is not the intention of this book to deny the worries of the population, but rather to question the dominant position of fear in society and to open up and sensitize social consciousness more strongly so that courage is recognized for what it is.

**Only when the potential of courage becomes visible, when its positive and constructive effects for the development of the personality, the strengthening of the community and the overcoming of societal challenges become more apparent, can bold decisions be made more readily and confidently whilst the courage of each individual citizen receives the recognition it deserves.**

# I. WHAT BEING COURAGEOUS REALLY MEANS

*"Between pride and humility*
*stands a third pillar to which life belongs,*
*and that is quite simply courage"*

*Theodor Fontane*

## Character traits of a courageous individual

Out of 100 interviewees state that they would use the following traits to characterize a courageous person:

| | |
|---|---|
| Self-confident | 87 |
| Assumes responsibility | 86 |
| Overcomes resistance | 85 |
| Steadfast/stands up for values | 85 |
| Optimistic | 80 |
| Strives for change | 76 |
| Willing to fail | 71 |
| Innovativ/ creative | 71 |
| Ready to take over risks | 67 |
| Unadjusted/individual | 50 |
| Bold | 39 |
| Reckless/naive | 19 |

A large majority of Germans associates courage primarily with the following four traits:

1. Self-confidence
2. Readiness to take responsibility
3. Preparedness to overcome resistance
4. Advocating for values

The first characteristic, *self-confidence*, is a trait that forms the basis of the other associations. This defines the type of self-esteem in which one recognizes and appreciates the importance and value of one's own personality. Both strengths and weaknesses are perceived as part of one's own personality and are translated into self-confident actions combined with an inner attitude of composure and satisfaction. In connection with courage, it is a strong character trait to „be oneself", even if the social environment expects or wants something else.

When individuals are aware of themselves and their own strengths, they can also develop the ability to take *responsibility* for themselves and others. Responsibility means using the leeway to shape things, to make courageous decisions and to put them into practice with confidence and determination. Other attributes include the *willingness to overcome resistance* and to accept obstacles and conflicts. The resistance can be both - structural (regulations, hierarchies, etc.) and personal (lack of support, mistrust, envy, etc.). The fourth aspect rounds off the courageous action of the character trait, the ability and willingness by adding the socio-moral component of value conviction, steadfastness and *standing up for one's convictions and actions.*

Other key characteristics from the point of view of German citizens are optimism, creativity, the willingness to take risks and to strive for change. Even if all of these are seen more as necessary basic attitudes than as skills, they can be learned or amplified by each individual. The decisive factor here is whether the private and social environment offers sufficient freedom to learn how to be courageous and to act fearlessly. Specifically, these characteristics are needed to strengthen the motivation (optimism) and decisiveness (willingness to take risks) as well as to promote the will to create and the variation of perspective (creativity). All of these are accompanied by a desire and willingness to see change as a positive development, and to question old patterns of thinking and behaviour. In this context, almost three quarters of the population also mention the willingness to fail, which is inherent in courageous behaviour and goes beyond the willingness to take risks - for example, in the form of financial losses, failed concepts or plans that do not materialize. Failure is not viewed in a fundamentally negative light since it is precisely the setbacks and mistakes that can pave the way to new perspectives. However, in this case, extraordinarily strong courage is needed, since in Germany in particular, mistakes are often viewed very critically and negatively.

### EXAMPLE OF COURAGE
**Odysseus was a brave hero in Greek mythology. He demonstrated his courage and bravery in the numerous challenges and adventures during his Odyssey. Whether it was defeating the cyclops Polyphemus, braving the cliffs of Scylla and Charybdis, or resisting the temptations of the seductive Sirens, Odysseus repeatedly put into action his determination, persistence and leadership to achieve his goals.**

# I. WHAT BEING COURAGEOUS REALLY MEANS
## a. Generational differences in understanding courage

*"The courage*
*to sense fear*
*is the beginning of courage as a whole"*

Jean-Paul Sartre

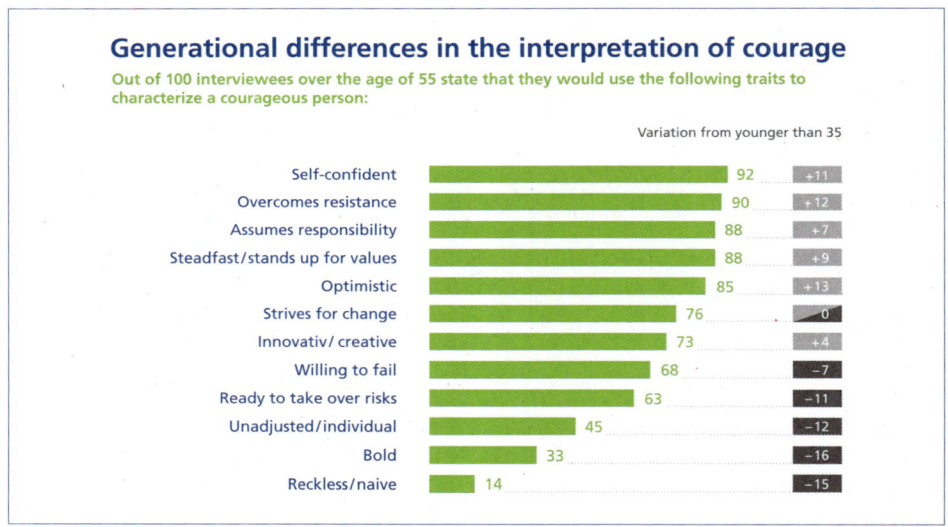

**Generational differences in the interpretation of courage**

Out of 100 interviewees over the age of 55 state that they would use the following traits to characterize a courageous person:

Variation from younger than 35

| Trait | Value | Variation |
|---|---|---|
| Self-confident | 92 | +11 |
| Overcomes resistance | 90 | +12 |
| Assumes responsibility | 88 | +7 |
| Steadfast/stands up for values | 88 | +9 |
| Optimistic | 85 | +13 |
| Strives for change | 76 | 0 |
| Innovativ/ creative | 73 | +4 |
| Willing to fail | 68 | −7 |
| Ready to take over risks | 63 | −11 |
| Unadjusted/individual | 45 | −12 |
| Bold | 33 | −16 |
| Reckless/naive | 14 | −15 |

Within the population, some differences can be noted with regard to age, although there is a similar emphasis. For both the older and younger generations, overcoming resistance, self-confidence, the willingness to take responsibility and standing up for values are the top priorities. Differences between the generations can be seen, among other things, when the assessment refers to optimism, overcoming resistance and self-confidence, as well as the associations with individuality, recklessness and bravado.

**Among older citizens, the character trait of self-confidence receives significantly higher consensus than among those under 35 years of age (+11 per cent).**

This can primarily be attributed to the fact that younger people have less life experience. The older ones define, according to their own experiences, self-awareness and confidence in their own abilities as a basic prerequisite for courageous action. Only those who are aware of themselves can also act outwardly courageous or can do so in social exchanges. This also includes, for instance, the understanding that as an individual one can represent one's convictions in a self-determined manner. Standing up for oneself is not reduced to expressing one's own opinion, but also includes being able to detach oneself more easily from group pressures and to confront a group or opinion that conforms to values. On the other hand, this self-confidence is often not yet as pronounced among the younger generation or is less strongly associated with courage. In addition, there is a self-image - shaped by a corresponding upbringing by parents and school - which perceives the expression of one's own convictions as normal and associates it less with courage.

With a similarly high level of consensus self-confidence attains, the older generation associates courage with overcoming resistance. The life experience of this generation has shown its members that challenges in life can not only be external, but also manifest themselves internally. Overcoming these to achieve a goal requires determination, perseverance and courage. More than younger people, this generation can rely on self-discipline, self-motivation and perseverance, and has learnt strategies for dealing constructively and courageously with failures, rejections and obstacles.

Another difference between the generations can be seen in optimism (+13 per cent). Although there is also a high level of consensus among the younger generation, its members have a more sceptical basic attitude towards courageous people, while being simultaneously considered more optimistic. In this sense, courage for the younger generation can also mean standing up for something, acting courageously and at the same time having doubts or lacking confidence about the success of one's own actions. What becomes clear is an attitude that is characterized by less clear-cut views and that also allows for doubt and scepticism. A current example in this context can be found in civil resistance actions addressing the subject matter of climate change. Thus, the aspect of optimism is not in the foreground in conjunction with these actions. On the contrary, the pessimistic attitude or outlook of many young people ("it is almost impossible to stop global warming") becomes the basis for courageous action.

**In this context, the stronger emphasis on the connection between courage and the willingness to take risks among younger citizens becomes self-evident (+11 per cent). This is not only revealed as a result of the age-related lessened need for security, but also in the willingness to take risks and to potentially fail (+7 per cent). This fearlessness can refer to a wide range of areas, such as courageous decisions concerning the choice of**

**vocations or study courses, sports challenges, civil protests in conjunction with political actions, risky financial endeavours, or bold moves of any kind.**

**The willingness to take risks and to possibly fail is fed by the youthful recklessness paired with the knowledge that it is certainly possible to fail at any time, but also to dare something new again and again, regardless of whether one will succeed or not.**

In addition, many younger individuals' financial and family scenarios are less associated with security and responsibility. Whenever there are no family members to look after, it is easier to take risks, and where no professional responsibility is expected yet, you can still try things and undertake ventures with uncertain outcomes.

The greatest differences between the age groups can be seen in the notion to take dare-devilish and reckless action. Significantly more young people associate these aspects with a courageous person. Once again, the differences can be explained by the rather daring lifestyle on the one hand and the restrained lifestyle on the other. Especially younger people consider daring and reckless behaviour positive endeavours. This may be related, for example, to social behaviour or a generally cool habitus. For both character traits, recognition within the social group has a particularly strong significance. Among older citizens, on the other hand, the characteristics are predominantly negative, and significantly fewer associate these traits with courage. What becomes clear is an age-related greater need for security and stability as well the less intense need to be part of a group.

**Significantly more young citizens equate unaligned individualism with courage (+12 per cent).**

This high level of consensus merely seems to contradict the above statements on the importance of group membership. Even if their social reference groups exert a strong influence, they still believe in the importance of individuality as an expression of a personality that resists rigid rules and norms. This individuality can also be realized in the respective youth subcultures within the group. The focus is on self-will, the unconventional or non-conformist. In everyday life, these character traits can be seen in the demarcation from other groups, in the distance to the adult world or in the resistance to the majority controlled society.

It is perceived as courageous above all when it contradicts general conventions, for example with regard to sexual orientation, political expression or life planning. In the later phase of life, the characteristic of resistance loses significance and focuses more on self-realization. In this context, the term "courageous" refers to someone who is willing to take risks and to resolutely pursue his or her personal goals, who realizes plans outside the mainstream. For instance, this may include the implementation of a creative business idea or embarking on an exotic holiday destination. The fact that the older generation agrees with the characteristic of non-conformist individuality in much smaller numbers shows the need to distinguish oneself from the majority controlled society, which often weakens with increasing age. Older citizens are also less susceptible to media influences and trends toward increasing individualization. They are sceptical in some cases about the increasing differentiation and efforts toward autonomy and do not associate them with courageous behaviour.

## b. Higher income earners associate significantly more terms with courageous individuals

*"It takes courage
to embark on new paths
and to learn from mistakes"*

*Elon Musk*

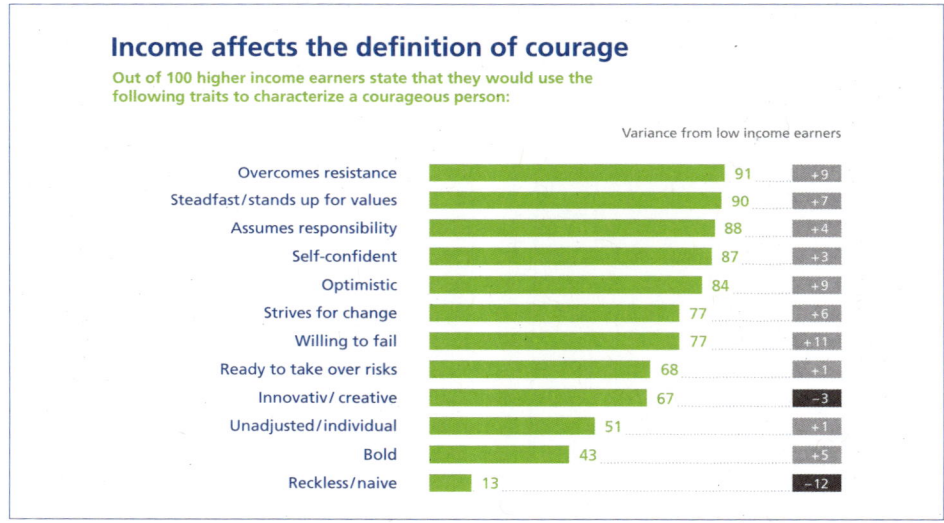

### Income affects the definition of courage

Out of 100 higher income earners state that they would use the following traits to characterize a courageous person:

Variance from low income earners

| Trait | Value | Variance |
|---|---|---|
| Overcomes resistance | 91 | +9 |
| Steadfast/stands up for values | 90 | +7 |
| Assumes responsibility | 88 | +4 |
| Self-confident | 87 | +3 |
| Optimistic | 84 | +9 |
| Strives for change | 77 | +6 |
| Willing to fail | 77 | +11 |
| Ready to take over risks | 68 | +1 |
| Innovativ/creative | 67 | −3 |
| Unadjusted/individual | 51 | +1 |
| Bold | 43 | +5 |
| Reckless/naive | 13 | −12 |

There are also numerous differences depending on income. For example, those with higher incomes (net household income over €5,000 per month) more frequently mention the aspects of overcoming resistance, steadfastness, optimism and the willingness to fail. By contrast, the concept of recklessness is cited less often. The reasons for the higher numbers can be explained, among other things, with the greater financial independence and the opportunities and experiences associated with higher income levels. For instance high income earners predominantly associate the above-mentioned terms with courage with their work environments and the challenges they face there. Often working in management positions themselves, they perceive courageous actions primarily in areas related to innovative concepts, individual investments, job changes and creative business start-ups. In order to succeed professionally, they emphasize the importance of an optimistic fundamental attitude and a determined way of moving forward. Cautious or hesitant behaviour, on the other hand, is considered a method that has only a minimal chance of succeeding. Particularly in rather tense financial times, it is important for them to continue to act with confidence and take a dynamic stance – be it with regard to personnel affairs, competency issues or capital investments. This also explains their higher appreciation of the character depiction of "overcoming resistance", which they see as a positive challenge to demonstrate their performance capabilities and assertiveness. A pronounced intrinsic motivation is thus additionally boosted by external incentives and reinforces courage. This also includes the willingness to fail and accept setbacks. On the one hand, this gives rise to new challenges; and on the other hand, these scenarios are easier to deal with if one has financial reserves. For higher income earners, a courageous risk assessment is not to be confused with recklessness, which is why they mention it less often. Low-income earners (net household income below €1,500 a month) are more risk averse overall – due to greater monetary uncertainty; and because it is more difficult for them to financially compensate for potential errors. Low-income earners are also more often affected by structural barriers (e.g. less access to information, networks), which offer them fewer opportunities to pursue bold decisions. Due to these preconditions, they tend to show a more negative attitude towards risks and change and tend to associate courageous decisions, especially in professional or financial terms, with recklessness and naivety.

## EXAMPLE OF COURAGE

**David is known for his courage in facing the giant warrior Goliath, who was considered invincible, despite his inexperience, youth and physical disadvantages. With a courageous heart and unwavering confidence, he faced Goliath and defeated him. His courage is an example of how faith in something greater (trust in God and His protection) can overcome one's fear and doubt.**

# II. ROLE MODELS – BETWEEN WISHES AND REALITY

*"A great role model is someone*
*Who spreads courage and hope,*
*not only through words,*
*but also action"*
Martin Luther King Jr.

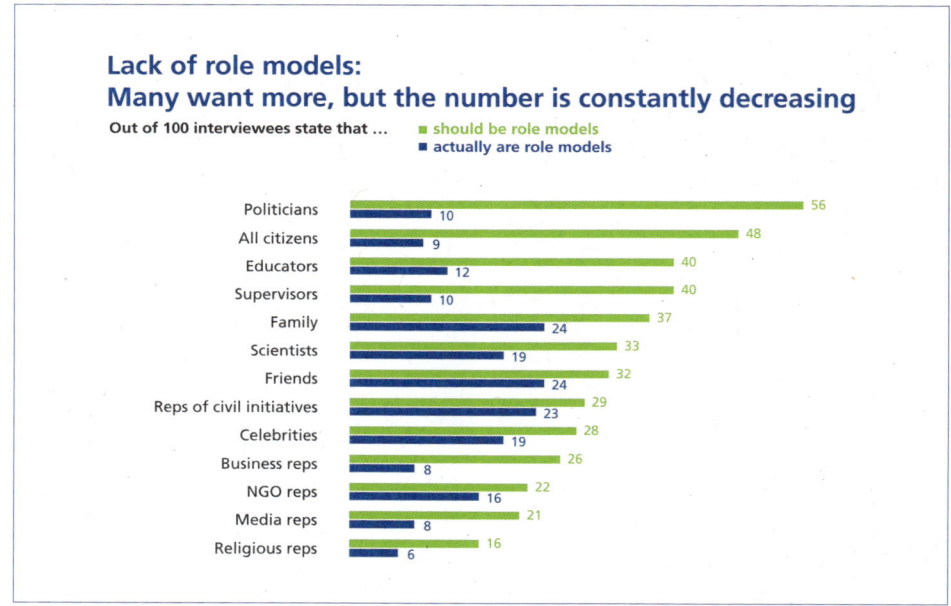

**Lack of role models:**
**Many want more, but the number is constantly decreasing**

Out of 100 interviewees state that ...   ■ should be role models
                                          ■ actually are role models

| | should be | actually are |
|---|---|---|
| Politicians | 56 | 10 |
| All citizens | 48 | 9 |
| Educators | 40 | 12 |
| Supervisors | 40 | 10 |
| Family | 37 | 24 |
| Scientists | 33 | 19 |
| Friends | 32 | 24 |
| Reps of civil initiatives | 29 | 23 |
| Celebrities | 28 | 19 |
| Business reps | 26 | 8 |
| NGO reps | 22 | 16 |
| Media reps | 21 | 8 |
| Religious reps | 16 | 6 |

While social values and norms are rather abstract concepts in their function as rules of conduct, role models offer concrete identification with a person whose attitude or life path inspires imitation. These persons can be, for example, friends or family members, politicians or celebrities, colleagues or media representatives.

**Role models accompany individuals consciously or unconsciously in certain phases of or throughout their lives. They educate, shape and influence them without forcing them into a rigid mould. As role models, they demonstrate promising behaviour that is judged to be effective and adopted.**

Young people use role models for self-discovery, orientation and differentiation. Adults, on the other hand, turn to them for support, especially in uncertain situations. There is a great discrepancy between the desire for courageous role models and the reality they experience. In conjunction with courageous conduct, people hope for role models from their close family circle, their own life environment, from social organizations and institutional forces. The coveting of role models is especially great in politics.

As elected officials at various levels, politicians not only represent the interests of their own party, but are also committed to the general formation of political will and being positive forces aiming at the common good. As public figures, constituents observe them carefully and often have high expectations when it comes to the performance of the elected leaders. Ideally, they are personalities of integrity who are characterized by authenticity, prudence, goal orientation and trustworthiness. Their exemplary character is cited above all in connection with social challenges and uncertain crisis situations. People hope that the decision-makers will be inspiring their constituents with their far-sightedness, conviction, confidence and drive and will point out possible solutions. These should extend beyond their own political interests and involve courageous, innovative decisions. Both national and global challenges are cited as examples, such as social grievances, high inflation rates, climate change or even standing up confidently for one's own convictions against the majority opinion. In terms of their public impact, the political role models should not only be worthy of emulation because of the lives they lead themselves, but should also have a signal effect on society. If possible, the individual courage of the personality should positively influence the confidence and courage of all citizens (and institutions).

Nevertheless, these expectations to be met by political representatives are not actually accommodated. To the contrary, the huge discrepancy between desire and reality is evident. Only one in ten agree that politicians are acting courageously and see them as role models who inspire the population with their positive leads. However, this is not a typically German perception, as various studies show an increasing distance between the governed and the governors in all Western industrial nations. One particular issue that gives rise to criticism is the lack of a culture of debate characterized by clear positions and not just intra-party compromises. There is also a lack of statements and actions that point optimistically to the future and do not focus only on problems or negative perspectives. Overall, to a broad spectrum of the population, most politicians represent an image that is counterproductive to courage and that is marred by uncertainty, undetermined procrastination, failure to be transparent, affairs and failures.

The fact is: the higher the expectations, the more impactful the disappointment. Consequently, politicians have a particularly hard time to address and resolve the mistrust of the people by making promises or attempts at courage.

In addition to politicians, almost half of the population sees itself and every other citizen as having a duty to be a courageous role model. This demonstrates a high level of awareness in civil society, in that the focus is not solely on authority, but rather on the ability of non-public individuals in society to act as role models. However, the granting of this ability is also accompanied by the call and expectation to behave courageously. In concrete terms, citizens want this courage, for instance, when it comes to showing civil courage and initiative, taking responsibility or standing up for their own convictions. Individuals would thus create spaces of opportunity and encourage other people to leave their comfort zone and courageously help shape society. In doing so, the influence can even reach beyond that of politicians, since they come from a similar life scenario, which results in a lower inhibition threshold of identification. Even this great potential of courage is not fulfilled in reality. Only one in ten identifies people in Germany who are acting as courageous role models. People are disappointed above all by „the others" – fellow citizens in general – and less by their own families and circle of friends. This perception is influenced on the one hand by corresponding surveys and reports, and on the other by a diffuse feeling of mistrust, insecurity, fear and pessimism in society. Both aspects are mutually interdependent. Thus, reports on the purported *German angst* reinforce the former and give rise to an image of resignation to fate, with no commitment, no chance of change, no perspective, no hope and no positive energy.

Two out of five citizens also name people from their own world as potentially courageous role model profiles. In most cases, these are authority figures with whom the people questioned have a direct relationship, e.g. from the professional and school environment, such as superiors and teachers. These people stand out as role models when their behaviour shows a high level of motivation and appreciation for others. They are perceived as courageous if they stand up for their employees or students, hold clear convictions and can authentically defend unpopular decisions. It is these qualities that are then perceived as worthy of emulation. Due to the special balance of closeness and distance, there is a high potential for identification with these role models and the option to find out what is possible on both an individual and a societal level.

Only a few teachers and supervisors can meet this demand, and only one in ten citizens feels inspired by them. In connection with courage, both persons/professional groups lack above all leadership qualities that express themselves in the form of commitment, optimism and decisiveness. For young people, it is particularly unfortunate that they find so few opportunities for identification or inspiration among their teachers, since they hope that these role models will provide them with important guidance for their own decisions and actions. Superiors are often criticized for their lack of interest in innovation, creative ideas and change, and for their sceptical or pessimistic attitude.

For about one third of Germans, family members or friends should have a high level of role model potential. As the closest reference persons, they are of great importance in early socialization and in the adolescence phase, both for self-discovery and for distancing. Their social influence takes place primarily in the areas of feeling, deciding, judging and acting. Within the family, their own actions motivate imitation at a young age, while in later development they are valued as advisors and emotional support.

In the context of courageous decisions, many adolescents and young adults especially want role models of the same age whose patterns of conduct they can apply themselves in specific situations, since they are closest to their own reality and thus also promise the most success. Courage here can also mean defying authority, overstepping given boundaries or rebelling against any kind of perceived paternalism. Depending on the situation, the less courageous friends can also assess the sanctions in case of a possible imitation. In addition to the peer group, adults should also act more frequently as courageous role models. Younger adults in particular are very receptive to their moral values and commitment. Accordingly, courageous family members often exert a strong influence on them with their determination and conviction.

**Studies show that in later life, too, many citizens draw primarily on role models from their youth or are guided by their courageous behaviour.**

People are often admired for questioning familiar behaviour patterns and decision-making processes, courageously standing up for their convictions, acting against resistance, planning new life plans or making risky decisions. They serve as a source of inspiration for courageous undertakings that one still shies away from oneself.

Compared to other role models, the gap between desire and reality is significantly smaller when family members and friends are mentioned. For around three quarters of Germans, the expectations placed on them are fulfilled. Disappointments often only occur where expectations were too high, for example those young people have of their parents. Due to their age, young people show a greater willingness to take risks and also hope for courageous guidance from their family caregivers, which the latter are not always able – or willing – to provide. These are important, though, since a lack of support or a pessimistic attitude can also be adopted and thus contribute to disappointment and frustration.

For around one in three, scientists and representatives of citizens' initiatives, and for just under one in four employees of non-profit organizations, are also people with great potential to become courageous role models. These groups of people can be assigned to the organizational and institutional spheres, with the latter also showing overlaps with their own life situations.

In recent years, science has increasingly become the focus of public interest, primarily due to the global challenges of climate change and the Covid-19 pandemic. For the general public, scientists are otherwise more in the background, responsible for the efficient transfer of theoretical knowledge into practice. Their technical approach is incomprehensible to most, and with their theorectic focus, they have had more of an advisory role in the public perception and are considered less of an authority to act or make decisions. However, since crises and conflicts have had an increasing impact on everyday life, scientific findings, and with them scientists, have become more visible. This applies above all to communication between science and various social actors. With regard to courageous behaviour, scientists are seen as being primarily committed to the truth and less guided by other interests, e.g. material, personal or party-political interests. Here, courageous role model means communicating even uncomfortable truths, not allowing oneself to be taken in, reflecting on findings and striving for interdisciplinary cooperation beyond one's own field of expertise. As public figures, they thus initiate a signal effect for confidence, honesty and trust.

Citizens' initiatives and non-profit organizations, such as NGOs are characterized by their basic democratic understanding of society. Engaged citizens form alliances for limited periods of time or longer term associations with the aim of jointly drawing attention to bad situations and to impact the decision-making processes.

Germans associate them with their own world and see them as courageous role models for energy, optimism and creative drive. Since role models help people to reflect on their own behaviour, Germans also value their confidence that they can actually initiate change through personal action. Even changes that they themselves may no longer believe in. Here, courageous role model means communicating even uncomfortable truths, not allowing oneself to be taken in, reflecting on findings and striving for interdisciplinary cooperation beyond one's own field of expertise. As public figures, they thus initiate a signal effect for confidence, honesty and trust.

**In times of general dissatisfaction and disenchantment with politics, it is seen as courageous when people resist this trend and believe in themselves and their own creative possibilities.**

In this sense, courage has a motivating effect on other individuals to overcome their own difficulties, even if internal and external stereotypes ("It's no use after all", "Better leave it to the experts") often hinder this confidence.

While citizens' initiatives and NGOs largely fulfil the trust placed in them, this is only partially true for scientists. This is due to the fact that they are often perceived as being (too) closely linked to politics and business, and that communication between them and the public is often incomprehensible. For example, many citizens associate the sometimes incomprehensible political actions during the Covid-19 pandemic with seemingly uncertain and contradictory statements by the scientific community. As a result, the impression is created of a fickle and uncertain science that shies away from bold and honest statements.

About a quarter of all German citizens hope to find courageous role models in celebrities and business representatives. Celebrities represent an individual phenomenon and are more likely to be equated with idols. Even though no clear line can be drawn between the two concepts, celebrities are subject to greater media staging and embody a certain image. They are valued as role models in two contexts in particular. On the one hand, they use their names to advocate for a "good cause", support certain campaigns or projects, encourage donations or draw attention to grievances. Secondly, their public success conveys courage, confidence, willpower and stamina. Their life stories show options to attain goals and wishes. Admiration is especially extended to individuals who had to address challenges (such as illnesses, accidents, poverty, problems starting out) or have had successful comebacks. The majority of these idols hail from the movie, sports and music scene.

Business representatives belong to the institutional sphere. Their exemplary character is based on their attitude, for example, by acting with particular integrity, courage or in a forward-looking manner. They are valued for their individuality, for offering an alternative to the usual economic concepts, for unusual ideas or for attaching great importance to their social responsibility – for example, through sustainable projects. In addition, people admire their financial achievements and see them as role models for determination and decisiveness. In the opinion of German citizens, business representatives often fail to live up to the hopes placed in them as courageous role models. Above all, they lack qualities such as farsightedness, determination and optimism. The (pre)judgment is that economic functionaries primarily have their own financial interests in mind and that their decisions are geared toward short-term profits. Their willingness to take risks, which is basically perceived as courageous, is reflected in reckless investments that show little consideration for the consequences employees may suffer. Longer-term or sustainable reforms or investments, on the other hand, are perceived rather rarely.

The need for courageous role models from the fields of media and religion is rarely mentioned. Yet courage plays a role in every faith. For example, the New Testament, the Torah and the Koran all call on believers to courageously stand up for their convictions, to fight against injustice and oppression and to stand up for the weak and those in need of help. Role models can be found in ancient writings, such as Fatima al-Fihri, who founded the first university in Morocco in 895, or the Maccabees, Jewish freedom fighters who defended themselves against Macedonian foreign rule in 168 BC. But Modernity also offers role models of determination and moral integrity, such as the theologian Dietrich Bonhoeffer, who paid for his resistance against the National Socialists with his life, the Baptist pastor Martin Luther King as a fighter for equal rights for coloured people in the USA, or the Buddhist Dalai Lama Tenzin Gyatso as a fighter for the autonomy of Tibet.

In Germany, until the 1950s, the Protestant and Catholic churches served as moral role models for a large part of the West German population (96% confessional affiliation). For instance, this concerned issues of social justice, the reconciliation with the Eastern European nations, the peace movement or the increased openness vis-à-vis other religions. As secular lifestyles continued to progress and the reunification of Germany was finalized, the trend to forego religious influences slowly progressed. This is also reflected in the growing rejection of Christian doctrine content and its application by churches (e.g. the role of women, the continued existence of celibacy) and the dwindling trust in religion as a moral authority (e.g., dealing with incidents of abuse). At present, not even one in two Germans is a member of the Protestant church (21.8 million members) or the Catholic church (19.7 million), and, at this time, there is no sign of that the mass exodus from the church will end any time soon. Accordingly, only about one in twelve Germans still sees Christian clergy as role models or as being associated with courageous behaviour. Germans feel that clergy hardly have any room left in public debates, that they withdraw too much into internal discussions after conflicts and accusations, and that they no longer stand up for courageous convictions, for example with regard to the social question, the radicalization of parts of society or climate change.

Media representatives are seen as possible role models for courage by only one in five. As the fourth power of the state, they have the potential of influencing the public and political events through their more or less autonomous options. In the past, journalists were seen as having a professional ethos, were committed to forming free opinions, acting independently, keeping their distance from those in power and focusing on relevant issues in their reporting. Courage here means exposing grievances, „putting one's finger on the wound", and, as the mouthpiece of the people, monitoring those in power. Now, this conduct is only attributed to them to a limited extent. Accordingly, media representatives are rarely perceived as resolute admonishers or courageous enlighteners. There is a lack of distance from government bodies and these days, people tend not to place their trust in journalists. Another point of criticism is that there is too little constructive reporting and an increasing focus on negative news. People miss optimistic and inspiring news and it would strengthen the perception of the media as courageous solution-oriented role models. In this context, it is also important to note the declining influence of traditional media and the simultaneous increase in the influence of social media.

## EXAMPLE OF COURAGE
**Citizens of the GDR – Despite the authoritarian regime and constant surveillance by the state security, many people dared to express their opinions and fight for their freedom and rights. They did this by demonstrating peacefully or even going on strike. The risk of sanctions did not deter many from standing up for change. The citizens of the GDR fought courageously against oppression and for freedom.**

## II. ROLE MODELS – BETWEEN WISHES AND REALITY

### a. Higher income earners demand more role models from politics, business and science

*"Courage is what it takes*
*to stand up and speak;*
*courage is also what it takes*
*to sit down and listen"*

Winston Churchill

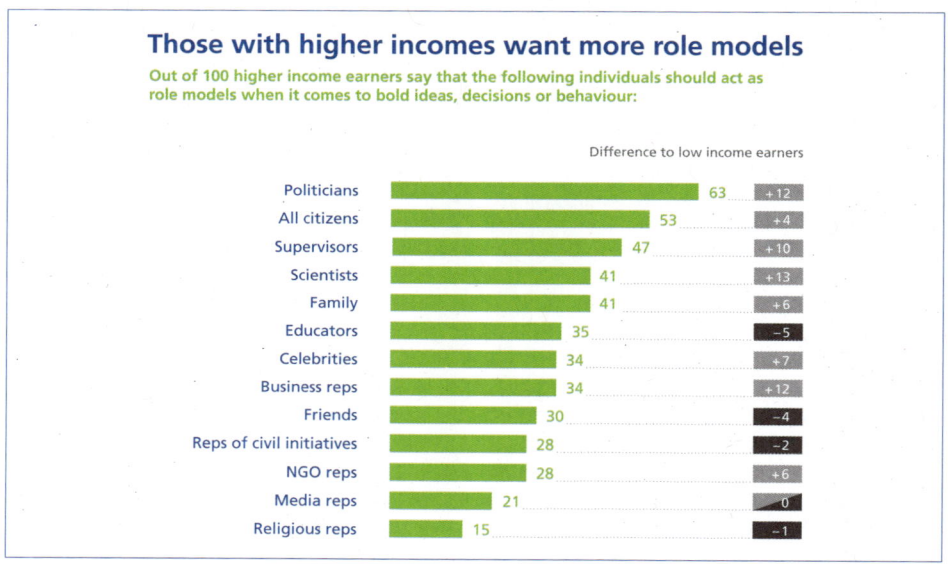

**Those with higher incomes want more role models**

Out of 100 higher income earners say that the following individuals should act as role models when it comes to bold ideas, decisions or behaviour:

Difference to low income earners

| | | |
|---|---|---|
| Politicians | 63 | +12 |
| All citizens | 53 | +4 |
| Supervisors | 47 | +10 |
| Scientists | 41 | +13 |
| Family | 41 | +6 |
| Educators | 35 | −5 |
| Celebrities | 34 | +7 |
| Business reps | 34 | +12 |
| Friends | 30 | −4 |
| Reps of civil initiatives | 28 | −2 |
| NGO reps | 28 | +6 |
| Media reps | 21 | 0 |
| Religious reps | 15 | −1 |

When asked whether they have a desire for a courageous role model, only just over half of Germans say they have such a need. The reasons for this vary from individual to individual and range from a disillusioned perception of reality, which classifies the existence of role models as unrealistic and thus the potential is not recognized at all, to the lack of necessity, since sufficient motivation and determination of one's own is at the ready, to other motives such as too great a distance between one's own world and possible role models or an existing lethargy.

There are only minor differences in the responses with regard to gender and place of residence, while there are more marked differences with regard to age and income. For example, higher earners increasingly express the desire for courageous role models. These are mainly in the fields of science, politics and business (+12 per cent). In a professional context, for example when changing jobs or positions, superiors can also act as suitable role models who help people to successfully prove themselves in the new organizational forms. In the context of courage, they could show meaningful ways of taking on increased responsibility, questioning old concepts, exercising self-reflection or developing innovative strategies for solving problems. This shows how important it is, also or especially in leadership positions, to build positive and courageous role models. In areas that are often associated with competition and hierarchy, people want inspiring and ground-breaking support that is not just focused on self-interest.

In the field of business, high earners show a stronger interest in particular in characteristics such as risk-taking, assertiveness, decisive investing and self-confidence. There is a strong desire not only to associate courage with social aspects, but also to recognize it in the economic sphere. For example, courage is required to dedicate oneself to a goal with all determination, to put safety concerns aside, to dare to make a new start or to accept challenges. Accordingly, courageous role models are people who, for example, have founded companies, implemented innovative concepts, created changes for themselves and possibly for others with creativity and a willingness to perform.

Similarly, high-income earners hope that society's political and scientific elite will have a stronger role model function. More than others, they believe in the power of authorities and place greater trust in them to make courageous decisions.

**High-income earners tend to see potential in role models rather than misconduct and grievances. They equate courage with determination, clarity and a willingness to take responsibility.**

Less consent is in evidence for the desired role model – the teacher. To that end the desire for a role model is more intense among citizens with lower incomes. They associate the profession with responsibility, commitment, expertise and passion. In the context of courage, they hope educators will have an inspiring influence on children and young people and help them develop a confident attitude and courageous plans for the future. When family backgrounds have few intangible resources (e.g. education), teachers can help build stronger self-confidence, broaden perspectives, and encourage adolescents to boldly pursue alternative paths, such as aiming to graduate from high school at a higher level than their parents. Against the background of their own school experiences, many low-income earners regret not having taken advantage of this support themselves.

*"Being a role model*
*is courageous"*
Maya Angelou

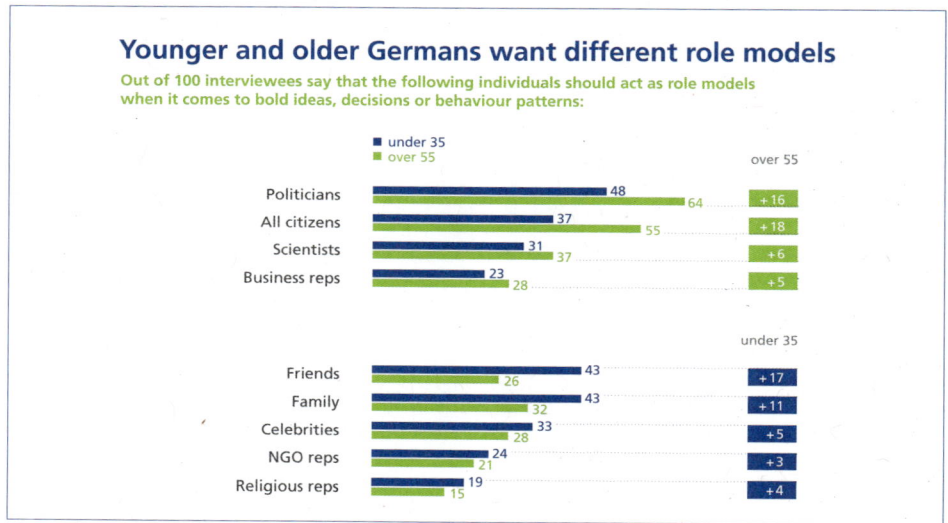

**Younger and older Germans want different role models**

Out of 100 interviewees say that the following individuals should act as role models when it comes to bold ideas, decisions or behaviour patterns:

The younger and older generations set different priorities as far as their desires to have role models are concerned. This applies to both – the order and the per centage of approval or disapproval. The group aged 55 and older, for instance, favour people from the political sector and „ordinary citizens" as courageous role models, and do so much more strongly than those who are younger than 35 Older people also place more trust in people from the business and science sectors and attribute to them a high potential for courageous decisions and actions.

**There is evidence of an appreciation of authority among the older generation and a belief that the former can exert a strong influence on citizens.**

The older generation has a generally positive attitude towards the institutions close to them and values them as role models for society in general. The emphasis in this case is on standing up for one's own convictions, self-confidence and an optimistic basic attitude. More often than not, those who are older than 55 hope that courageous behaviour will send an inspiring signal to the public. Nevertheless, the responsibility for constructive and confident coexistence is not just left up to the country's political, economic and scientific elite; as this group is convinced that this is just as much in the hands of each individual. Far removed from a fatalistic attitude, they see every citizen as being called upon to set an example of courage and confidence with his or her attitude and actions. In social scenarios this may be expressed by standing up for one's values, supporting other citizens, showing civil courage or following one's own convictions instead of the majority opinion. It is furthermore evident in fearless decisions, by taking responsibility in one's own professional and private environment and by conveying optimism. The fact that around one-fifth of older people believe more in the potential of every citizen can be attributed to life experience. This group has already experienced how much courage, confidence and commitment can pay off and have an inspiring effect on the social environment.

On the other hand, older citizens expect less courage and inspiration from family and friends; after all, in most cases they are firmly established in their (professional) lives and accordingly require less guidance from their immediate social environment. In their lives, they have already received a lot of advice, have had role models in or received guidance from relatives and friends, which means that they have less of a desire for personal role models in their private sphere. For them, role models are more of an important inspiration for society as a whole, which is why they want more institutional (politicians, scientists, business) and abstract role models (citizens in general).

**People under 35 have other priorities. They mainly expect friends and family members to act as courageous role models.**

This can be explained by the desire for orientation and support. Their own parents usually play a special role here: through their own behaviour, they can show how to deal with challenges, overcome crises and fears, learn from mistakes and realize their own goals and dreams. Likewise, they can also help in the fortification of children's self-confidence and self-esteem. While friends in adolescence serve primarily as role models who impress with their daredevilry and non-conformist behaviour, in later development they are more likely to provide stimulation, initiative, and a sense of belonging.

Given that they have experienced similar circumstances in life, friends have the potential to be an incentive to leave one's own comfort zone, to break through routines through diversity, or even to embark on completely new paths. These may involve, for example, a job, a change of relationships or residences, but also a social commitment.

On average, Germans younger than 35 name celebrities, religious and NGO representatives slightly more often as role models for courage. This shows the lesser association of young citizens with institutional role models or authorities and the greater proximity to individuals or an idea. Especially at a young age, people are receptive to moral values, support ethical goals, and look for inspiration for their own behaviour. In the case of celebrities, they admire above all their specific life stories and commitment to certain content. In a similar way, they appreciate NGOs and religious representatives, who are usually committed to people in need, justice or environmental protection. In addition to their social commitment, they are also close to their own lives, which is expressed, for example, in their personal membership.

### EXAMPLE OF COURAGE
**Pakistani Malala Yousafzai publicly campaigned for the right to education for girls as a young schoolgirl, despite threats from the ruling Taliban. However, she refused to be intimidated and continued her campaign for education and women's rights undeterred. Then, at the age of 15, she was shot and seriously injured by a Taliban fighter in her school bus. Despite this attack, she continued to stand up for her beliefs and founded an organization that campaigns for education and women's rights. She is a role model not only for young people in her home country, but around the world, because she shows what one person can achieve when you act with courage, perseverance and determination.**

# III. WHERE AND WHEN WE ARE BOLD

*"Those who are bold and take positive action*
*inspire others to do the same"*

Confucius

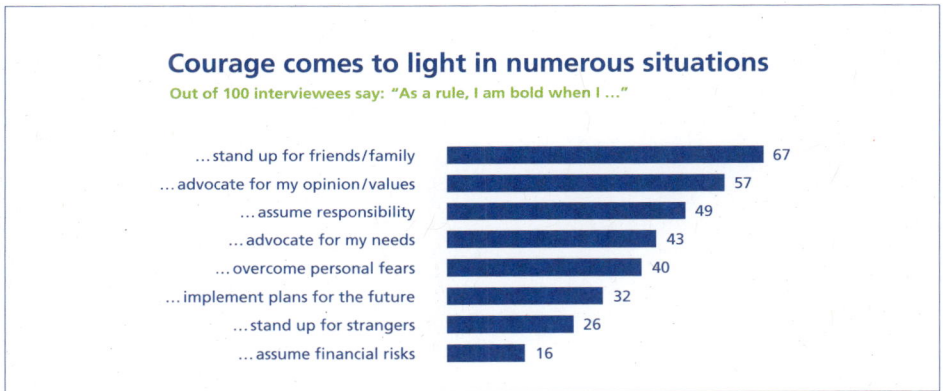

## Courage comes to light in numerous situations

Out of 100 interviewees say: "As a rule, I am bold when I ..."

| | |
|---|---|
| ...stand up for friends/family | 67 |
| ...advocate for my opinion/values | 57 |
| ...assume responsibility | 49 |
| ...advocate for my needs | 43 |
| ...overcome personal fears | 40 |
| ...implement plans for the future | 32 |
| ...stand up for strangers | 26 |
| ...assume financial risks | 16 |

Courage as an abstract term allows for many associations, can be understood as a form of behaviour, a wish or a value, but can also be associated with people, events and decisions. Yet, when do Germans describe their own behaviour as courageous? In what situations do they act fearlessly? Who or what makes them act fearlessly and overcome angst? As different as the aspects mentioned are, they all draw their strength from the same source.

**Courage develops through the combination of empathy, honesty, trust and self-reflection. It does not develop through external demands (for instance demands imposed by any authority), but from the innermost value system, reflection and social exchange.**

Two out of three citizens describe themselves as courageous in standing up for family and friends. This is expressed, for instance, in emotional support, help when facing challenges, conflicts with others or concrete assistance in emergency situations. People act courageously when they stand up together against something or someone, avoid being forced into groups and put their own ideas aside, and instead look after and defend the interests of their friends or relatives. For instance, this may involve siblings who are in a dispute with their parents, a friend embroiled in conflict within a circle of friends, a girlfriend confronted with career-related issues, or children who have to make a difficult decision about a field of study. Help may be extended that is financial, moral, social or emotional in nature and may be provided in a wide variety of contexts. Courageous support is borne out of a sense of responsibility, empathy and familiarity.

Courage also manifests itself in conflicts in which one's own values or convictions are at the centre of the discussion. In controversies with family or friends, it takes courage to oppose the other person, to contradict him or her, and to stand up for one's own opinion. Such situations might arise, for instance, from political convictions, plans for the future or professional and private decisions. Especially since all of these are individuals we are close to and because they often expect us to agree with them or anticipate consensus, it takes courage not to comply. Reflection on one's own values, the assertiveness of wanting to be understood, strengthens the power of decision-making and the courage to take this path. In case of conflict at school or at work, the courageous approach focuses primarily on the support of colleagues or classmates. Courageous resolution is shown, for example, when others need emotional support, are treated unfairly or are bullied. In addition, courage is demonstrated, albeit to a much lesser extent, in disputes with superiors or authorities. The more strongly one's inner values are affected, the more likely one is to resolutely take on the confrontation on behalf of others. In other cases, people strive to find a balance between courage and understanding.

Every second person interviewed also said that courage is expressed by assuming responsibility. As is clear from the other questions, this responsibility is expressed above all in the personal sphere. On the one hand, it refers to situations in which courageous communication is central to resolving social conflicts and disputes. On the other hand, it refers to a level of action in which directional decisions are the focus. This may mean that one person feels solely responsible for rearing a child, caring for sick family members or taking on binding responsibilities.

**Courage means being responsible for one's actions, not transferring them to others and also taking responsibility for the consequences.**

The assumption of sole responsibility is particularly challenging in this context. In these scenarios, it is impossible to hide behind a superior authority and one does have to stand up for the respective achievement or failure all alone. Germans primarily associate this challenge with professional concerns. In a society in which mistakes and failures are often stigmatized and success is regarded as the highest goal, it takes a great deal of courage to  embrace these challenges and to be fully accountable.

In this context, around two out of five citizens say they are courageous when it comes to representing their own interests and overcoming personal fears. It takes courage to represent one's own needs aggressively and to accept any resistance or rejection from others that may arise. If this statement is placed in the context of the high level of consensus of aligning courage with self-confidence, the reciprocal relationship between self-confidence, courage and standing up for one's own interests becomes clear. To that end, it is somewhat irrelevant as to which fields these interests can be allocated to and whether they are of a private or professional nature. What is decisive is the courageous and self-confident standing up for one's own needs, even in the face of resistance. This resistance can come from both, the outside or from within, for example in the form of fears. In this context, Germans refer to the issue of having to confront the challenges and, if possible, overcoming them. These are not pathological fears, but deeper-rooted worries and concerns that regularly or sporadically interfere with personal everyday life. Examples include fears of failure, decision-making or conflicts with authority. Facing up to these fears requires courage, as they require a change in habitual behaviour and their successful outcome is questionable.

For around one in three citizens, courage is a central requirement when planning and implementing personal plans for the future. Despite the existing freedom and numerous opportunities for self-realization in Germany, almost one third of Germans find it difficult to realize them. In addition to the financial risks, the main concerns in the professional sphere are bureaucratic obstacles, rigid structures, lack of understanding and lack of recognition. Here, those who allow themselves to be minimally influenced by the former and who resolutely keep their eyes on their goals, demonstrate bravery. In this context, plans for self-employment, incorporating an enterprise, making a career change, while also consciously foregoing a career step in order to have more time for other things are mentioned. In the private sphere, plans and changes are often integrated into a social context, which is why it is important to communicate courageously, to be convincing and to trigger enthusiasm.

**Acting courageously when planning changes is a particular challenge, since there is no certainty when it comes to determining how something will develop in the future.**

In contrast to the fearless commitment in the personal environment, only just under a third say that they would bravely stand up for strangers. The reasons can be explained in part by the rather abstract concept of „stranger" and a lesser need to engage. In contrast to family and friends, there is less emotional closeness and attachment, which reduces the moral obligation. In addition, there is a general trend towards the withdrawal into the private sphere, which results in fewer points of contact with people outside one's own life scenario. This is also evidenced by the above statements, in which courage is shown almost exclusively in personal surroundings and hardly ever in social contexts and commitment. Therefore, when citizens commit themselves to strangers, it requires more effort for many than it does when they advocate for people they trust. The hurdle to be courageous seems disproportionately higher because the stranger's reaction or behaviour is unpredictable and it is harder to assess whether the support is wanted. In addition, there is greater uncertainty about how the environment will react to the assistance we provide. If one bravely intervenes despite these adversities, a high level of empathy, willingness to help, open-mindedness as well as a sense of social responsibility is demonstrated. Examples of courageous behaviour on behalf of strangers can manifest itself in a variety of ways, for example in advocacy for refugees, the homeless or minorities, in defending individuals in discriminatory or dangerous situations. Common to all aspects is the effect of direct individual help as well as a general improvement in social trust. The latter is of central importance in this context, as trust is the social glue that holds a society together. This must be improved through opportunities for sharing, communication and cooperation, as otherwise increasing division, discrimination and prejudice will begin to evolve.

### EXAMPLE OF COURAGE

**Health care workers showed great courage during the Covid-19 pandemic as they took care of patients when little was initially known about the potential infection risks. Despite this uncertainty and under the most difficult conditions, they worked to the breaking point. Their dedication, determination and selflessness helped save lives and contain the virus. The commitment of doctors and nurses is an expression of extending brave help to others.**

## III. WHERE AND WHEN WE ARE BOLD

### a. Money inspires bravery – Individuals with higher incomes appear to be more determined

*"Courage is essential when you take risks and explore new opportunities"*

Steve Jobs

**Higher income earners are self-confident and assertive**

Out of 100 higher income earners say: "As a rule, I am bold when I ..."

Variance from low income earners

| | | |
|---|---|---|
| ...stand up for friends/family | 75 | +16 |
| ...advocate for my opinion/values | 60 | +6 |
| ...assume responsibility | 59 | +18 |
| ...advocate for my needs | 47 | +7 |
| ...overcome personal fears | 46 | +8 |
| ...implement plans for the future | 44 | +19 |
| ...stand up for strangers | 29 | +1 |
| ...assume financial risks | 26 | +10 |

When comparing the different groups of people, the responses of those with higher incomes show clear differences from those with lower incomes. This applies not only to their priorities, but also to the level of their percentage agreement, as they express a greater willingness to behave courageously in all areas.

The greatest deviation is seen in the willingness to boldly implement personal plans for the future. In this context, they not only demonstrate consensus that comes in 19 per centage points higher, but they also make this parameter the top priority of their list of brave undertakings. This was already evident from the analysis of other issues: the plans focus mainly on professional matters such as a change of position or job, a change of residence (including abroad), a professional reorientation, an investment or a new business cooperation.

**High earners find it easier than others to put potential security concerns to the back of their minds and make bold decisions.**

In the event of failure or withdrawal, they have to fear fewer negative monetary consequences. In addition, they frequently boast a high level of competence in financial matters, which spurs on their willingness to take more financial risks.

The higher the income, the higher the position in the company. Accordingly, higher earners can or must more often take on responsibility, make decisions or implement projects that also affect colleagues or clients. This requires determination and foresight, but above all also the willingness to take on responsibility, which higher earners are significantly more willing to do (+18 per cent). To do so, they use their experience and knowledge, as well as existing networks and support.

Although the above-mentioned characteristics are mainly related to the professional sphere, they always have an impact on private life as well. For example, risky financial investments and career changes could lead to conflicts within the family or circle of friends. However, people with a high incomes also act more boldly in their private lives and achieve predominantly positive effects. They provide social support and inspire others, show their confident and positive attitude and stand up for family and friends. This rarely involves financial support, but mostly social or emotional support. Influenced by their own successes and the firm conviction that courage and determination are worthwhile, they also defend others against resistance, support their decisions, encourage them in their plans and accompany them in conflicts, even if they themselves may have to fear disadvantages as a result.

**Earners of higher incomes demonstrate the confidence of being able to jointly master any and all challenges.**

They also show above-average courage in overcoming fears, standing up for their own needs and expressing their own opinions. As has already become clear, self-confidence and self-assurance are an important source of courageous behaviour. In terms of this characteristic, too, higher earners are often in a more privileged position, so that they can show their courage more often and more easily in these situations as well.

b. More senior people are oftentimes bolder

*"Courage rises with opportunity"*

*William Shakespeare*

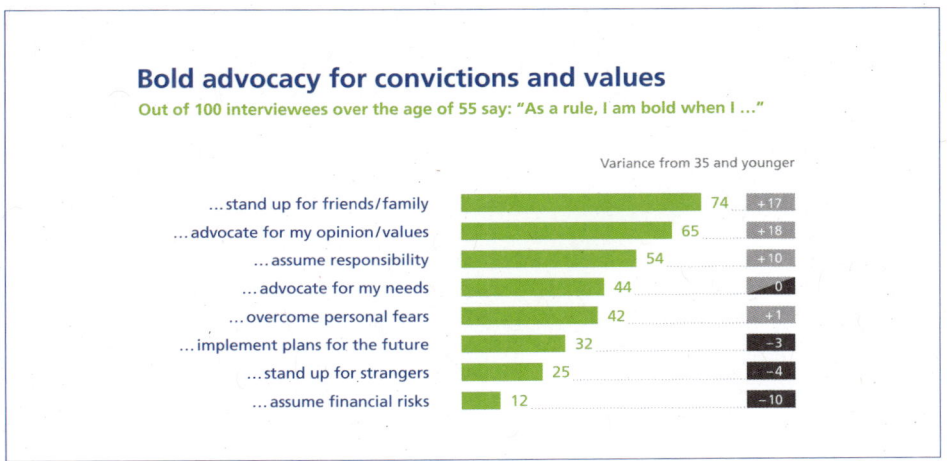

### Bold advocacy for convictions and values

**Out of 100 interviewees over the age of 55 say: "As a rule, I am bold when I …"**

Variance from 35 and younger

| | | |
|---|---|---|
| …stand up for friends/family | 74 | +17 |
| …advocate for my opinion/values | 65 | +18 |
| …assume responsibility | 54 | +10 |
| …advocate for my needs | 44 | 0 |
| …overcome personal fears | 42 | +1 |
| …implement plans for the future | 32 | −3 |
| …stand up for strangers | 25 | −4 |
| …assume financial risks | 12 | −10 |

However, higher income earners are not the only once who are more likely to act courageously in many situations. The 55+ generation is also more determined and courageous on numerous occasions than the younger generation. This applies above all to standing up for one's own opinion, friends and family, and to taking responsibility. While people who are financially well off show courage primarily in their professional lives, this also applies to the private lives of the older generation. For them, expressing their own opinions and convictions openly and honestly, regardless of whether they concern personal or professional matters, is a sign of inner strength. If they are still involved in work processes, they are less likely to shy away from questioning instructions, discussing matters with colleagues or superiors, and voicing alternative considerations or dissenting thoughts.

This is not only due to their greater self-confidence and knowledge of their own experience, but also to their confidence in finding a balance between the needs of the other person and the implementation of their own priorities. In addition, they are less likely than young people to face rebuke simply because of their age and can therefore act more fearlessly. When they are no longer working, their courage comes into play, for example, in volunteer work.

In personal disputes or conflicts, they also show greater composure and steadfastness than those under 35. They courageously defend their convictions, even if this leads to disputes or distancing from their social environment. The older generation's own values are not only important to them in professional matters; they also transfer them to their commitment to family and friends. Just like the group of high income earners, they are more likely than others to stand up for them, defend them against opposition and advocate for them in conflicts.

**The aforementioned aspects are embedded in a general sense of responsibility towards oneself and others, whereby the courage of the elderly is revealed as a moral obligation of steadfastness.**

At first glance, young people seem to be less brave than the older generation. One exception is when it comes to taking financial risks, even though they often have little experience in this area and can only assess the risks and consequences to a limited extent. In line with their age, they often act impulsively and are more easily influenced by promises or advice without questioning claims made more thoroughly. At the same time, they have a lower need for security, have less consideration and responsibility for other people, and are less concerned about setbacks. Thus, their plans, projects or investments in monetary matters are often quite daring and are intensified the more often they are rewarded with success for their bold moves.

**In addition to the willingness to take financial risks, the younger generation is also somewhat bolder than older generations when it comes to implementing plans for the future.**

People under 35 are often still in a phase of orientation in their lives, both professionally and privately, and are more open to change and more flexible in their objectives. They often meet challenges with sporting ambition and are more willing to turn uncertain plans or mental games into reality. Finally, it should be noted that the lower level of consensus among younger people when it comes to the aspects of „Courage in standing up for one's own opinion" and „Courage in standing up for friends and family" does not necessarily mean a lower level of commitment. More than the generations before them, they have grown up in a social milieu that promotes independent, free and critical thinking. For example, voicing one's own opinion or standing up for friends is taken for granted by many and is not associated with courage. In contrast, they act with above-average courage when supporting strangers.

## EXAMPLE OF COURAGE

Born into a simple peasant family and later canonized, Joan of Arc was a remarkably courageous woman in the 15th century. As a young female, she had visions of saints that motivated her to help liberate France from the English rule and to leave the safe shelter of her family and home to serve the French King Charles VII in the war. She led the French troops in the Hundred Years War against England, although as a woman she had to go into combat with initial opposition in her own army. With her determination, audacity and optimism, she inspired and motivated the soldiers, giving them the confidence they needed to win several significant victories together. Joan of Arc's courage to stand up for what she believed in made her a symbol of courage, strength and bravery.

# IV. WHY COURAGE OFTEN FAILS US

*"Courage is not being flawless,*
*but making mistakes*
*and going on anyway"*
John F. Kennedy

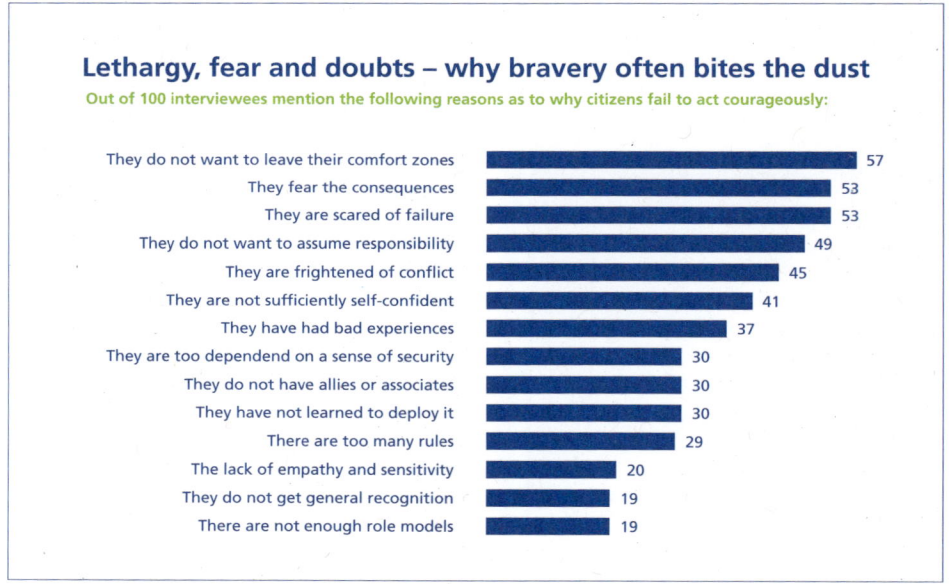

### Lethargy, fear and doubts – why bravery often bites the dust

Out of 100 interviewees mention the following reasons as to why citizens fail to act courageously:

| | |
|---|---|
| They do not want to leave their comfort zones | 57 |
| They fear the consequences | 53 |
| They are scared of failure | 53 |
| They do not want to assume responsibility | 49 |
| They are frightened of conflict | 45 |
| They are not sufficiently self-confident | 41 |
| They have had bad experiences | 37 |
| They are too dependend on a sense of security | 30 |
| They do not have allies or associates | 30 |
| They have not learned to deploy it | 30 |
| There are too many rules | 29 |
| The lack of empathy and sensitivity | 20 |
| They do not get general recognition | 19 |
| There are not enough role models | 19 |

Above all, being courageous requires self-confidence paired with the willingness to take responsibility, a willingness to take risks and optimism. Depending on the situation, it is also important to stand up for one's own convictions or values. Courageous behaviour is particularly evident in one's personal life. But what prevents many Germans from performing this action, which is perceived as positive, more often and outside their immediate environment? Are external circumstances responsible for this or rather inner motives?

The fact is: from the point of view of the population, it is not possible to draw a clear line between internal and external obstacles. Although the individual aspects can be roughly classified between the two motives, they are generally mutually dependent and influence each other. One impairment that is definitely intrinsic and is the one that is most often mentioned, is having to leave one's own comfort zone. Courage means action, commitment, possible risk, can be arduous and burdensome. The opposite poles are passivity, comfort and security. These are qualities with which one can be comfortable in one's usual everyday life. One is content to master the professional and private challenges and wants to make little effort for further tasks. People who take an active part in political and social events, sometimes plan to become more involved and dream of personal changes and goals, but in most cases this remains a theoretical intellectual game of courage and concrete action and implementation.

**The thought of effort and the possible consequences is too daunting for many Germans and prevents them from taking bold stances.**

For two out of five citizens, the inner motives also include a lack of self-confidence and, for one in three, an overly strong need for security. As with the question about the character traits of a courageous person, self-confidence is also a key prerequisite here. If it is not present, even bold considerations – and even more so courageous decisions – can become daunting challenges. In combination with a high need for security and the constant weighing of possible risks, assertive action thus becomes unlikely. People's need for security varies from person to person and can undoubtedly not be generalized. But it is also always socially determined when interacting with public opinion, social structures, general values, and so on. German society, which is often referred to as a fully comprehensive society, protects its citizens from as many imponderables as possible. Early warning systems of all kinds aim at minimizing risks, and controls and rules seem to guarantee security. Probably nowhere else in the world are there so many insurance policies that offer protection against every possible misfortune, ranging from healthcare coverage, liability insurance as well as household, life and long-term care insurance to disability, accident, legal protection and glass breakage insurance to cell phone, eyeglasses, luggage or pet health insurance. Many citizens find it difficult not to be influenced by this security-focused thinking and not to internalize it. Thus, the individual need for security is not only an internal obstacle for courage to be expressed, but also points to a societal problem: a culture that tends to be suspicious and dismissive of risks and changes.

**Courageous action also always leads to a change to what already exists.**

A majority of Germans also cite fear of failure and fear of responsibility as major obstacles. These two fears can only be superficially attributed to internal motives. From the analyses of further research findings, it becomes clear that they are primarily learnt behaviours and cha-racteristics and thus exhibit a reciprocal relationship between individual and societal moti-ves. The aforementioned prevailing full-casualty mentality makes life appear as an all-around secure construct that does not provide leeway for mistakes or failure. Everything seems to take its safe and orderly course. Added to this is a societal tendency toward optimization and the complete absence of an error culture, which provides little room for failure or risks that are always inherent in courageous behaviour. In this context, the general preference for se-curity and success can lead to an internalized fear of failure. This, in turn, has a direct impact on how willingly and intently citizens take on responsibility. The idea of exercising personal responsibility in the professional or private sphere is all the more negatively connoted the more obviously any potential failure is viewed as a mistake from the outside.

Most people make courageous decisions mainly in the personal sphere and, accordingly, only take responsibility for the consequences there. Consequently, the mention of responsi-bility as an obstacle to courage relates primarily to the professional and public spheres of life.

**It is the public's responsibility to promote a culture that minimizes fears of responsibi-lity and failure and integrates and promotes risks, mistakes and courageous decisions as something positive.**

This statement is confirmed by another obstacle to courage - also mentioned by a majority of respondents: fear of the economic and social consequences of one's actions. In the eco-nomic sphere, this refers primarily to financial risks, such as the start-up capital required, un-secured income, debts incurred or the lack of security in the event of failure. The fear of not receiving sufficient monetary support and the fear of the hurdles of creditworthiness often causes many innovative ideas to fail in the planning phase. Combined with a very high wor-kload, bureaucratic regulations and external uncertainties (e.g. inflation, Corona, Ukraine war, etc.), every second citizen is reluctant to make bold decisions in this area. Among other things, this is also evident in the declining interest in professional autonomy, which began in 2000. In an international comparison, the country that was once a nation of innovators and inventors and a location where many start-ups were initiated, now trails far behind coun-tries such as the United States, South Korea and even Great Britain, whose "TEA Quota" is twice as high. TEA stands for „Total Early Stage Entrepreneurial Activity" and shows the percentage of citizens who have established a business over the past 3.5 years. The low rate in Germany cannot simply be explained by a lack of personal courage, but is also rooted in inadequate scholastic start-up education and structural obstacles.

On the one hand, fears of the possible social consequences are linked to the economic risks resulting from monetary uncertainties, high workloads, stress-prone work atmospheres and reduced social life. On the other hand, almost every second German citizen also names the fear of disputes and conflicts.

Courageous behaviour means not only overcoming inner fears, but also dealing with them in one's personal environment, since this is usually directly or indirectly affected. Courage means change or unrest, as the status quo changes and new circumstances are formed. It is of secondary importance what kind of courageous behaviour is involved, whether it is standing up for convictions, confronting unfamiliar decisions, demanding needs and expectations or expressing unusual plans. In each case, it changes social relationships, whether at the professional or personal level. In the positive case, courage is perceived as constructive, innovative, inspiring or fearless; in the negative case, however, it is perceived as unsettling, rash or presumptuous. Those who act courageously often quickly find themselves in a position of justification.

**In a prevailing climate of security thinking, it is particularly challenging to realize the desire for change while at the same time not straining social relationships.**

Almost one in three citizens cites greater freedom as a prerequisite for making a courageous decision or acting with confidence and commitment. Once again, social structures that do not offer individuals sufficient opportunities to initiate projects or to implement them courageously become clear. In this context, rigid regulations, hierarchies or entrenched patterns are mentioned, which often limit or even prevent alternative thoughts or projects even in the concept phase. These are embedded in a fully comprehensive society that tends to reject risks and changes.

Yet, openness, innovation and the questioning of old concepts are the exact prerequisites that have been and continue to be forward-looking for every society. This not only concerns economic concepts, but extends into all areas of everyday life, such as concepts of the sharing economy, sustainability, integration, the development of local training programs, digital promotion, neighbourly coexistence, etc.

The interaction between societal, external and internal resistance to courage is also evident in the aspect of experiences. Two out of five Germans cite negative experiences as an obstacle to courageous action. Yet numerous studies on strategies and mechanisms with which people overcome challenges show how important positive experiences are for accepting challenges and acting innovatively. The more often conflict resolution is experienced as successful and constructive, the more confident people are in facing new problems. Conversely, however, unsatisfactory solutions or avoidance strategies lead to frustration, discontent and uncertainty.

**Fear of failure as well as negative experiences often lead to avoiding new challenges or to their perception as stressful events.**

The negative experiences affiliated with courageous action take different forms, such as financial failure, social conflicts, a lack of understanding from others, subsequent sanctions or a lack of recognition, which is also named by one in five as an important obstacle to courageous action. It is clear here that courageous action always has a social context and that positive feedback, whether private or public, is conducive to it. Precisely because courage also means overcoming fears and concerns, many would like to see appreciation that also rewards courage.

Almost one in three cites the lack of learning experience as an obstacle to courage. Social reasons are even more important here than negative experience. From family and school socialization to a lack of opportunities in student or vocational training and everyday working life, younger people in particular complain that they have hardly been given any knowledge and strategies or opportunities to learn or try out courageous behaviour. This happens albeit these disciplines offer innumerable options, as the environments of family and school offer a protected framework within which, in a relatively low risk setting, certain bold behaviour patterns, such as civil courage and self-accountability or even outlandish projects can be learnt, initiated and completed. Thus armed, strengthened by positive feedback, experience and success, young people could learn to calculate risks and take possible setbacks or failures as an incentive and internalize a culture that rewards courageous action and sees mistakes and risks not only as negative, but rather as a learning process and knowledge advantage for future decisions.

**To behave courageously, to think self-confidently and confidently takes place in an interactive learning process that does not focus on the teachers but on the learners who take an active role in the exchange with others.**

The goal is to develop one's own ways of thinking, solutions and ideas in a self-motivated, committed and team-oriented manner. In this context, in addition to the aforementioned inhibitions, such as a lack of positive experiences and rewards, the importance of a lack of role models is also apparent, whether in the private sphere (family, friends, teachers, trainers, neighbours, etc.) or in the public sphere (politicians, entrepreneurs, athletes, artists, etc.). Role models make an important contribution to the social-cognitive development of the individual, and not only in childhood, to the formation of one's own identity. If parents initially take on the function of role models as the closest reference persons, other role models later also provide orientation for one's own behaviour. Particularly in situations that are not so familiar or are associated with uncertainty, these are not simply imitated, but are often also subjected to critical reflection in order to be able to better classify one's own behaviour.

**Without role models, there is a lack of positive impulses and models that show how worthwhile it is to follow one's own ideas, ideals or dreams, how resistance can be overcome and how a venture can be successful.**

Another obstacle worth mentioning is the lack of fellow campaigners, which is also cited by one in three Germans. This aspect forms an intersection between the importance of a lack of role models, a lack of recognition and the fear of responsibility and failure. It reflects the individual's desire to find like-minded people who have a similar idea or vision and who also want to implement it courageously and confidently. The individual's fear of failure or responsibility can be much more effectively distributed and mitigated when joining forces with others. This also means that the individual is less vulnerable and the team can address the consequences of actions as a group. This does not mean that the individuals hide behind the group, it means that they stand up together. This also implies mutual recognition, the lack of which is often cited as an obstacle to courageous behaviour. The role of fellow campaigners is thus that of supporters who inspire and strengthen confidence when doubts or fears about one's own courage make it difficult to take action.

## EXAMPLE OF COURAGE
**Egyptian Queen Hatshepsut was courageous because she defied the common gender roles and cultural conventions of her time and became the first woman to hold the office of Egyptian pharaoh. Despite opposition and threats from those around her, she successfully ruled for more than 20 years and led Egypt into a time of prosperity and progress. She promoted trade as well as building projects, undertook expeditions to other countries, and initiated prosperity programs. Hatshepsut was a trailblazer for women and inspired future generations to pursue her goals and raise their voices.**

# IV. WHY COURAGE OFTEN FAILS US
## a. Women complain about fear and the couch potato mentality

*"There is only one kind of courage*
*that really matters:*
*The courage to be oneself"*
Ernest Hemingway

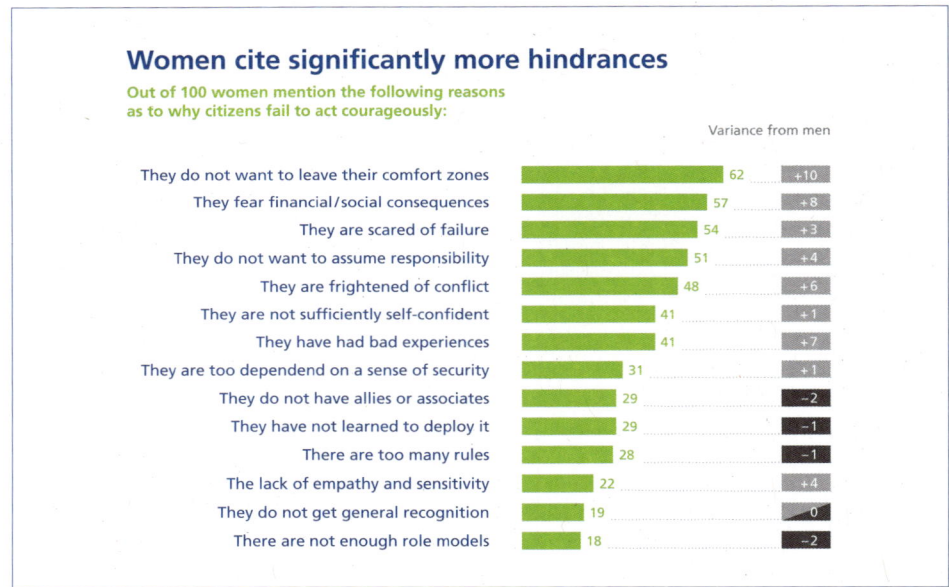

### Women cite significantly more hindrances

Out of 100 women mention the following reasons
as to why citizens fail to act courageously:

Variance from men

| Reason | Value | Variance |
|---|---|---|
| They do not want to leave their comfort zones | 62 | +10 |
| They fear financial/social consequences | 57 | +8 |
| They are scared of failure | 54 | +3 |
| They do not want to assume responsibility | 51 | +4 |
| They are frightened of conflict | 48 | +6 |
| They are not sufficiently self-confident | 41 | +1 |
| They have had bad experiences | 41 | +7 |
| They are too dependend on a sense of security | 31 | +1 |
| They do not have allies or associates | 29 | -2 |
| They have not learned to deploy it | 29 | -1 |
| There are too many rules | 28 | -1 |
| The lack of empathy and sensitivity | 22 | +4 |
| They do not get general recognition | 19 | 0 |
| There are not enough role models | 18 | -2 |

There are few differences in priorities between the genders. However, women cite significantly more obstacles to being courageous. This relates above all to the aspects of comfort, fear of consequences, negative experiences and shyness about confrontations. Due to their gender-specific socialization, they have a different view of certain forms of behaviour, so that some differences in their statements can be attributed to this. In addition, their specific experiences help to broaden the analysis and to view the respective characteristics and their meaning in a more differentiated way.

Women more often than men consider personal comfort and retreat into the comfort zone to be factors that can impair courageous behaviour. From a positive perspective, the latter offers a protected space for regeneration and relaxation. Free from constraints and requirements, one feels safe, content and self-determined there. The environment, fellow human beings and one's own behaviour are familiar and convey a feeling of comfort. In a negative sense, this can be associated with stagnation and comfort. Our own comfort zone then no longer serves as an important outlet for activity but has developed a momentum of its own that prevents us from taking on new challenges.

**The more one becomes accustomed to avoiding unpleasant or unknown situations, the less motivation, curiosity about change, and willingness to take risks develop.**

More often than men, women attribute great importance to inner motives. On the one hand, they draw on their own experiences and observations, and on the other, they focus more often on internal explanations for grievances, while men more often blame external circumstances for individual behaviour.

Negative experiences can hinder courageous people in their determination. Women, for example, report numerous negative experiences in their lives with a courageous demeanour. This mainly concerns professional activities. Women complain about the presence of prejudices in the form of gender stereotyping. They are often given less credit for courageous concepts and undertakings, denied leadership and assertiveness, and their determination and willingness to take risks are doubted. Since courageous behaviour requires a lot of energy, patience and strength, this additional resistance is seen as demotivating and obstructive. Because women are more likely than men to associate failures with inner motives, they complain about the extent to which negative experiences can manifest themselves internally, reduce self-awareness and lead to doubts about their own competence.

This is also evident in the higher level of consensus expressed by women when it comes to the obstacle of fear of consequences, especially in professional matters. More often than men, women are affected by low income, lack of access to resource networks and lack of mentoring support, and they are underrepresented in higher hierarchical levels. As a result, they have to anticipate to be exposed to stricter benchmarks, ignorance and more negative consequences when they introduce courageous projects, unconventional proposals, assertive demands – for instance disadvantages in their career advancement or with regard to salary increases.

In addition, women attribute a higher relevance to fear of confrontation as an obstacle. Here, too, their statements relate primarily to the work sector and their experiences there.

Gender-specific socialization still influences women's inner attitudes and perceptions. Accordingly, many of them tend to prefer harmonious and empathetic cooperation and to strive for balance and cooperation. By contrast, they tend to avoid decisive confrontations, uncompromising action and bold advances. In private contexts, on the other hand, such as courageous confrontations with family members, this fear is attributed more to men. They, too, cannot completely free themselves from social stereotypes and role models, such as the attribution of control and objectivity. Like women, they fear emotional injury and damage to relationships, but are often unable to communicate their needs and feelings and avoid emotional confrontations.

# IV. WHY COURAGE OFTEN FAILS US

## b. Older people primarily complain about complacency and the lack of responsibility

*"Courage does not mean,*
*having the strength to go on;*
*courage is going on*
*when you have no strength"*

Theodore Roosevelt

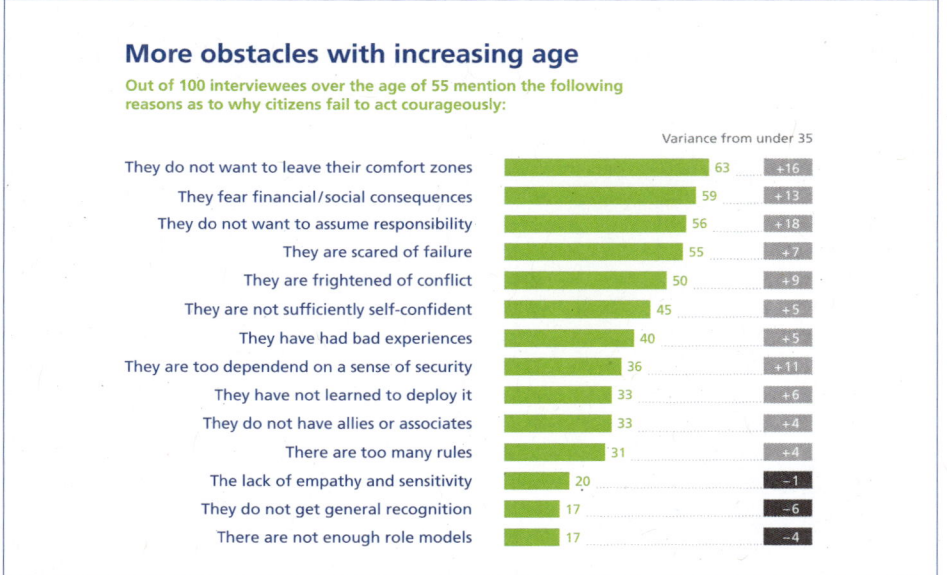

**More obstacles with increasing age**

Out of 100 interviewees over the age of 55 mention the following reasons as to why citizens fail to act courageously:

Variance from under 35

| Reason | Value | Variance |
| --- | --- | --- |
| They do not want to leave their comfort zones | 63 | +16 |
| They fear financial/social consequences | 59 | +13 |
| They do not want to assume responsibility | 56 | +18 |
| They are scared of failure | 55 | +7 |
| They are frightened of conflict | 50 | +9 |
| They are not sufficiently self-confident | 45 | +5 |
| They have had bad experiences | 40 | +5 |
| They are too dependend on a sense of security | 36 | +11 |
| They have not learned to deploy it | 33 | +6 |
| They do not have allies or associates | 33 | +4 |
| There are too many rules | 31 | +4 |
| The lack of empathy and sensitivity | 20 | -1 |
| They do not get general recognition | 17 | -6 |
| There are not enough role models | 17 | -4 |

When asked about possible obstacles to courage, the differences between the generations amount to up to 20 per cent. It is almost exclusively the older generation that achieves higher values. Only in the case of the characteristics of a lack of role models and recognition do they vote somewhat below average. The highest differences can be found for reasons stemming from intrinsic motivation.

According to many older people, many remain too much in their comfort zone, have an excessive need for security and are not prepared to take on responsibility. Given the absence of inner drive and the consistent focus on security and consistency, their focus is on their own welfare and keeps them from bravely embracing challenges. According to the older generation, however, this hardly applies to their own generation. The only motive they admit to themselves is convenience, which is not due to a lack of motivation, but rather to their age and declining energy.

**The older generation draws a direct comparison with their own living environment and misses values such as a willingness to perform, a sense of responsibility and a sense of community, especially among young people.**

Looking back, they remember how often in their lives they have met resistance and conflicts with determination and acted with perseverance and daring. In doing so, they not only pursued their own interests, but also acted with responsibility for the family or the community. They see the courage of many citizens today mainly in the form of self-interest, risk-taking, naivety and recklessness. Motives to which they tend to have a negative attitude. These different perceptions between young and old can be explained, among other things, by a glorified view of the past and of one's own history – for example, many a daring act was more like a determined appearance. In addition, a change in values and definitions is taking place. For example, many younger people no longer find their life fulfilment only in a performance-oriented workday or duty-filled family life with numerous positive and negative challenges. They strive for a balance between work and leisure and do not always have the ambition for leadership positions, careers and family commitments. Authoritarian structures that used to be widespread in professional and private life and accordingly offered opportunities for resistance are now in the process of dissolution, which is why courageous action in this context is not very necessary.

Further differences can be seen with regard to fear, which tends to encompass the professional rather than the personal sphere. Older professionals miss from their colleagues the willingness to settle disputes, to stand up for their own convictions, to make courageous suggestions or to implement plans courageously without always thinking of the consequences immediately. In their estimation, most of them are afraid to venture into uncertain territory and prefer to hide behind the silent majority. Trapped in their striving for security, they dare little for fear of possible professional disadvantages. This is accompanied by a fear of failure and of confrontation. This perception provides insights into a past working world that hardly exists in this form today. On the one hand, this refers to the previously mentioned authoritative structures that provided more of an occasion for brave behaviour, and on the other hand a different error culture. For instance, many older citizens criticize the lack of acceptance of errors and, at the same time, the prevailing tendency towards optimization.

More mature people still experienced mistakes as learning and growth opportunities and accordingly made many decisions without a safety net. Although they did not always perceive the working atmosphere as harmonious, and often even as tough, they also perceived it as lively, full of energy and marked by a thirst for action.

**Overall, older Germans often appear more determined, motivated and courageous than younger Germans.**

For them, the lack of courage is primarily a matter of individual responsibility. In doing so, they sometimes forget how much changes in values, living and working conditions also entail a changed interpretation of courage, which results in bravery appearing in new forms that are not always immediately apparent to them.

### c. People from East Germany are more likely to mention negative experiences, a lack of recognition and fear

*"Courage is not the absence of fear,*
*but the decision*
*that something else is more important*
*than fear"*

Ambrose Redmoon

## East Germans identify more hurdles for courageous conduct

Out of 100 East Germans mention the following reasons as to why citizens fail to act courageously:

Variance from West Germans

| Reason | Value | Variance |
|---|---|---|
| They do not want to leave their comfort zones | 58 | +1 |
| They fear financial/social consequences | 58 | +6 |
| They are scared of failure | 56 | +4 |
| They do not want to assume responsibility | 50 | +2 |
| They are frightened of conflict | 46 | +1 |
| They have had bad experiences | 44 | +8 |
| They are not sufficiently self-confident | 40 | −1 |
| They have not learned to deploy it | 33 | +4 |
| There are too many rules | 33 | +5 |
| They do not have allies or associates | 31 | +1 |
| They are too dependend on a sense of security | 27 | −4 |
| They do not get general recognition | 25 | +7 |
| The lack of empathy and sensitivity | 21 | +1 |
| There are not enough role models | 21 | +2 |

When it comes to naming obstacles to courageous behaviour, East and West Germans are almost of one mind. However, more citizens in the east agree with the respective reasons. This applies in particular to negative experiences, lack of recognition and fear of economic and social consequences. In contrast, their agreement with the obstacle reason "great need for security" is less pronounced.

Even when citizens talk about obstacles for the population in general, their own experiences are always included. This derives from experiences they have had with their personal, social, economic and historical backgrounds that have shaped their perceptions of the outside world. Perceptions of the behaviour of others are thus also always a mirror of their own lifeworld and offer explanatory approaches for differences in responses.

Even a quarter of a century after reunification, the responses of East Germans are still directly or indirectly linked to its economic and social consequences. For example, they see the negative experiences much more strongly than their West German counterparts as a significant hurdle to courage.

**East Germans criticize stereotypical ideas and prejudices that lead to inhibited – not only financial – support for courageous ideas and concepts, as well as a purely negative view of mistakes or setbacks.**

The more often they have had these experiences, not only personally but also among acquaintances or friends, the more they perceive a social climate of disillusionment and retreat into a safe comfort zone. According to their own statements, they themselves have had negative experiences, particularly in their social and professional environment, in that they have been denied courage, for example, and have been met with prejudice regarding their motivation, willingness to perform and entrepreneurial spirit, and in some cases still are.

In this context, they also criticize the often very one-dimensional view of courage and the focus on professional performance and success. In contrast, for many East Germans, courage in the context of their family biography means the willingness and ability to integrate in a relatively short time into a society that contradicted their previous life worlds. Thus, they had to overcome economic changes, forego social security and reject entire life plans. At the same time, they tried not to completely abandon their own behaviours and habits and courageously drew up new plans for the future. Based on this courageous behaviour, they regret more than West Germans that the various forms of courage are not given enough attention, past achievements are not appreciated enough, and a lack of recognition discourages people. Positive resonance is demanded not only from the personal environment, but also from social institutions, for example, by making courageous behaviour more visible.

Against this background, the above-average consensus of East Germans with the obstacles fear of consequences and fear of failure becomes clear:

Where family histories have been influenced over generations first by repression and conformity and later by job loss and social insecurity, it is more difficult to approach courageous projects with an open mind and without fear. The external constraints, material disadvantages and existing prejudices can also become internally entrenched and reinforce insecurities.

The lower level of approval for the aspect of a high need for security is also due to the historical biography of many East Germans. The older population in particular, with its socialization in GDR society, developed a special talent for improvisation. They learned to deal with the existing material deficiencies and to compensate for them independently and creatively. After the fall of communism, new challenges came to the fore, such as the search for jobs, the need for retraining, or the recognition of qualifications. The ability to deal with these changes and the experience they have gained do not protect them from the fear of failure or the broader consequences of courageous behaviour, but they are strengthened in their awareness that they can rely on their own strategies of adaptation and flexibility and attach less importance to the need for security than West Germans.

d. Lower income earners see negative experiences and lack of empathy, higher income earners identify an excessive need for security

*"Courage is like a muscle.*
*The more you use it,*
*the stronger it gets"*

Ruth Gordon

## Low and high income earners see different reasons for obstacles

Out of 100 high income earners mention the following reasons as to why citizens fail to act courageous:

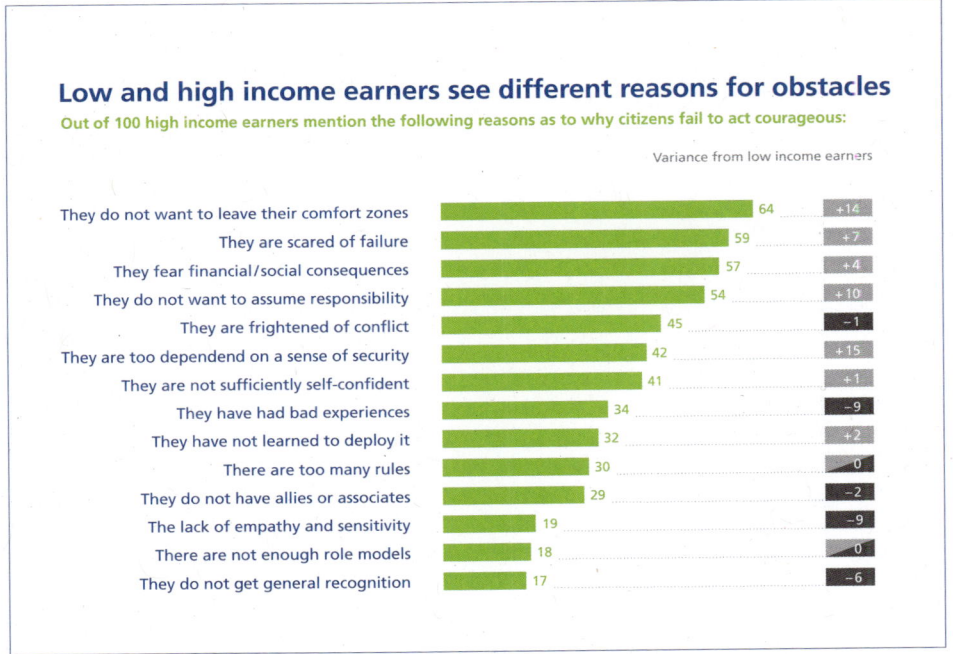

Variance from low income earners

| | | |
|---|---|---|
| They do not want to leave their comfort zones | 64 | +14 |
| They are scared of failure | 59 | +7 |
| They fear financial/social consequences | 57 | +4 |
| They do not want to assume responsibility | 54 | +10 |
| They are frightened of conflict | 45 | −1 |
| They are too dependend on a sense of security | 42 | +15 |
| They are not sufficiently self-confident | 41 | +1 |
| They have had bad experiences | 34 | −9 |
| They have not learned to deploy it | 32 | +2 |
| There are too many rules | 30 | 0 |
| They do not have allies or associates | 29 | −2 |
| The lack of empathy and sensitivity | 19 | −9 |
| There are not enough role models | 18 | 0 |
| They do not get general recognition | 17 | −6 |

Interesting similarities become apparent when comparing age and income. The higher earners, for example, have an almost identical focus as the older generation. Both agree more often than average with the obstacles of convenience, security, lack of responsibility and fear of failure. And both claim for their own reference group and for themselves that they are little influenced by these obstacles, but rather assign them to the "others."

Whereas the considerations of older people can be explained primarily based on their ages, their experience and their value concepts, the values of higher income earners lie mainly in their monetary starting position and their professional positions. This also, to a large extent, explains the differences between them and the lower income earners. If we relate the statements of the financially well-off to their other statements, such as personal courage, certain behaviours and thought patterns emerge. Based on their own experiences, they do not see challenges as a threat or hurdle, but as a positive incentive to fully exploit their own potential and to present themselves to the outside world as a determined and courageous individuals.

Their thinking tends to be optimistic, future-oriented and resolute, and their courage is mainly evident in the realization of professional and personal changes. Accordingly, they miss characteristics in their fellow citizens that they themselves perceive as promising for their own happiness in life and also realize. As a result, they are more likely than average to criticize an existing laziness that leads them to avoid risks and not show any daring.

**The high security mindset focuses too much on negative consequences, according to high earners, and makes many citizens hesitant and fearful to act without recognizing the positive consequences of courage and change.**

This also explains their dissatisfaction with the lack of responsibility. Often working in managerial positions themselves, they see the assumption of professional responsibility as a matter of course or even as an attractive challenge that they are happy to take on. Accordingly, they react with incomprehension to the lack of willingness to do so. They sometimes underestimate their privileged situation and overlook their lack of financial resources and access to information and networks from others. Thus, their statements focus primarily on individual obstacles and neglect the importance of certain societal characteristics, such as low income and less access to educational resources.

Fellow low-income citizens agree with the above reasons to a much lesser extent due to these lack of resources. More often than average, they cite a lack of empathy and negative experiences as arguments for a lack of courage. Similar to many East Germans and women, they also associate failed attempts at courageous action with a lack of support, recognition and prejudice. Due to their (professional) life situation, they find it much more difficult to pursue new plans decisively and optimistically. When options arise, they have to reckon with more disappointments and rejections. In this context, they also show the highest agreement of all groups of people on the obstacle of lacking empathy. Empathy means the ability to empathize with the feelings and perspectives of others and to understand their needs and fears. The lack of empathy can affect not only the interpersonal sphere, but also society as a whole.

**Lower income earners feel that courageous people are often not shown enough empathy, their decisions and plans tend to be viewed sceptically and from a distance, and they are therefore disillusioned and disappointed.**

This lack of empathy is also one reason why some citizens are focused only on their own views and interests. As a result, the motivation to support other people or stand up for them decreases. Combined with other motives, such as convenience or fear of risks, this can create a social climate of passivity, in which civil courage is seen as an unnecessary risk that does not affect one personally. In particular, citizens with a low income would like to see a strengthening of empathy and courageous and resolute solidarity for the cohesion of society.

## EXAMPLE OF COURAGE
**The first responders and firefighters who worked in New York after the September 11 terrorist attacks showed great courage. They ran into the collapsing buildings amid the rubble and chaos to save people. Their selfless dedication and determination to help in the midst of one of the greatest disasters on American soil is a prime example of courage and service to others in dangerous situations.**

*"There is no courage without fear,*
*but we must still dare"*

Madeleine Albright

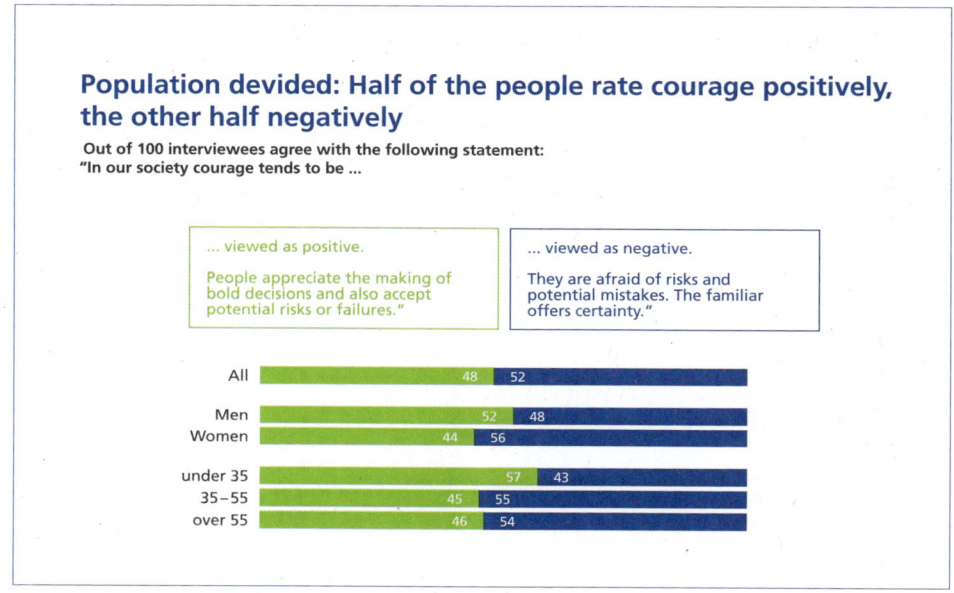

## Population devided: Half of the people rate courage positively, the other half negatively

**Out of 100 interviewees agree with the following statement:**
**"In our society courage tends to be ...**

... viewed as positive.

People appreciate the making of bold decisions and also accept potential risks or failures."

... viewed as negative.

They are afraid of risks and potential mistakes. The familiar offers certainty."

| | positive | negative |
|---|---|---|
| All | 48 | 52 |
| Men | 52 | 48 |
| Women | 44 | 56 |
| under 35 | 57 | 43 |
| 35–55 | 45 | 55 |
| over 55 | 46 | 54 |

Is courage viewed positively or negatively in German society? The German population is split on this issue. As was evident from the other questions, on the one hand people recognize the positive significance of courageous behaviour, value determination and optimism, believe in the importance of role models and show their courage themselves in various situations. On the other hand, however, they also name numerous aspects that hinder such behaviour, whether of an individual or structural nature. These range from a lack of self-confidence to a lack of freedom to rigid institutional regulations. Only very few citizens express a purely positive or purely negative opinion, but rather a differentiated assessment. The question on the general societal assessment of courage reveals which motives are more important to citizens, what their respective perceptions are, and which factors influence them.

**More than every second German citizen believes that courage is viewed rather negatively in our society.**

This applies to individuals and to public and state institutions. With regard to institutions, the political and economic spheres in particular are perceived as lacking in courage. Both are characterized by a climate that feels particularly committed to security and stability. Risks are seen as a threat, either to the status quo, to reliability, and stability or regulated structures. In the economic sphere, concepts that are too bold or too expeditious are often met with terms such as "endangering prosperity" as a counterargument, while politicians often speak of "stability as the highest premise" in order to reject uncertain reforms. The culture is geared toward security and optimization. Risk minimization concepts must be available in all areas, everything must be considered twice, and the outcome should be known in advance. As a result, mistakes are viewed primarily negatively, risks and uncertainties are rejected, and the familiar is the primary goal.

Here, the statements also point to the importance of structures that inhibit people's bold behaviour. This relates, for example, to discrimination against minorities, the unequal distribution of material and immaterial resources and gender inequality. Stereotyping and discrimination can affect people's courage to stand up for their interests, ideas or plans, thus reinforcing the general climate of reticence.

Whenever citizens show little willingness to express courage, certainty and habits become all the more visible instead. These are expressed not only in the restrained behaviour of political and business leaders, but also in numerous laws, regulations, rules and insurance policies. Citizens feel surrounded by a secure framework that protects them from imponderables, gives them direction and influences their personal behaviour in terms of courage and determination. Structural protection can lead to a retreat into the comfort zone, preference for comfort and avoidance of challenges. This behaviour becomes visible when the social environment increasingly withdraws into the private sphere, reacts opposingly to courageous life plans and perceives change as a disruption or danger. Particularly regrettable in this context is a reluctance to get involved in society and a lack of civil courage.

The perception of a safety-oriented society is influenced by a multitude of complex contexts and aspects, such as personality, gender, age, social environment, individual experiences with courageous or safety-oriented behaviour, and the influence of public or private structures and institutions (e.g. education, school, media). These motives are in a continuous exchange, shaping, affecting and inspiring each other. As a result, it is often not possible to name any clear causes for the respective perceptions, but rather to speak of complex reciprocal influences that shape one's own assessment and the social climate.

The same applies to those who have a positive view of courage in German society. They speak of an optimistic climate, with an appreciation for courageous decisions and a multitude of opportunities to realize individual life designs. Both the closer social environment and public opinion are described as determined and confident. Although hesitancy and a strong need for security are not denied, a generally unafraid awareness dominates for them. In particular, this is perceived in personal life and professional settings and less so within institutional spheres, such as politics or the media. In the private realm, citizens speak of numerous examples in which friends or family members themselves act courageously or regard and support daring on the part of others with admiration and praise. This may include taking on a leadership role in a community group, championing a good cause on social media, civic engagement, living abroad, or alternative life choices. These are often the subject of open and interested discussion and are positively evaluated in a feedback culture. In the professional sector, a courageous climate is perceived in small and medium-sized enterprises and in all forms of self-employment. Particularly among the self-employed, a high-energy determination, innovative ideas, belief in oneself, overcoming resistance and financial investment are mentioned.

**Citizens are certain that the courageous conviction of individuals has an inspiring and motivating effect on their friends, family, colleagues or neighbours. As a result, they encourage others and each other to express their assertiveness.**

People who are initially less bold also reap the benefits of this interchange. Moreover, brave action in one life realm may also have a positive effect on another.

For example, any professional fearlessness can be transferred to bold civil conduct. An encouraging and supportive social network is helpful here. This fortifies an open and learning society in which versatility, change, mistakes and risks are seen positively and as opportunities for improvement.

Notwithstanding the positive perception of courage, the statements also point to possible dangers and motives that could be weakened by acting too courageously. This applies, for example, to certain groups of people who are more concerned with security and stability and feel overwhelmed by a constantly changing climate. Here, fears can be intensified and courage as such can only be associated with recklessness, arrogance and naivety.

When comparing educational or income groups, only marginal differences can be found, as with marital status or East-West comparisons. Only gender and age show different perceptions. For example, women express a higher level of agreement with a negative perception of courage in society than men. This can be attributed, among other things, to the structural obstacles mentioned above. Women are confronted more strongly than men with role attributions, prejudices and rejections, both in the professional and private spheres. They perceive their social environment as more rigid and security-oriented – more fixated on the status quo than open to change. Women are more committed than others to achieving a better work-life balance, flatter hierarchies and fewer gender stereotypes, for example. However, their commitment is only successful to a limited extent and thus reinforces the female perception of a less courageous society.

In terms of age, those under 35 show above-average agreement with the perception of a courageous society. This can be explained on the one hand by their (age-related) lack of experience, but on the other hand also by their greater curiosity, their stronger idealism or their greater affinity for further development and change. They act more decisively, more daringly and are less afraid of risks. They are often still in an orientation phase, both professionally and privately, and strive to try out or realize their ideas and life plans. Surrounded by peers, they experience their own environment as energetic and innovative, whereby their view of the outside world is significantly influenced by their own attitude. This is why young people also transfer their own perspectives to society as a whole and perceive it as more courageous than the other groups in society. In this way, they can be an important source of inspiration for others when it comes to shaping society more courageously based on their own responsibilities.

## EXAMPLE OF COURAGE
**American James Shaw Jr. provides an example of courageous action in a dangerous situation. In 2018, he witnessed an armed attack in a Nashville restaurant in which four people were killed. Shaw Jr. acted boldly by confronting the perpetrator and disarming him, preventing further death or injury. This act demonstrates not only his courage, but also his determination as an individual to stand up for the unknown, even when it can be risky and life-threatening.**

*"I've never tried this before,
so I'm completely sure I can do it"*

Pippi Longstocking

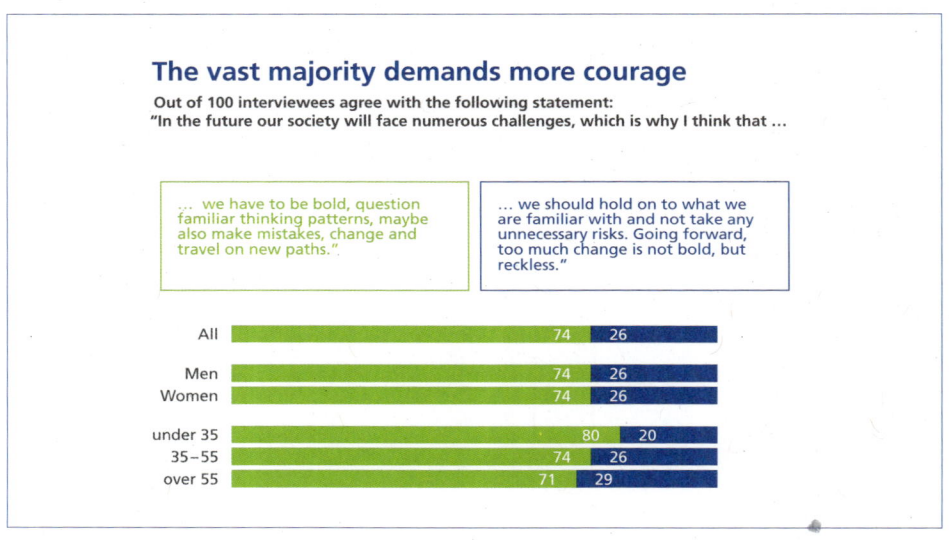

### The vast majority demands more courage

Out of 100 interviewees agree with the following statement:
"In the future our society will face numerous challenges, which is why I think that ...

| ... we have to be bold, question familiar thinking patterns, maybe also make mistakes, change and travel on new paths." | ... we should hold on to what we are familiar with and not take any unnecessary risks. Going forward, too much change is not bold, but reckless." |

| | | |
|---|---|---|
| All | 74 | 26 |
| Men | 74 | 26 |
| Women | 74 | 26 |
| under 35 | 80 | 20 |
| 35–55 | 74 | 26 |
| over 55 | 71 | 29 |

A large majority agrees that the challenges of the future can only be met if society is prepared to question old thought patterns and openly embrace bold change. The challenges are to be found at both national and global level and will occupy Germany in the short term as well as in the longer term. In terms of national priorities, citizens name problems such as the oft-cited shortage of skilled workers, the uncertain energy supply, necessary reforms to the education and healthcare systems, urban or housing development, the integration of refugees and migrants, increasing social division, demographic change, the rise of political extremism, digitization or faltering competitiveness and rising inflation. In the global context, the main issues highlighted are European integration, international security, armed conflicts, the spread of pandemics, and the consequences of global warming. What is typical for all challenges without a doubt is that they are highly complex and cannot be considered single-handedly. They are all interconnected and subject to economic, political and social developments and dependencies. Therefore, they cannot be solved by simple political measures or legislation. Instead, a variety of measures and approaches are needed to identify constructive and sustainable solutions. Most citizens are aware of this complexity and recognize that not only structural obstacles must be overcome, but all citizens are required to reflect on their own thinking and behaviour. This is where the importance of courage comes into focus, as it is seen as an indispensable prerequisite for facing future challenges.

In this case, for the German people, courage is not just one character trait among many, but a central prerequisite for individual and social development. Courage manifests itself in a wide variety of forms, always involves social interaction with others, and affects not only the person acting courageously, but often also his or her social environment, the broader public, or even society as a whole. And it always brings about change, creates new constellations and perspectives.

**Due to future challenges, citizens will have to experience changes, accept modifications and adapt to new condition.**

In order to not only passively let this happen, but to actively help shape it, courage is seen as a significant characteristic. Old patterns of thinking will also only be able to solve future problems to a limited extent or even to grasp them at all. Habitual ways of looking at things – whether from an individual or a group, whether they concern institutional structures or the social climate – tend to prioritize concerns and negate opportunities. In the personal sphere, this can be evident when, at an early age, adolescent rebellion against authority is curbed by parents with reference to possible sanctions, studies or career aspirations are discounted with the risk of lacking career opportunities, or sabbaticals/stays abroad are disapproved of with disadvantages in terms of pension payments. Later, traditional attitudes, such as an increased need for security or comfort, can lead to a retreat into the familiar comfort zone and a refusal to take risks, whether in private or professional decisions. Within businesses and institutions, for instance in work flow processes or when decision-makers take action, the focus on benefitting oneself, on paths often travelled and stringent traditions, lead us to perceiving alternative concepts or ground-breaking reforms as dangers that will affect the status quo. The constant concerns about possible risks, the hesitant waiting and the cautious reassurances superficially offer a false vision of security and reason, but also translate into a lack of confidence, a lack of self-assurance and a lack of visibility. With regard to the high level of approval for social courage, there are hardly any differences within the individual groups. Only the younger generation shows above-average approval, at 80 percent. As was already clear from other questions, they are also more open, curious and willing to take risks.

In line with their own behaviour, they also want and demand more of society. In addition, future challenges affect and influence them, e.g. in education (more digitization), work (better compatibility of career and family) or climate change (more sustainability), affect and influence young people in particular, which is why they are in favor of new approaches and ways of thinking. In connection with the majority approval of bold changes, there is also criticism of a culture of error, which is perceived as too rigid and negative. In its most visible form, it is reflected in the current trend toward optimization, which is seemingly goal-oriented and effectively erected. But where mistakes or setbacks are not foreseen, optimization becomes a compulsion and subsequently inhibits courageous decisions for fear of failure. This is also confirmed in the critical view of the increasing optimization of more than two thirds of the population.

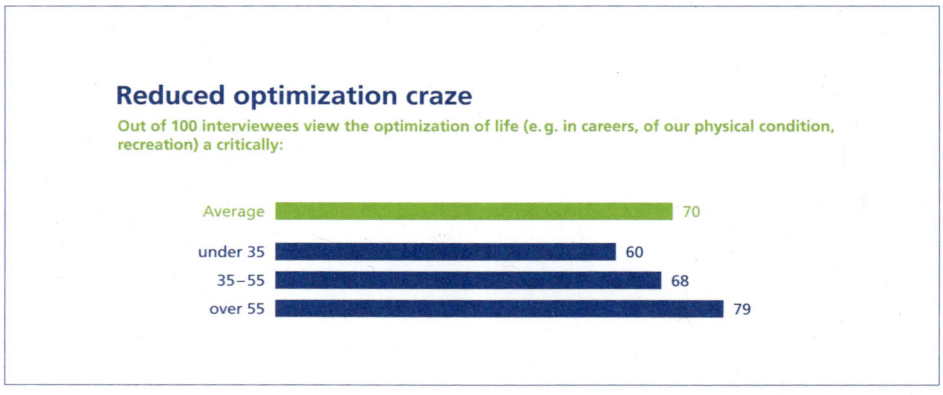

**Reduced optimization craze**

Out of 100 interviewees view the optimization of life (e.g. in careers, of our physical condition, recreation) a critically:

| | |
|---|---|
| Average | 70 |
| under 35 | 60 |
| 35–55 | 68 |
| over 55 | 79 |

The search term "optimize your life" returns around 27 million entries on Google. The topics range from nutrition and career to dating and sports tips, to topics such as time management or mindfulness. Optimization affects all areas of society and, in its pronounced form, is also accompanied by risks. In the area of leisure, for example, the search for the most effective activities can lead to a feeling of overload and exhaustion, combined with a lack of relaxation and leisure. With regard to physical optimization, tendencies toward perfect fitness and beauty must be critically questioned, as they can lead to a loss of one's own body acceptance and one-sided beauty ideals. In the professional sector, constant optimization and the associated increase in performance can lead to increased competition, mistrust and envy, to an increased risk of burnout and to a poorer compatibility of work and leisure.

Common to all optimization tendencies is the danger of changing the orientation towards externally determined, external ideals and requirements, which leads to self-disciplining, at the end of which is inner dissatisfaction and the loss of diversity and individuality. There is also the risk of no longer behaving courageously since the uncertainties involved cannot be optimally calculated in a risk-benefit calculation. With regard to the differences within the population, the older generation expresses itself much more critically. They have lived most of their lives in a time when the focus was not as strongly on optimization and performance as it is today. Thus, the idea of constantly optimizing life is perceived by them as too superficial and rigid. Because of their life experiences and their age, they are also less susceptible to fads and trends and know that life is not always perfect or predictable. Their critical appraisal also reflects existing disadvantages compared with the younger generation e.g., in terms of physical resilience or the use of technical possibilities, which make it more difficult for them to adapt to optimization.

The younger generation, on the other hand, is more susceptible to group pressures, fads and trends and cannot always escape the demands of optimization. Nevertheless, the majority of them also view the increasing optimization of life critically, blaming social media platforms in particular for this trend, as people try to present themselves as perfectly as possible there.

**Particularly in connection with challenges that affect social interaction in society, whether in the personal or professional sphere, young and old alike would like to see an end to increasing optimization and instead a constructive culture of error in which mistakes are seen as an opportunity for learning and improvement.**

This culture is characterized by open communication, learning orientation, support and co-operative solution orientation. On the other hand, demotivating structures, one-sided blame and sanctions should be avoided.

For citizens, a courageous social climate contributes to broadening their own perspectives, strengthening their motivation and sense of responsibility, facing up to personal challenges and dealing courageously with future social requirements. In addition, a courageous social climate also supports and obliges institutional organizations and political and economic leaders to detach themselves more strongly from particular interests, to think more openly, to act more innovatively and to make courageous decisions. In their mutual closeness to influence, all citizens could thus confidently and fearlessly help to shape society.

## EXAMPLE OF COURAGE

Steve Jobs was willing to take risks for his dreams and visions. He was not swayed by the sceptical opinions of others, nor discouraged by industry rejection. Instead, he believed in himself and his ideas, revolutionizing the computer industry. With the introduction of the Apple Macintosh computer, the iPods, the iPad or the iPhone, he managed to make electronic devices simple and intuitive. Jobs also did not hesitate to leave the company in an interim when it was going in a direction he thought was wrong. His determination and courage to take risks helped him achieve great success and leave a lasting impact on the technology industry.

# VII. CONCLUSION

*"You have to be bold*
*to be happy"*
Anne Frank

*German courage* instead of *German fear* is the title of this book. After evaluating all the interviews, data and research results, this appeal can only be underscored. The generally prevailing view that Germany is characterized by *German angst*, and in some cases almost paralyzed, can be countered by numerous positive and hopeful facts, attitudes and examples. However, the challenges, obstacles and necessary preconditions that should be addressed constructively and creatively have also become clear.

## THE CORE RESULTS
– **The associations with the term "courage" are largely positive.**
– **People have an intense desire to have courageous role models in their lives.**
– **People are willing to exude a determined advocacy for bold action within the families and circles of friends.**
– **Courage is adversely affect by lethargy and uncertainties.**
– **Society is taking a split stance towards courage.**
– **Courage is considered valuable for addressing future challenges.**

Contrary to the often cited *German angst*, the potential of *German courage* becomes clear. The term "potential", from the Latin "potentia", means something like power, strength, performance, influence, ability or capability, and implies the option of achieving something and exploiting existing possibilities without falling prey to optimization tendencies at the expense of health or emotional balance. This potential is reflected in the courageous basic attitude of the vast majority of citizens, which, however, has so far often failed to materialize in practice due to internal and external obstacles. Courage is associated with people who are self-reliant and responsible, who courageously stand up for their values and are willing to overcome internal and external resistance. This idea coincides with the desire for courageous role models from whom Germans hope to draw inspiration for their own lifestyles. Germans would like to see these role models from their immediate family environment or their own lives, as well as from politics and fellow citizens in general. Role models that arise from these groups are sending strong signals out to society to get all citizens to assume responsibilities and to act courageously. However, this longing is often disappointed in reality, as none of the people or groups mentioned above currently fulfil the hopes placed in them.

With regard to their own courageous behaviour, this is particularly evident in the private sphere, in their commitment to family and friends and in standing up for their own convictions. Apart from this, the figures and statements as a whole suggest a rather restrained idealistic determination in practice. The reasons for this are rooted in individual sensitivities as well as institutional and social structures, which influence and reinforce each other. The obstacles range from comfort, a lack of self-confidence and a sense of responsibility, to fear of failure and conflict, to restrictive structures such as too many regulations, too little recognition, a prevailing culture of error or a lack of support. These obstacles are also reflected in the social awareness and climate, which is perceived differently by the citizens. Roughly half of the respondents have a positive or negative view of the understanding of courage in society. In contrast, the population is largely unanimous about the importance of courage for future national and global challenges and fearless thinking and acting. For the vast majority, courage is an indispensable attribute for shaping society constructively. The latter two statements in particular highlight the contradiction between theoretical conviction and the reality check. Thus, a large majority is convinced of the positive and innovative power of courage and recognizes the importance of courageous role models and the high significance of courage for both personal development and that of society. In practice, however, they see few opportunities for courageous behaviour, are mainly involved within their close social environment, complain about a lack of fearless role models, are often disappointed by their fellow citizens in terms of decisive action, and many also see society as a whole as too security oriented.

On the one hand, the analysis of individual population groups points to structural obstacles, but on the other hand, apparent self-evident facts are refuted. Obstacles are found in the areas of work and leadership structures, material inequality, lack of recognition and discrimination. These particularly affect low-income earners, women and East Germans and prevent them from acting more confidently and courageously. But higher earners also criticize certain professional constellations as well as framework conditions that hinder innovative and unusual ideas. There are many opportunities for all decision-makers to overcome these barriers and prejudices to give more liberty and justice a much higher priority. The seemingly self-evident issues specifically affect the older generation in terms of their perception of courage and security. They are often said to have a greater need for security, a greater affinity for the status quo and a more negative attitude toward innovation and risks. However, this assessment cannot be confirmed. Although many older people are more reluctant to embrace new trends and developments, are less willing to take risks and rate some past conditions and behaviours more positively than current ones, they do not rate courage lower overall than others. On the contrary, due to their age, experience and socialization, they have had to face resistance more often in their lives and have had to assert themselves more strongly against authority and tradition. They have learned to act self-confidently and optimistically, to take responsibility and to stand up for their convictions. On the basis of these experiences, they miss courageous commitment and courage from their fellow citizens and express the intention of behaving courageously themselves in the future as well.

The high level of agreement among Germans on the need for courage and confidence to tackle future challenges is also evident when asked about their own optimism. Around three quarters of the population want to be more optimistic in the next twelve months. Optimism can be defined as a positive attitude or outlook on life that is focused on future events. Regardless of the content, people are convinced that things will change for the better. This basic attitude is shaped by the family situation (upbringing, parental behaviour, home environment, material circumstances) and other socialization influences (school, working world, peer groups).

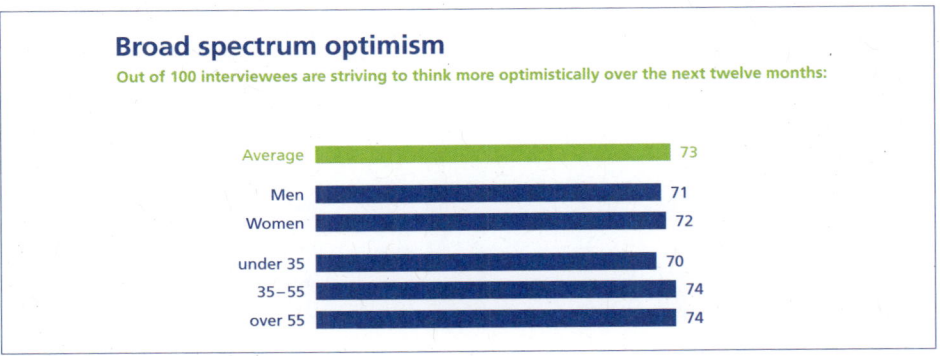

**Broad spectrum optimism**
Out of 100 interviewees are striving to think more optimistically over the next twelve months:

| | |
|---|---|
| Average | 73 |
| Men | 71 |
| Women | 72 |
| under 35 | 70 |
| 35–55 | 74 |
| over 55 | 74 |

**Optimism may be fortified, fostered, encumbered and learnt.**

In the private sphere, optimism can help strengthen mental and emotional health and develop a sense of hope and confidence. The positive is put in the foreground, whereas rejections and inhibitions become less important. Both in everyday life and during extraordinary events or crisis situations (illness, conflicts, losses, failures, etc.), positive thinking helps to reduce stress, overcome setbacks and focus on possibilities and opportunities.

People express a desire to internalize optimism more and focus less on obstacles and uncertainties. This also applies to the professional and social spheres. Here they intend to overcome resistance, accept challenges and focus less on grievances, annoyances and problems. In concrete terms, they mention an improvement in the working atmosphere, career aspirations and more favourable working conditions. Many people would also like to take a more intensive and serious look at life's dreams, perhaps take some time off, go abroad or take a longer vacation. In the social context, the vast majority would like to be more optimistic about challenges, tackle them, shape them themselves and act with confidence. Almost three quarters (72%) also want to criticize less and instead act more tolerantly, recognize more and support more.

Neighbourhood or voluntary work are mentioned as possible fields of action in this context. Particularly in interpersonal interaction, citizens hope this will lead to a better community, less egoism and more cohesion. This also points to another effect of optimism: Optimism not only has great significance for the individual, but also strengthens social ties, interactions and the sense of community. Individual members experience and show more interest, support, motivation and inspiration. In short, optimism is contagious.

**Although citizens use different strategies to think and act more optimistically, they are united by a desire for optimism and an effort to seize more opportunities to have positive experiences.**

Optimism can not only be learned, but also strengthened and developed through positive experience. The more often people experience that a positive attitude can help them achieve their goals, the more their self-esteem increases and they take on new challenges with greater confidence. Citizens want to expand their social lives to gain inspiration and motivation from others. They hope to have a support system beyond their circle of friends and family. This can be, for example, like-minded people with common interests, club members, neighbours, but also strangers who can offer them a model of motivation and confidence and who can also encourage them themselves with their optimism. Accordingly, nine out of ten Germans (89%), for example, would like to have a neighbourhood in which people help each other and are optimistic even in difficult situations. Almost all citizens want to broaden their mental perspectives by not condemning contrary convictions or life plans, but also accepting them as an opportunity for reflection and recognizing positive aspects in them. The importance of reflection also becomes apparent in connection with the public and the media. Many citizens regret how much their own perceptions are influenced by the media, which often focus on negative reporting.

**Too much bad news**
Out of 100 interviewees feel that primarily bad news is published by the media:

| | |
|---|---|
| Average | 84 |
| Men | 82 |
| Women | 86 |
| under 35 | 81 |
| 35–55 | 84 |
| over 55 | 86 |

More than eight out of ten Germans are convinced that they see, hear or read predominantly negative headlines in the news. There is widespread agreement within the population, and gender, place of residence, income, educational background or age hardly play a role.

"Only bad news is good news" is a well-known phrase from the media industry. According to this assumption, bad news sells better than good news and often reaches the public's attention more quickly. The content of the news is not decisive and can range from economic downturns and natural disasters to personal tragedies or misconduct. Although some bad news may have a positive impact (e.g, serving as a warning or stimulating action to improve), bad news is almost always accompanied by negative consequences. One of the most serious is the emotional toll it can take on many citizens. When most reports revolve around wars, recessions, climate disasters, political malfeasance, scandals, or divisions, there is often a sense of fear and hopelessness. Also, too much bad news can reinforce a loss of trust in politicians and institutions and foster a resigned defensiveness. This view makes it difficult to tackle problems in a constructive way.

**Citizens do not want glossed-over news, but they miss information, reports, accounts and narratives that speak of confident developments, lasting successes, optimistic concepts or practices.**

In addition to the media, other parameters also influence an optimistic or pessimistic attitude, such as difficult living conditions (e.g. material deficiencies, unemployment), structural inequality (e.g. discrimination) and unstable economic or political conditions. Thus, the resolution for more individual optimism must also be seen against the backdrop of the social challenges of recent years (pandemic, Ukraine war or inflation).

Advances in science and technology, economic developments and trends, political decisions and demographic developments are all driving forces for change in society. But the actual implementation is also up to each individual to help shape the social climate with courage and confidence. Courage is not just a character trait but manifests itself in a wide variety of facets: *Moral courage*, for example, refers to the ability to stand up for convictions and values, even if they are not popular. *Emotional courage* becomes visible when one overcomes injuries or losses. *Physical courage* involves going into dangerous situations to protect oneself or others, while *creative courage* comes into play when pursuing innovative ideas. *Self-reflective courage* refers to the ability to make, accept and learn from mistakes. *Cultural courage* challenges values and norms. *Intellectual courage* does not shy away from new ideas and reflection, even if they contradict previous knowledge, and *social courage* emerges in interpersonal situations when initiating interactions and advocating for the rights of others.

There is undoubtedly no simple answer to what is needed to make German society more courageous. However, numerous measures and opportunities emerge that can help promote courage within a society and strengthen the existing potential.

1. Upbringing and education: Both are without question among the most effective tools for promoting courage. Early on, self-confidence and social intelligence can be strengthened in families and kindergartens. Later, critical thinking should be promoted in school, broadening students' perspectives and encouraging them to undertake courageous projects on their own responsibility. Universities and colleges could also include courage as one of the key competencies in their curricula.

2. Encouraging open dialogue and discussion: Allowing and encouraging open dialogue can help individuals to share their fears and concerns, overcome them, encounter other perspectives, ways of thinking and behaving, and challenge their own prejudices.

3. Fostering solidarity and community engagement: Supporting and recognizing community service projects, volunteering and voluntary work that encourage people to contribute to the

community and support others. One focus here could be on reaching out to young people, giving them more freedom and decision-making opportunities to actively shape their future.

4. More media competence and "good news": Only with sufficient media competence is one able to classify and critically question the information received and its origins. This also reduces the fear of apparent manipulation by the media. In addition, a stronger visibility of positive news is recommended to strengthen a general confident basic attitude.

5. Promoting political participation: Encouraging people to actively shape society, whether through elections, online platforms, citizens' forums or memberships in political organizations or NGOs, can help strengthen individual responsibility and reduce feelings of helplessness and powerlessness. Citizens need to know that their opinions and needs are being heard and that they will be involved in decision-making.

6. Promoting entrepreneurship and innovation: Establish support programs and resources to help entrepreneurs and innovators develop new and bold ideas and business models.

7. Creating open working conditions: Develop programs and measures that encourage companies and employers to create attractive and supportive development opportunities for their employees, thereby giving them more room for bold ideas and self-responsible work.

8. Leadership: Determined, confident and inspiring leadership, whether political, economic, scientific, social or media, can help a society to act more courageously. This requires open communication, an authentic demeanour and clear formulations of convictions, visions and goals that both motivate and can be understood.

9. Culture of errors: Promoting a culture characterized by openness, learning orientation, responsibility and optimism, and seeing errors not as failures but as important opportunities for growth.

10. Positive role models: Increased recognition of courageous people, projects, concepts, ideas, in order to give them the recognition they deserve and to meet the citizens' desire for positive role models.

**The realization of each of these proposals requires effort, a sense of responsibility and the willingness to overcome resistance. In short, IT REQUIRES COURAGE.**

# MORE COURAGE

Christiane Goetz-Weimer
Wolfram Weimer

# CHRISTIANE GOETZ-WEIMER, WOLFRAM WEIMER

Publisher WEIMER MEDIA GROUP

Philosopher Sören Kierkegaard turned German angst into a term used around the globe in 1844. Martin Heidegger and Karl Jaspers polished it up from an existential perspective. World wars, ideologies and dictatorships were associated with German angst – the alleged character trait of a nation that due to its central geographical location was dominated and driven by primal fear. "Like hypochondriacs, Germans are always afraid of the worst", is the diagnosis of historian Frank Biess, whose book "Republik der Angst" (Republic of Fear) sheds light on Germany's trauma. It is indeed possible that the "last generation" feels more comfortable here than any where else. The term itself has actually landed in the Oxford Dictionary.

Nevertheless, the noun "German angst" travels through this country like counterfeit cash. After all, the other major German characteristics are lots of vigour paired with optimism. The nation of poets, intellectuals, exporters and engineers as well as travel and patent champions would not be nearly as successful if it were not also curious and confident. Is Germany possibly much bolder than many think?

We set out to discover more about that. We asked more than forty pioneers from the disciplines of science, business, politics and well as journalism. Those who at our Ludwig Erhard Summit charge our meeting that takes place each and every year on the Tegernsee so progressively with their creative thoughts and actions. After all, doing is being willing, except more drastically.

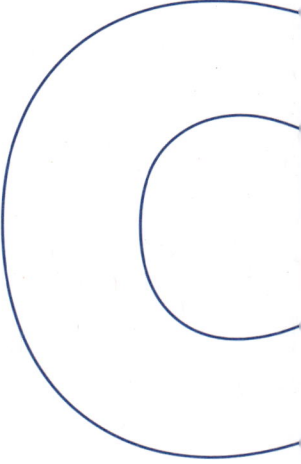

# OUR

## more COURAGE

So what is really going on with German angst? What encourages us? What keeps Germany from being bold? How do the multipliers and those who have the power to define things encourage others to go out on a limb? The answers to these questions are featured in this book. They are smart, contemplative and pioneering – all at the same time. Sometimes they are surprising and counter intuitive. Always characterized by "MOVE" – Mut, Optimismus, Vertrauen und Engagement (courage, optimism, trust and engagement). This book shows that angst does not even talk about half of the cultural history. It ends with a panopticum of new courage. The other half begins here.

*We hope that this book will inspire contemplation and that you will enjoy reading about our pioneers.*

*Yours,*
Christiane Goetz-Weimer und Wolfram Weimer

# 44 INTERVIEWS

# ILSE AIGNER

President of the Bavarian State Parliament,
Member of the Landtag

### In your opinion, what is the association between German angst and the changes that are necessary to overcome current and future societal challenges?

I think it is actually a scary thought that people talk so much about German angst. Who would even do that and why? I actually know of more people and also businesses who are the exact opposite of fearful: they have definitive, bold strategies for the future and amazingly see opportunities in crises. And that is precisely the right attitude! Obviously, we had or have to tackle a lot of crises all at once. First, we faced two years of the pandemic, and then the Russian warfare attacks targeting Ukraine. Moreover, all of this is topped by climate change – another crisis and possibly the most humongous challenge. People have to deal with a lot – being in crisis mode for a long time is taxing. Many have big problems finding their way out again. Yet that is exactly what we have to do: look ahead. We do have to accept the fact that changes, challenges and even crises will become the norm. The world is not what it used to be. Here in Germany, we lived in a comfort zone for decades and it literally turned us into passive creatures: a stable democracy paired with lasting prosperity and social justice – peace in Europe. Now we actively have to go into battle for these values as we now know what has been achieved is no longer a given.

### Which societal developments or movements inspire you to boldly approach the future?

The sole fact that Germany came out of the pandemic so well, gives me courage. Other nations did not master this problem nearly as effectively. I find it emboldening that young people are once again taking an interest in politics and that they advocate for their interests – even if the spectrum of issues is sometimes still very limited. I also think that we have made a lot of progress in terms of equality, even if we have not yet attained the ultimate goal. During the crisis we realized that economic dependency is potentially fatal. Hence, many companies are taking a broader approach and are bravely rethinking their original strategies. I am encouraged by the revitalization and fortification of our transatlantic defence alliance and by the fact that everyone understands that lasting peace can only be achieved through defence readiness. Moreover, I'm inspired by so many people – especially in Bavaria, where the numbers are extraordinarily high – volunteering. After all, volunteer work is one of the pillars of our society.

## What do you consider the most daunting societal obstacles that keep us from thinking and acting more confidently and boldly?

Unfortunately, I frequently come away thinking that we do not always set our priorities straight and that we often take the second step before we have completed the first one. I feel that we act emotionally – from a short sighted perspective. Also, that ideologically we impose roadblocks when people expect pragmatic solutions. I am specifically referring to our debate of securing our energy supply. The shock of Fukushima led to our early withdrawal from nuclear energy. Now we are finding out that we absolutely should have hung on to this gap bridging technology a bit longer instead of counting on gas supplies from Russia. Ideological blinders are currently preventing the extended operation of our nuclear energy plants. I often think that this ideological inflexibility is the most paralyzing hindrance when it comes to being bolder.

## How do you encourage others and yourself to go out on a limb?

By advocating for engagement as the President of the State Parliament. I want people to act on behalf of our democracy or to volunteer at the centre of society. By emboldening them and telling them "Do not be afraid of change!" By also stating that things that are positive and have proven themselves should be retained and maintained. It also takes courage to retain values by protecting them from the fickle impact of zeitgeist.

# HUBERT AIWANGER

Vice State Premier of Bavaria, Minister of Economy,
State Development and Energy, Member of the Landtag

### In your opinion, what is the association between German angst and the changes that are necessary to overcome current and future societal challenges?

What some like to call German angst is not necessarily a negative association. A healthy dose of prudence and critical questioning make an important contribution to thinking things through, becoming aware of our own strengths and to acting intelligently. This is what made it possible for us to become a high-tech nation that now allows us to participate in the top league of critical future disciplines.

But it is also clear that German angst must not paralyze us. Especially given the numerous challenges we have to master as competitors, we cannot afford to act hesitantly and in the absence of resolve. However, principally, I am convinced that we must not lose a certain amount of basic optimism as we face the many enormous challenges, we will undoubtedly find ourselves confronted with.

### Which societal developments or movements inspire you to boldly approach the future?

Especially three issues give me confidence when it comes to the challenges and developments in Bavaria, Germany, and the world.

First, the energy crisis ultimately led to a noticeable change in awareness in our nation. It has impressed upon citizens, companies, and all political players that changes are unavertable. That is also why critical issues of the future are finally beginning to feel wind beneath their wings. Hydrogen is one example. Due to the high energy costs and the risk of gas bottlenecks, many businesses, assisted by political players are now – for the first time – concretely working towards the conversion to $H_2$ technology.

Second, in Bavaria and Germany we boast bold and innovative companies that actively participate in the technological shifts. In this context, I am especially referring to many dynamic start-ups that are proving to be true drivers of innovation. Not only do they develop solutions aiming at the efficient protection of the climate and digitization, they also come up with tomorrow's export best sellers.

Third, we are in a position to effectively position ourselves in the domestic and international comparison when it comes to well-trained skilled workers. Besides colleges and universities, vocational training is a big plus in global competition. This model will absolutely survive in the future and the willingness of businesses to offer apprenticeships continues to be high despite the crisis.

## What do you consider the most daunting societal obstacles that keep us from thinking and acting more confidently and boldly?

Regrettably, federal and European politicians do not have sufficient confidence in the market's innovative forces. This is a shame, given that they are the strongest drivers of progress. Hence, directorial approaches are frequently implemented that hamper technological openness. The best example is the ban of combustion engines as of 2035, which cancels out the efficiency measures and use of e-fuels before they even materialize.

We need activating impulses instead of these planned approaches to the economy, especially also for fledgling start-ups. In Germany, it is still relatively difficult to secure sufficient capital to fund their entrepreneurial ideas. Hence, we have not only initiated a start-up fund in Bavaria but have also added a scale-up fund that specifically assists founders with the scaling of their business.

## How do you encourage others and yourself to go out on a limb?

Looking at everything we have already achieved is encouraging. Since the end of World War II, our nation has evolved into one of the world's leading economic powerhouses and has defended its position against numerous obstacles for decades, most recently against the effects of the Covid-19 pandemic. This could be done only based on our trust in our own capabilities, a willingness to take risks, by being open to the new and thanks to a confidence-fuelled basic attitude. The countless small and medium sized companies, the large number of successful start-ups, but also the global players who call our free state home, are the best role models for the high level of innovative forces and entrepreneurial foresight. Hence, I am certain that this spirit will help us to also master the challenges of the future.

# BURKHARD BALZ

Board Member
of the Deutsche Bundesbank

### In your opinion, what is the association between German angst and the changes that are necessary to overcome current and future societal challenges?

I do not like the term "German angst" because it suggests that Germany is in a general state of panic and powerlessness. Our management of the Corona crisis and currently, of the energy crisis caused by the Russian war against Ukraine gives us a different perspective. I see a broad political discourse that carefully weighs the risks and identifies appropriate measures. When it comes to the major global challenges such as climate change, demographics and digitization, Germany could definitely play a more prominent European and international leadership role.

### Which societal developments or movements inspire you to boldly approach the future?

I am actually encouraged by how we as a society respond to the latest challenges caused by crises. For instance, during the Covid-19 pandemic, which was a dramatic health crisis and led to a never-before-seen breakdown of the global economy, we mastered both. I found it to be particularly impressive how expeditiously businesses, politicians and society assimilated with the latest conditions. Just one example: as the responsible member of the board for payment transactions at the German Federal Bank, I observed how card payments and touchless payments established themselves at a record pace. Such innovative forces will also carry us through future challenges.

## What do you consider the most daunting societal obstacles that keep us from thinking and acting more confidently and boldly?

The most daunting obstacles in my opinion are the amount of red tape that is still excessive and what I call the still often domineering "church tower politics." New approaches, future-oriented solutions and promising projects often fail because of excessively stringent regulations or take too much time to implement because of the coordination between federal, state, and communal governments.

## How do you encourage others and yourself to go out on a limb?

In this context, I second the Albert Einstein quote "We can't solve problems by using the same kind of thinking we used when we created them." Even things that appear to be impossible at first can be attained. Yet, we will have to engage in out of the box thinking more often and choose new paths, even if not all of them lead to success.

# ELKE BENNING-ROHNKE

Advisor, Supervisory Board and Advisory Board
Benning & Company GmbH

## In your opinion, what is the association between German angst and the changes that are necessary to overcome current and future societal challenges?

A brief historic travelogue in this context: the Chinese Empire once considered itself the centre of the universe that was surrounded by barbarian nations. Even Europe, which was prospering at the time, was thought of as marginal. This overestimation of its own power led to Cathay sleeping through the industrial revolution. China fell into poverty.

We should look at history as a warning. Nowadays, in Germany, we risk missing the boat. We are boasting about our economic strength, are in love with our position as the champions of export sales and believe that we are in an untouchable position. Prior to her first re-election, Chancellor Angela Merkel, at a private event I attended stated: "Germans cannot be expected to tolerate reforms, which is why I will not implement any." Given her re-election, this might have been the right move for her. Yet it is a fatal attitude for our country: our positioning in many future-driving disciplines is obsolete. Politics of recent years have missed the opportunity to get the population ready for change from a position of strength and to initiate debates as to how we will have to align ourselves in a pluralistic world full of newcomers. The latest crises have amplified the pressure to act. Given a latent sense of decline, many parts of society are now increasingly afraid of loss, upset and exhausted. In turn, the parties are trying to calm us down. They are deferring essential reforms. Billions of euros are invested to compensate for economic consequences and to retain a sense of prosperity in society. Truths are being concealed and resources are not being allocated in a future-compliant manner. It is not German angst that blocks the way. Instead, it is the short term political tactics of the parties aiming at presumed constituent approval.

## Which societal developments or movements inspire you to boldly approach the future?

Generation Z is comprised of young, well-trained digital natives who are joining the career world and allow for more "play in a flexible world." Hopefully, this is a mindset that will have an impact on the innovative force and attractiveness of Germany as a business venue. Moreover, a lot of young people today believe in cooperation instead of competition. I hope that this will not only boost the quality of our output, but also strengthen our societal sense of community. Ultimately, we have a well-integrated second generation of migrants. Many of its members are responsible participants and highly motivated to enrich our society.

## What do you consider the most daunting societal obstacles that keep us from thinking and acting more confidently and boldly?

We are at a crossroads. However, too many of us still keep their eyes shut. "Let's continue as we always have", may feel more comfortable. However, if in the future, we aim to carry our democratic values into this pluralistic world, we have to amplify our competitiveness. This goes hand in hand with thorough change and investments. Consequently, we need competent politicians at these crossroads who shape a new framework for our future survival based on facts and with foresight.

## How do you encourage others and yourself to go out on a limb?

I get out of my comfort zone every day. Daily, I recommend a woman who is in my network whom I support because of her abilities. I try to be a role model every single day.

# MARCUS BERRET

Senior Partner, Global Managing Director
Roland Berger

## In your opinion, what is the association between German angst and the changes that are necessary to overcome current and future societal challenges?

Fear must neither guide political nor entrepreneurial decisions since angst does not give rise to innovation. From my perspective, Germany does in fact not have so much of a fear-based issue, but a problem driven by lethargy: we stay in our comfort zone because over the past decades, our society did very well and has developed this basic sense of trust that everything will work out for us. However, now, instead of protecting the status quo, we have to live with risks, have to make decisions without an "airbag", as only this will allow us to initiate the transformation that will let us keep our global competitive standing in the long run.

## Which societal developments or movements inspire you to boldly approach the future?

I derive courage especially from the activism of the younger generation and from the exponential technological progress. Young adults are frequently accused of being unwilling to perform and being disinterested in politics. Nonetheless, they are the ones who primarily question apparent certainties and drive change. "Fridays for Future" have led to the more critical discussion of even abstract issues, such as the climate crisis, at the heart of our society. Technological achievements of recent years have not only made possible the expeditious vaccine developments during the Covid-19 pandemic, they will also help us to drastically reduce our energy dependency.

Looking back, it is evident that vast reforms can definitely be successful: while Germany was still referred to as "Europe's sick man" in the early 2000s, the controversial Agenda 2010 has turned us into Europe's strongest economy.

## What do you consider the most daunting societal obstacles that keep us from thinking and acting more confidently and boldly?

The demographic transition is a factor that should not be underestimated when it comes to the German "Culture of Persistence." The interests as well as the higher risk aversion of older generations are extra-proportionally reflected in political decisions. Change requires courage – and this is also true for Germany's world of business, which must undergo radical transformation.
We need to understand that established business models will, in some cases, reach their limits and we must create an investment environment that encourages companies to make bold decisions. After all, in recent years, Germany has made insufficient investments and is now being increasingly overtaken in a world of global competition. To ensure that Germany will remain an attractive business venue, it will have to implement a broad structural change, which will have to be jointly supported by the public and the private sector.

## How do you encourage others and yourself to go out on a limb?

To get ahead as a society, we need a positive vision of the future. Instead of wondering what could go wrong, we will have to recognize the opportunities inherent in change and we will have to seize its potential. New ideas will frequently lead to achievements that are not yet covered in any management manual. This is why we regularly join our clientele as we investigate the world outside our own sector. Principally, it is true that entrepreneurship has always been associated with certain risks and nowadays, given multiple crises that make uncertainty fester, we have to learn to embrace the risks and to manage more resiliently.

# MARKUS DUESMANN

Chairman of the Board of the AUDI AG,
Member of the Volkswagen Group Board

**In your opinion, what is the association between German angst and the changes that are necessary to overcome current and future societal challenges?**

One thing is certain: Our willingness to change and our speed of adaptation are more important than ever given the multiple crises we are facing. We must respond flexibly to the current and future challenges, and we must be willing to make fast decisions in an uncertain world. Also, given the background of protectionist trends in North America and China, now would be the worst time to hesitate. Germany and Europe must act with more determination and less red tape. In this context, we should clearly state what our own interests are without aiming to uncouple. At the same time, I am convinced that the need for a secure future can be an additional incentive for us to position ourselves more resiliently and to develop our own European position in the world of global competition.

**Which societal developments or movements inspire you to boldly approach the future?**

The amazing solidarity people demonstrated during the Covid-19 pandemic and in conjunction with the war in Ukraine left a deep impression on me. The cohesiveness of our society is one of our greatest strengths. We should avert any split-up no matter what happens. If we are to master the challenges of the future, it is important that we join forces to work on them.

### What do you consider the most daunting societal obstacles that keep us from thinking and acting more confidently and boldly?

We need to trust more. Trust is within us and it is one of our positive qualities. Thankfully, the term "German angst" is not the one and only thing Germany is renowned for in the world. I tend to rather think of "made in Germany" as an international quality seal of approval. Hence, we should never give up the high standard we impose upon ourselves. Simultaneously, though, our tendency to aim for perfection should not prevent us from trying new things – even if we have no way of knowing for sure that the results will ultimately be excellent.

### How do you encourage others and yourself to go out on a limb?

I first and foremost look for opportunities. Now is actually the perfect time to seize the opportunity to claim our position in the world by launching sustainable technical innovations that are "made in Germany." We should seize this opportunity quickly – right now. One example is the combustion engine ban as of 2035 passed by the EU. It is an important step that creates forecasting certainty for manufacturing and offers the perfect incentives to prove our innovative power.

# KIRSTEN FEHRS

Bishop in diocese Hamburg and Lübeck
of the North Church

## In your opinion, what is the association between German angst and the changes that are necessary to overcome current and future societal challenges?

First and foremost, I think it is important to give the fear in the current situation its legitimacy. I have never experienced a time when I saw people as fearful as they have been recently, specifically because of concrete threats: war in Europe, climate change, the Corona crisis, fatigue related to democracy, existential fears because the money runs out before you pay your heating bill or buy bread, commodity shortages, sales slumps. In my opinion, those are not phenomena that are typical syndromes of the German condition but have to be attributed to a deeply troubling risk scenario.

However, the determining factor is how we deal with these fears. Do we get stuck, or do we find a way out based on hope? Perhaps, the first thing we should address is not strategies to manage this fear, but to foster an attitude that fortifies our hears and our resilience. And what do we focus on, what can we do to counter these threats, despite of it all? For instance, the beautiful side of humanity that does not overlook suffering, distress and pain but takes an empathetic stance. The beauty of words that advocate for others. The beauty of music, theatre and ballet that shows us the preciousness of life. If we have hearts emboldened by this beauty, we will be able to act confidently and will be ready for the future.

## Which societal developments or movements inspire you to boldly approach the future?

I am encouraged by the variety of small steps. People who simply do things, are pragmatic and amazingly empathetic. Those who do not stand still when they receive devastating news, projections and look at the balance sheets of our war and crisis times, but reach out with a helping hand. Right on the spot, in their own professional, family or neighbourhood context, so many of us provide to the people loving empathetic services aiming at peace: at shared tables, in childcare centres and hospitals, in their neighbourhoods, at refugee facilities, cultural initiatives, as neighbourhood and homeless aides, etc., etc. The fact that so many are not just working for their own personal wealth and growth projections, but for the community, positive interactions, as well as social and ecological transformation – those are all things that fill my heart with hope.

## What do you consider the most daunting societal obstacles that keep us from thinking and acting more confidently and boldly?

Our culture of perfectionism and sometimes our "know it all" attitudes frequently end up being roadblocks. We give things too much thought, plan too much and no longer focus on action. We have a hard time compromising and we prefer to lose ourselves in debates aiming at finding solutions that meet a hundred per cent of our expectations. The church participates in this process. Our large, very well organized institutions did contribute to advancement, prosperity, and certainty for a long time. However, they also degenerated into inflexible and slow to respond organizations. It would be nice if we could arrive at dynamic community interaction that prompts more people to first ask what they can do for society and that do not set themselves up to make righteous claims as to what those in charge are doing wrong.

## How do you encourage others and yourself to go out on a limb?

As Christians we are blessed by the fact that we do not have to rely only on ourselves. We believe in a power greater than ourselves: the dynamic spiritual power of God, inspiration. I actually experience it at work as an impulse of change that fervently counters the fear of action with the joy of living. The objective is active listening and acting. King Salomon in the Bible speaks of a listening heart. A listening heart is brave. It is a wonderful vision, also a leadership principle. Finding it through meditation and silence, going to the sources that God has placed within me is the best encouragement to go into the world with hope, in other words, inspired and ready to act. Not everything I do has to work out, but what I do has heartfelt meaning – for me and others.

# ISABEL FROMMELT-GOTTSCHALD

Ambassador of the Principality of Liechtenstein

**In your opinion, what is the association between German angst and the changes that are necessary to overcome current and future societal challenges?**

German angst as the definition for an entire nation is not something I can identify with. In fact, there were or are parts of the population who exuded a fundamental mood that can likely be described in more detail as a blend of hesitancy, fears of the future and a need to feel safe, which can also be attributed to the catastrophes experienced in the first half of the 20th century. Those always teach humans facts that will characterize their lives for years or decades. Yet even countries that had more or fewer war experiences have such fears. In politics, a certain amount of hesitancy and the desire to avert risks can actually also be positive. Nations who practice these patterns are often trying especially hard and are successful at attaining joint resolutions despite differing views. The basic fearful attitude is of course being fuelled by the various crises of recent years, and particularly by the war attacks targeting Ukraine. Questions as to whether things could get worse and how long the state of uncertainty will continue hover over everything all the time. The post war order we had become used to is no more – and a new one is still not on the horizon. I think that for Germany, this poses a huge opportunity along with all of the facets that the new epoch will bring. Germany should seize them to become actively and courageously engaged. After all, from the global perspective, Germany is still a model country with enormous achievements in terms of economic, political and cultural aspects. In the new security-political order, Germany can assume an important leadership role given its prominence and size in Europe, its geographical location, its transatlantic proximity as well as its closeness to the east, in particular also because of its historic experience. Moreover, Germany is in an excellent position to assume a leadership role in climate change. This is a long term risk aversion and wealth guarantee.

## Which societal developments or movements inspire you to boldly approach the future?

We are all working towards a positive future and look forward to it with confidence. However, this is contingent upon engagement, sometimes the forfeiture of things and the courage to overcome dry patches. I believe in our Western values of democracy and constitutional rule of the law, so that there is no alternative to advocating for it and to take advantage of all available leeway. I am encouraged by our distinctive civil society, the "Fridays-for-Future" movement that is willing to advocate for its issues even in the face of resistance, or the creative start-up scenario in Germany.

## What do you consider the most daunting societal obstacles that keep us from thinking and acting more confidently and boldly?

One of the prime obstacles is the fact that we live in wealthy societies that have experienced forward-moving trends since the end of World War II. There is a dominant sense that in recent decades everything was always associated with more – more growth, financial resources and mobility. Virtually all regions of the world can now be reached and the world can be brought into our homes (medially). As a result, we appear to have infinite opportunities. In my eyes, this has also led to a kind of lethargy. However, now the pandemic and the worsening climate crises have shown us how contingent this standard of living is on our networks and that we are unable to keep many crises away from us. For many, this results in concerns about wealth, along with a loss of control with regard to these developments that we, in our own perception, have hardly any control over. In this situation, politics can introduce critical impulses and incentives to become more receptive to risks and a willingness to change as well as evolve.

## How do you encourage others and yourself to go out on a limb?

When it comes to projects that require courage, I imagine what opportunities they offer and what could possibly go wrong. I frequently find it helpful to visualize the scenarios and to "feel them out." In my experience, bold steps usually pay off.

# ANGELIKA GIFFORD

Vice President EMEA at Meta
& Supervisory Board Member

**In your opinion, what is the association between German angst and the changes that are necessary to overcome current and future societal challenges?**

Digitization is the answer. By now digital technologies transform all aspects of life. Given these revolutionary changes, we in Germany and Europe should participate in the creation and application of these technologies – especially since Europe is already setting global standards as far as the regulation of the digital world is concerned. The pre-requisite for this is that we overcome our hesitation when it comes to investments into digitization: especially medium-sized companies could still implement more measures. If we aim to keep up with other countries, the investments, based on the latest computations, would have to increase from currently 18 billion euros to 35 to 50 billion euros per annum.

**Which societal developments or movements inspire you to boldly approach the future?**

I am impressed by our self-confidence affiliated with our objective to utilize to their full potential the possibilities of digital technologies. Digitization is the top priority on the to-do-lists of the leaders of any nation. The conversations I had in conjunction with the book "Deutschlands digitale Dekade" (Germany's Digital Decade) clearly confirm that we no longer have an insight issue in this country. The aim now is to implement: pilot, iterate and scale.

For instance, the development of the AI sector in Germany clearly shows how innovation can be designed and moved forward on location. With its National AI Strategy, the German federal government also already supports AI made in Germany. Plans call for the investment of five billion euros by 2025. I am very optimistic that this will be a success.

### What do you consider the most daunting societal obstacles that keep us from thinking and acting more confidently and boldly?

We still have to make greater investments into the next generation and its interests. In terms of digital education, Germany, among the 32 OECD countries, currently only comes in 18th. Katrin Suder, in her article "Deutschlands digitale Dekade" correctly states that schools should introduce children to topics such as data and technologies early-on. This of course means that we will also need a contemporary digital infrastructure, which is still not available at 33 per cent of all German schools. We also have some catching up to do when it comes to diversity and equality. Germany ranks 11th in the EU Equality Index. However, the objective is not how we fare in the international rankings. Diversity and inclusion are essential for future-ready development, innovation and business success.

### How do you encourage others and yourself to go out on a limb?

As an executive, it is my strategy to create a culture of trust. The aim is to give people assignments and to give them the freedom to "simply do." The fostering of an error culture that considers mistakes as an opportunity to learn, has the potential of motivating people to perform even better and to encourage them to try new things.

# GREG HANDS

Minister without Portfolio at the Cabinet Office,
Chairman of the Conservative Party, MP (UK)

## In your opinion, what is the association between German angst and the changes that are necessary to overcome current and future societal challenges?

My first impressions of Germany date back to my adolescence since I learnt German at school in 1978 through 1984 and subsequently, after I graduated from high school, always spent some time in Germany between 1985 and 1988. To be concise, I was in West Berlin, where I had a job at the Summer Pool Kreuzberg near the Wilhelmstraße (and other history laden iconic sites).

At the same time I was studying history at the University of Cambridge, primarily German and Central European history. One of the first books I worked with during my history education had just been published – "Nach Hitler. Der schwierige Umgang mit unserer Geschichte" (Post Hitler. Difficult Interactions with Our History) by Martin Broszat. This book was my – the 20-year-old student's – first introduction to the concept of "dealing with the past" and I learnt that Germany handles its past in a very unique way.

Visitors can see this all over the country time and again. It demonstrates the profound background of German society over the past 80 years. Germany has to be given a lot of credit for its "dealing with history" and can by and large be called a success. Germany is now a role model for other countries that have dark chapters in their history. I am convinced of this some 40 years after my initial experiences. At this time, from the perspective of its international partners, Germany must play an even larger key role on the international stages since it is the fourth most powerful business powerhouse in the world and Western Europe's most populated nation.

### Which societal developments or movements inspire you to boldly approach the future?

Some criticize Germany's contributions to the war in Ukraine. I, on the other hand, am impressed by Germany's contributions, for instance the sensitive topic that German tanks might be deployed near Dnjepr. According to Broszat, the relationship with Russia is part of the "difficult interaction with Germany's history." In my opinion, Germany delivered a lot to Ukraine and we are cooperating closely.

The German response to the energy crisis is impressive as well. Who would have thought that a politician like Robert Habeck would, just a year after the Russian invasion, commission the construction of liquid gas terminals? I can still recall the power struggle within the Green Party between the fundamentalists and the reality supporters in the 1980s while I was striving to pass my high school exam. Perhaps Mr. Habeck is now the "Realo in Chief!" Historically – and from the outside perspective – Germany always moved a little slowly and within the consensus. While this now appears to have changed, I am still hoping for a more positive attitude vis-à-vis nuclear energy.

### What do you consider the most daunting societal obstacles that keep us from thinking and acting more confidently and boldly?

I was always under the impression that Germany needs to enter into a more intensive internal discourse. Consensus is a good thing, but rethinking and questioning are definitely not inappropriate. It appears to me that Germans are usually very well educated. However, their education is highly congruent. Controversies and diversity, on the other hand improve both, the decision-making process and ultimately the outcome.

### How do you encourage others and yourself to go out on a limb?

In my career as a minister, which spans eleven years, I have learnt that it is quite simple to align oneself along government lines. To do the job more effectively, it is however advisable to think independently and to question the consensus. The world is constantly changing and political brains and decision-makers have to adapt – like Germany did last year.

Personally, I often see myself as a bridge builder between Great Britain and Germany and I want to encourage others to also work toward the deepening of the German-British relationship.

# STEFAN HARTUNG

Chairman of the Management Board
Robert Bosch GmbH

## In your opinion, what is the association between German angst and the changes that are necessary to overcome current and future societal challenges?

These days, Germany is a nation that is a cosmopolitan, global network and thankfully also a country that engages in discourse. Lively exchanges, if possible without any bans on thought and without prejudice, provide the best foundation for a society that aims to be positioned in a manner that secures the future. Obviously, a consensus-oriented communal structure does sometimes lead to hesitant debates or rulings that are perceived as too cautious or half-hearted by some. However, the German angst so many conjure up time and again, is not in evidence from my perspective at this time, just like I do not see any major impact of pessimists or concerned individuals. We most certainly could not afford it: we have to accelerate our speed in many disciplines, including digitization, sustainable energy, or education. These things take courage, international collaboration and, if possible clear roads for the huge desire for improvement so many people harbour.

## Which societal developments or movements inspire you to boldly approach the future?

Paradoxically, it was the simultaneous occurrence of several grave crises that showed clearly that dodging the bullet is not a solution. What is growing in much of Germany and Europe, is not resignation – it's resilience. The war in Ukraine has demonstrated how unified, pragmatic, consistent and also balanced many countries can respond given the extraordinary challenges they are facing. These are encouraging signs. We at Bosch are convinced that technology is a determining factor in the efforts to combat climate change and the scarcity of energy. And we are not the only ones, as evident from the results of our most recent Bosch Tech Compass: two of three Germans agree with the assessment that technological progress makes the world a better place. That is a significant increase over last year. Hence, the trend is on point.

## What do you consider the most daunting societal obstacles that keep us from thinking and acting more confidently and boldly?

It is a known fact that confidence and trust rarely evolve from the small details of daily politics and daily business, but only if a society develops a clear concept of a positive future on the broadest possible foundation. To that end, we should not forget, given the immediately imminent tasks, to also develop a strategy for the next decade. Being first and foremost an optimist, I would hope that we discuss the opportunities just as passionately and openly as we talk about our concerns. Ideological reservations or the call for special paths do not move us ahead. The major challenges, such as climate change, cannot be mastered single-handedly, but only as a global community.

## How do you encourage others and yourself to go out on a limb?

By and large, life today is better for many people than it was 50 or 100 years ago. I am convinced that this trend will continue – however, it will be contingent upon the participation of all of us. The future is more pliable than many of us believe, especially since there is no lack of ambitious visions. Just one example: Bosch is currently further developing the manufacturing process for MEMS, i.e. microelectromechanical systems, in great strides. At our chip factory in Dresden, we aim to also produce MEMS sensors on 300-millimetre wafers as one of the first companies in the world. This is an important step that will render the European semiconductor sector even more competitive. In other industries, a whole lot of similarly ambitious projects are underway. Overall, they consistently point into one direction: forward. And that is encouraging.

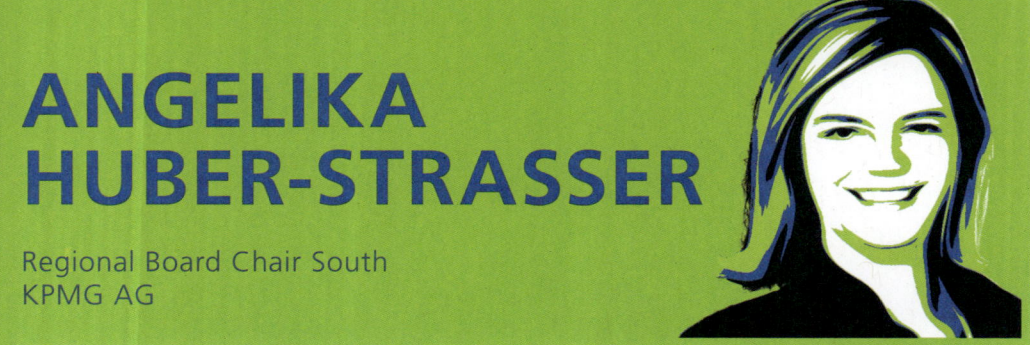

# ANGELIKA HUBER-STRASSER

Regional Board Chair South
KPMG AG

## In your opinion, what is the association between German angst and the changes that are necessary to overcome current and future societal challenges?

German angst is a term that describes German hesitancy from the perspective of outsiders. However, one must not forget that the hesitancy is largely based on German thoroughness and the aim to "do everything correctly and well." This level of perfectionism was a building block of our economy and of our business success in the past. In this era of dynamic change, courage is another necessity to ensure that we do not get stuck in the obsolete, but use new technologies and opportunities to create a better world.

## Which societal developments or movements inspire you to boldly approach the future?

I am encouraged by the German peoples' broad societal involvement: so many people, regardless of whether they are young or seniors, work in associations, NGOs, social and caritative facilities or advocate for the protection of the environment – in other words, simply with the objective of creating a better world.

### What do you consider the most daunting societal obstacles that keep us from thinking and acting more confidently and boldly?

The biggest challenge in my eyes is the loss of trust in society and the lack of tolerance towards the different. Those who trust themselves, others and society overall and who also have the ability to live in and with the community, have the capability of acting boldly and confidently. We need executives who have concisely these capabilities.

### How do you encourage others and yourself to go out on a limb?

What should always be the basis for encouragement is the intent to change ourselves! A young man once asked a wise woman: "How can I change the world?" She responded: "I once wanted to change the world when I was your age. I attempted to change it, but the world was so large, and I failed. So, I tried to change my country, but that did not work out either. Finally, I wanted to change my town and those attempts were unsuccessful as well. So, I resolved to change my family – to no avail. I finally realized that the one thing I could change was myself. Had I changed myself, my family would have changed as a result. My family would have changed the town, the town the country and the country could have changed the entire world." Changes always have to begin with us and this takes reflection paired with the courage to actually do it.

# MICHAEL KÄFER

Chairman of the Käfer AG

### In your opinion, what is the association between German angst and the changes that are necessary to overcome current and future societal challenges?

Let me say these two things to start with: I am not a fearful person, in fact, quite the opposite is true. On occasion, my enthusiasm and impulsivity tend to run amok. I am not the only one, as I know from my personal and professional interactions. This is why I feel that it is wrong to associate the character trait of German angst with all Germans in general. That's too simplistic an approach. On the other hand, a certain amount of a critically negative perspective is in fact a strong point since we tend to resolve problems instead of waiting them out.

However, I also have to assert that German politics and society have a tough time when it comes to changing the status quo. New ideas – regardless in which field they arise – always come with some inherent risks and not everything works out perfectly right away. Nevertheless, as an entrepreneur I know that nothing is more damaging to business than being deadlocked, which is the result of hesitancy or the desire to do everything perfectly. Everyone longs for a future of prosperity and security, and one does not get either one by waiting. Hence, a reasonable balance between waiting and taking risks is indispensable. However, I think we are well on our way despite all of the criticism.

### Which societal developments or movements inspire you to boldly approach the future?

I am under the impression helpful attitudes paired with social advocacy are once again gaining ground despite of or especially because of the difficult general conditions we find ourselves confronted with right now. Awareness is another trend that I consider very positive when it comes to interacting with others and the environment. Moreover, the young people who represent Generation Z are now beginning to assume societal responsibilities. Sustainability, diversity, tolerance, and freedom are particularly important values in their eyes. This generation, albeit it is also already concerned about the future and has fears, will have to be convinced by politicians, employers and associations through their arguments and actions.

## What do you consider the most daunting societal obstacles that keep us from thinking and acting more confidently and boldly?

We need more pioneers who motivate others and talk about the positive aspects of change. We have to be mindful of how much better we are doing in comparison to many other nations and that we have so many opportunities, which we will, of course, also have to seize. However, whenever you listen, you hear from those who have concerns and only see obstacles along any new path. In the media, every second headline now contains terms such as "warning", "fearful" and other negative statements because apparently, alarmism generates the most clicks. We should not goad and block each other; after all, history has shown that crises frequently are far less impactful than the alarmists projected. Moreover, things always continued in the aftermath. We should have a lot more confidence in our resilience and strength and should share this attitude with others.

## How do you encourage others and yourself to go out on a limb?

There is this German saying: "Those who don't dare will not win." As an entrepreneur I have had to live with several defeats in my life, but I have definitely landed a lot more victories. The proper ratio is the deciding factor. Success is a huge motivator. I strive to encourage others through positive thinking and actions as well as by being a role model. Life is simply so much more fun in the absence of diffuse fear and constant worries.

# GEORG KELL

Chairman of the Board
Arabesque Group

**In your opinion, what is the association between German angst and the changes that are necessary to overcome current and future societal challenges?**

German angst – understood as the tendency to be fearful and gloomy – has a political upside and an economic downside. It helps to keep political extremism in check for fear of repeating past mistakes. But at the same time, it is an enormous drag on innovation and entrepreneurship. Business failure, which in other cultures is seen as a badge of honor and a reason to try even harder, is regarded as a social stigma and holds back risk taking and creativity in Germany. Collective fear also leads to costly overregulation and irrational decisions. Recent examples include the decision to switch off nuclear high-standard power plants, while importing electricity produced with nuclear power from neighboring countries or prohibiting "fracking" of gas from domestic sources at low costs with low emissions and risks, while importing more expensive gas with high emission contents from other countries.

**Which societal developments or movements inspire you to boldly approach the future?**

Three trends stand out: First, Germans have a strong sense for social fairness and inclusion which is an important foundation for broad-based renewal. Second, there is a deep pool of scientific and technical expertise and there are many professionals who are proud of their work and who love to improve what they are doing. Third, Germans are far ahead of the rest of the world (except for a few other European countries) in understanding that climate change is a system-changing force. These are the building blocks upon which a successful rejuvenation of the German economy can be accomplished. If successful, Germany can become a lighthouse for the future.

## What do you consider the most daunting societal obstacles that keep us from thinking and acting more confidently and boldly?

Overall, it seems that high incomes and high living standards are taken for granted in German politics and in the public opinion. The question of how to secure future competitiveness is neither sufficiently understood nor discussed, as it is overshadowed by the seemingly endless debates about entitlements and distributing wealth generated in the past. This could prove fatal. Germans are now more obsessed with administering the past than with investing in the future. Success makes lazy and builds entitlement mentalities. This systemic problem is also reflected in the world-famous German bureaucracy and overregulation. The current system clearly is not designed to support renewal and change but rather to defend the status quo.

## How do you encourage others and yourself to go out on a limb?

After nearly three decades of building new global networks with the United Nations, I now find excitement in giving my full support to Arabesque, a technology firm that aims to disrupt finance powered by AI and sustainability. I always look ahead and try to recognize opportunities. When it comes to execution, I find it motivating to think in "potentials" and explore ways to activate them though narratives and encouragement. Often people have great skills but lack confidence and willpower. I find it very motivating and rewarding to support others in unlocking their full potential. I often tell young people that one of the most important choices we have in life is between criticizing what others are doing – which is easy but cheap – or building something, by ourselves or with others, that we can be proud of. Instead of being a cynic, aspire to be a "homo ludens"!

# LARS KLINGBEIL

Federal Chair of the Social Democratic Party,
Member of the Bundestag

**In your opinion, what is the association between German angst
and the changes that are necessary to overcome
current and future societal challenges?**

Transformation and change are not higher powers we have to succumb to. They are processes and we have a lot of control over them. Hence, we do not have to be afraid of them. Instead, we need confidence to shape them.

One thing is certain: lots of changes are ahead of us. I want us to identify the opportunities in the former, so that we turn changes into improvements. The coming decade offers an enormous economic potential. We have the ability to establish and fortify Germany in Europe as a technology leader, and an innovation and industrial venue in the long term. We have the capability to set standards and create jobs. The affiliated decisions are made in the present tense and I am happy that a strong Social Democratic Party is involved in the decision-making processes that will determine our future.

**Which societal developments or movements inspire you
to boldly approach the future?**

After what now marks the third year of diverse challenges, we have learnt that Germany's people are strong and that we are well positioned to fight our way out of crises. Fundamentally, this makes me take a very optimistic stance.

I am especially emboldened by the high level of willingness to help, for instance, refugees and the solid societal bond we have – despite attempts by political players such as the AfD, who attempt to come between us. The people of this nation have great strength and want to stand together. We can be proud of this fact. And we can build upon it.

### What do you consider the most daunting societal obstacles that keep us from thinking and acting more confidently and boldly?

I believe that we, as a society, can take a more self-confident stance focusing on what we can jointly achieve. As politicians, it is our responsibility to bring all of our constituents along to give them security as we go through the changes. This is also a matter of respect – respect for personal life time achievements and life paths. Anyone who feels disconnected these days often lacks confidence in tomorrow. This is why transformative politics must not continue as an abstract tale of opportunities. It is the responsibility of politics to emphasize that we work, day after day, to safeguard perspectives and to create new ones – for everyone. We must fortify societal cohesiveness since it is the foundation of progress. If we do this, we can courageously work towards our joint future. This is also one of the core promises of the Social Democrats: keeping a changing society together.

### How do you encourage others and yourself to go out on a limb?

Courage is also always a question of confidence. Social Democrats have always been a force that advocates for bold progress, because they see the strengths in all of us and stand for the political standard of placing trust in people. We also apply this trust to concrete solutions – whether they are related to public funding, modern immigration policies and Germany's international responsibilities within the world. Right now, we are on a very positive path to establishing a society that is bold enough to believe in positive changes. This is encouraging to me.

# JULIA KLÖCKNER

Member of the Bundestag,
Scientific Speaker of the Christian Union,
Editor in Chief, ret. Minister

In your opinion, what is the association between German angst
and the changes that are necessary to overcome
current and future societal challenges?

As a rule, fear is not a reliable advisor when it comes to making smart decisions. Fear is paralyzing, angst takes away our freedom. However, I don't primarily associate Germany with fearfulness. After all, the proverbial German angst is not the only thing that defines us; we also have to remember that Germany produces high quality products with German precision and dependability. The British actually came up with the classification "Made in Germany" to indicate that merchandise sourced in Germany was of lesser quality. However, the term evolved to become an internationally recognized seal of approval for quality, solidity, inventiveness, dependability and an eagerness to compete. These are other qualities that define our nation. So, what do we need to face the challenges of the future? Not minimalism. We need large-scale, bold thinking, for instance to implement a governmental reform that aims at doing away with some mandates, impositions, competencies and red tape. This also means that we have to take risks. The government is incapable of safeguarding and compensating for everything.

## Which societal developments or movements inspire you to boldly approach the future?

Entrepreneurship, inventiveness and the young generation's start-up scenarios.

## What do you consider the most daunting societal obstacles that keep us from thinking and acting more confidently and boldly?

Fear of loss is a huge hurdle. On average, Germans enjoy a high standard of living, for instance if you consider the government benefits and services. This may result in a focus on individualization instead of communal thinking, which in turn hampers our much needed willingness to change. Standards, once attained, such as income, government benefits and others are not things we want to do without – even if the taxes generated decline and the federal debt ceiling rises, if the economy declines or social security systems are overburdened. Instead of being open to reforms, we tend to penalize politicians and parties who substantiate the need for reforms.

## How do you encourage others and yourself to go out on a limb?

More optimism citing more examples that document that bold moves pay off.

# ANNEGRET KRAMP-KARRENBAUER

Federal Defense Minister, ret.

**In your opinion, what is the association between German angst and the changes that are necessary to overcome current and future societal challenges?**

The world has changed over the past two decades. The terror attacks of September 11, 2001 targeting the World Trade Centre, the economic and financial crises, the refugee crisis, the Covid-19 pandemic and the Russian war fighting Ukraine have dominated our everyday lives. In the long term, the climate crisis, new technologies and the advancement of China will change the world even more fundamentally. These challenges instigate fears. Those are normal responses. However, our fears must not be more monumental than the challenge on hand. And they do not have to since there are, of course, developments that give us hope. The EU did not crumble under the economic and financial crisis. The pandemic revealed great international solidarity. Ukraine still stands. To the contrary, our economy has proven to be robust despite rising energy costs and inflation. Hence, there are plenty of reasons to be bold.

**Which societal developments or movements inspire you to boldly approach the future?**

Our past and the people of Germany. Post the NS dictatorship, nothing but rubble was left of our country – we were quite literally, devastated. The courage of individuals and politicians, including Konrad Adenauer, Robert Schumann and Charles de Gaulle achieved the feat of re-construction and the establishment of a united Europe. The bravery of demonstrators in the GDR, the boldness of Helmut Kohl to seize the cloak of history, gave us the re-unification of our nation. Whenever major challenges were at stake, Germany passed the test of its courage.

In J. R. R. Tolkien's "The Hobbit", Gandalf, the sorcerer, says: "I have found that it is the small everyday deeds of ordinary folk that keep the darkness at bay." An entire army of very common people keep the darkness at a distance in our nation. They work, get involved and face challenges. As long as we have more of them than worriers, we will be on the right path.

### What do you consider the most daunting societal obstacles that keep us from thinking and acting more confidently and boldly?

Max Frisch said "crisis is always a productive state of mind. All you have to do is get rid of the undertow of disaster." It is not easy to take such a stand. We all know that from our very own lives. If something happens that drastically changes the way of life we are used to, we grieve for what we have lost and get mad at the imposed changes and hold on to the past as if our life depended on it. All of that is just normal human nature. However, we also know that we cannot get stuck in this place. We have to go on, as hard as it may be. It's the same with politics. If, here in Germany, we first and exclusively envision disasters in every development, instead of the opportunities inherent in it, our evolution will stall.

### How do you encourage others and yourself to go out on a limb?

I strive to set a good example. My mantra is: if I see a chance, I take it. I will do it even if it's risky. Ask yourself what the worst thing that could happen to you really is. If you are willing to live with it, you don't have to be scared of anything.

# RICARDA LANG

Federal Chair of the Alliance 90/The Greens,
Member of the Bundestag

**In your opinion, what is the association between German angst and the changes that are necessary to overcome current and future societal challenges?**

I do not think that the term German angst is appropriate here. During any crisis, there will be people who are concerned for good reasons. They wonder if they will still be able to pay their bills and whether they will have enough money to live on. I take this very seriously. As politicians, we have to give them answers and we do just that. Focusing on future societal challenges we must however deploy courage and innovative strengths. Over the past 16 years, we have seen the stagnation of the expansion into renewable energy, we've seen the solar industry falter, how China was booming and how Bavaria slept on the job when it came to expanding the power grid. This has nothing to do with German angst but was caused by the blinders and a lack of political precautions. In the first year, a lot of important decisions were made and that is one thing many entrepreneurs acknowledge. Now all of society needs to be determined to make decisions – on the federal, state and communal levels. Businesses will also have to join forces to ensure the transformation will be successful. The economy of the future is climate neutral and renewable energy is one of the drivers that creates jobs. Germany's continued success as a business nation will be contingent on us moving ahead as described.

**Which societal developments or movements inspire you to boldly approach the future?**

I am encouraged by the staying power of the shared solidarity, which bonds our nation time and again despite multiple crises and gives us the courage to face the future. Of course, I have a whole list of movements in my head. In Germany, as well as internationally, I still hold the work of "Fridays for Future" in high esteem. This initiative regularly motivates thousands of young people all over the world to demonstrate peacefully for the protection of the climate. But I'm also inspired by the incredible courage of women in Iran who risk their lives every day to offer their children a better future. It is absolutely essential.

## What do you consider the most daunting societal obstacles that keep us from thinking and acting more confidently and boldly?

Justice is a huge issue. It starts with the educational system and does not end there. Especially among young people I currently detect a lot of hesitancy when it comes to the overlapping crises and global inequality. Politicians and businesses will have to join forces to demonstrate that there is a better way. I believe that growth and sustainability are not mutually exclusive, and neither are growth and justice. The deciding factor is how things are distributed. This also means that we will have to make certain that future technologies such as renewable energies or green industries still can grow while fossil options do not.

## How do you encourage others and yourself to go out on a limb?

Change is possible if we all work together, encourage and inspire each other, learn from one another and find compromises. Ultimately, government work is precisely that: expressing ideas, convincing others to jointly optimize them, arriving at a consensus and ultimately putting them into action. Personally, reading encourages me again and again. One of my favourite writers, James Baldwin, penned this statement in the 1960s: "Not everything that is faced can be changed, but nothing can be changed until it is faced." I follow this lead.

# CHRISTIAN LINDNER

Federal Minister of Finance,
Member of the Bundestag,
Federal Chair of the Free Democratic Party

**In your opinion, what is the association between German angst and the changes that are necessary to overcome current and future societal challenges?**

In 2015, the Free Democrats embarked on our internal renewal process. Our mission statement was: German courage Instead of German angst. Back then, much like nowadays, German angst kept the people of our country down; our ability to act, and be determined was paralyzed. German courage, on the other hand, supports people, fosters inspiration, and prevents the flight into the crippling paralysis of fear.

There is no doubt that this vision can also be applied to the current and future challenges our society finds itself confronted with. We will need to pass through ecological, economic, infrastructural and security related transformation processes. While German angst, in the past caused us politicians to miss the opportunities to change, we need the German qualities of courage even more today. We have to keep looking ahead, recognize the challenges and embody the ambition to reform. The good news is: if a nation raises its own roadblocks, it can just as easily remove them!

## Which societal developments or movements inspire you to boldly approach the future?

I am impressed by the extent that people and businesses in our country have proven to be resilient and to have innovative strength against the backdrop of the consequences of the Russian war attacks. Projected scenarios depicting the industrial collapse of our nation did not materialize. Many businesses survived without funding from the government, notably reduced their energy consumption, adapted their processes and thus made considerable contributions to the stabilization of Germany as well as Europe.

## What do you consider the most daunting societal obstacles that keep us from thinking and acting more confidently and boldly?

In our country we were happy with the status quo for a long time. We persistently held on to our past successes. Thus, we missed the opportunity to initiate important projects aiming at the modernization of our nation. Hence, we now must go forward with new determination and a clear intention to implement change. I am emboldened by the fact that this intent is already evident in vast parts of the country.

## How do you encourage others and yourself to go out on a limb?

Based on my own experiences, I strive to encourage others: risk something, go out on a limb, even if you fail. And if you fail, it's a chance for all of us to learn from it. For me, taking risks and offering new opportunities in the event of failure is a critical issue.

# CARSTEN LINNEMANN

**Deputy Federal Chairman,
Christian Democratic Union,
Member of the Bundestag**

### In your opinion, what is the association between German angst and the changes that are necessary to overcome current and future societal challenges?

In Germany we have given up on the mentality to "simply do something." Instead of trying new options driven by courage, we hide behind regulations because we are afraid that we might make a mistake. This is true albeit the pandemic has shown us that everything is possible if only we truly want it. Hence, I want Germany to evolve into a nation that is willing to experiment. Why don't we test novel ideas in pilot regions where restrictions are lifted for a certain amount of time? Later, we can analyse what went well and what did not. We stop the flops and roll out the successful results all over Germany. Consequently, we could stop the naysayers and worriers in Germany who say "This won't work because…" in their tracks.

### Which societal developments or movements inspire you to boldly approach the future?

According to a study of adolescents conducted by the Bertelsmann Foundation in August 2022, 80 percent of our youth want to actively work on their future and assume more responsibilities. Based on the study, three of five young people are looking forward to their own career future with confidence. Also, many youngsters are bold enough to think about starting their own businesses. The willingness to donate and help others are also very positive trends and remain consistently high in Germany despite the inflation and the energy crisis.

## What do you consider the most daunting societal obstacles that keep us from thinking and acting more confidently and boldly?

From my perspective, one thing that undermines a higher level of courage is the lack of an error culture in our society. We will have to overcome the paralyzing fear that our mistakes may cause us to fail. We are obviously all striving to be successful. However, the fear of failure must not lead us astray into a realm where we don't even try things. Consequently, we must identify mistakes as opportunities because they help us learn new things. This includes that we do not degrade others who were bold enough to try something. Overall, we have to give citizens more freedom and instil greater self-accountability. After all, whenever a high level of faith in the government, or worse a mentality of having comprehensive insurance, spreads, courage, self-drive and entrepreneurial spirit are stifled, and innovation comes to a halt.

## How do you encourage others and yourself to go out on a limb?

I recently published a book titled "'Die ticken doch nicht richtig!': Warum Politik neu denken muss" (They've gone berserk. Why Politicians Have to Change Their Way of Thinking"). In it I ask Germany to change its mentality – more courage and more "just do it". I call upon our nation to leave its comfort zones and to implement true structural reforms – even if it might be painful here and there.
It is the only way for us to be victorious in the future.
Consequently, I also call my new podcast "Einfach mal machen" (Just Do it). Once a month I bring interesting guests to the table who share my optimism and are eager to change our nation. In live interviews on Instagram, I also introduce exciting role models who have dared to do something and are bursting with energy.
However, it does not suffice for us to admire the top performers, we also have to especially encourage the weaker members of society. Hence, I have established a foundation more than ten years ago. It is called the LEBENSlauf Foundation. It is our aim to give adolescents on the fringes of society a positive perspective. In these projects, which take nine months to complete, we introduce participants to the joy of movement, games and sports. Through this athletic project we give them a new sense of self and show them that in the long run, courage and industriousness will pay off.

# JOCHEN MAAS

Managing Director, Research & Development
Sanofi-Aventis Deutschland GmbH

**In your opinion, what is the association between German angst and the changes that are necessary to overcome current and future societal challenges?**

In Germany, the glass is almost always half empty when it comes to new technologies, while other countries consider it half full. The result is often an innovation interrupting technology scepticism. Among the historic examples are nuclear power debates or green gen technology. The latest examples include the use of health information for research, customised medicine or gene therapy. In that context it is extremely rare that a technology is the per se fear factor or, worse, dangerous. It is always a person who uses them incorrectly. We should be mindful of the fact that we can manage the great societal challenges only with new and innovative technologies and that we must not oppose them. This does not only pertain to healthcare, but also many other critical issues, such as climate research, biodiversity research, the investigation of the migrant streams and backgrounds and many others. To be ready to manage all of these responsibilities, we need a broad societal consensus as it is the only way to ultimately minimize German angst. Comprehensive communication supported by scientists, theologians, ethics experts, journalists as well as politicians and many other groups is essential in the efforts to achieve this.

## Which societal developments or movements inspire you to boldly approach the future?

It is encouraging that people are able to change their thinking so quickly, especially during times of crises. The pandemic, for instance, has demonstrated to many of us how important and lifesaving gen technology can be. Today, were it not for this technology, we would not have a single vaccine. The understanding that there are potential scenarios that make health protection more important than data privacy, has risen to the top as a result of comparing Covid death rates in other countries that have effective infection tracking in place and countries that do not. One question remains: Why does it take a crisis for us to gain such insights?

## What do you consider the most daunting societal obstacles that keep us from thinking and acting more confidently and boldly?

We have become used to critically questioning matters and to trying to always think processes all the way through before we even initiate them at the latest since the era of enlightenment. We must welcome this attitude as it has taken us a long way as a society and scientifically. It even earned us a lot of recognition around the world. However, sometimes it would be better to be bold enough to start things and to correct the course while we are moving forward and not to write every detail of the process in stone all the way to the end.

## How do you encourage others and yourself to go out on a limb?

Courage, forthrightness, honesty and transparency are sine qua non conditions. Overall, we would be far more optimistic if we used these basic elements to first investigate the opportunities inherent in new approaches without neglecting their inherent risks. We should not start with the risks and address the opportunities only at the end. Our future outlook would be based on more confidence. Societies, such as the United States, would be fitting role models.

# ROBERT MAYR

Chairman of the Board
DATEV eG

**In your opinion, what is the association between German angst and the changes that are necessary to overcome current and future societal challenges?**

Even though this keyword is catchy – the much cited angst is merely the tip of the iceberg. The caution allegedly inherent in the "nature of Germans" is indeed problematic in any situation that makes a willingness to change absolutely essential. What we are talking about are general positions, the mindset of society that hinders progress. In Germany we tend to test an invention once again to escape the risk of the failure of an idea. However, digital products work differently: they are never really finished and the development quasi continues "live." It is difficult to align this with the mentality of making certain. That's why we have to focus a lot more on opportunities than risks. We have to foster people and their ideas, create structures they can work in that also tolerate failure.

**Which societal developments or movements inspire you to boldly approach the future?**

In my eyes, the digital transformation is a top favourite. During the pandemic we experienced a digital push and even now this trend continues – albeit not always with spectacular projects. One example: the number of businesses that have archived their accounting relevant receipts on the DATEV Cloud in a digital format recently exceeded one million. I think this is exciting since the digitization of receipts is the indispensable foundation for the next digitization steps in commercial processes. It offers a huge potential for efficiency gains – all the way to the completely automated further processing of this data in the individual process steps. This will help make our enterprises more expeditious and effective.

### What do you consider the most daunting societal obstacles that keep us from thinking and acting more confidently and boldly?

Given the objective of fostering progress and innovation in Germany, we clearly have way too much government regulation in place. We will have to fortify entrepreneurship while eliminating the red tape. Being in business for yourself has to be worthwhile so that creative ideas can be transformed into strong companies that deliver innovative products and services. One huge obstacle is our traditional "Prussian administration system." Digitization and the transition into a data driven economy require a digital mindset. The objective is to turn data streams into added value for everyone, so that individual government agencies will no longer manage data silos that do not have any economic benefits. Nevertheless, in terms of administration, digitization unfortunately still translates into the simple digital depiction of paper-based processes. This means that citizens and businesses are unable to take advantage of a lot of efficiency potential as soon as they have to depend on government administrators.

### How do you encourage others and yourself to go out on a limb?

In my eyes, the primary objective is to remain open to new ideas, to recognize opportunities and to subsequently seize them, for instance with the aim of creating added value for the customers. This intellectual attitude, this mindset is what I consciously promote in my environment. It must be acceptable and standard practice to get off the beaten paths, to think differently and to share ideas with others. Let's try things, let's fail, let's learn to never give up until a problem has been resolved. This does, of course, also include an error culture that does not assign blame.

# FRIEDRICH MERZ

Chairman of the Christian Democratic Union,
Germany, Member of the Bundestag

### In your opinion, what is the association between German angst and the changes that are necessary to overcome current and future societal challenges?

We, the Germans, sometimes appear to actually enjoy scaring ourselves. A vast tendency to torture ourselves as we wonder about the future is afoot.

German angst mutates into an immense problem if it has followers in the highest political circles. The German federal government and chancellor Olaf Scholz model this dilemma for us time and again. The Scholz Administration hesitates and procrastinates whenever doing the job is the task at hand. Political staffers have to be role models. This means that the more daunting the challenges, the more we must have faith in mastering them. The only way to approach the future is with confidence and trust in our own abilities.

### Which societal developments or movements inspire you to boldly approach the future?

Since February 24, 2022, we have been witnesses of the Russian war attacks targeting Ukraine. We are standing by as Vladimir Putin attempts to eradicate an entire nation. We are also witnessing the efforts of the Ukrainians to heroically defend against this terror. Yes, Ukraine is also going to battle for our freedom. And Estonian prime minister Kaja Kallas was right when she said: "the cost of energy may go up, but freedom is priceless." Many people are again becoming mindful of what freedom means and what its value actually is. We also need this spirit of liberty, this attitude, in many other areas. The problems of our day and age can be solved and we should proliferate this message.

### What do you consider the most daunting societal obstacles that keep us from thinking and acting more confidently and boldly?

Politicians have a responsibility in this context and in my opinion, they do not always meet these objectives. All too often, they only describe what is happening or try to keep up with the zeitgeist. Politicians should make an impact on the zeitgeist and make mission statements that go beyond the current day. Humility is important, but it must not result in courage being pushed under the table. "Prosperity for all" – a promise made by Ludwig Erhard - was not representative of zeitgeist. In fact, the opposite was true. He took a courageous stance toward the future that appeared unattainable to most Germans so soon after World War II. We must get back to bold and courageous thinking.

### How do you encourage others and yourself to go out on a limb?

Those who dare assume responsibility. But assuming responsibility as part of a party, a corporation, on behalf of the nation and its people most of the time is extremely fulfilling. I follow the lead of Karl Popper: "Optimism is mandatory."

# FRANK ULRICH MONTGOMERY

Chairman of the Board
World Medical Association

In your opinion, what is the association between German angst
and the changes that are necessary to overcome
current and future societal challenges?

In my eyes, Germany has the makings of a paralyzed giant. German dwarfs have tied Gulliver Germany down to the ground. This although we need nothing more urgently than a pioneering spirit paired with innovation, perspective and being excited about our future. We must learn to bypass the minute dispute over every little detail. We must take action and not merely talk (things down). We have to relearn reasonable use and stop to prevent every ounce of progress out of our fear of "misuse."

Which societal developments or movements inspire you
to boldly approach the future?

Young people in this country are the ones who give us a chance. They are self-confident, innovative, rebellious – and that's our future. "Fridays for Future" is one of these movements. Young people have never been this politically engaged in our country before. We have to return from the gerontocracy to the representation of future interests. My generation (in politics and society) must cease to just think about its own needs and must do much more to ensure that we leave a world with solvable problems to our successors.

### What do you consider the most daunting societal obstacles that keep us from thinking and acting more confidently and boldly?

At some point we have by and large lost the immense sense of community in our society. Instead of concentrated action and community we are ruled by a sense of I instead of we. The societal individualization results in individual egotism – and this turns into a level of isolation that loses sight of the things outside of our individual boxes and the interest in others and other subject matters. Politics have become a game aiming at the protection of self-interest. We no longer have great plans or great personalities. Yes, we are at a turning point. But why did it have to be imposed on us by outside forces? We did not change the times, we were compelled to change out of necessity.

### How do you encourage others and yourself to go out on a limb?

Openness, transparency, and truth are the only truly reasonable drivers of societal change. Those will make it possible to motivate reasonable people to stand for something. However, fake news will also have to be identified, named and eradicated. Those who have doubts, feel insecure or confused will not be able to act in a future-oriented and forward-looking manner.

# HILDEGARD MÜLLER

President
German Association
of the Automotive Industry

**In your opinion, what is the association between German angst
and the changes that are necessary to overcome
current and future societal challenges?**

In Germany, we have to leave the outdated thinking patterns behind us if we want to successfully tackle today's and tomorrow's major challenges. German angst will not move us forward and neither will continuing to do things the way we've always done them. While we are still hesitating and procrastinating, other parts of the world are creatively working towards the future. I am in particular considering the challenges climate change confronts us with.

Of course, we also see other issues we frequently fail to move along as fast as we want to. This includes the consequences of Russia's brutal attacks of Ukraine, which must be us betting more rigorously on the international collaboration with reliable partners. We must immediately diversify our trading partners, we need new energy and commodities partnerships right now. When it comes to digitization and infrastructure projects, we can no longer act reluctantly, but we must create the proper general conditions quickly to ensure that new projects can be implemented expeditiously.

## Which societal developments or movements inspire you to boldly approach the future?

It is first and foremost the innovative development of the German industry that gives me the courage to look into the future. Companies representing a vast variety of sectors are currently demonstrating a never-before-seen process of transformation. All are eager to make contributions to climate protection and are adapting their manufacturing processes. In Germany, this is evident in the automotive industry, but also in countless other sectors. Businesses are going forward with an incredible amount of commitment that remains un-rivalled. If the government would create general conditions that unfetter this force and if companies would no longer be confronted with more stringent regulations, I would not be concerned about our future.

## What do you consider the most daunting societal obstacles that keep us from thinking and acting more confidently and boldly?

The pressure to reform our nation is immense. The tax, benefit and allocation burdens are too extreme – for citizens as well as enterprises. The sources from which we procure energy and commodities are not diverse enough. Analogue technology can still be found in too many places. We have known this for quite some time. But not enough is happening at this point. We are often too slow and we are not willing to embark on new avenues and to leave our old ways of thinking behind. In Germany, as well as Europe we have to become better and bolder. Otherwise, we will be overtaken by more courageous and determined nations in the international competition for production venues.

## How do you encourage others and yourself to go out on a limb?

I am convinced that we should, time and again, expose ourselves to situations that take us out of our own comfort zones. I keep sharing this idea with my employees. In new situations, we learn something new, and this contributes to our personal growth. We must not remain in a state of personal lethargy but must challenge ourselves time and time again.

# ANGELIKA NIEBLER

Member of the European Parliament,
Chair of the Europe Group
of the Christian Social Union

**In your opinion, what is the association between German angst
and the changes that are necessary to overcome
current and future societal challenges?**

German angst? I notice that businesses are very interested in making changes, innovating, in rethinking things consistently and in trying new ideas all the time. Especially in the world of business, I am not aware of much German angst. What I do see is the concern because of overreaching regulations and general conditions that are extremely innovation averse.

On the other hand, I am very worried about the hostility vis-à-vis technology and policies that feed into the illusion that the government is able to eradicate all of the constituents' concerns. Of course, we have to help people in crisis situations, and we must support companies who depend on government funding. However, the benchmark should always be the social market economy, which demands self-accountability along with social security. Politicians must encourage, set goals, demonstrate visions and strengthen the trust in one's own capabilities. With the right mindset we can also manage societal challenges, such as the demographic transition, more effectively.

**Which societal developments or movements inspire you
to boldly approach the future?**

During the pandemic, we stuck together, the Ukrainian refugees who escaped from the Russian attacks and arrived in Germany found homes in many families, while a lot of families also provide homecare for their family members, are active in associations, volunteer to help others or advocate for the improvement of climate protection measures. We have so many citizens who advocate for others or good causes, and this is encouraging. Scientists, including Ugur Sahin and Özlem Türeci, who developed Corona vaccines, also set brave examples. These scenarios impress upon us what society and businesses can achieve when it matters. The scientists and vast numbers of staff members gave everything to find a way to counteract the vicious virus. In my eyes, this is also the greatest testament as to why the social market economy is the most successful societal model especially in times of upheaval. In 1957, Ludwig Erhard said: "The ideal scenario that comes to my mind is based on the power of one person being able to say: I want to prove myself by deploying my own strength; I want to assume the risk of living myself, I want to be in charge of my own fate. Now, you, the government, make certain that I will be able to do that."

The many years of wealth we were able to enjoy in Germany have their roots in this vision. Provided we once again focus more intensively on the basic principles of the social market economy, I have no doubt that we will successfully manage the multiple crises of this day and age.

## What do you consider the most daunting societal obstacles that keep us from thinking and acting more confidently and boldly?

We have successfully worked towards great prosperity and now we are scared that we might lose it all due to all of the changes. Defending what we already have is a response that is easy to understand. Yet, raising a defence is not enough. A lot will have to change if we want to retain prosperity. Standing still is the equivalent of regressing. Politicians have to encourage us as well, they must offer us opportunities for the future, especially in times of crisis. People have to know that their concerns are being taken seriously. It is their right to expect honest answers.

## How do you encourage others and yourself to go out on a limb?

I can only tell myself and others: get out of your comfort zone! We have to trust in ourselves and must not fear occasional failures. I like to encourage others to try or attempt something new. This may trigger action, overcoming personal hurdles or remaining persistent in difficult situations. We all make mistakes. The main objective is that we learn something from our mistakes. Our future successes require us to be courageous.

# FRANK NIEHAGE

CEO of the flatexDEGIRO AG

**In your opinion, what is the association between German angst and the changes that are necessary to overcome current and future societal challenges?**

Angst is never a good advisor when it comes to changes. However, there are lots of fields that urgently require us to do away with obsolete behaviour patterns if we want to conserve our societal prosperity. This pertains to every single one of us. Most of us will find it impossible to enjoy a financially secure retirement if we do not obtain private pension insurance. The implementation of the nationalized stock pension is a positive sign. However, to lastingly overcome German angst, which causes concerns about long term investments into the capital market, direct incentives offered to all private households by politicians are essential. Other countries, including France, Sweden or Great Britain are already a step ahead of us.

**Which societal developments or movements inspire you to boldly approach the future?**

Education, specifically financial education. Only those who understand the capital markets will be able to successfully generate assets. To achieve this, we have been in a cooperation with the Frankfurt School of Finance & Management for many years. In 2016, we inaugurated the first "FinTech-Bachelor "course. And our documentary film "Die Kunst des Investierens" (The Art of Investing), has already reached more than a million viewers. And I also think that it was the right move to spend an extra 100 billion euros when we in Germany realized that given the geopolitical situation, it is a worthy cause to build an army that can defend us.

## What do you consider the most daunting societal obstacles that keep us from thinking and acting more confidently and boldly?

There is a German saying: "despair drives invention." This definitely sounds true. In Germany, the past two or three generations have enjoyed the blessing of not being victims of despair. As prosperous as this may be for society, our "economic miracle" and "quality made in Germany" have left us lethargic over the years. Many now give the protection of what is more priority than the assumption of entrepreneurial risks. Improper incentive systems do the rest. Let's just look at the banking sector: as a board member I have to assume personal liability for ten years, which is twice as long of a term than those practiced by non-banks. At the same time, the Institution Compensation Policy limits the success-based compensation to an amount equivalent to the annual fixed salary. For the board members of a bank this means that they have to assume more risk while the chance to generate additional income is smaller. It is hardly surprising that the German financial sector does not evolve into an innovative pioneer but continues to fall behind on the international stage.

## How do you encourage others and yourself to go out on a limb?

Courage must be rewarded. This is why "entrepreneurial engagement" is not just lip service for all of the flatexDEGIRO staff. It is what we live day in and day out. Moreover, thanks to an employee program, about half of our workforce of 1,300 is directly participating in the bank's financial success. These employees are flatexDEGIRO shareholders. Making bold decisions, we achieve this success as a team. Hence, in just a few years, we have evolved from being a niche provider to being Europe's leading online brokerage.

# SUSANNE PORSCHE

German Film Producer and Investor

**In your opinion, what is the association between German angst and the changes that are necessary to overcome current and future societal challenges?**

German angst, in my opinion, is the result of the desire to always be perfect, not to fail, not to become the target of criticism and not being attackable. The fear of failure is evident in public and personal life. On the one hand, it prompts us to be cautious, prudent, industrious and dependable, while it also makes us keenly aware of the importance of rules and order. On the other hand, the fear of failure has the potential of hampering or restraining positive developments. It is key to remember that falling down is not something to be ashamed of, and that it is a misstep not to get up after we fall. Anyone who has ever fallen and stood up again, can feel and deserves the respect of the community. We can learn a lot from the Americans as far as this subject is concerned. We are on a positive path given that we have learned from start-ups against the backdrop of failures that we certainly have the capability to master societal, economic and political challenges.

### Which societal developments or movements inspire you to boldly approach the future?

What encourages me looking ahead into the future is that we, despite all of the obstacles and challenges have a fantastic proven education and training culture that we are renowned for around the globe. It fosters an elite, inspires creativity and gives us future opportunities. This is a great treasure that has to be protected and that must not be placed into jeopardy as a result of cost cuts or debates inspired by jealousy.

### What do you consider the most daunting societal obstacles that keep us from thinking and acting more confidently and boldly?

The most imposing hurdle in our society is that we can only be proud of our politicians in rare cases. Among politicians, it tends to be much harder to identify the above described lofty culture of training and education. In fact, politicians who never completed an apprenticeship and/or gained life skills based on professional experience want to dictate to their constituents how things should be done. A lot of people do not accept that. Politicians focus on getting re-elected and don't dare to develop long term perspectives. They lack the courage to stand up for their decisions because they are afraid that it could cost them their re-election.

### How do you encourage others and yourself to go out on a limb?

We have to stand side by side with the young generation, communicate values while living them and let youngsters share our wealth of experience. We should enable them to be bold, to get back up again if they fall, to believe in themselves and their goals and to recognize that it is important to always stay focused on the goals we set for ourselves, even if the path is full of obstacles and challenges. My lifelong experiences have taught me that every loss allowed me to gain strength and moved me forward another step of the way.

# KATHERINA REICHE

Board Chair
Westenergie AG

**In your opinion, what is the association between German angst and the changes that are necessary to overcome current and future societal challenges?**

As easy it is to empathize with the longing for peace and security, in particular in times of multiple crises, we need to be brave and trust in our own strengths. Ludwig Erhard was a very firm and dedicated believer in social market economics and their foundational pillars: freedom and responsibility, market and competition. These days, the objective must be to fortify this belief more than ever before as the principles still apply. Erhard wanted every single person to be able to say "I aim to prove myself based on my own strengths and I want to be responsible for my own fate." This though does not take fear – it takes courage.

**Which societal developments or movements inspire you to boldly approach the future?**

In public, we have rarely ever discussed the availability of energy as passionately as we do today. In this, I can see a huge opportunity as I believe in the inventive spirit of humans. In fact, many fields of energy production and supply are now making impressive progress: batteries are becoming increasingly powerful, kerosene and automotive fuels can now be manufactured synthetically and the natural gas grids that were based on fossil fuels to date can now transport 100 per cent hydrogen instead of natural gas. Furthermore, the construction of the liquid gas terminal in Wilhelmshaven demonstrates that if the pressure is daunting enough, Germany cannot only be thorough, but also fast. I find these things encouraging.

### What do you consider the most daunting societal obstacles that keep us from thinking and acting more confidently and boldly?

In keeping with Ludwig Erhard's philosophy, we must not rely on directive government enforced solutions, but trust in the interaction of the market forces inherent in competition. Erhard had a positive vision of humanity: he believed in creativity, the willingness to assume responsibility and a pioneering spirit. He optimistically believed that liberalized competition enables progress. Hence, we should interpret a crisis as an opportunity. Let's overcome the old and dare to try new things.

### How do you encourage others and yourself to go out on a limb?

Courage requires us to leave our comfort zones. First, it can be helpful to analyse our own fears. What are we afraid of and what is the worst thing that could happen? Those who know this will find relief, combat their fears and find the courage to do things differently. The next step would be to become aware of the fact that any new idea will first face resistance as any change will be met with doubt. No progress without courage, regardless of whether it is economic or societal progress. Those who dare do not always have to win. But those who don't dare have already lost.

# HAGEN RICKMANN

Managing Director, Business Customers
Telekom Deutschland GmbH

### In your opinion, what is the association between German angst and the changes that are necessary to overcome current and future societal challenges?

It depends on how you define German angst. I think that our angst consists of two facets: one is the fear of the future and it does not oppose change. To the contrary, it may even drive us to make changes since uncertainty about the future prevents us from simply continuing to do what we have always done. The other facet is a certain amount of reluctance and with regard to change, it is anything but beneficial. We should learn to master this facete. In an era during which much of the world is being re-distributed, this hesitancy is not appropriate. Germany is a technology nation – we place great emphasis on quality. It is extremely important that in the future we focus on innovation even more.

### Which societal developments or movements inspire you to boldly approach the future?

Today's young generation emboldens me. The fact that the term "today's youth" has something of a negative connotation is impossible for me to understand. The young generation is far more active than the generation that preceded it. It is more reflective, more self-critical and it does not shy away from questioning the lifestyles older generations model for it. When I, for instance, discuss climate protection with my children, I hardly dare to take a taxi later. But let's be real – it inspires confidence in me that our upcoming generations are advocating for change.

## What do you consider the most daunting societal obstacles that keep us from thinking and acting more confidently and boldly?

Traditionally, we have a love affair with processes and perfection. Being open-minded, agile and willing to live with failure every once in a while, – those are attributes we rarely appreciate. If we could overcome the pressure to take everything imaginable into account from the start, we would already make considerable progress. After all, we do have bold ideas. But we still put a lot more effort into finding "but" excuses than we put into the pragmatic implementation of these ideas.

## How do you encourage others and yourself to go out on a limb?

By emulating role models or referring to them. Around 1,500 companies in Germany are considered Hidden Champions – i.e., businesses who are hardly known to the public eye, but have established themselves as global market leaders in their industries. They hold this status because they have demonstrated courage. They have either invented new products, technologies or services and launched them, or they have recognized trends early in the game and have made them work for medium-sized companies. Learning more about them is incredibly inspiring. I tell my customers the same thing. Incidentally, the conditions for making bold moves are much better in Germany than one would think. We have, for instance, more funding programs than most other countries in Europe. Therefore, it is not surprising that Germany is considered the number 2 nation for start-ups on our continent – Great Britain is the only country that invests even more risk capital into fledgling enterprises.

# SARNA RÖSER

Federal Chairwoman of the Business Alliance
DIE JUNGEN UNTERNEHMER

## In your opinion, what is the association between German angst and the changes that are necessary to overcome current and future societal challenges?

Brain studies tell us that caution affiliated with changes works ten times harder in us than the excited anticipation of better times. This dates back to the era of cave dwellers and sabre tooth tigers. Nevertheless, we have successfully emerged from the stone age. From the perspective of our young generation, changes are once again an absolute must! This takes courage and we prove that we have it, time and time again, despite the German angst we are legendary for. In many disciplines, we have won admiration as a country of inventors, quality suppliers and innovators. The number of innovative global market leaders among German medium-sized companies is the best example. Nevertheless, it is time to take action!

We are now more well-versed at handling societal challenges due to the pandemic, inflation, and the energy crisis than we were just a few years ago. Our resilience has been further amplified. Moreover, we have all learnt that the social market economy is a model for success. We have also determined that our economy is more fragile than most of us imagined. Prosperity is not a given, it is something we have to work for. To achieve this, all of us must participate, wherever we can. The government should build the bridges to make sure that each individual can move forward and can tell his or her story. However, education programs and the conditions at business locations have to be rapidly improved to give German courage a lasting platform for take-off.

## Which societal developments or movements inspire you to boldly approach the future?

Globalization and networking expand the horizons for the new and for change all around the globe. Especially young people in Germany are eager to play a leading role in these endeavours. This is evident in the large number of future-oriented start-ups that have been established in recent years. One of the major location advantages in Germany is the fact that the grown structures of numerous family owned and operated enterprises are in place. They evolved into large businesses because they are innovative, and they show newcomers how new ideas can be converted into lasting business success.

However, more than ever before foreign locations attract entrepreneurs thanks to often more promising overall conditions. To allow companies to be well positioned in case of market changes, they must have operational leeway and positive conditions for investments into research & development. Action is required to reposition Germany more solidly in the contest of business venues, and to again make it a competitor who is ready to do business.

## What do you consider the most daunting societal obstacles that keep us from thinking and acting more confidently and boldly?

The unfettered expansion of the socialist approach to governing in Germany has its roots in German angst. Every election serves more constituents and votes are secured by making immense financial promises. By offering a safety net for everyone in every life situation and by carrying people well-padded through any crisis, the government is compelling mature citizens to become dependent on our government. As a consequence, people increasingly believe that the government will somehow fix things – time and again. However, to be able to do this, the government needs to collect taxes here and make certain that the invention and innovation forces and therefore ultimately the self-realization of many is not hampered by ever growing government intervention. I call on the government to always also under-stand crises as opportunities and not just reasons for ever growing government benefits. Instead, what we need are measures aiming at creating a future, in particular advanced education in the fields of business and digital applications and, ultimately a reduction of red tape paired with an understanding that politicians and government employees definitely do not have better knowledge of the technologies that have a chance to manifest themselves with citizens in the future.

## How do you encourage others and yourself to go out on a limb?

Based on my experience, positive examples, role models and an "information toolbox" play the biggest roles. Many young people have fantastic ideas but still don't know where to take them. It is our responsibility to show courageous young people what is possible. That's why talking about these issues in alliances such as "Die jungen Unternehmer", solid public relations work and the dialogue with politicians are so important to me. However, the intent to create and move changes ahead is the first step. Nevertheless, it is also the responsibility of politics to ensure that these things can subsequently be implemented.

# ANDREAS RÜTER

Managing Director and Local Market Leader
AlixPartners Deutschland

**In your opinion, what is the association between German angst and the changes that are necessary to overcome current and future societal challenges?**

German angst probably has its roots in the deeply unsettling experiences of the first half of the 20th century. It is not helpful when trying to handle and manage crises. As a rule, Germans collectively view the extent of a crisis as much worse than it actually turns out in hindsight.

This is counterproductive as far as the mastering of challenges is concerned. While the German economy has consistently emerged strongly from crises such as the 1970s oil crisis, the bursting of the dot.com bubble or the financial crisis, one must ask oneself: does it always take a crisis to catapult us into making the necessary changes? Does the current multi-crisis impose enough pressure to unify forces, push ideologies down to the bottom of the barrel and to loosen the German fear brakes so that the switch in favour of change can be activated?

"It won't work is not an option." It makes one yearn for a new consciousness of German qualities – the art of engineering and innovative force, courage, and confidence – so that we can now approach the challenges of geopolitical change and climate objectives in harmony with business success. And in conjunction with this, we have to engage in medium term instead of short term thinking paired with individual ad-hoc actions.

**Which societal developments or movements inspire you to boldly approach the future?**

The stability of the job market and the continued entrepreneurial bravery exuded by medium sized companies. Thanks to its financial prowess and, at the core, very stable political and governmental systems, the German society boasts a high level of resilience, provided we succeed in keeping the public discourse within an objective framework governed by reason. I think it is encouraging if even restructuring or investor conferences discuss environmental standard compliance and not merely profitability criteria. If we bet on our innovative strength, we will not only master the climate crisis, but also reel in profits in the future.

A politically active and sensitized young generation that has the courage to rethink fundamental priorities in life planning and that is willing to question the status quo, has the potential to trigger positive effects.

### What do you consider the most daunting societal obstacles that keep us from thinking and acting more confidently and boldly?

The rise of prohibitive policies and regulation: excessive amounts of red tape and regulation are restrictive factors.

The tendency to aim for perfection: too many hurdles prevent us from transforming a good idea quickly and efficiently to create a market relevant product and business.

A healthy debate and dispute culture: in the past, it was one of the responsibilities of the media to keep the level of the discourse culture high. Today's media landscape, in particular due to the influence of social media and in some cases targeted manipulation, drives polarization and has an unproductive impact on societal development.

Egalitarianism: the degradation of the elites while attempting to level everything down to the lowest commonality is counterproductive for an innovative and progressive industry and society.

### How do you encourage others and yourself to go out on a limb?

Trying and driving forward the new as a team. Offering leeway, motivation, positive reinforcement. Talking more about opportunities and not just the risks. Practicing an openminded attitude towards the new and encouraging others if they fail. And always remember to have good friends, partners, people you trust on your side.

# SONJA SCHWETJE

Editor-in-Chief, ntv

### In your opinion, what is the association between German angst and the changes that are necessary to overcome current and future societal challenges?

Changes do not only trigger uncertainties and resistance among the employees of businesses, but frequently also among citizens of a country. The more complex a crisis, the greater the challenges, the more intense these resistant forces will be. Especially after a long period of stability and prosperity gains, it consequently makes sense that many people will grab on to this phase and regard any change processes, especially those that are disruptive in nature, with suspicion. Just like in any organization, intense communicative accompaniment is a determining factor for the success of change. In a nation of around 83 million, this is not an easy feat. However, in addition to a uniform strategy for the future that is subsequently allocated to the individual sectors, a compatible communications strategy is equally essential.

### Which societal developments or movements inspire you to boldly approach the future?

I am observing a high level of energy and willingness to participate in parts of our society. Far more people are willing to change, while fewer are doing their very best to keep what already exists at any cost. Finding the right combination is a balancing act. There are certain values and capabilities that have provided the foundation for the success of the German economy. They can help us implement the next stage of this transformation. However, at the same time, we will have to sever ties with some earlier success factors, because they tend to slow us down in this digitized world.

### What do you consider the most daunting societal obstacles that keep us from thinking and acting more confidently and boldly?

The flood of information, the simultaneous occurrence of crises and the virtually unsolvable global and local challenges of our day and age are overwhelming for many people and trigger a sense of helplessness. From a humanitarian perspective, it is absolutely conclusive that this can have a paralyzing effect. If the situation is further compounded by individual incidents that have to be attributed to the failure of the administration or public institutions, some will lose faith in the conviction that our society offers the proper general conditions to implement good ideas. One example is the mishap election of Berlin's Senate in 2021, which will now have to be conducted a second time.

### How do you encourage others and yourself to go out on a limb?

Communication and reflection play a deciding role in all areas that require change. Time and again, we have to sharpen our awareness of the extent of our action radius and ask ourselves if we are making full use of it. It often turns out to be larger than we think. And it is helpful to keep in mind that the solution for a complex problem cannot be a one-step incident, but must consist of several targeted partial solutions that everyone can make contributions to.

# RAINER SESSNER

Managing Director
Bayern Innovativ

In your opinion, what is the association between German angst
and the changes that are necessary to overcome
current and future societal challenges?

I think that the term "German angst" is a stereotypical, prejudicial term that implies that the German business world is acting fearfully. At Bayern Innovativ, we frequently find the opposite to be true when we interact with Bavarian businesses, who are indeed very ready for change. This is why I am convinced that the negative ramifications in journalistic reporting are given much more attention than they deserve.

We have to keep in mind how innovative and capable our economy really is – and this is particularly evident with medium-sized companies. And that is exactly what we need to be ready for the future. Change is the key to the management of current and future societal challenges. At the same time we must be aware of the fact that a functioning social and sustainable market economy will still need a meritocracy.

Which societal developments or movements inspire you
to boldly approach the future?

History attests that humanity has arisen stronger from virtually every crisis. This encourages me. To that end, our current time may be an important phase. However, the price that so many people have to pay is much too high – war, draught, flooding or other disasters.

Our Bayern Innovativ customers give me a sense that things are going well. Most of them have recognized the need for change and see its opportunities. The primary question that generates uncertainty is the "how." Especially small and medium-sized companies need impulses and support. We provide them with both by offering our knowledge of future-oriented technologies and trends, and by providing the proper tools or even partners. This approach comprises a multitude of industries.

### What do you consider the most daunting societal obstacles that keep us from thinking and acting more confidently and boldly?

A satiated public that is no longer interested in and thus blocks change is a major obstacle. If we restrict ourselves from the start, by for instance failing to use new technologies, we will not be able to create a positive future. Moreover, in some cases, a legal and administrative system has emerged that prevents a liberal, social market economy. It fuels the in part out-of-synch relationship between entitlement, performance and the willingness to assume societal responsibility. You have to wonder – what is the hen and what is the egg.

### How do you encourage others and yourself to go out on a limb?

This has been part of our DNA for 27 years – something we do very passionately. We help Bavarian companies who are striving to reposition themselves and manage change – either with new technologies or business models. In this context, networks and knowledge transfer are more important than ever. I am convinced that businesses, science and research will have to cooperate even more intensively in the future and that they will do it. Our "Thinknet Bayern" is the perfect point of departure. Boasting more than 75,000 contacts, it is the largest network in the free state of Bavaria and links businesses, science and politics with industry, technology and partnership networks.

# MARGRET SUCKALE

Member of the Infineon Technologies AG
Supervisory Board

**In your opinion, what is the association between German angst and the changes that are necessary to overcome current and future societal challenges?**

It is a fact that Germans are considered particularly fearful by many and there is indeed some truth to that. We clearly have many worriers in this country. Having said that, I do not want to minimize the huge challenges we are facing. To the contrary, war, the pandemic, inflation and the gas shortage are all things that raise immense concerns. However, the question is, how do we best address these enormous challenges. Fear is definitely the worst advisor. What we need is more self-confidence; trust in our own strengths and join forces in our commitment to tackle necessary changes. Other countries handle even complex matters with more ease. The United States actually have integrated the "Pursuit of Happiness" into the nation's constitution. What I'd like to see in Germany as well is a lot more positive energy.

**Which societal developments or movements inspire you to boldly approach the future?**

Reality thankfully regularly cancels out the countless pessimistic projections. Contrary to what quite a few experts have predicted, the gas tanks are full this winter and the first LNG terminals have been built in record time. Industrial production has declined, but not nearly as much as we feared. So far, the job market also has not weakened. In fact, the opposite is true. All in all, truly positive signs. I would also like to underscore the continued strong innovative capabilities of German enterprises. Many actually – justifiably – envy us for our bio scientists' and engineers' know-how. In fact, our scientists are the ones who make this daunting transformation even possible.

## What do you consider the most daunting societal obstacles that keep us from thinking and acting more confidently and boldly?

Being considered a country of poets and intellectuals is not a bad thing at all. However, we have evolved into a nation that is much too complicated and often also too complacent. We want to regulate everything; get tangled up in an enormous amount of red tape. Construction projects, for instance, take far too long. The digitization of the government administration should also progress much more rapidly. Numerous good ideas fail here because we don't follow through. It does not have to be this way. We should change that. The motto should be "just do it" instead of "ifs and buts."

## How do you encourage others and yourself to go out on a limb?

In discussions, I tend to – more than ever – focus on the strengths of German businesses: we boast well-trained staff, German technicians and engineers have the spirit of inventors, we have great companies that offer positive work environments, and our interesting world of start-ups continues to expand. The investments made by international venture capitalists into newly established companies in Germany are increasing and the number of "unicorns" in Germany is on the rise. The courage and enthusiasm of the young founders is truly remarkable and just one example is that only those who dare have a chance to win.
I am an optimistic realist. My motto is: "What is, simply is." That's why I strive not to waste time over bemoaning things I cannot change and focus on situations we can tackle and improve.

# HORST M. TELTSCHIK

Honorary Professor
Technical University Munich

**In your opinion, what is the association between German angst and the changes that are necessary to overcome current and future societal challenges?**

The term "German angst" is popular right now, primarily in the Anglo-Saxon media. The term is used to express a certain amount of schadenfreude to profile the helplessness of German politics when it comes to making compelling and especially unambiguous decisions concerning our military support of Ukraine.

Fears do in fact arise from scenarios that put us in a position to experience obvious problems, such as the Ukrainian war or imminent environmental disasters or the pandemic and many other things through the mass media or individually, while the responsible parties in politics and society fail to present conclusive decisions or even answers. Based on my experience in politics and business, it would help many people if someone would explain the causes and complexity of these problems in a way they can understand to emphasize that quick and easy answers are not possible. When I understand an issue I can adapt to it much more effectively as an individual.

## Which societal developments or movements inspire you to boldly approach the future?

Courage to move forward into the future – this is a challenge we all have to embrace first and foremost. Nowadays, knowledge and information are available all around the globe in mere seconds. It can be used positively or negatively. This was, for instance, evident in the Arabian Spring and the ongoing protests mounted by young Iranians, but also in those of the climate activists or in the marches of radical right-wingers in some parts of Eastern Germany. What emboldens me looking into the future is the fact that it is becoming increasingly difficult to uphold closed societies and to conceal human rights violations.

## What do you consider the most daunting societal obstacles that keep us from thinking and acting more confidently and boldly?

Whining is always easier than thinking of solutions for problems and to actually work towards these solutions by getting involved. The latter requires knowledge, after all. Who will teach us and how? Are parents, schools, associations, or the media willing and capable when it comes to passing on knowledge and self-accountability? Does a person's failure result in him or her being excluded from the community or, do we, out of solidarity, give this person supportive encouragement to try new things?

## How do you encourage others and yourself to go out on a limb?

By inspiring intellectual curiosity to acquire the essential knowledge. By fostering and promoting self-confidence. By celebrating achievements, analysing failures, and encouraging new attempts to resolve issues.
The way to get there is to never give up!

# FRANK THELEN

European Serial Founder,
Technology Investor and TV Personality

### In your opinion, what is the association between German angst and the changes that are necessary to overcome current and future societal challenges?

Changes are always painful. In Germany, we face the problem that thanks to our strong past we are still doing well today. We are slumbering in what one could call a prosperity nap and now we suddenly have to come to grips with the fact that we are resting on our laurels, eating away at our foundation. We recognize problems but not opportunities, albeit the daunting challenges of our day and age are actually also our biggest opportunity to reinvent Germany and Europe. This also means that we have to establish a new error culture to let go of our German angst. A lot of German businesses do not deliver innovation because their employees will not dare to pursue new ideas and visions. They are not given incentives to deviate from existing processes every now and then. "We have always done it this way", will not move us ahead. In fact, what we really should be afraid of is that if we perpetuate this approach, we will soon no longer be on par to negotiate with global powers, i.e. the United States and China. What we need is German courage, not German angst.

### Which societal developments or movements inspire you to boldly approach the future?

We have outstanding universities and are global research leaders. Our Hidden Champions remain strong, and we also boast the phenomenon of medium-sized global niche market leaders who only exist here. What we need now are NextGen Champions, who will walk in the footsteps of Ferdinand Porsche and Robert Bosch. I have the pleasure of supporting some hopefuls through Freigeist Capital: Lilium Aviation is one of the leading players in the EVTOL Taxi market hailing from Germany, while Kraftblock has developed an energy storage solution that will soon decarbonize our industry and that in the long term has the potential of making the conversion to renewable energy tenable. However, it will also take reinforcing political impulses – I am hoping for future political decisions that are based more on scientific insights and the laws of nature. Climate change is one of humanity's most daunting challenges. Technical solutions exist, however, we are boosting the output of our coal power plants.

## What do you consider the most daunting societal obstacles that keep us from thinking and acting more confidently and boldly?

In Germany, we do not pursue a culture of heroism. Things are different in Silicon Valley, where individuals like Elon Musk or Jeff Bezos are celebrated for their achievements, even if they sometimes make controversial decisions and manage their companies in a highly progressive manner. To that end, it is irrelevant whether we have to necessarily approve of their decisions. Nevertheless, the positive momentum that drives Silicon Valley ultimately draws its energy from the fact that founders find a lot more support there – and that includes investors and the media.

## How do you encourage others and yourself to go out on a limb?

I have experienced frequent failures in my life and have learnt to get up after every fall. At this time, I am also facing numerous challenges related to the tech sell-off. I frankly address these issues in my books and at my presentations. I hope that the path I have chosen will inspire others to pursue great ideas and to, occasionally, take chances to do so. I also model a healthy error culture in my businesses. My team proceeds self-accountably, in lean hierarchies, while seeing eye to eye. I get much more enthusiastic about an opportunity than I worry about a potential mistake.

# ANGELA TITZRATH

Chairwoman of the Board
Hamburger Hafen und Logistik AG

### In your opinion, what is the association between German angst and the changes that are necessary to overcome current and future societal challenges?

We Germans are definitely not a nation of fear mongers. What we are is consensus-driven and we act in a thoughtful, cautious manner. These efforts to be reasonable and take the middle road also stabilize our democratic community. Thoroughness instead of speed frequently works better than the taking of unpredictable risks. This is obviously a German character trait that is often interpreted as German angst. We certainly have the skills and opportunities to drive change forward, in particular if it is truly important to focus and act with determination. It is remarkable, how quickly the anti-Covid vaccine was developed and manufactured. Also, the way we ultimately managed the pandemic evidences that we have the capability of mastering the challenges we have to.

### Which societal developments or movements inspire you to boldly approach the future?

Courage is the positive energy we need to overcome the huge challenges humanity is facing. Whether it's climate change, the effects of the demographic transition or the consequences of the growing world populations with regard to nutrition and energy supplies, or the consumption of resources by the industrial nations – bold and responsible decisions have to be made by politicians and entrepreneurs. The fact that a movement like "Fridays for Future" has managed to increase the awareness of the need for accelerated climate protection is encouraging. The large number of outstanding scientific achievements in the fields of medicine and healthcare also documents that we, the people, are the strongest movement that has the capacity to create a liveable future.

## What do you consider the most daunting societal obstacles that keep us from thinking and acting more confidently and boldly?

Our stance is a deciding factor that allows us or prevents us from taking courageous action. We have reaped the benefits of globalization because there is a worldwide demand for products "made in Germany." Yet staying successful is a continuous challenge. In recent years, we have not pursued some work with the passion and determination that would have been necessary given the global changes that started at the end of the 1990s. What is evident instead is the tragic disparity between the willingness to act self-accountably and the now vast opinion that the government will take care of everything, especially in times of crisis. We should be grateful for the fact that government benefits assist many people and that our social safety net is so dense that nobody will easily "fall into the mine", as the saying in the Ruhr Area calls it. Yet there is a price we pay for all of this…

The virtual cornucopia of regulation and the endless options to file appeals in court interfere with self-initiated and personal advocacy. We must find a balance in this context since the speed decisions are being made at and actions are being taken in the global world of competition for solutions is still high. One concerning result of this is the fact that Germany lags behind in the digitization of its government administration and infrastructure. The condition of schools and university facilities as well as the quality of our education are alarming as well. As a country devoid of commodities, investments into our population's intellect are the most promising when it comes to our chance to remain one of the leading industrial nations in the future.

## How do you encourage others and yourself to go out on a limb?

I grew up in the Ruhr Region and saw the region go through changes. It was not always the kind of success story that can be planned out on a drawing board. Whenever we fail, we have to roll up our sleeves and move forward. This attitude has shaped my own. That's why I will support anyone who dares to try something new. Taking risks also means learning something new. It is critical to offer the kind of leeway that makes it possible to try something outside of the established processes. I have great trust in the capability of humans to take new paths and bold action. Our attitude makes the difference. If a lot is uncertain, that also means that a lot is possible.

# JOHAN VANDERMEULEN

Chief Transformation Officer, BAT plc
Chairman of the Supervisory Board,
BAT Germany Group

### In your opinion, what is the association between German angst and the changes that are necessary to overcome current and future societal challenges?

For the past years, I have had the privilege of being chairman of the supervisory board for BAT Germany. When I, as an engineer, think of Germany, I not only think of the land of poets and thinkers, but above all of the land of inventors. Change can be a springboard for inventions. But by the same token, inventions can also be the motor for change. In a time characterised by uncertainty and constant change, we as a society should courageously and optimistically develop innovative, sustainable solutions for our future. Through our company and our social commitment, and especially through our Foundation for Future Studies, we are accepting our responsibility to address future concerns. As pioneers and trend setters, we provide positive impulses aimed at helping us prepare for tomorrow, today.

### Which societal developments or movements inspire you to boldly approach the future?

At BAT, we want to create a culture that supports us in achieving corporate success as well as in making a contribution to society. The driving force behind this is our ethos. An ethos that responds to constant change and embodies a learning culture committed to continuous improvement: bold, fast, empowered, responsible and diverse. These are values I am also noticing more and more in society. Courage, optimism, solidarity, personal responsibility and the willingness to question one's own actions for the sake of a sustainable way of life.

### What do you consider the most daunting societal obstacles that keep us from thinking and acting more confidently and boldly?

The German dramatist and poet Friedrich Hebbel once said "It often takes more courage to change one's opinion than to stay true to it". Thinking and acting courageously requires openness. Openness in the sense of a willingness to embrace changes and new ideas and, where necessary, change the way we think. BAT has defined a clear corporate purpose: to build A Better Tomorrow™ by minimising the health impact of our business. The corporate purpose is based on the principle of harm reduction. Adult consumers should have a choice and be able to make an informed decision. Creating an environment that clearly identifies the harms caused by smoking, while holistically and consistently recognising where real public health benefits can be achieved, requires a willingness to accept our industry as part of the solution. If this can be achieved, I am convinced that we can improve public health by applying the concept of harm reduction in order to mitigate harm.

### How do you encourage others and yourself to go out on a limb?

Being able to shape and influence things is a privilege, but also a responsibility. Accepting this responsibility, thinking big, being innovative, valuing different points of view, challenging and encouraging one another, sharing experiences, questioning oneself and acting with integrity builds a framework that rewards those who dare. What you end up with is not just results, but meaningful action along the way. Or, in the words of Greek philosopher Democritus: "Courage is at the beginning of an action, happiness at the end."

# MATTHIAS VOELKEL

CEO of the Börse Stuttgart Group

## In your opinion, what is the association between German angst and the changes that are necessary to overcome current and future societal challenges?

In our complex, volatile word we will only survive if we change. Let's create, not react. Unfortunately, we Germans have had trouble doing that for years. German angst is not a reliable advisor. However, I do not want to paint it all black. In Germany, we still have a lot of doers and entrepreneurs that do the right thing without getting scared, who deliver ground-breaking innovation and tackle the problems of our day and age. This country has the potential to establish itself as a politically value-driven, not a morals admonishing leader and to assume our position once again at the helm of economic and technological endeavours. Provided we embrace this potential and stop tolerating the flourishing German mediocrity in many areas, I am optimistic. The current crisis gives us an extraordinary opportunity to re-invent ourselves.

## Which societal developments or movements inspire you to boldly approach the future?

On the one hand, the engagement and solidarity exuded by the people of this nation. One thing that comes to mind is the admirable rebuilding efforts of the Ahrtal residents after the horrific disaster and the impressive nationwide wave of solidarity. On the other hand, the dynamics that drive the start-up landscape. For instance, the eco system Digital Finance, we at the Group "Börse Stuttgart" are participating in on a Pan-European level. Creative founders who come up with new ideas join forces with established enterprises. Digitization is underway here that will not only optimize the financial markets, but also our everyday lives. It emboldens me that I see so much energy being dedicated to positive change.

### What do you consider the most daunting societal obstacles that keep us from thinking and acting more confidently and boldly?

I see the emerging etatism and the constant proliferation of government as well as quasi-government structures as hindrances. We definitely do not need more red tape. We need smart regulation. Another obstacle is the tendency of some German opinion-makers to combine cautious, alarming and wise guy approaches. Obviously, reflection is important. But it is just as important to develop the intuition that tells us when it is time to try new things. Moore's Law tells us that every other year, digital capabilities complete another exponential growth leap. We must stop letting the United States and China from speeding ahead of Germany. Our sometimes umbilical self-satisfaction is another hurdle. We should ask ourselves whether our basic political stance really works. In the case of energy and defence policy, after the shock of Russia's war of aggression against Ukraine, this is now fortunately happening gradually. So, let us take a step back: Would any ambitious nation actually follow our path in terms of fundamental political issues? My answer: not a single one. That should give us food for thought.

### How do you encourage others and yourself to go out on a limb?

I am personally curious by nature – I find creativity fulfilling. This means I need less encouragement. I embolden others by striving to draw an enthusiasm generating vision of the future. This is true: those who don't dare will have their future determined by others. By those, who risk things. We must make sure that we are part of the latter group.

# FRANK WALTHES

Chairman of the Board
Versicherungskammer Bayern

In your opinion, what is the association between German angst and the changes that are necessary to overcome current and future societal challenges?

Angst, in my eyes, is actually a fundamentally positive, helpful thing. For instance, think about stage fright – it is one form of fear. If you don't allow it to paralyze you, and if you think of it as normal, it will motivate you to be particularly well prepared and to approach the scenario with much greater focus.

German angst is quite often intangible, imprecise and nebulous. By now, it has made a name for itself internationally, although we all know that most of the things Germans worried about in the past 70 years or so did not materialize. Frequently, German angst is a historic chimaera in the collective memories of all Germans that is not rarely evident in the wait and see attitude – a hesitant attitude characterized by opportunism. I consider it dangerous. As communities, we should deploy this fear to mobilize our (defensive) forces, to take the initiative and to fortify our economic and social solidarity. We should use it to overcome the fear and to manage conditions that trigger fear. It is often a fear of loss, largely driven by concerns about declining wealth. I am convinced that none of this will happen since we are embedded into numerous alliances today, such as the EU or NATO and can thus trust in respective solidarity and support.

### Which societal developments or movements inspire you to boldly approach the future?

In conjunction with the Russian combat attacks targeting Ukraine, we have witnessed great declarations of solidarity in Europe. The European Union is standing behind the rule of law principles and largely acts accordingly. I can also identify economic and social cohesion among the liberal and democratic forces. This should encourage all of us and continue to solidify our intent to keep trying to establish a discourse and agree on a choice of moderate resources combating the many consequences of Russian aggression.

### What do you consider the most daunting societal obstacles that keep us from thinking and acting more confidently and boldly?

I would like to quote Nelson Mandela who said, "It always seems impossible until it's done." It is important for us to stay willing and able to overcome social boundaries and to recognize the value or the precious asset of equality. I think it is an important opportunity to give all citizens future perspectives, regardless of their social backgrounds. This means that our level of solidarity must still increase well above the level we are familiar with now. Another aspect for which I do not see an alternative if we want our society to continue to make progress, is more diversity in all positions and hierarchies. We need this level of diversity since people who have had different experiences, are of different ethnicities and who have intercultural contacts reinforce each other a lot more than homogenous groups. The aim is to think and act interdisciplinarily, cross-functionally, and cross-hierarchically.

### How do you encourage others and yourself to go out on a limb?

I can recommend Psalms 23 for encouragement.

# FALCO WEIDEMEYER

Head of EY-Parthenon EMEIA,
Global Head of Turnaround & Restructuring

### In your opinion, what is the association between German angst and the changes that are necessary to overcome current and future societal challenges?

It is a fact that Germans are not commonly known for their optimism. In six month intervals, we ask CEOs what their current professional focus is – and 98% of German CEOs ultimately say that they are anticipating a downturn in 2023; and 57 per cent actually say that it will be a grave recession. Nevertheless, I have never interpreted German angst as a stance that actually refers to fear, but a tendency to have a conservative basic outlook, quasi a dependency on the path. This yearning for orientation and the stance to pursue values and goals, also offers an inherent opportunity. After all, the entrepreneurial goal system will have to be enhanced with ecological, social and geopolitical aspects and the subsequent transformation will not be easy.

The persistence that creates a lofty initial hurdle can, in this case, be the very strong point companies will need to make to move forward on the new path. The numbers say the same – investments are still a top priority on the agenda of German CEOs. Every other respondent stated that the continuation of digital technology and technological transformation are still top priorities.

## Which societal developments or movements inspire you to boldly approach the future?

Two things – first of all, the fact that the immense social and ecological challenges have arrived in the mainstream of political and economic discussions, and second, the relevancy these issues have for the younger generation. This creates a push and pull scenario that turns these issues into subject matters that are permanent fixtures in the economic, political and societal discourse.

## What do you consider the most daunting societal obstacles that keep us from thinking and acting more confidently and boldly?

In a society that tends to strive for relief instead of absolution and common welfare instead of community, our much loved prosperity appears to be the biggest hurdle. It is likely that it will be impossible to further increase it in its current form. A new definition may be required. Perhaps our economic growth will be somewhat slower, but the ecological and social balance will be greater priority. This will equally affect companies and individuals – the goal system of businesses complements financial goals with social and ecological ones. The very personal terms of wealth or riches will have expanded meaning as well. This will not change the temporary setbacks and slumps in terms of growth, but it is helpful to reclassify them.

## How do you encourage others and yourself to go out on a limb?

First and foremost, with a logical chain. If we were to presume that the necessary ecological and social actions are existential in nature and will not just go away, consumers and markets are likely to integrate these facts sooner rather than later, which means that the process will evolve into an entrepreneurial necessity. This is definitely true if one wants to continue to fund companies, enthuse customers and inspire employees. This is further compounded by the fact that the transformation can be achieved only if consumers, regulators and businesses all rethink the situation, albeit companies will have a particular creative responsibility. And ultimately, being a father of two sons, I would not like to be accused of having spent decades influencing the executives and the management of companies as a consultant without introducing new impulses.

# VOLKER WISSING

Federal Minister of Digital and Transportation,
Member of the Bundestag

**In your opinion, what is the association between German angst
and the changes that are necessary to overcome
current and future societal challenges?**

There is clearly a gap between what we intend to do and what we are willing to change in our lives. Our society sets extremely lofty goals for itself. However, when it comes to actually doing things, many of us tend to fight to keep everything the way it has always been. We must work on this obstacle. After all, fundamental change, for instance in favour of climate neutral mobility comes with considerable upheaval. Hence, as a society, we have to be forthright and clearly question what we can achieve and what will overwhelm us. We have to manage things in a manner that allows us to push changes ahead at the rate the community is willing to support them. Otherwise, we risk losing the solidarity it takes within society. This would be fatal. We all have to depend on each other.

**Which societal developments or movements inspire you
to boldly approach the future?**

Our young generation encourages me. There is nothing worse for any society than adolescents who have no direction. Our youths know what they want, they are politically involved and make contributions – while they also have their own vision of values. This is a fantastic opportunity for our society. The vision of many young people is also an important mirror the older and middle-aged generations should look at. It helps us reflect on what we can do better. If we do, we also have to address the issues and when necessary, change the structures to move our society forward.

## What do you consider the most daunting societal obstacles that keep us from thinking and acting more confidently and boldly?

Being confronted with new crises all the time is a gigantic hurdle for change. The occurrence of new international conflicts gives rise to issues that are difficult to manage. We have made a lot of plans to engage in climate protection in Europe and now we are suddenly confronted with war. We have spent a lot of efforts on stabilizing Europe's finances – and suddenly we faced a pandemic. We had plans to invest a lot into transformative processes and now we are suddenly putting money into arms. May people are wondering what else will happen. Not having answers to these questions makes it more and more difficult to make bold decisions.

## How do you encourage others and yourself to go out on a limb?

With my conviction that change is the only chance we have. Standing still is not an option. Once you internalize this vision you will also have the courage to change. The deciding factor is to always look one step ahead and not to worry whether a decision made yesterday or the day before was the correct one. Today, I have the opportunity to make the right decision. Every path can lead to the destination, since we can always correct the course we are on. This is a vision that makes it very easy for me to motivate myself. It is also great that humans have both: emotions and intellect. We should absolutely deploy both when we make decisions.

# DAGMAR WÖHRL

Entrepreneur,
Attorney and Politician

## In your opinion, what is the association between German angst and the changes that are necessary to overcome current and future societal challenges?

The outcome of our national soccer team's performance during the recent Soccer World Cup in Qatar still haunts me because it is on par with the current situation in Germany. Our athletes, who were once known as a competitive team left behind a rather uncoordinated and wildly disparaged impression. The intent to walk away victoriously was not in evidence. I get the same sense when I survey Germany right now. We are in a lethargic phase, hopeless, do not have any drive and are waiting for the government to remove all the roadblocks for us.

Yes, times are difficult. One crisis follows another. However, we should not only focus on the obstacles. We should recall the things we have already achieved and leave behind the loss of direction – the right path is the one going forward. As Germans, we should know that changes that happen all around us are not necessarily bad. History has certainly taught us that fantastic things can arise from the ashes. For instance, more than 30 years ago, a divided Germany finally was reunited. Hence, we should boldly embrace the challenges of our day and age.

## Which societal developments or movements inspire you to boldly approach the future?

I have to admit that I am a huge fan of our youth! Many of us need to stop criticizing our young generation over and over again. We have truly engaged and participating young folks in our nation. What we have to learn is to keep these creative and productive heads in

our country. We have to offer these strong performers perspectives and incentives paired with the recognition they deserve. Politicians also need to rethink their approaches in a lot of areas. Members of every older generation claim that life was more difficult for them and that they achieved more. However, I think that today's challenges cannot be compared to those of the past. Developments evolve at lightning speed and if we're honest, we the "Best Agers", sometimes find this situation tough to manage. Those who have diverse teams consisting of both, experienced staff members and young talent are definitely winners.
This is why my motto is a slightly edited version of Herbert Grönemeyer's lyrics: "Gebt den Jungen das Kommando!" (Let Young People Rule)

### What do you consider the most daunting societal obstacles that keep us from thinking and acting more confidently and boldly?

We have lost our faith in our own abilities, albeit we have good reasons to believe. We are a nation that gets closer when life situations are especially hard. We face obstacles with courage. We now need this courage and this sense of community. Only if we realize that we have the potential to do great things, we will make it through these tough times.

### How do you encourage others and yourself to go out on a limb?

I do not consider myself a motivator, but I strive to give my founders that fundamental trust in their own abilities. They have to learn that it is absolutely fine and even necessary to make mistakes as we go through life. We have to make mistakes to learn and make progress. This is also why I personally immerse myself into new projects without fear. The worst that will ultimately happen is that I've gained more experience.

# GERMAN COURAGE
## instead of GERMAN ANGST

für unsere Gesellschaft. Die Sichtweise vieler junger Menschen ist außerdem ein wichtiger Spiegel für die ältere und mittlere Generation. Sie hilft dabei zu reflektieren, was wir besser machen können. Darauf müssen wir dann aber auch eingehen – und, wo notwendig, Strukturen verändern, um unsere Gesellschaft voranzubringen.

### Worin sehen Sie die größten Hindernisse in unserer Gesellschaft, zuversichtlicher und mutiger zu denken und zu handeln?

Ständig mit neuen Krisen konfrontiert zu sein, ist ein großes Hindernis für Veränderungen. Das Aufbrechen neuer internationaler Konflikte wirft Fragen auf, die schwer zu bewältigen sind. Wir haben uns sehr viel vorgenommen in Europa, um Klimaschutz zu betreiben – und plötzlich haben wir Krieg. Wir haben uns sehr viel vorgenommen, die europäischen Finanzen zu stabilisieren – und plötzlich hatten wir eine Pandemie. Wir wollen sehr viel investieren in Transformationsprozesse – und plötzlich investieren wir in Rüstung. Viele Menschen fragen sich: Was kommt denn noch? Diese unbeantworteten Fragen machen es immer schwieriger, mutige Entscheidungen zu treffen.

### Wie ermutigen Sie andere und sich selbst, etwas zu wagen?

Mit der Überzeugung, dass nur in der Veränderung eine Chance liegt. Stillstand ist keine Option. Das muss man einmal verinnerlicht haben – und dann hat man auch Mut zur Veränderung. Das Entscheidende ist, immer nach vorn zu schauen und nicht zu grübeln, ob eine Entscheidung von gestern oder vorgestern die richtige war. Heute habe ich die Chance, richtig zu entscheiden. Jeder Weg kann zum Ziel führen, weil wir ja immer wieder den Kurs korrigieren können. Das ist eine Lebenseinstellung – und damit kann ich mich sehr gut motivieren. Das Großartige ist außerdem, dass wir Menschen beides haben: Gefühl und Verstand. Und wir sollten bei Entscheidungen auch ruhig beides einsetzen.

# DAGMAR WÖHRL

Unternehmerin,
Rechtsanwältin und Politikerin

**Wie sehen Sie das Verhältnis zwischen der German Angst und der Notwendigkeit von Veränderungen, um aktuelle und zukünftige gesellschaftliche Herausforderungen zu bewältigen?**

Das Abschneiden unserer Fußballnationalmannschaft bei der vergangenen Fußballweltmeisterschaft in Katar ist für mich immer noch ein Sinnbild der derzeitigen Situation in Deutschland. Unsere früher als Turniermannschaft bekannten Spieler haben eher einen unkoordinierten und wild miteinander agierenden Eindruck hinterlassen. Der Wille, als Sieger vom Platz zu gehen, war nicht erkennbar. Und dieses Gefühl habe ich, wenn ich mich derzeit in Deutschland umschaue. Wir befinden uns in einer lethargischen Phase, hoffnungslos, antriebslos, und warten darauf, dass vonseiten der Regierung alle Steine aus dem Weg geräumt werden.

Ja, es sind schwierige Zeiten. Eine Krise wechselt sich mit der nächsten ab. Doch wir sollten uns nicht zu sehr nur auf die Widrigkeiten konzentrieren. Wir sollten uns daran erinnern, was wir alles bereits geschafft haben, und die Orientierungslosigkeit hinter uns lassen, denn der Weg führt nach vorn. Wir als Deutsche sollten wissen, dass Veränderungen, die um uns herum passieren, nicht zwangsläufig etwas Schlechtes bedeuten. Die Geschichte hat uns bereits gezeigt, dass daraus großartige Dinge hervorgehen können: Wie vor mehr als 30 Jahren, als aus einem geteilten Deutschland endlich wieder eins wurde. Insofern sollten wir uns mit breiter Brust den Herausforderungen der Zeit stellen.

**Welche gesellschaftlichen Entwicklungen oder Bewegungen machen Ihnen Mut für die Zukunft?**

Ich bekenne mich hier als ein großer Fan unserer Jugend! Viele sollten damit aufhören, immer wieder unsere junge Generation schlechtzureden. Wir haben wirklich engagierte und teilhabewillige junge Menschen in unserem Land. Wir müssen nur verstehen, diese kreativen und leistungsstarken Köpfe im Land zu behalten. Diesen Leistungsträgern müssen Perspektiven und Anreize geboten werden und die Anerkennung geschenkt, die sie verdienen. Hier hat auch die Politik in vielen Bereichen umzudenken.

Jede ältere Generation behauptet von sich, sie hätten es schwerer gehabt und sie hätten viel mehr geleistet. Ich denke, die Herausforderungen in der heutigen Zeit sind aber mit den früheren Jahren nicht vergleichbar. Die Entwicklungen schreiten in einem rasanten Tempo voran und wenn wir ehrlich sind, haben wir „Best Ager" manchmal Mühe, da mitzukommen. Wenn man dann ein diverses Team hat, das sowohl erfahrene Mitarbeiter als auch junge Talente umfasst, ist man ganz klar auf der Gewinnerseite.

Von daher lautet meine Devise leicht abgewandelt nach Herbert Grönemeyer: „Gebt den Jungen das Kommando!"

## Worin sehen Sie die größten Hindernisse in unserer Gesellschaft, zuversichtlicher und mutiger zu denken und zu handeln?

Wir haben verlernt, an uns zu glauben. Dabei haben wir allen Grund dazu. Wir sind ein Volk, das besonders in schwierigen Lebenslagen enger zusammenrückt, sich mit Mut den Widrigkeiten stellt. Diesen Mut und diese Gemeinschaft brauchen wir jetzt. Wenn wir erst wieder erkennen, zu welchen großartigen Dingen wir in der Lage sein können, dann schaffen wir es auch durch diese schwierigen Zeiten.

## Wie ermutigen Sie andere und sich selbst, etwas zu wagen?

Ich sehe mich selbst nicht als Motivator, aber ich versuche, auch meinen Gründerinnen und Gründern Urvertrauen in sich selbst mitzugeben. Sie müssen lernen, dass es völlig in Ordnung, ja sogar notwendig ist, dass man im Leben Fehler macht. Nur aus Fehlern können wir lernen und uns weiterentwickeln. Deshalb gehe ich persönlich auch ohne Angst in neue Projekte. Das Schlimmste, was am Ende passieren kann, ist, dass ich um eine Erfahrung reicher bin.

# GERMAN MUT
## statt GERMAN ANGST

## GERMAN MUT statt GERMAN ANGST
### 44 IDEEN FÜR EINE BESSERE ZUKUNFT

Die Deutsche Bibliothek – CIP Einheitsaufnahme:

German Mut statt German Angst
44 Ideen für eine bessere Zukunft

Deutscher Wirtschaftsbuch Verlag, Tegernsee 2023
ISBN 978-3-949981-01-2

Herausgeber: Prof. Dr. Ulrich Reinhardt,
Stiftung für Zukunftsfragen – eine Initiative von BAT,
in Kooperation mit der WEIMER MEDIA GROUP GmbH

Gestaltung: Ulrike Mieth
Porträt-Illustrationen: Andrea Rexhausen
Druck und Bindung: Westermann Druck Zwickau GmbH

Printed in Germany

ULRICH REINHARDT [HG.]

# GERMAN MUT
## statt GERMAN ANGST

**44 IDEEN FÜR EINE BESSERE ZUKUNFT**

DEUTSCHER
WIRTSCHAFTSBUCH
VERLAG

# INHALT

# 01
## ÜBER MUT

Ulrich Reinhardt

# 02
## MEHR MUT

# 03
## 44 INTERVIEWS

# ÜBER MUT

Ulrich Reinhardt

# ULRICH REINHARDT

Wissenschaftlicher Leiter der Stiftung für Zukunftsfragen –
eine Initiative von BAT

*German Mut* statt *German Angst*. Dieser Appell steht im
Zentrum dieses Buches. Auf der Basis von 24 qualitativen Ein-
zelinterviews, vier Fokusgruppen sowie einer Repräsentativ-
befragung mit über 3.000 Personen wird ein Einblick in die
derzeitige emotionale Stimmung der Deutschen gegeben.
Ist die Mehrheit der Bundesbürger, wie es die Medien und
die Öffentlichkeit gern suggerieren, tatsächlich gefangen in
einem Korsett von Bedenken und Sicherheitsbedürfnissen,
die eine optimistische Einstellung auf die Zukunft verhindern? Oder verdeckt diese Einschätzung nur ein brachliegen-
des Potenzial von Mut und Zuversicht, welches den zukünftigen Herausforderungen mit Optimismus begegnen könnte?

Um sich den Ursprüngen und Möglichkeiten von Mut anzu-
nähern sowie die Hemmnisse und Gründe für mutiges Verhalten zu erfassen, ist es wichtig, auch das Gegenteil, die
Angst, zu verstehen. Welche Bedeutung hat Angst für die
Bundesbürger, wie beeinflusst sie ihr Verhalten und wie lässt
sie sich überwinden? Blickt man in die Geschichte zurück,
wird deutlich, wie sich der Charakter von Angst im Laufe der
Zeit gewandelt hat. Der Begriff „Angst" stammt aus dem
Althochdeutschen und leitet sich von dem Wort „angust"
oder „angustia" ab, das mit Bedrängnis oder Enge gleichge-
setzt werden kann. In der antiken Mythologie äußerte sich
diese vor allem im Zusammenhang mit konkreten Bedrohungen wie zum Beispiel Erdbeben, Stürmen, Gewitter oder
Vulkanausbrüchen. In der Figur des Helden, der in allen antiken Kulturen einen hohen Stellenwert besaß, trat ein Vorbild
in Erscheinung, welches die Ängste in Gestalt von Dämonen,

**über MUT**

Meeresungeheuern oder Drachen mit seinem Heldenmut besiegen und überwinden konnte. Die damaligen Beschreibungen der Angst in Bezug auf körperliche Symptome finden sich noch heute in unserem Sprachgebrauch wieder, wenn sich beispielsweise vor Angst die Haare sträuben, die Augen weit aufgerissen und die Pupillen geweitet sind, die Ohren sausen, der Atem stockt, die Stimme versagt, das Herz unregelmäßig schlägt, der Puls rast und die Knie weich werden. Griechische Philosophen empfahlen, die Angst mit Rationalität und der inneren Reflexion von Emotionen zu überwinden, sahen sie aber auch als eine nützliche Reaktion an, um vernünftige Schutzmaßnahmen bei Gefahr zu ergreifen. In der Bibel zeigt sich Angst als Zeichen des Staunens über Wunder und Erscheinungen ebenso wie als Zeichen des Respektes und der Ehrfurcht vor Gott. „Fürchtet den Herrn, ihr seine Heiligen! Denn die ihn fürchten, haben keinen Mangel", heißt es in Psalm 34,9.

In der Zeit der Aufklärung wurde Angst ausschließlich negativ betrachtet und stand in Zusammenhang mit Irrationalität und abergläubischen Vorstellungen. Statt sich diesen furchtsam zu unterwerfen, wurde dazu aufgerufen, seinen eigenen Verstand zu nutzen und intellektuelle Vernunft und Freiheit zu beweisen. „Habe Mut, dich deines eigenen Verstandes zu bedienen", schrieb Kant 1784. Ende des 19. Jahrhunderts, im Übergang zur Moderne, sah die aufkommende Disziplin der Psychologie Angst als einen komplexen emotionalen Zustand an, der sowohl eine Reaktion auf äußere Bedrohungen sein konnte als auch ein Hinweis auf innere Konflikte. Nach dem Psychoanalytiker Freud entspringt sie unbewältigten Konflikten des Unterbewusstseins und ist ein wichtiger Anhaltspunkt, um das menschliche Verhalten verstehen zu können.

Heute ist die Bedeutung von Angst stark von Werten, Überzeugungen und kulturellen Besonderheiten geprägt. Obwohl die direkten äußeren Bedrohungen – zumindest in Industrieländern – stark abgenommen haben, zeigt sich oftmals auf persönlicher Ebene eine Vielzahl von Ängsten. Durch die Zunahme von globalen Herausforderungen, abnehmenden sozialen Bindungen, zunehmender Digitalisierung und einer Multioptionsgesellschaft verspüren viele Bürger ein Gefühl von Unübersichtlichkeit und fehlender Kontrolle über die eigenen Lebensentwürfe, woraus sich ein Empfinden von allgemeiner Überforderung und Ohnmacht entwickelt. Die Angst ist dabei nicht immer greifbar, sondern wird als ein diffuses Gefühl der Unsicherheit und Instabilität wahrgenommen.

In diesem Zusammenhang erscheint auch die *German Angst* nicht als ein alleiniges Phänomen der deutschen Gesellschaft, sondern reiht sich ein in eine allgemeine Befindlichkeit der westlichen Welt. Gleichwohl lassen sich einige deutsche Besonderheiten nachweisen.

**Der Begriff *German Angst*, der auch in den englischen Sprachgebrauch eingegangen ist, bezeichnet eine allgemein negative und zögerliche Haltung der Bundesbürger gegenüber der Zukunft.**

In der Folge werden Veränderungen nur sehr zurückhaltend angenommen und ihr Handeln ist von Bedenken und einem starken Sicherheitsbedürfnis geprägt. Die Gründe hierfür liegen unter anderem in der Geschichte mit ihren unterschiedlichen Angstzyklen verankert. Diese reichen von der Angst vor Vergeltung in den frühen Nachkriegsjahren über die (in Westdeutschland herrschende) Kommunistenangst im Zusammenhang des Kalten Krieges in den 1950er-Jahren, die revolutionäre Angst in den 1960er- und 1970er-Jahren bis hin zur Angst vor dem Waldsterben und einem Atomkrieg in den 1980er-Jahren. Nach der Wiedervereinigung weckten unter anderem der Golfkrieg, die Terroranschläge des 11. Septembers 2001, die Reaktorkatastrophe von Fukushima, die Vogelgrippe, die Herausforderungen der Fluchtmigration, die Coronapandemie oder der Ukrainekrieg die Befürchtungen, Ängste und Sorgen der Deutschen. Jede dieser Perioden bestärkte dabei die nachfolgende und schuf so allmählich ein Klima der allgemeinen Verunsicherung. Oftmals wird hierbei aber unterschätzt, welchen Einfluss positive historische und aktuelle Ereignisse und Entwicklungen auf die deutsche Befindlichkeit hatten und noch heute haben. Sei es die Einführung der sozialen Marktwirtschaft, der Ausbau des Sozialsystems, Innovationen in den Bereichen der erneuerbaren Energien, der Automobilindustrie oder Biotechnologie, die Aussöhnung mit osteuropäischen Nachbarn, die Wiedervereinigung, die europäische Integration oder die Förderung von Gleichberechtigung und kultureller Vielfalt. Alle diese Entwicklungen prägen sowohl den Einzelnen als auch die Gesellschaft als Ganzes und zeugen von Entschlossenheit, Mut und Zuversicht. Dieses bestätigt sich auch bei einem Jahresvergleich über die Zukunftssorgen der deutschen Bevölkerung.

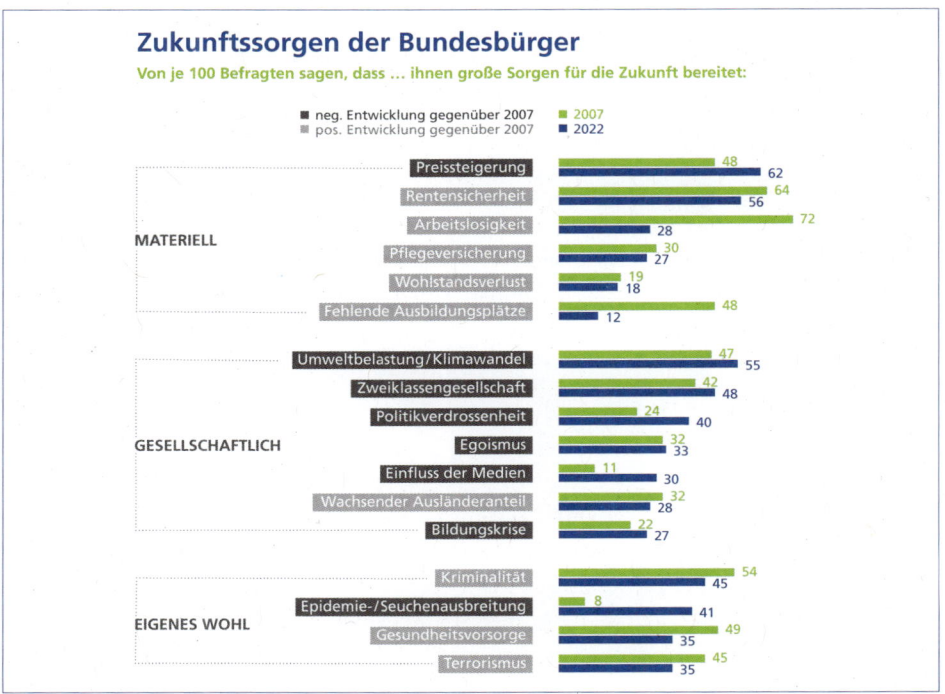

**Zukunftssorgen der Bundesbürger**

Von je 100 Befragten sagen, dass ... ihnen große Sorgen für die Zukunft bereitet:

■ neg. Entwicklung gegenüber 2007   ■ 2007
■ pos. Entwicklung gegenüber 2007   ■ 2022

**MATERIELL**
- Preissteigerung — 48 / 62
- Rentensicherheit — 64 / 56
- Arbeitslosigkeit — 72 / 28
- Pflegeversicherung — 30 / 27
- Wohlstandsverlust — 19 / 18
- Fehlende Ausbildungsplätze — 48 / 12

**GESELLSCHAFTLICH**
- Umweltbelastung/Klimawandel — 47 / 55
- Zweiklassengesellschaft — 42 / 48
- Politikverdrossenheit — 24 / 40
- Egoismus — 32 / 33
- Einfluss der Medien — 11 / 30
- Wachsender Ausländeranteil — 32 / 28
- Bildungskrise — 22 / 27

**EIGENES WOHL**
- Kriminalität — 54 / 45
- Epidemie-/Seuchenausbreitung — 8 / 41
- Gesundheitsvorsorge — 49 / 35
- Terrorismus — 45 / 35

So sind sowohl in zahlreichen materiellen Bereichen als auch bei Sorgen um das eigene Wohl die Ängste der Bevölkerung geringer geworden. 2007 blickten beispielsweise noch fast zwei Drittel skeptisch auf die zukünftige Höhe der Rente und knapp drei Viertel machten sich Sorgen um die Sicherheit des eigenen Arbeitsplatzes beziehungsweise fürchteten die Arbeitslosigkeit. Auch fehlende Ausbildungsplätze wurden als ernstes Zukunftsproblem wahrgenommen. Im Jahr 2022 wurden die Entwicklungen am Arbeitsmarkt deutlich weniger kritisch bewertet. Auch sahen nur jeweils halb so viele Bürger Arbeitslosigkeit und fehlende Ausbildungsplätze als dringende Zukunftsprobleme an. In gleichem Maße reduzierten sich die Bedenken gegenüber der Gesundheitsvorsorge und Pflegeversicherung sowie die Angst vor Terrorismus und Kriminalität.

Große Sorgenzuwächse verzeichneten dagegen die Aspekte Preisanstieg und Seuchen, was mit den aktuellen Herausforderungen durch die steigende Inflation infolge des Ukraine-krieges und der Coronapandemie erklärt werden kann. Im Gegensatz zu den materiellen und persönlichen Sorgen stiegen jedoch die gesellschaftlichen Ängste erkennbar an. Besonders deutlich ist hierbei die hohe Zunahme von Sorgen bezüglich des Einflusses von Medien und der Politikverdrossenheit. Die Diskussionen um Fake News sowie eine zunehmende Meinungsmache in den sozialen Medien haben Spuren hinterlassen. Mehr und mehr Bürger sind besorgt über den Einfluss der Medien auf die eigene Meinungsbildung und die Beeinflussung der jungen Generation durch soziale Netzwerke. Die Besorgnis vor dem Anstieg der Politikverdrossenheit zeigt zum einen bestehende Zweifel an der Leistungs- und Leitungsfähigkeit der Akteure auf – unter anderem in den Bereichen Zukunftsfähigkeit der sozialen Systeme, aktuelle Herausforderungen durch Globalisierung, Klimawandel, Kriege, Pandemien und der Integrität von Einzelpersonen (echte und vermeintliche Lobby- und Korruptionsaffären). Zum anderen wird aber auch eine hohe Sensibilität und Reflexionsfähigkeit der Zivilgesellschaft deutlich, die Vertrauen in die politischen Entscheidungsträger als unerlässliche Grundlage einer demokratischen Gesellschaft ansieht.

**Insgesamt zeigt sich die Bedeutung einer Differenzierung von Ängsten. Es kann nicht von einer pauschal vorherrschenden *German Angst* ausgegangen werden.**

Wie steht es nun aber konkret um den Mut in Deutschland? Und wie wandelte sich seine Bedeutung im Laufe der Geschichte? Der Begriff „Mut" lässt sich auf unterschiedliche Wurzeln zurückführen. Im Indogermanischen stammt er vom Wort „mo" ab, während es im Althochdeutschen „mout" hieß. Beide Begriffe haben die Bedeutung von starkem Willen, Anstrengung und Sinn sowie der Kraft des Wollens. Im Lateinischen „virtus" bezieht sich das Wort auf Integrität, Entschlossenheit und die Fähigkeit, Risiken einzugehen, während es im Griechischen „andreia" in Bezug auf Tapferkeit im Krieg verwendet wurde. Das französische Wort „courage" wiederum leitet sich vom lateinischen „cor" ab, was Herz bedeutet und damit die emotionale Fähigkeit betont, Ängste zu überwinden. Im Laufe der Geschichte wandelte sich die symbolische Begrifflichkeit. Während Mut in der Antike und im Mittelalter als ein wichtiger Teil der Kriegskunst galt und als Wert der Kühnheit und Tapferkeit mit Heldentum und Ehre verbunden wurde, stand er in der Renaissance, etwa bei Shakespeare, für eine unerlässliche Tugend zur Ausbildung eines vollständigen Charakters. In der Aufklärung mit ihrer Betonung der Vernunft symbolisierte Mut dagegen den Willen und die Fähigkeit, sich gegen Vorurteile und Unterdrückung einzusetzen und für Freiheit und Vernunft einzustehen. Im Übergang zum 20. Jahrhundert verstärkte sich dieser Bedeutungswandel vom körperlichen Wagemut zu einer emotionalen oder moralischen Ebene.

Gegenwärtig wird Mut mit einer breiten Palette von Verhaltensweisen verbunden, wie Entschlossenheit und Motivation, der Bereitschaft, sich für seine Überzeugungen, Ideale oder andere Menschen einzusetzen, oder auch der Neigung, Risiken einzugehen und Entscheidungen zu treffen, die mit Unsicherheit und möglichen Konsequenzen verbunden sind. Diese Merkmale sind individuell und kulturell sehr verschieden, weisen aber alle das Motiv der Überwindung von Ängsten auf. Dabei müssen es nicht immer nur die großen Herausforderungen sein, die uns mutig erscheinen lassen. Oft zeigt sich Mut auch in den kleinen Dingen des Alltags. Sie alle kräftigen den eigenen Willen, helfen Widerstände zu überwinden und stärken die individuelle Zuversicht – denn schließlich gehört den Mutigen die Welt. In diesem Sinne ist es auch nicht die Absicht des vorliegenden Buches, die Sorgen der Bevölkerung zu verneinen, sondern vielmehr soll die dominante Stellung der Angst in der Gesellschaft hinterfragt und das gesellschaftliche Bewusstsein stärker für den Mut geöffnet und sensibilisiert werden.

**Erst wenn das Potenzial von Mut sichtbar wird, wenn seine positiven und konstruktiven Effekte für die Entwicklung der Persönlichkeit, die Stärkung der Gemeinschaft und die Bewältigung der gesellschaftlichen Herausforderungen deutlicher erkennbar werden, können mutige Entscheidungen leichter und zuversichtlicher getroffen werden und der Mut jedes einzelnen Bürgers die Anerkennung erfahren, die ihm gebührt.**

*„Zwischen Hochmut und Demut*
*steht ein Drittes, dem das Leben gehört,*
*und das ist der Mut"*

Theodor Fontane

**Charaktereigenschaften eines mutigen Menschen**

Von je 100 Befragten sagen, dass sie einen mutigen Menschen
durch folgende Eigenschaften charakterisieren:

| | |
|---|---|
| Selbstbewusst | 87 |
| Verantwortung übernehmend | 86 |
| Widerstände überwindend | 85 |
| Standhaft/für Werte einstehend | 85 |
| Optimistisch | 80 |
| Veränderungen anstrebend | 76 |
| Bereitschaft zu scheitern | 71 |
| Innovativ/kreativ | 71 |
| Risikobereit | 67 |
| Unangepasst/individuell | 50 |
| Draufgängerisch | 39 |
| Leichtsinnig/naiv | 19 |

Eine große Mehrheit der Bürger verbindet Mut vor allem mit vier Eigenschaften:

1. Selbstbewusstsein
2. Verantwortungsbereitschaft
3. Bereitschaft, Widerstände zu überwinden
4. Einstehen für Werte

Das erste Merkmal *Selbstbewusstsein* bildet als Wesenszug die Grundlage der weiteren Assoziationen. Hierunter wird ein Selbstwertgefühl verstanden, bei dem man die Wichtigkeit und den Wert seiner eigenen Persönlichkeit erkennt und schätzt. Dabei werden sowohl Stärken als auch Schwächen als Teil der eigenen Persönlichkeit wahrgenommen und in einer inneren Haltung der Gelassenheit und Zufriedenheit in selbstbewusste Handlungen übersetzt. Im Zusammenhang mit Mut zeugt es von einer starken Eigenschaft, „man selbst zu sein", auch wenn das soziale Umfeld etwas anderes erwartet beziehungsweise wünscht.

Wenn der Einzelne sich seiner selbst und seiner eigenen Stärken bewusst ist, kann er auch die Fähigkeit entwickeln, für sich und andere *Verantwortung* zu übernehmen. Verantwortung bedeutet, Freiräume zur Gestaltung zu nutzen, mutige Entscheidungen zu treffen und mit Zuversicht und Entschlossenheit praktisch umzusetzen. Hier schließt sich die *Bereitschaft an, Widerstände* zu überwinden und Hindernisse und Konflikte in Kauf zu nehmen. Die Widerstände können dabei sowohl struktureller (Regularien, Hierarchien etc.) als auch persönlicher Natur sein (fehlende Unterstützung, Misstrauen, Neid etc.). Der vierte Aspekt rundet das mutige Agieren von Wesenszug, Fähigkeit und Bereitschaft mit der sozio-moralischen Komponente der Werteüberzeugung ab, der Standhaftigkeit und dem *Einstehen für seine Überzeugungen und Handlungen.*

Weitere zentrale Eigenschaften sind aus Sicht der Bürger Optimismus, Kreativität, Risikobereitschaft sowie das Streben nach Veränderungen. Auch wenn alle eher als notwendige Grundhaltung denn als Fähigkeit angesehen werden, können sie von jedem Einzelnen erlernt beziehungsweise verstärkt werden. Hier ist entscheidend, ob das private und gesellschaftliche Umfeld genügend Freiräume bietet, um Mut erlernen und unerschrocken agieren zu können. Konkret werden diese Merkmale benötigt, um die Motivation (Optimismus) und die Entschlossenheit (Risikobereitschaft) zu stärken sowie den Gestaltungswillen und die Variation der Perspektive (Kreativität) zu fördern. Damit einher gehen der Wunsch und die Bereitschaft, Veränderungen als positive Entwicklung zu sehen und alte Denk- und Verhaltensmuster infrage zu stellen. In diesem Zusammenhang wird von fast drei Vierteln der Bevölkerung auch die Bereitschaft zum Scheitern genannt, die einem mutigen Verhalten innewohnt und noch über die Risikobereitschaft hinausreicht – beispielsweise in Form von finanziellen Verlusten, fehlgeschlagenen Konzepten oder gescheiterten Plänen. Das Scheitern wird dabei nicht grundsätzlich negativ gesehen, da gerade Rückschläge und Fehler neue Perspektiven eröffnen können. Allerdings ist in diesem Fall ein besonders starker Mut vonnöten, da gerade in Deutschland Fehler oftmals sehr kritisch und negativ bewertet werden.

### BEISPIEL FÜR MUT
**Odysseus war ein mutiger Held in der griechischen Mythologie. Er zeigte seinen Mut und seine Tapferkeit bei den zahlreichen Herausforderungen und Abenteuern während seiner Odyssee. Sei es beim Sieg über den Zyklopen Polyphem, beim Trotzen der Klippen von Skylla und Charybdis oder beim Widerstehen der Versuchungen der verführerischen Sirenen – Odysseus bewies immer wieder seine Entschlossenheit, Zielstrebigkeit und Führungsstärke, um seine Ziele zu erreichen.**

> *„Der Mut,*
> *Angst zu empfinden,*
> *ist der Anfang allen Mutes"*
>
> Jean-Paul Sartre

**Generationenunterschiede im Verständnis von Mut**

Von je 100 befragten über 55-Jährigen sagen, dass sie einen mutigen Menschen durch folgende Eigenschaften charakterisieren:

Unterschied zu unter 35-Jährigen in Prozentpunkten

| Eigenschaft | Wert | Unterschied |
|---|---|---|
| Selbstbewusst | 92 | +11 |
| Widerstände überwindend | 90 | +12 |
| Verantwortung übernehmen | 88 | +7 |
| Standhaft/für Werte einstehend | 88 | +9 |
| Optimistisch | 85 | +13 |
| Veränderungen anstrebend | 76 | 0 |
| Innovativ/kreativ | 73 | +4 |
| Bereitschaft zu scheitern | 68 | −7 |
| Risikobereit | 63 | −11 |
| Unangepasst/individuell | 45 | −12 |
| Draufgängerisch/Gefahren eingehend | 33 | −16 |
| Leichtsinnig/naiv | 14 | −15 |

Innerhalb der Bevölkerung lassen sich mit Blick auf das Alter einige Unterschiede verzeichnen, wobei eine ähnliche Schwerpunktsetzung vorliegt. Sowohl für die ältere als auch für die jüngere Generation stehen das Überwinden von Widerständen, das Selbstbewusstsein, die Bereitschaft, Verantwortung zu übernehmen, und das Einstehen für Werte an oberster Stelle. Abweichungen zwischen den Generationen zeigen sich unter anderem bei den Begriffen Optimismus, Überwinden von Widerständen und Selbstbewusstsein sowie den Assoziationen zu Individualität, Leichtsinn und Draufgängertum.

**Bei älteren Bürgern erhält das Merkmal des Selbstbewusstseins eine deutlich höhere Zustimmung als bei den unter 35-Jährigen (+11 Prozentpunkte).**

Dies ist vor allem im Zusammenhang mit der geringeren Lebenserfahrung der jungen Menschen zu sehen. Die Älteren definieren, entsprechend ihren eigenen Erfahrungen, die Selbst-erkenntnis und das Vertrauen in eigene Fähigkeiten als Grundvoraussetzung für mutiges Agieren. Nur wer sich seiner selbst bewusst ist, kann auch nach außen beziehungsweise im sozialen Austausch mutig agieren. Dieses schließt zum Beispiel auch das Verständnis ein, als Individuum selbstbestimmt seine Überzeugung zu vertreten. Das Einstehen reduziert sich dabei nicht auf das Äußern der eignen Meinung, sondern umfasst auch, sich von Gruppenzwängen leichter lösen zu können und sich einer wertekonformen Gruppe oder Meinung gegenüberzustellen. Im Gegensatz dazu ist bei der jüngeren Generation dieses Selbstbewusstsein oftmals noch nicht so stark ausgeprägt beziehungsweise wird weniger stark mit Mut assoziiert. Hinzu kommt ein Selbstverständnis – geprägt durch eine entsprechende Erziehung der Eltern und der Schule –, welches das Äußern der eigenen Überzeugung als normal empfindet und weniger mit Mut in Verbindung bringt.

Mit einer ähnlich hohen Zustimmung wie beim Selbstbewusstsein verbindet die ältere Generation Mut mit dem Überwinden von Widerständen. Ihre Lebenserfahrung hat ihnen gezeigt, Herausforderungen des Lebens können nicht nur äußerlich sein, sondern sich auch im Inneren manifestieren. Diese zu überwinden, um ein Ziel zu erreichen, erfordert Entschlossenheit, Ausdauer und Mut. Stärker als Jüngere können sie sich dabei auf Selbstdisziplin, Selbstmotivation und Ausdauer verlassen, haben Strategien erlernt, um mit Fehlschlägen, Zurückweisungen und Hindernissen konstruktiv und mutig umzugehen.

Ein weiterer Unterschied zwischen den Generationen zeigt sich beim Optimismus (+13 Prozentpunkte). Obwohl auch bei den Jüngeren eine hohe Zustimmung vorliegt, zeigt sich doch eine skeptischere Grundeinstellung darüber, ob mutige Menschen auch gleichzeitig optimistisch sind. In diesem Sinne kann Mut für die junge Generation auch bedeuten, sich für etwas einzusetzen, mutig zu agieren und gleichzeitig Zweifel oder fehlende Zuversicht, ob des Erfolges der eigenen Aktion, zu haben. Deutlich wird eine Einstellung, die durch weniger eindeutige Ansichten gekennzeichnet ist und die auch Zweifel und Skepsis zulässt. Ein aktuelles Beispiel lässt sich in diesem Zusammenhang etwa bei Aktionen des zivilen Widerstandes zum Thema Klimawandel finden. So steht der Aspekt des Optimismus bei diesen Aktionen nicht im Vordergrund. Im Gegenteil: Die pessimistische Grundhaltung oder Zukunftsaussicht vieler junger Menschen (*„Die Erderwärmung ist kaum noch aufzuhalten"*) wird zur Grundlage des mutigen Handelns.

**In diesem Zusammenhang wird auch die stärkere Betonung der Verbindung zwischen Mut und Risikobereitschaft bei den jungen Bürgern deutlich (+11 Prozentpunkte). Hier zeigt sich nicht nur ein altersbedingtes geringeres Sicherheitsbedürfnis, sondern auch**

die Bereitschaft, Risiken einzugehen und eventuell zu scheitern (+7 Prozentpunkte). Diese Furchtlosigkeit kann die unterschiedlichsten Bereiche betreffen, wie etwa mutige Entscheidungen der Berufs- oder Studienwahl, sportliche Herausforderungen, Bürgerproteste bei politischen Aktionen, riskante finanzielle Unternehmungen oder Wagnisse jeglicher Art.

Die Bereitschaft zum Risiko und zum möglichen Scheitern speist sich aus der jugendlichen Unbekümmertheit mit dem Wissen, jederzeit scheitern zu können, aber auch immer wieder aufs Neue etwas zu wagen, egal ob man Erfolg haben wird oder nicht.

Hinzu kommt bei vielen Jüngeren eine finanzielle und familiäre Situation, die weniger mit Sicherheit und Verantwortung verbunden ist. Wo keine Familienmitglieder versorgt werden müssen, lassen sich Risiken leichter eingehen, und wo noch keine berufliche Verantwortung erwartet wird, kann man sich noch ausprobieren und unsichere Wagnisse eingehen.

Die größten Unterschiede zwischen den Altersgruppen sind bei den Eigenschaften des Draufgängertums und des Leichtsinns zu betrachten. Deutlich mehr junge Bürger verbinden diese Aspekte mit einem mutigen Menschen. Erneut können die Unterschiede mit der einerseits eher waghalsigen, andererseits zurückhaltenden Lebensführung erklärt werden. Besonders bei der Gruppe der Jüngeren wird waghalsiges und leichtsinniges Verhalten positiv gesehen. Dieses kann beispielsweise das soziale Agieren oder einen allgemein coolen Habitus betreffen. Bei beiden Merkmalen hat die Anerkennung innerhalb der sozialen Gruppe eine besonders starke Bedeutung. Bei den älteren Bürgern hingegen sind die Merkmale vorwiegend negativ besetzt und deutlich weniger assoziieren diese Eigenschaften mit Mut. Deutlich wird dabei ein altersbedingt größeres Bedürfnis nach Sicherheit und Stabilität sowie eine geringere Bedeutung von Gruppenzugehörigkeit.

Deutlich mehr junge Bürger setzen unangepassten Individualismus mit Mut gleich (+12 Prozentpunkte).

Diese hohe Zustimmung steht nur scheinbar im Widerspruch zu den oben genannten Aussagen zur Bedeutung der Gruppenzugehörigkeit. Auch wenn deren soziale Bezugsgruppen einen starken Einfluss ausüben, glauben sie doch an die Wichtigkeit der Individualität als Ausdruck einer Persönlichkeit, die sich starren Regeln und Normen widersetzt. Diese Individualität kann sich auch in den jeweiligen jugendlichen Subkulturen innerhalb der Gruppe verwirklichen. Im Vordergrund steht die Eigenwilligkeit, das Unkonventionelle oder Nichtkonforme. Im Alltag zeigt sich dieses Merkmal in der Abgrenzung zu anderen Gruppen, in der Distanz zur Erwachsenenwelt oder im Widerstand zur Mehrheitsgesellschaft. Als mutig wird es vor allem wahrgenommen, wenn es den allgemeinen Konventionen widerspricht, etwa bezüglich der sexuellen Orientierung, der politischen Meinungsäußerung oder der Lebensplanung. In der späteren Lebensphase verliert das Merkmal des Widerstandes an Bedeutung und konzentriert sich mehr auf die Selbstverwirklichung. Mutig ist hier, wer risikobereit und entschlossen seine persönlichen Ziele verfolgt, wer Pläne abseits des Mainstreams verwirklicht. Das kann zum Beispiel die Umsetzung einer kreativen Geschäftsidee sein oder auch eine exotische Urlaubsreise. Dass die ältere Generation dem Merkmal der unangepassten Individualität in sehr viel geringerer Zahl zustimmt, zeigt das mit steigendem Alter oft weniger starke Bedürfnis, sich von der Mehrheitsgesellschaft abzugrenzen. Auch sind ältere Bürger den medialen Einflüssen und Trends hinsichtlich einer zunehmenden Individualisierung gegenüber weniger anfällig. Den zunehmenden Ausdifferenzierungen und Autonomiebestrebungen stehen sie zum Teil skeptisch gegenüber und assoziieren diese nicht mit einem mutigen Verhalten.

b. Besserverdienende verbinden deutlich mehr Begriffe
mit einem mutigen Menschen

*„Es braucht Mut,*
*um neue Wege zu gehen*
*und aus Fehlern zu lernen"*

Elon Musk

### Einkommen beeinflusst Verständnis von Mut

**Von je 100 Besserverdienenden sagen, dass sie einen mutigen Menschen durch folgende Eigenschaften charakterisieren:**

Unterschied zu gering Verdienenden in Prozentpunkten

| Eigenschaft | Wert | Unterschied |
|---|---|---|
| Widerstände überwindend | 91 | +9 |
| Standhaft/für Werte einstehend | 90 | +7 |
| Verantwortung übernehmend | 88 | +4 |
| Selbstbewusst | 87 | +3 |
| Optimistisch | 84 | +9 |
| Veränderungen anstrebend | 77 | +6 |
| Bereitschaft zu scheitern | 77 | +11 |
| Risikobereit | 68 | +1 |
| Innovativ/kreativ | 67 | −3 |
| Unangepasst/individuell | 51 | +1 |
| Draufgängerisch/Gefahren eingehend | 43 | +5 |
| Leichtsinnig/naiv | 13 | −12 |

Auch beim Einkommen zeigen sich zahlreiche Unterschiede. Beispielsweise nennen die Besserverdienenden (Haushaltsnettoeinkommen über 5.000€) häufiger die Aspekte der Überwindung von Widerständen, der Standhaftigkeit, des Optimismus und der Bereitschaft des Scheiterns. Im Gegensatz dazu wird der Begriff des Leichtsinns weniger häufig angegeben. Die Gründe für die höheren Zahlen können unter anderem mit einer größeren finanziellen Unabhängigkeit und den damit verbundenen Möglichkeiten und Erfahrungen erklärt werden. So verbinden sie die oben genannten Assoziationen zu Mut überwiegend mit der Arbeitswelt und den dortigen Herausforderungen. Oftmals selbst in Führungspositionen tätig, nehmen sie mutige Handlungen vor allem in Bereichen wahr, die im Zusammenhang mit innovativen Konzepten, individuellen Investitionen, Arbeitsplatzwechseln und kreativen Unternehmensgründungen stehen. Um beruflich erfolgreich bestehen zu können, betonen sie die Bedeutung einer optimistischen Grundhaltung und einer entschlossenen Vorgehensweise. Zaghaftes oder zögerliches Verhalten wird dagegen als wenig Erfolg versprechende

Methode gewertet. Besonders in finanziell eher angespannten Zeiten ist es für sie wichtig, weiterhin mit Zuversicht zu agieren und eine dynamische Position zu vertreten – sei es bei Personalbelangen, Kompetenzfragen oder Kapitalanlagen. Dieses erklärt auch ihre höhere Wertschätzung des Statements Überwindung von Widerständen, die sie als positive Herausforderung sehen, um ihre Leistungs- und Durchsetzungsfähigkeit zu zeigen. Eine ausgeprägte intrinsische Motivation wird so durch äußere Anreize zusätzlich erhöht und verstärkt den Mut. Eingeschlossen ist hierin auch die Bereitschaft, zu scheitern und Rückschläge anzunehmen. Zum einen erwachsen dadurch neue Herausforderungen, zum anderen lassen sich diese bei finanziellen Rücklagen leichter annehmen. Eine mutige Risikoeinschätzung ist für die Besserverdienenden dabei nicht mit Leichtsinn zu verwechseln, weshalb sie diese seltener nennen. Geringverdienende (Haushaltsnettoeinkommen unter 1.500€) zeigen sich – aufgrund einer höheren monetären Unsicherheit – insgesamt risikoaverser, können sie doch schwerer mögliche Fehler finanziell ausgleichen. Auch sind Geringverdienende häufiger von strukturellen Barrieren (z.B. geringerer Zugang zu Informationen, Netzwerken) betroffen, die ihnen weniger Möglichkeiten bieten, mutige Entscheidungen zu verfolgen. Aufgrund dieser Voraussetzungen zeigen sie eine eher ablehnende Einstellung gegenüber Risiken und Veränderungen und tendieren dazu, mutige Entscheidungen, vor allem in beruflicher oder finanzieller Hinsicht, mit Leichtsinnigkeit und Naivität zu verbinden.

## BEISPIEL FÜR MUT

David ist bekannt für seinen Mut, sich dem riesenhaften, als unbesiegbar geltenden Krieger Goliath trotz seiner Unerfahrenheit, seiner Jugend und seiner körperlichen Nachteile zu stellen. Mit mutigem Herzen und unerschütterlichem Selbstvertrauen trat er gegen Goliath an und besiegte ihn. Sein Mut ist ein Beispiel dafür, wie man durch den Glauben an etwas Größeres (Vertrauen auf Gott und dessen Schutz) seine Angst und Zweifel überwinden kann.

*„Ein großes Vorbild ist jemand,*
*der nicht nur durch seine Worte,*
*sondern auch durch seine Taten*
*Mut und Hoffnung verbreitet"*

Martin Luther King Jr.

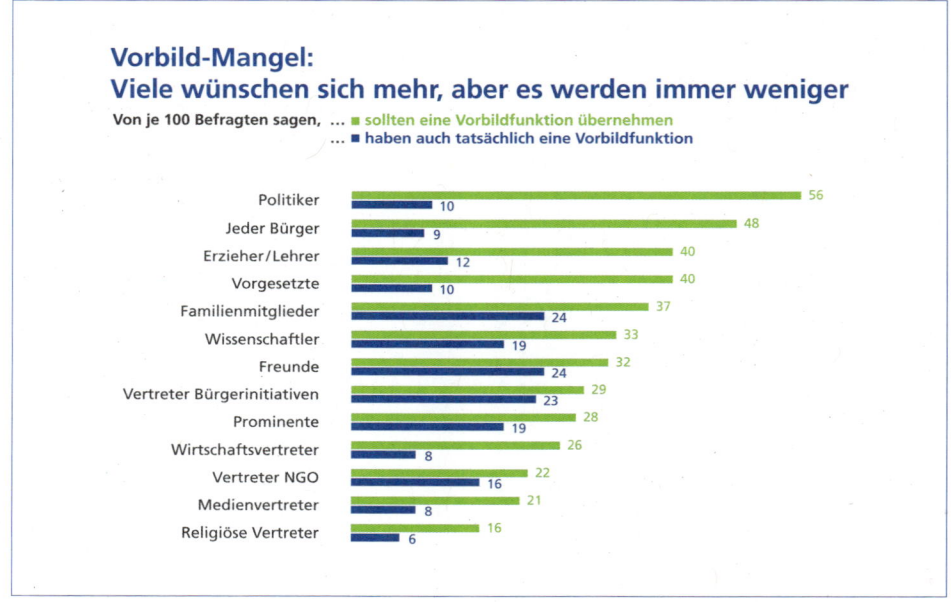

**Vorbild-Mangel:**
**Viele wünschen sich mehr, aber es werden immer weniger**

Von je 100 Befragten sagen, … ■ sollten eine Vorbildfunktion übernehmen
… ■ haben auch tatsächlich eine Vorbildfunktion

| | |
|---|---|
| Politiker | 56 / 10 |
| Jeder Bürger | 48 / 9 |
| Erzieher/Lehrer | 40 / 12 |
| Vorgesetzte | 40 / 10 |
| Familienmitglieder | 37 / 24 |
| Wissenschaftler | 33 / 19 |
| Freunde | 32 / 24 |
| Vertreter Bürgerinitiativen | 29 / 23 |
| Prominente | 28 / 19 |
| Wirtschaftsvertreter | 26 / 8 |
| Vertreter NGO | 22 / 16 |
| Medienvertreter | 21 / 8 |
| Religiöse Vertreter | 16 / 6 |

Während gesellschaftliche Werte und Normen in ihrer Funktion als Verhaltensregeln eher abstrakte Konzepte sind, bieten Vorbilder eine konkrete Identifikation mit einer Person, deren Einstellung oder Lebensweg zur Nachahmung inspiriert. Diese Personen können zum Beispiel Freunde oder Familienangehörige, Politiker oder Prominente, Kollegen oder Medienvertreter sein.

**Vorbilder begleiten den einzelnen Bürger bewusst oder unbewusst in bestimmten Phasen oder auch das ganze Leben lang. Sie bilden, prägen und beeinflussen ihn, ohne ihn in eine starre Form zu pressen. Als Role Models zeigen sie Erfolg versprechendes Verhalten, welches als wirkungsvoll beurteilt und übernommen wird.**

Jungen Menschen dienen Vorbilder zur Selbstfindung, Orientierung sowie zur Abgrenzung. Erwachsene greifen dagegen vor allem in verunsicherten Situationen auf sie zurück beziehungsweise suchen bei ihnen nach entsprechender Unterstützung. Dabei herrscht eine große Diskrepanz zwischen dem Wunsch nach mutigen Vorbildern und der erlebten Realität. Im Zusammenhang mit einem mutigen Verhalten hoffen die Bürger auf Vorbilder aus dem engen Familienverband, der eigenen Lebenswelt, aus sozialen Organisationen und institutionellen Bereichen. Besonders groß ist hierbei die Sehnsucht nach Vorbildern in der Politik.

Als Mandatsträger auf unterschiedlichen Ebenen vertreten Politiker nicht nur die Interessen der eigenen Partei, sondern sind der allgemeinen politischen Willensbildung und Gestaltung zum Wohle der Gesellschaft verpflichtet. Als Person der Öffentlichkeit stehen sie im besonderen Fokus der Bürger, die an ihr Verhalten oft hohe Ansprüche stellen. Im Idealfall sind sie integre Persönlichkeiten, die sich durch Authentizität, Umsicht, Zielorientierung und Vertrauenswürdigkeit auszeichnen. Ihr Vorbildcharakter wird vor allem im Zusammenhang mit gesellschaftlichen Herausforderungen und unsicheren Krisensituationen genannt. Man hofft auf Entscheidungsträger, die mit Weitsicht, Überzeugung, Zuversicht und Tatkraft die Bürger durch ihr Verhalten inspirieren und mögliche Lösungswege aufzeigen. Diese sollten über die eigenen politischen Interessen hinausreichen und mutige, innovative Entscheidungen beinhalten. Als Beispiele werden sowohl nationale als auch globale Herausforderungen genannt, wie etwa soziale Missstände, hohe Inflation, Klimawandel oder auch das selbstbewusste Einstehen für die eigenen Überzeugungen gegen die Mehrheitsmeinung. Im Hinblick auf ihre öffentliche Wirkung sollen die politischen Vorbilder nicht nur nachahmenswert für die eigene Lebenswelt sein, sondern eine Signalwirkung für die Gesellschaft haben. Der individuelle Mut der Persönlichkeit soll möglichst die Zuversicht und den Mut aller Bürger (und Institutionen) positiv beeinflussen.

Diese Erwartung an politische Vertreter wird in der Realität allerdings nicht erfüllt. Vielmehr zeigt sich die größte Diskrepanz zwischen Wunsch und Wirklichkeit. Lediglich jeder Zehnte erkennt bei Politikern ein mutiges Agieren und sieht sie als eine positive Inspiration für die Bevölkerung. Dies ist jedoch keine typisch deutsche Wahrnehmung, zeigen doch verschiedene Studien eine zunehmende Distanz zwischen Regierten und Regierenden in allen westlichen Indusrienationen. Bemängelt wird besonders eine fehlende Debattenkultur, die sich durch klare Positionierungen auszeichnet und sich nicht in parteiinternen Kompromissen erschöpft. Daneben werden Aussagen und Handlungen vermisst, die optimistisch in die Zukunft weisen und sich nicht nur auf Probleme oder negative Perspektiven fokussieren. Insgesamt vermitteln die meisten Politiker für breite Bevölkerungsgruppen ein Bild, welches dem Mut entgegensteht und gekennzeichnet ist von Unsicherheit, unentschlossenem Lavieren, Intransparenz, Affären und Verfehlungen. Dabei gilt: Je höher die Erwartungen sind, desto stärker wird die Enttäuschung empfunden. Folglich fällt es Politikern auch besonders schwer, das Misstrauen der Bevölkerung durch Beteuerungen oder Versuche des Mutes wieder aufzulösen.

Neben Politikern sieht fast die Hälfte der Bevölkerung sich selbst und jeden anderen Bürger in der Pflicht, ein mutiges Vorbild zu sein. Hier zeigt sich ein hohes zivilgesellschaftliches Bewusstsein, indem kein alleiniger Fokus auf Autoritäten gelegt wird, sondern den nichtöffentlichen Individuen der Gesellschaft die Fähigkeit zugesprochen wird, eine Vorbildfunktion zu übernehmen. Mit dem Zuspruch dieser Fähigkeit gehen jedoch auch die Aufforderung und Erwartung einher, sich mutig zu verhalten. Konkret wünschen sich die Bürger diesen Mut zum Beispiel, wenn es darum geht, Zivilcourage und Eigeninitiative zu zeigen, Verantwortung zu übernehmen oder seine eigene Überzeugung zu vertreten. Der Einzelne würde damit Möglichkeitsräume erschaffen und andere Menschen dazu ermutigen, ihre Komfortzone zu verlassen und mutig die Gesellschaft mitzugestalten. Dabei kann die Einflussnahme sogar noch über die der Politiker hinausreichen, kommen sie doch aus einer ähnlichen Lebenswelt, wodurch eine niedrigere Hemmschwelle der Identifikation besteht. Auch dieses große Potenzial des Mutes erfüllt sich in der Realität nicht. Nur jeder Zehnte sieht die Menschen in Deutschland als mutige Vorbilder agieren. Enttäuscht zeigt man sich vor allem von „den anderen", den Mitbürgern im Allgemeinen und weniger von dem eigenen Familien- und Freundeskreis. Beeinflusst wird diese Wahrnehmung zum einen von entsprechenden Umfragen und Berichterstattungen, zum anderen durch ein diffuses Gefühl des Misstrauens, der Unsicherheit, der Angst und des Pessimismus in der Gesellschaft. Beide Aspekte bedingen sich wechselseitig. So verstärken die Meldungen über die vermeintliche *German Angst* diese noch und lassen ein Bild der Schicksalsergebenheit entstehen, ohne Engagement, ohne Veränderungschance, ohne Perspektive, ohne Hoffnung und positive Energie.

Zwei von fünf Bürgern nennen auch Personen aus der eigenen Lebenswelt als potenziell mutige Vorbildcharaktere. In den meisten Fällen handelt es sich dabei um Autoritätspersonen, zu denen man in einem direkten Verhältnis steht, zum Beispiel aus dem beruflichen und schulischen Umfeld, wie Vorgesetzte und Lehrer. Diese Personen zeichnen sich dann als Vorbild aus, wenn sie in ihrem Verhalten eine hohe Motivation und Wertschätzung dem anderen gegenüber aufweisen. Als mutig werden sie wahrgenommen, wenn sie sich für ihre Mitarbeiter oder Schüler einsetzen, klare Überzeugungen vertreten und unpopuläre Entscheidungen authentisch vertreten können. Diese Eigenschaften sind es dann auch, die als nachahmenswert empfunden werden. Durch die besondere Balance von Nähe und Distanz besteht bei diesen Vorbildern eine hohe Identifikationsmöglichkeit und die Option herauszufinden, was sowohl auf individueller als auch gesellschaftlicher Ebene möglich ist.

Diesen Anspruch können nur wenige Lehrer und Vorgesetzte erfüllen und nur jeder zehnte Bürger fühlt sich von ihnen inspiriert. Bei beiden Personen-/Berufsgruppen fehlen im Zusammenhang mit Mut vor allem Führungsqualitäten, die sich in Engagement, Optimismus und Entschlossenheit äußern. Für Jugendliche ist es besonders bedauerlich, bei ihren Lehrkräften so wenige Möglichkeiten der Identifikation oder Inspiration zu finden, erhoffen sie sich durch diese Vorbilder doch wichtige Orientierung für ihre eigenen Entscheidungs- und Handlungsmöglichkeiten. Bei Vorgesetzten wird das oftmals geringe Interesse an Innovation, kreativen Ideen und Veränderungen bemängelt sowie ihre eher skeptische oder pessimistische Grundhaltung.

Für etwa jeweils ein Drittel der Bundesbürger sollten Familienmitglieder oder Freunde einen hohen Vorbildcharakter haben. Als engste Bezugspersonen sind sie in der frühen Sozialisation und in der Adoleszenzphase sowohl zur Selbstfindung als auch zur Distanzierung von großer Bedeutung. Ihr sozialer Einfluss findet vor allem in den Bereichen Fühlen, Entscheiden, Urteilen und Handeln statt. Innerhalb der Familie motivieren sie in jungen Jahren durch ihr eigenes Handeln zur Nachahmung, während sie in der späteren Entwicklung als Ratgeber und emotionaler Beistand geschätzt werden.

Im Zusammenhang mit mutigen Entscheidungen wünschen sich zahlreiche Jugendliche und junge Erwachsene vor allem gleichaltrige Vorbilder, deren Verhalten sie in spezifischen Situationen nachahmen können, da sie der eigenen Realität am nächsten sind und so auch am meisten Erfolg versprechen. Mut kann hier auch bedeuten, sich Autoritäten zu widersetzen, vorgegebene Grenzen zu überschreiten oder gegen jede Art von empfundener Bevormundung zu rebellieren. Je nach Situation können von den weniger mutigen Freunden auch die Sanktionen bei einer möglichen Nachahmung eingeschätzt werden. Neben der Peergroup sollten zudem auch Erwachsene häufiger als mutige Vorbilder fungieren. Insbesondere jüngere Erwachsene zeigen sich sehr empfänglich für deren moralische Werte und Engagement. Entsprechend üben mutige Familienmitglieder mit ihrer Entschlossenheit und Überzeugung nicht selten einen starken Einfluss auf sie aus.

**Wie Studien zeigen, greifen viele Bürger auch im späteren Leben vor allem auf Vorbilder aus ihrer Jugendzeit zurück beziehungsweise orientieren sich an deren mutigem Verhalten.**

Es werden häufig Personen bewundert, die gewohnte Verhaltensmuster und Entscheidungsprozesse hinterfragen, mutig für ihre Überzeugung eintreten, gegen Widerstände agieren, neue Lebensentwürfe planen oder riskante Entscheidungen treffen. Sie dienen dabei als Inspirationsquelle für mutige Unterfangen, vor denen man selbst noch zurückschreckt.

Im Vergleich zu anderen Vorbildern ist die Lücke zwischen Wunsch und Wirklichkeit bei der Nennung von Familienmitgliedern und Freunden deutlich geringer. Für etwa drei Viertel der Deutschen werden die an sie gesetzten Ansprüche erfüllt. Zu Enttäuschungen kommt es oftmals nur dort, wo die Erwartungen zu hoch waren, etwa von Jugendlichen an ihre Eltern. Altersbedingt weisen junge Menschen eine höhere Bereitschaft auf, Risiken einzugehen, und erhoffen sich auch von ihren familiären Bezugspersonen mutige Orientierungshilfen, die sie nicht immer geben können – oder wollen. Diese sind jedoch wichtig, da fehlende Unterstützung oder eine pessimistische Grundhaltung ebenfalls übernommen werden kann und so zu Enttäuschung und Frustration beitragen könnte.

Für etwa jeden Dritten sind zudem Wissenschaftler und Vertreter von Bürgerinitiativen sowie für knapp jeden Vierten Mitarbeitende aus gemeinnützigen Organisationen Personen mit einem großen Pozential zum mutigen Vorbild. Diese Personengruppen sind den organisatorischen und institutionellen Bereichen zuzuordnen, wobei sich bei den beiden Letzteren auch Überschneidungen zur eigenen Lebenswelt zeigen.

Die Wissenschaft ist in den letzten Jahren vornehmlich durch die globalen Herausforderungen des Klimawandels und der Coronapandemie verstärkt in den Fokus des öffentlichen Interesses gelangt. Für die Bevölkerung agieren die Wissenschaftler sonst eher im Hintergrund, zuständig für den effizienten Wissenstransfer von theoretischen Erkenntnissen in die Praxis. Ihr fachspezifisches Vorgehen ist für die meisten unverständlich und mit ihrem theoretischen Schwerpunkt hatten sie in der öffentlichen Wahrnehmung eher eine Beratertätigkeit und weniger eine Handlungs- oder Entscheidungsbefugnis. Seit Krisen und Konflikte aber immer stärker einen Einfluss auf das alltägliche Leben nehmen, werden wissenschaftliche Erkenntnisse, und mit ihnen die Wissenschaftler, stärker wahrgenommen. Dies betrifft vor allem die Kommunikation zwischen Wissenschaft und verschiedenen gesellschaftlichen Akteuren. In Bezug auf mutiges Verhalten wird Wissenschaftlern zugestanden, dass sie sich vor allem der Wahrheit verpflichtet fühlen und weniger von anderen, zum Beispiel materiellen, persönlichen oder parteipolitischen Interessen geleitet werden. Mutiges Vorbild bedeutet hier, auch unbequeme Wahrheiten zu kommunizieren, sich nicht vereinnahmen zu lassen, Erkenntnisse zu reflektieren und über das eigene Fachgebiet hinaus die interdisziplinäre Zusammenarbeit anzustreben. Als Personen der Öffentlichkeit initiieren sie damit eine Signalwirkung für Zuversicht, Ehrlichkeit und Vertrauen.

Bürgerinitiativen und gemeinnützige Organisationen wie NGOs zeichnen sich durch ihr basisdemokratisches Verständnis aus. Engagierte Bürger schließen sich zeitlich begrenzt oder auch längerfristig zusammen, um gemeinsam auf bestimmte Missstände aufmerksam zu machen und Einfluss auf Entscheidungen zu nehmen. Die Bundesbürger ordnen sie ihrer eigenen Lebenswelt zu und sehen sie als mutiges Vorbild für Tatkraft, Optimismus und Gestaltungswillen. Da Vorbilder helfen, das eigene Verhalten zu reflektieren, schätzen die Deutschen an ihnen auch die Zuversicht, durch persönliches Handeln Veränderungen tatsächlich anstoßen zu können. Auch solche, an die sie selbst vielleicht nicht mehr glauben.

**In Zeiten einer allgemeinen Unzufriedenheit und Politikverdrossenheit wird es als mutig empfunden, wenn Menschen sich diesem Trend widersetzen und an sich und die eigenen Gestaltungsmöglichkeiten glauben.**

In diesem Sinne wirkt Mut motivierend für andere Individuen, die eigenen Schwierigkeiten zu überwinden, auch wenn innere und äußere Stereotypen („Das bringt ja doch nichts", „Lieber den Fachleuten überlassen") diese Zuversicht oftmals behindern.

Während Bürgerinitiativen und NGOs das in sie gesetzte Vertrauen zum größten Teil erfüllen, trifft das für Wissenschaftler nur teilweise zu. Verantwortlich hierfür ist ihre oftmals als (zu) eng wahrgenommene Verzahnung mit der Politik und Wirtschaft sowie die oft unverständliche Kommunikation zwischen ihnen und der Öffentlichkeit. So verbinden viele Bürger das zuweilen für sie nicht nachvollziehbare politische Agieren während der Coronapandemie mit scheinbar unsicheren und widersprüchlichen Aussagen der Wissenschaft. In der Folge entsteht der Eindruck einer wankelmütigen und unsicheren Wissenschaft, die vor mutigen und ehrlichen Aussagen zurückschreckt.

Ungefähr ein Viertel der Bürger hofft bei Prominenten und Wirtschaftsvertretern mutige Vorbilder zu finden. Prominente stellen ein Einzelphänomen dar und sind eher mit einem Idol gleichzusetzen. Auch wenn keine eindeutige Grenze zwischen beiden Begrifflichkeiten gezogen werden kann, unterliegen Prominente doch einer stärkeren medialen Inszenierung und verkörpern ein bestimmtes Image. Als Vorbilder werden sie vor allem in zwei Zusammenhängen geschätzt. Zum einen, wenn sie ihren Namen für eine „gute Sache" einsetzen, bestimmte Kampagnen oder Projekte unterstützen, zum Spenden anregen oder auf Missstände aufmerksam machen. Zum anderen vermitteln sie durch ihren öffentlichen Erfolg Mut, Zuversicht, Willensstärke und Durchhaltevermögen. Ihre Lebenswege zeigen die Möglichkeit, Ziele und Wünsche zu erreichen. In besonderem Maße werden dabei Personen bewundert, die mit Herausforderungen (z. B. Krankheiten, Unfällen, Armut, Startschwierigkeiten) zu kämpfen hatten oder es nach Misserfolgen (wieder) zum Erfolg geschafft haben. Die Mehrheit dieser Vorbilder stammt aus der Film-, Sport und Musikszene.

Wirtschaftsvertreter gehören dem institutionellen Bereich an. Deren Vorbildcharakter speist sich aus ihrer Haltung, indem sie etwa besonders integer, mutig oder zukunftsweisend handeln. Sie werden für ihre Individualität geschätzt, dafür, dass sie den üblichen wirtschaftlichen Konzepten eine Alternative gegenüberstellen, ungewöhnliche Ideen oder ihrer gesellschaftlichen Verantwortung – etwa durch nachhaltige Projekte – eine hohe Bedeutung zumessen. Daneben bewundert man ihren wirtschaftlichen Erfolg und sieht sie als Vorbild der Entschlossenheit und Entscheidungsstärke. Nach Meinung der Bundesbürger können Wirtschaftsvertreter die in sie gesetzte Hoffnung auf ein mutiges Vorbild oftmals nicht erfüllen. Vor allem Eigenschaften wie Weitsicht, Entschlossenheit und Optimismus werden vermisst. Das (Vor-)Urteil lautet: Ökonomische Funktionäre haben in erster Linie ihre eigenen finanziellen Interessen im Blick und ihre Entscheidungen sind auf kurzfristigen Gewinn ausgerichtet. Die grundsätzlich als mutig empfundene Risikobereitschaft zeigt sich bei ihnen in waghalsigen Investitionen, die wenig Rücksicht auf Folgen für die Arbeitnehmenden nehmen. Längerfristige oder nachhaltige Reformen oder Anlagen werden dagegen eher selten wahrgenommen.

Relativ selten wird das Bedürfnis nach mutigen Vorbildern aus den Bereichen Medien und Religion genannt. Dabei spielt Mut in jeder Glaubensrichtung eine Rolle. So fordert zum Beispiel sowohl das Neue Testament als auch die Thora oder der Koran die Gläubigen auf, mutig für ihre Überzeugungen einzutreten, gegen Ungerechtigkeit und Unterdrückung anzukämpfen und sich für Schwache und Hilfsbedürftige einzusetzen. Vorbilder finden sich in den alten Schriften, wie etwa in Gestalt von Fatima al-Fihri, die 895 die erste Universität in Marokko gründete, oder den Makkabäern, die sich als jüdische Freiheitskämpfer 168 vor Christus gegen die makedonische Fremdherrschaft wehrten. Aber auch die Moderne bietet Vorbilder der Entschlossenheit und der moralischen Integrität wie etwa den Theologen Dietrich Bonhoeffer, der seinen Widerstand gegen die Nationalsozialisten mit dem Leben bezahlte, den baptistischen Pfarrer Martin Luther King als Kämpfer für die Gleichberechtigung der Farbigen in den USA oder den buddhistischen Dalai Lama Tenzin Gyatso als Streiter für die Autonomie Tibets.

In Deutschland übten bis in die 1950er-Jahre hinein, für einen Großteil in der westdeutschen Bevölkerung, die protestantischen und die katholischen Kirchen eine moralische Vorbildfunktion aus (96 % Konfessionszugehörigkeit). Diese betraf etwa Fragen der sozialen Gerechtigkeit, die Aussöhnung mit osteuropäischen Ländern, die Friedensbewegung oder die Annäherung an andere Religionen. Mit der zunehmenden Säkularisierung und der

Wiedervereinigung Deutschlands vollzog sich allmählich eine Tendenz der schwindenden konfessionellen Einflussnahme. Diese zeigt sich auch an der zunehmenden Ablehnung von Inhalten des Christentums und deren Anwendung in den Kirchen (z. B. Rolle der Frauen, Bestand des Zölibats) sowie dem schwindenden Vertrauen als Moralinstanz (u. a. Umgang mit Missbrauchsvorfällen). Derzeit ist nicht einmal mehr jeder zweite Bundesbürger in der protestantischen (21,8 Millionen Mitglieder) oder der katholischen Kirche (19,7 Million) und ein Ende der Kirchenaustritte zeichnet sich aktuell nicht ab. Entsprechend üben christliche Geistliche nur noch für etwa jeden zwölften Bundesbürger eine Vorbildfunktion aus beziehungsweise werden nicht mit einem mutigen Verhalten in Verbindung gebracht. Nach ihrer Empfindung nehmen sie in der öffentlichen Diskussion kaum noch einen Raum ein, ziehen sich nach Konflikten und Vorwürfen zu sehr in die interne Diskussion zurück und stehen nicht mehr für eine mutige Überzeugung ein, beispielsweise hinsichtlich der sozialen Frage, der Radikalisierung von Teilen der Gesellschaft oder des Klimawandels.

Medienvertreter werden nur von jedem Fünften als mögliches Vorbild für Mut gesehen. Als vierte Macht des Staats können sie durch ihre mehr oder weniger unabhängigen Möglichkeiten die Öffentlichkeit und das politische Geschehen beeinflussen. Journalisten wurde in der Vergangenheit ein Berufsethos zugestanden, das sich der freien Meinungsbildung verpflichtet fühlt, unabhängig agiert, Distanz zu den Regierenden hält und relevante Themen in den Fokus seiner Berichterstattung stellt. Mut bedeutet hier, Missstände aufzudecken, „den Finger in die Wunde zu legen" und als Sprachrohr des Volkes die Regierenden zu kontrollieren. Dieses Verhalten wird ihnen nur noch bedingt zugesprochen. Entsprechend selten werden Medienvertreter als entschlossene Mahner oder mutige Aufklärer wahrgenommen. Man vermisst eine fehlende Distanz zu den Regierungsorganen und schenkt den Journalisten wenig Vertrauen. Ein weiterer Kritikpunkt ist eine zu geringe konstruktive Berichterstattung und eine zunehmende Fokussierung auf negative Nachrichten. Vermisst werden optimistische und inspirierende Neuigkeiten, welche die Medien als mutige lösungsorientierte Vorbilder stärken würden. Zu beachten ist in diesem Zusammenhang auch der sinkende Einfluss der traditionellen Medien sowie der zeitgleich steigende Einfluss der sozialen Medien.

## BEISPIEL FÜR MUT
**Bürger der DDR – Ungeachtet des autoritären Regimes und der ständigen Überwachung durch die Staatssicherheit, wagten es viele Menschen, ihre Meinung zu äußern und für ihre Freiheit und Rechte zu streiten. Sie taten dies, indem sie friedlich demonstrierten oder auch streikten. Das Risiko von Sanktionen hielt viele nicht davon ab, sich für Veränderungen einzusetzen. Die Bürger der DDR kämpften mutig gegen Unterdrückung und für die Freiheit.**

## a. Besserverdienende fordern mehr Vorbilder aus Politik, Wirtschaft und Wissenschaft

*„Mut ist das, was man braucht,*
*um aufzustehen und zu sprechen;*
*Mut ist auch das, was man braucht,*
*um sich hinzusetzen und zuzuhören"*
Winston Churchill

### Besserverdienende wollen mehr Vorbilder

Von je 100 befragten Besserverdienenden sagen, dass folgende Personen eine Vorbildfunktion haben sollten, wenn es um mutige Ideen, Entscheidungen oder Verhaltensweisen geht:

Unterschied zu Geringverdienenden in Prozentpunkten

| Person | Wert | Unterschied |
|---|---|---|
| Politiker | 63 | +12 |
| Jeder Bürger | 53 | +4 |
| Vorgesetzte | 47 | +10 |
| Wissenschaftler | 41 | +13 |
| Familienmitglieder | 41 | +6 |
| Lehrer/Erzieher | 35 | −5 |
| Prominente | 34 | +7 |
| Wirtschaftsvertreter | 34 | +12 |
| Freunde | 30 | −4 |
| Vertreter Bürgerinitiativen | 28 | −2 |
| Vertreter NGO | 28 | +6 |
| Medienvertreter | 21 | 0 |
| Religiöse Vertreter | 15 | −1 |

Bei der Frage, ob sie einen Wunsch nach einem mutigen Vorbild haben, geben nur etwas über die Hälfte der Bundesbürger an, ein solches Bedürfnis zu haben. Die Gründe hierfür sind individuell unterschiedlich und reichen von einer desillusionierten Wahrnehmung der Realität, die das Vorhandensein von Vorbildern als unrealistisch einstuft und so das Potenzial gar nicht erkennt, über die fehlende Notwendigkeit, da über genügend eigene Motivation und Entschlossenheit verfügt wird, bis hin zu anderen Beweggründen wie zum Beispiel eine zu große Distanz zwischen der eigenen Lebenswelt und den möglichen Vorbildern oder einer vorhandenen Lethargie.

Bei den Antworten zeigen sich bezüglich der Geschlechter und des Wohnortes nur geringe Differenzen, während hinsichtlich des Alters und des Einkommens deutlichere Unterschiede zu verzeichnen sind. So äußern Besserverdienende vermehrt den Wunsch nach mutigen Vorbildern. Diese sind vor allem im Bereich der Wissenschaft, der Politik und der Wirtschaft angesiedelt (+12 Prozentpunkte). Im beruflichen Zusammenhang, etwa beim Wechsel des Arbeitsplatzes oder der Position, können auch Vorgesetzte als geeignete Role Models fungieren, die dabei helfen, sich in den neuen Organisationsformen erfolgreich zu bewähren. Im Zusammenhang mit Mut könnten sie sinnvolle Möglichkeiten aufzeigen, eine erhöhte Verantwortung zu übernehmen, alte Konzepte zu hinterfragen, Selbstreflexion auszuüben oder innovative Strategien zur Problemlösung zu entwickeln. Hier zeigt sich, wie wichtig es auch oder gerade in Führungspositionen ist, positive und mutige Rollenbilder aufzubauen. In Bereichen, die häufig mit Konkurrenz und Hierarchie assoziiert werden, wünscht man sich inspirierende und wegweisende Unterstützung, die nicht nur auf das Eigeninteresse fokussiert ist.

Im Bereich der Wirtschaft zeigen Besserverdienende insbesondere ein stärkeres Interesse an Merkmalen wie Risikobereitschaft, Durchsetzungsvermögen, entschlossene Investitionen und Selbstsicherheit. Der Wunsch ist groß, Mut nicht nur mit sozialen Aspekten zu assoziieren, sondern auch im ökonomischen Bereich anzuerkennen. So erfordert es beispielsweise Mut, sich mit aller Entschlossenheit einem Ziel zu widmen, Sicherheitsbedenken beiseitezuschieben, einen Neuanfang zu wagen oder Herausforderungen anzunehmen. Mutige Vorbilder sind dementsprechend Personen, die zum Beispiel Unternehmen gegründet, innovative Konzepte umgesetzt, mit Kreativität sowie Leistungsbereitschaft Veränderungen für sich und möglicherweise auch für andere geschaffen haben.

In ähnlicher Weise erhoffen sich die Besserverdienenden von der politischen und wissenschaftlichen Elite der Gesellschaft eine stärkere Vorbildfunktion. Mehr als andere glauben sie an die Kraft von Autoritäten und schenken diesen auch ein größeres Vertrauen hinsichtlich mutiger Entscheidungen.

**Besserverdienende sehen bei Vorbildern eher das Potenzial und weniger Verfehlungen und Missstände. Mut setzen sie dabei mit Entschlossenheit, Klarheit und Verantwortungsbereitschaft gleich.**

Eine schwächere Zustimmung lässt sich beim gewünschten Vorbild des Lehrers erkennen. Hier ist der Wunsch nach einem Vorbild bei Bürgern mit einem geringen Einkommen ausgeprägter. Diese assoziieren mit dem Berufsstand Verantwortung, Engagement, Fachkenntnis und Leidenschaft. Im Zusammenhang mit Mut erhoffen sie sich von Pädagogen einen inspirierenden Einfluss auf Kinder und Jugendliche sowie Hilfestellung, um eine zuversichtliche Grundhaltung und mutige Zukunftspläne zu entwickeln. Wenn der familiäre Hintergrund nur geringe immaterielle Ressourcen (z. B. Bildung) aufweist, können Lehrer dabei helfen, ein stärkeres Selbstbewusstsein aufzubauen, Perspektiven zu erweitern und die Heranwachsenden darin zu bestärken, mutig alternative Wege zu beschreiten, wie zum Beispiel das Ziel eines höheren Schulabschlusses, als ihre Eltern ihn haben. Vor dem Hintergrund ihrer eigenen schulischen Erfahrungen bedauern viele Geringverdienende, diese Unterstützung selbst nicht genutzt zu haben.

### b. Generationen-Gap bei der Wahl von Vorbildern

*„Es ist mutig,
ein Vorbild zu sein"*

Maya Angelou

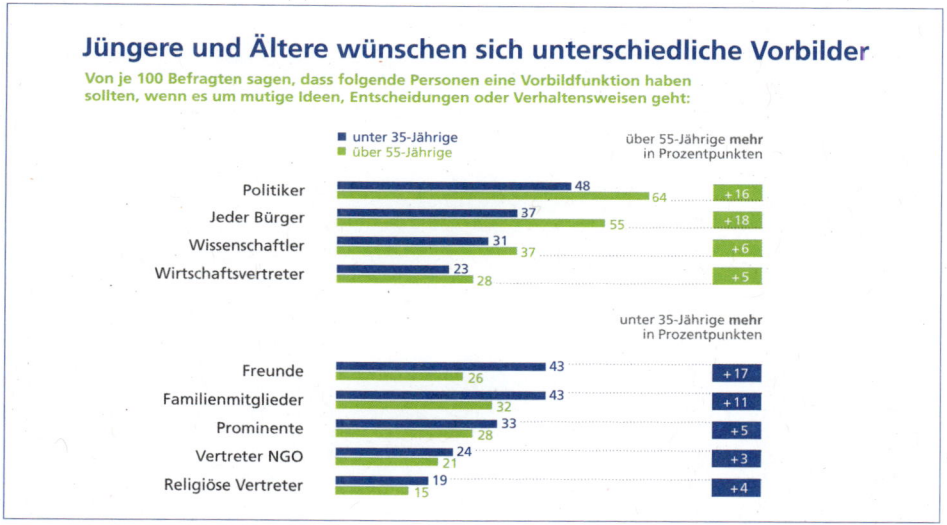

**Jüngere und Ältere wünschen sich unterschiedliche Vorbilder**

Von je 100 Befragten sagen, dass folgende Personen eine Vorbildfunktion haben sollten, wenn es um mutige Ideen, Entscheidungen oder Verhaltensweisen geht:

- ■ unter 35-Jährige
- ■ über 55-Jährige

über 55-Jährige **mehr** in Prozentpunkten

| | unter 35-Jährige | über 55-Jährige | mehr in Prozentpunkten |
|---|---|---|---|
| Politiker | 48 | 64 | +16 |
| Jeder Bürger | 37 | 55 | +18 |
| Wissenschaftler | 31 | 37 | +6 |
| Wirtschaftsvertreter | 23 | 28 | +5 |

unter 35-Jährige **mehr** in Prozentpunkten

| | unter 35-Jährige | über 55-Jährige | mehr in Prozentpunkten |
|---|---|---|---|
| Freunde | 43 | 26 | +17 |
| Familienmitglieder | 43 | 32 | +11 |
| Prominente | 33 | 28 | +5 |
| Vertreter NGO | 24 | 21 | +3 |
| Religiöse Vertreter | 19 | 15 | +4 |

Die jüngere und ältere Generation setzt bei ihren Wünschen nach Vorbildern unterschiedliche Prioritäten. Dies betrifft sowohl die Reihenfolge als auch die prozentuale Zustimmung oder Ablehnung. So favorisieren die über 55-Jährigen vor allem Personen aus dem politischen Sektor sowie den „normalen Bürger" als mutige Vorbilder und das deutlich stärker als die unter 35-Jährigen. Auch Personen aus der Wirtschaft und der Wissenschaft schenken die Älteren mehr Vertrauen und gestehen ihnen ein hohes Potenzial für mutige Entscheidungen und Handlungen zu.

**Es zeigt sich eine Wertschätzung von Autoritäten bei der älteren Generation und die Überzeugung, dass diese eine starke Einflussnahme auf die Bürger ausüben können.**

Die ältere Generation ist den ihnen nahestehenden Institutionen grundsätzlich positiv zugewandt und schätzt sie als Leitbilder für die Gesellschaft allgemein. Betont werden hierbei das Einstehen für die eigene Überzeugung, Selbstbewusstsein und eine optimistische zielgerichtete Grundhaltung. Überdurchschnittlich oft erhoffen sich die über 55-Jährigen durch mutiges Auftreten eine inspirierende Signalwirkung für die Bevölkerung. Die Verantwortung für ein konstruktives und zuversichtliches Miteinander wird aber nicht nur der politischen, wirtschaftlichen und wissenschaftlichen Elite des Landes überlassen, sondern liegt nach ihrer Überzeugung ebenso stark in den Händen jedes Einzelnen. Weit entfernt von einer fatalistischen Haltung sehen sie jeden Bürger gefordert, mit seiner Haltung und seinen Handlungen ein Beispiel für Mut und Zuversicht zu geben. Dies kann sich unter anderem im sozialen Bereich äußern, indem man für seine Werte einsteht, andere Mitbürger unterstützt, Zivilcourage zeigt oder der eigenen Überzeugung statt der Mehrheitsmeinung folgt. Ebenso auch durch unerschrockene Entscheidungen, indem Verantwortung im eigenen beruflichen und privaten Umfeld übernommen und Optimismus vermittelt wird. Dass rund ein Fünftel der Älteren mehr an das Potenzial eines jeden Bürgers glauben, kann auf ihre Lebenserfahrung zurückgeführt werden. Sie haben bereits erlebt, wie sehr sich Mut, Zuversicht und Engagement auszahlen und eine inspirierende Wirkung auf das soziale Umfeld haben können.

Im Gegensatz dazu erwarten die älteren Bürger weniger Mut und Anregungen von Familie und Freunden, stehen sie doch in den meisten Fällen fest im (Berufs-) Leben und benötigen entsprechend weniger Orientierung aus dem direkten sozialen Umfeld. Sie haben in ihrem Leben bereits zahlreiche Ratschläge, Rollenmuster oder Orientierungshilfen von Verwandten und Freunden erhalten, wodurch der Wunsch nach persönlichen Vorbildern in ihrem privaten Umfeld geringer ist. Für sie sind Vorbilder eher eine wichtige Inspiration für die Gesellschaft insgesamt, weshalb sie sich mehr institutionelle (Politiker, Wissenschaftler, Wirtschaft) und abstrakte Vorbilder (Bürger allgemein) wünschen.

**Die Generation der unter 35-Jährigen setzt andere Prioritäten. Sie erhofft sich hauptsächlich von Freunden und Familienmitgliedern eine mutige Vorbildfunktion.**

Erklärt werden kann dieses mit dem Wunsch nach Orientierung und Unterstützung. Eine besondere Rolle kommt hierbei meist den eigenen Eltern zu: Sie können durch ihr eigenes Verhalten zeigen, wie man mit Herausforderungen umgeht, Krisen und Ängste überwindet, aus Fehlern lernt und eigene Ziele und Träume verwirklicht. Ebenso können sie auch dazu beitragen, das Selbstbewusstsein und die Selbstachtung der Kinder zu stärken. Während Freunde im Jugendalter vor allem als Role Models dienen, die durch Waghalsigkeit und unangepasstes Verhalten beeindrucken, erhofft man sich von ihnen in der späteren Entwicklung eher Anregung, Initiative und Ansporn. Freunde haben durch ähnliche Lebensumstände das Potenzial zum Ansporn, um die eigene Komfortzone zu verlassen, Routinen durch Abwechslung zu durchbrechen oder auch gänzlich neue Wege einzuschlagen. Diese können zum Beispiel einen Arbeitsplatz-, Beziehungs- oder Wohnwechsel, aber auch ein gesellschaftliches Engagement betreffen.

Leicht überdurchschnittlich oft nennen die unter 35-Jährigen Prominente, Religionssowie NGO-Vertreter beim Wunsch nach Vorbildern für Mut. Hier zeigt sich die geringere Verbindung von jungen Mitbürgern zu institutionellen Vorbildern oder Autoritäten und die größere Nähe zu Einzelpersonen oder einer Idee. Besonders in jungen Jahren ist man empfänglich für moralische Werte, unterstützt ethische Ziele und sucht nach Inspirationen für das eigene Verhalten. Bei den Prominenten bewundern sie vor allem deren spezifischen Lebenswege und Einsatz für bestimmte Inhalte. In ähnlicher Form schätzen sie NGO- und Religionsvertreter, die sich in der Regel für Menschen in Not, Gerechtigkeit oder den Umweltschutz einsetzen. Bei ihnen kommt zum gesellschaftlichen Engagement noch die Nähe zur eigenen Lebenswelt hinzu, die sich zum Beispiel auch in einer persönlichen Mitgliedschaft äußert.

## BEISPIEL FÜR MUT

**Die Pakistanerin Malala Yousafzai setzte sich bereits als junge Schülerin öffentlich für das Recht auf Bildung für Mädchen ein, trotz der Drohungen durch die regierenden Taliban. Sie ließ sich jedoch nicht einschüchtern und setzte ihre Kampagne für Bildung und Frauenrechte unbeirrt fort. Als 15-Jährige wurde sie dann von einem Taliban-Kämpfer in ihrem Schulbus angeschossen und schwer verletzt. Trotz dieses Anschlags setze sie sich weiterhin für ihre Überzeugungen ein und gründete eine Organisation, die sich für Bildung und Frauenrechte einsetzt. Sie ist nicht nur für junge Menschen in ihrer Heimat ein Vorbild, sondern weltweit, da sie zeigt, was eine einzelne Person bewirken kann, wenn man mit Mut, Beharrlichkeit und Entschlossenheit agiert.**

*„Wer mutig ist und gut handelt,*
*inspiriert andere, dasselbe zu tun"*

Konfuzius

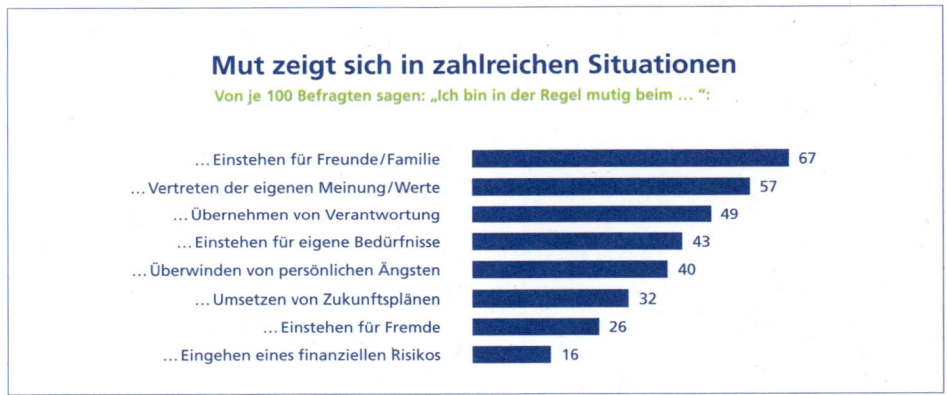

### Mut zeigt sich in zahlreichen Situationen

Von je 100 Befragten sagen: „Ich bin in der Regel mutig beim … ":

| | |
|---|---|
| … Einstehen für Freunde / Familie | 67 |
| … Vertreten der eigenen Meinung / Werte | 57 |
| … Übernehmen von Verantwortung | 49 |
| … Einstehen für eigene Bedürfnisse | 43 |
| … Überwinden von persönlichen Ängsten | 40 |
| … Umsetzen von Zukunftsplänen | 32 |
| … Einstehen für Fremde | 26 |
| … Eingehen eines finanziellen Risikos | 16 |

Mut als abstrakter Begriff lässt viele Assoziationen zu, kann als Verhaltensform, Wunsch oder Wert verstanden werden, genauso aber auch mit Personen, Geschehnissen und Entscheidungen verbunden werden. Wann aber bezeichnen die Bürger ihr eigenes Verhalten als mutig? In welchen Situationen handeln sie unerschrocken? Wer oder was lässt sie furchtlos agieren und Ängste überwinden? So unterschiedlich die genannten Aspekte auch sind, entwickeln doch alle ihre Kraft aus derselben Quelle.

**Mut entsteht durch die Verbindung von Empathie, Ehrlichkeit, Vertrauen und Selbstreflexion. Er entwickelt sich dabei nicht durch äußere Forderungen (z. B. einer Autorität), sondern aus dem innersten Wertesystem, der Reflexion und dem sozialen Austausch.**

Zwei von drei Bürgern bezeichnen sich selbst als mutig beim Einstehen für die Familie und Freunde. Dieses äußert sich etwa durch emotionalen Beistand, Unterstützung bei Herausforderungen, Konflikten mit anderen oder der konkreten Hilfe in Notsituationen. Mutig agiert man, indem man sich gemeinsam gegen etwas oder jemanden stellt, sich dabei Gruppenzwängen entzieht sowie eigene Vorstellungen zurückstellt und stattdessen die Interessen des Freundes oder der Verwandten wahrnimmt und verteidigt. Das können die Geschwister in der Auseinandersetzung mit den Eltern sein, der Freund bei Konflikten im Freundeskreis, die Freundin bei beruflichen Problemen oder die Kinder bei der schwierigen Studienfachentscheidung. Die Hilfe kann dabei finanzieller, moralischer, sozialer oder emotionaler Art sein und in den unterschiedlichsten Zusammenhängen stattfinden. Getragen wird die mutige Unterstützung aus einem Gefühl der Verantwortung, Empathie und Vertrautheit heraus.

Mut zeigt sich auch bei Konflikten, bei denen die eigenen Werte oder Überzeugungen im Mittelpunkt stehen. Bei familiären oder freundschaftlichen Kontroversen braucht es Mut, sich dem anderen entgegenzustellen, ihm zu widersprechen und seine eigene Meinung zu vertreten. Dieses können zum Beispiel politische Überzeugungen, Zukunftspläne oder berufliche und private Entscheidungen sein. Gerade weil es sich um vertraute Personen handelt, die oftmals Zustimmung erwarten oder einen Konsens voraussetzen, erfordert es Überwindung, diese nicht zu erfüllen. Die Besinnung auf die eigenen Werte, die Zuversicht, Verständnis zu erfahren, stärkt die Entscheidungskraft und den Mut, diesen Weg zu gehen. Bei Auseinandersetzungen im schulischen oder beruflichen Kontext konzentriert sich das mutige Vorgehen vor allem auf die Unterstützung von Kollegen oder Mitschülern. Mutige Entschlossenheit zeigt sich zum Beispiel, wenn andere emotionale Unterstützung benötigen, ungerecht behandelt oder gemobbt werden. Daneben zeigt sich Mut, wenn auch in deutlich geringerem Maße, bei Auseinandersetzungen mit Vorgesetzten oder Autoritäten. Je stärker dabei die inneren Werte betroffen sind, umso eher stellt man sich entschlossen der Auseinandersetzung für andere. Ansonsten wird versucht, eine Balance zwischen Mut und Verständnis zu finden.

Für jeden Zweiten äußert sich Mut auch darin, Verantwortung zu übernehmen. Wie bei anderen Fragestellungen deutlich wird, zeigt sich diese Verantwortung vor allem im persönlichen Bereich. Zum einen werden damit Situationen angesprochen, in denen eine mutige Kommunikation im Mittelpunkt steht, um soziale Konflikte und Auseinandersetzungen zu lösen. Zum anderen betrifft es eine Handlungsebene, bei der richtungsweisende Entscheidungen im Mittelpunkt stehen. Das kann zum Beispiel bedeuten, sich allein verantwortlich für die Erziehung eines Kindes zu fühlen, die fürsorgliche Betreuung kranker Familienmitglieder oder verbindliche Aufgaben zu übernehmen.

**Mut bedeutet, für seine Handlungen verantwortlich zu sein, sie keinem anderen zu übertragen und für ihre Folgen auch einzustehen.**

Als besonders herausfordernd ist hierbei der Aspekt der alleinigen Verantwortung zu nennen. Man kann sich nicht hinter einer höheren Autorität oder anderen verstecken, sondern muss mit seiner Persönlichkeit für den jeweiligen Erfolg oder auch Misserfolg geradestehen. Dieses wird von den Bürgern vornehmlich mit beruflichen Belangen in Verbindung gebracht. In einer Gesellschaft, in der Fehler und Misserfolge oftmals stigmatisiert werden und Erfolg als das höchste Ziel betrachtet wird, erfordert es besonders viel Mut, sich dieser Herausforderung zu stellen und Verantwortung zu übernehmen.

Jeweils etwa zwei von fünf Bürgern geben an, sich mutig zu verhalten, wenn es darum geht, die eigenen Interessen zu vertreten und persönliche Ängste zu überwinden. Es braucht Mut, die eigenen Bedürfnisse offensiv zu vertreten und dabei eventuell auftretende Widerstände oder Ablehnung von anderen in Kauf zu nehmen. Stellt man diese Aussage in Zusammenhang mit der hohen Zustimmung zur Assoziation von Mut mit Selbstbewusstsein, wird die wechselseitige Beziehung von Selbstvertrauen, Mut und dem Einstehen für die eigenen Interessen deutlich. Dabei ist es eher nebensächlich, in welche Bereiche sich diese Interessen einordnen lassen, seien sie nun privater oder beruflicher Natur. Entscheidend ist das mutige und selbstbewusste Eintreten für die eigenen Bedürfnisse, auch gegen Widerstände. Diese Widerstände können sowohl von außen als auch von innen kommen, beispielsweise in Form von Ängsten. Die Bürger sprechen in diesem Zusammenhang von der Herausforderung, sich diesen zu stellen und sie möglichst zu überwinden. Dabei geht es nicht um pathologische Ängste, sondern um tiefer greifende Sorgen und Befürchtungen, die regelmäßig oder sporadisch den persönlichen Alltag beeinträchtigen. Beispiele hierfür sind Versagensängste, Entscheidungsängste oder Ängste vor Konflikten mit Autoritäten. Sich diesen Befürchtungen zu stellen, erfordert Mut, da sie eine Änderung des gewohnten Verhaltens voraussetzen und in ihrem Erfolg ungewiss sind.

Für etwa jeden dritten Bürger ist Mut eine zentrale Voraussetzung bei der Planung und Umsetzung von persönlichen Zukunftsentwürfen. Trotz der vorhandenen Freiheit und den zahlreichen Möglichkeiten zur Selbstverwirklichung in Deutschland empfindet es fast ein Drittel der Bundesbürger als schwierig, diese zu realisieren. Im beruflichen Bereich werden neben den finanziellen Risiken vor allem bürokratische Hemmnisse, starre Strukturen, Unverständnis und fehlende Anerkennung befürchtet. Hier zeigt sich mutig, wer sich von diesen wenig beeinflussen lässt und seine Ziele entschlossen im Blick behält. Genannt werden in diesem Zusammenhang zum Beispiel Planungen zur Selbstständigkeit, Unternehmensgründungen, ein Berufswechsel, aber auch der bewusste Verzicht auf einen Karriereschritt, um mehr Zeit für andere Dinge zu haben. Im privaten Bereich sind Pläne und Veränderungen oftmals in einen sozialen Zusammenhang eingebunden, weshalb es wichtig ist, mutig zu kommunizieren, überzeugend zu sein und Begeisterung auszulösen.

**Mutiges Agieren beim Planen von Veränderungen ist eine besondere Herausforderung, da keine Gewissheit besteht, wie sich etwas in Zukunft entwickeln wird.**

Im Gegensatz zum unerschrockenen Einsatz im persönlichen Umfeld gibt nur ein knappes Drittel an, sich mutig für fremde Personen einzusetzen. Die Gründe können zum Teil mit der recht abstrakten Begrifflichkeit des „Fremden" sowie einer geringeren Notwendigkeit erklärt werden. Im Gegensatz zu Familie und Freunden besteht weniger emotionale Nähe und Verbundenheit, was die moralische Verpflichtung verringert. Dazu kommt noch der allgemeine Trend zum Rückzug ins Private, welcher weniger Berührungspunkte mit Menschen außerhalb der eigenen Lebenswelt nach sich zieht. Dies belegen auch die obigen Aussagen, bei denen sich Mut fast ausschließlich im persönlichen Umfeld und kaum im gesellschaftlichen Zusammenhang und Engagement zeigt. Wenn sich die Bürger daher für Fremde einsetzen, erfordert es für viele eine höhere Überwindung als bei Personen des Vertrauens. Die Hürde, mutig zu sein, erscheint ungleich höher, da die Reaktion oder das Verhalten des Fremden unvorhersehbar ist und man schlechter einschätzen kann, ob die Unterstützung auch gewollt wird. Zudem besteht eine größere Unsicherheit darüber, wie das Umfeld auf den Beistand reagiert. Wenn man sich trotz dieser Widrigkeiten mutig einsetzt, zeigt sich eine hohe Empathie, Hilfsbereitschaft, Aufgeschlossenheit genauso wie ein gesellschaftliches Verantwortungsgefühl. Beispiele für ein mutiges Verhalten für Fremde können sich auf unterschiedliche Weise zeigen, etwa beim Engagement für Flüchtlinge, Obdachlose oder Minderheiten, bei der Verteidigung Einzelner in diskriminierenden oder gefährlichen Situationen. Allen Aspekten gemeinsam ist der Effekt der direkten individuellen Hilfe sowie eine allgemeine Verbesserung des gesellschaftlichen Vertrauens. Letzteres ist in diesem Zusammenhang von zentraler Bedeutung, ist Vertrauen doch der soziale Klebstoff, der eine Gesellschaft zusammenhält. Diese gilt es durch Möglichkeiten des Austausches, der Kommunikation sowie der Zusammenarbeit zu fördern, ansonsten droht eine zunehmende Spaltung, Diskriminierung und Vorurteilsbildung.

## BEISPIEL FÜR MUT

**Das Gesundheitspersonal hat während der Coronapandemie großen Mut bewiesen, indem es sich um Patienten kümmerte, über deren Infektionsrisiko zunächst nur wenig bekannt war. Trotz dieser Unsicherheit und unter schwersten Bedingungen arbeiteten sie bis an die Belastungsgrenze. Ihr Einsatz, ihre Entschlossenheit und ihre Selbstlosigkeit haben zur Rettung von Menschenleben und zur Eindämmung des Virus beigetragen. Das Engagement von Ärzten und Pflegekräften ist ein Ausdruck der mutigen Hilfe für andere.**

### a. Geld gibt Mut – Besserverdienende zeigen mehr Entschlossenheit

*„Mut ist notwendig,*
*um Risiken einzugehen und*
*neue Möglichkeiten zu erschließen"*

Steve Jobs

**Besserverdienende sind selbstbewusst und selbstsicher**

Von je 100 befragten Besserverdienenden sagen:
„Ich bin in der Regel mutig beim ... "

Unterschied zu Geringverdienenden
in Prozentpunkten

| | | |
|---|---|---|
| ... Einstehen für Freunde/Familie | 75 | +16 |
| ... Vertreten der eigenen Meinung/Werte | 60 | +6 |
| ... Übernehmen von Verantwortung | 59 | +18 |
| ... Einstehen für eigene Bedürfnisse | 47 | +7 |
| ... Überwinden von Ängsten | 46 | +8 |
| ... Umsetzen von Zukunftsplänen | 44 | +19 |
| ... Einstehen für Fremde | 29 | +1 |
| ... Eingehen eines finanziellen Risikos | 26 | +10 |

Beim Vergleich der unterschiedlichen Personengruppen zeigen die Antworten der Besserverdienenden deutliche Differenzen zu den Beziehern eines geringen Einkommens. Dieses betrifft nicht nur ihre Prioritäten, sondern auch die Höhe ihrer prozentualen Zustimmung, äußern sie doch in allen Bereichen eine größere Bereitschaft für ein mutiges Verhalten.

Die größte Abweichung zeigt sich bei der Bereitschaft, persönliche Zukunftspläne mutig umzusetzen. In diesem Bereich weisen sie nicht nur eine um 19 Prozentpunkte höhere Zustimmung auf, sondern setzen diese Handlung auch an erster Stelle ihrer mutigen Aktionen. Die Pläne konzentrieren sich – wie auch schon bei der Betrachtung von anderen Fragestellungen deutlich wurde – hauptsächlich auf berufliche Angelegenheiten wie einen Positions- oder Arbeitsplatzwechsel, einen Wohnortwechsel (auch ins Ausland), eine berufliche Neuorientierung, eine Investition oder eine neue geschäftliche Kooperation.

**Den Besserverdienenden fällt es leichter als anderen, mögliche Sicherheitsbedenken in den Hintergrund zu rücken und mutige Entscheidungen zu treffen.**

Im Falle eines Misserfolges oder eines Rückzuges müssen sie weniger negative monetäre Konsequenzen fürchten. Hinzu kommt ihre oftmals vorhandene hohe Kompetenz bei Finanzfragen, die ihre Bereitschaft, mehr finanzielle Risiken einzugehen, unterstützt.

Je höher das Einkommen, desto höher ist die Position in den Unternehmen. Entsprechend können oder müssen Besserverdienende häufiger Verantwortung übernehmen, Entscheidungen treffen oder Projekte umsetzen, die auch Kollegen oder Kunden betreffen. Dies erfordert Entschlossenheit und Weitsicht, vor allem aber auch die Bereitschaft, Verantwortung zu übernehmen, wozu Besserverdienende deutlich häufiger bereit sind (+18 Prozentpunkte). Dafür nutzen sie ihre Erfahrungen und ihr Wissen, ebenso wie auch vorhandene Netzwerke und Unterstützung.

Obwohl die genannten Merkmale hauptsächlich auf den beruflichen Bereich bezogen sind, haben sie immer auch Auswirkungen auf den privaten. So könnten zum Beispiel riskante finanzielle Investitionen und berufliche Veränderungen Konflikte innerhalb der Familie oder des Freundeskreises nach sich ziehen. Jedoch agieren Personen mit einem hohen Einkommen auch im privaten Umfeld mutiger und erzielen hierbei überwiegend positive Effekte. Sie leisten soziale Unterstützung und inspirieren andere, zeigen ihre zuversichtliche und positive Einstellung und setzen sich für Familie und Freunde ein. Dieses betrifft in seltenen Fällen eine finanzielle, meistens eine soziale oder emotionale Unterstützung. Geprägt von den eigenen Erfolgen und der festen Überzeugung, wie sehr Mut und Entschlossenheit sich lohnen, verteidigen sie auch andere gegen Widerstände, befürworten deren Entscheidungen, ermuntern sie bei Plänen und begleiten sie bei Konflikten, auch wenn sie gegebenenfalls selbst dadurch Nachteile befürchten müssen.

**Besserverdienende zeigen sich zuversichtlich, sämtliche Herausforderungen gemeinsam meistern zu können.**

Überdurchschnittlich mutig verhalten sie sich zudem bei der Überwindung von Ängsten, dem Einstehen für eigene Bedürfnisse und dem Vertreten der eigenen Meinung. Wie bereits deutlich wurde, bilden Selbstvertrauen und Selbstbewusstsein eine wichtige Quelle für mutiges Verhalten. Auch hinsichtlich dieses Merkmals befinden sich Besserverdienende häufig in einer privilegierteren Position, sodass sie öfter und leichter auch in diesen Situationen ihren Mut zeigen können.

*„Es steigt der Mut mit der Gelegenheit"*

William Shakespeare

**Mutiges Eintreten für Überzeugung und Werte**

Von je 100 befragten über 55-Jährigen sagen:
„Ich bin in der Regel mutig beim ... "

Unterschied zu unter 35-Jährigen
in Prozentpunkten

| | | |
|---|---|---|
| ... Einstehen für Freunde/Familie | 74 | +17 |
| ... Vertreten der eigenen Meinung/Werte | 65 | +18 |
| ... Übernehmen von Verantwortung | 54 | +10 |
| ... Einstehen für eigene Bedürfnisse | 44 | 0 |
| ... Überwinden von Ängsten | 42 | +1 |
| ... Umsetzen von Zukunftsplänen | 32 | −3 |
| ... Einstehen für Fremde | 25 | −4 |
| ... Eingehen eines finanziellen Risikos | 12 | −10 |

Nicht nur Besserverdienende agieren in vielen Situationen häufiger mutig, auch die Generation der über 55-Jährigen zeigt sich bei zahlreichen Gelegenheiten entschlossener und beherzter als die jüngere Generation. Dies betrifft vor allem das Einstehen für die eigene Meinung, Freunde und Familie sowie die Übernahme von Verantwortung. Während finanziell wohlsituierte Menschen vornehmlich in beruflicher Hinsicht Courage zeigen, trifft dies für die älteren Jahrgänge auch auf den privaten Bereich zu. Für sie zeugt es von einer inneren Stärke, die eigene Meinung und Überzeugung offen und ehrlich zu äußern, unabhängig davon, ob es sich um persönliche oder berufliche Belange handelt. Wenn sie noch in Arbeitsprozessen tätig sind, scheuen sie sich seltener, Anweisungen zu hinterfragen, mit Kollegen oder Vorgesetzten zu diskutieren sowie alternative Überlegungen oder abweichende Gedanken zu äußern. Dieses liegt nicht nur an ihrem stärkeren Selbstbewusstsein und ihrem Wissen um die eigenen Erfahrungen, sondern auch an ihrer Zuversicht, eine Balance zwischen den Bedürfnissen des Gegenübers und der Umsetzung eigener Prioritäten zu finden. Zudem haben sie weniger als junge Menschen, allein aufgrund ihres Alters, mit Zurechtweisungen zu rechnen und können so unerschrockener agieren. Wenn sie nicht mehr beruflich tätig sind, kommt ihr Mut zum Beispiel bei einem ehrenamtlichen Engagement zum Tragen. Bei persönlichen Auseinandersetzungen oder Konflikten zeigen sie ebenfalls größere Gelassenheit und Standhaftigkeit als die unter 35-Jährigen. Mutig werden Überzeugungen vertreten, auch wenn das zu Streitigkeiten oder einer Distanzierung des sozialen Umfelds führt. Die eigenen Werte sind den Älteren nicht nur bei beruflichen Belangen wichtig, sie übertragen sie auch auf ihren Einsatz für Familie und Freunde. In ähnlicher Weise wie die Gruppe der Besserverdienenden setzen sie sich überdurchschnittlich oft für diese ein, verteidigen sie gegen Widerstände und unterstützen sie bei Konflikten.

**Eingebettet werden die genannten Aspekte in einem allgemeinen Gefühl der Verantwortung sich selbst und anderen gegenüber, wodurch sich der Mut der älteren Menschen als eine moralische Verpflichtung der Standhaftigkeit zeigt.**

Auf den ersten Blick scheinen die jungen Menschen im Gegensatz zur älteren Generation weniger mutig zu agieren. Eine Ausnahme zeigt sich beim Eingehen von finanziellen Risiken und das, obwohl sie in diesem Bereich oftmals nur über geringe Erfahrung verfügen und die Risiken sowie Auswirkungen nur bedingt einschätzen können. Ihrem Alter gemäß handeln sie dabei öfters impulsiv und lassen sich leichter von Versprechungen oder Ratschlägen beeinflussen, ohne diese genauer zu hinterfragen. Gleichzeitig haben sie auch ein geringeres Sicherheitsbedürfnis, müssen weniger Rücksicht auf sowie Verantwortung für andere Menschen übernehmen und sind Rückschlägen gegenüber unbekümmerter. So sind ihre Pläne, Vorhaben oder Investitionen in monetären Belangen oft recht wagemutig und werden intensiviert, je öfter sie für ihren Mut mit Erfolg belohnt werden.

**Neben der finanziellen Risikobereitschaft zeigt sich die junge Generation auch bei der Umsetzung von Zukunftsplänen etwas mutiger als die ältere.**

Unter 35-Jährige befinden sich sowohl beruflich als auch privat oft noch in einer Orientierungsphase ihres Lebens, sind Veränderungen gegenüber aufgeschlossener und flexibler in ihren Zielsetzungen. Herausforderungen begegnen sie häufig mit einem sportlichen Ehrgeiz und sind eher bereit, unsichere Pläne oder Gedankenspiele in die Realität umzusetzen. Abschließend ist anzumerken: Die geringere Zustimmung der Jüngeren hinsichtlich der Aspekte „Mut beim Eintreten für die eigene Meinung" und „Mut beim Einstehen für Freunde und Familie" bedeutet nicht unbedingt ein geringeres Engagement. Stärker als die Generationen vor ihnen sind sie in einem gesellschaftlichen Milieu aufgewachsen, welches ein selbstständiges, freiheitliches und kritisches Denken fördert. So ist das Äußern der eigenen Meinung oder der Einsatz für Freunde für viele selbstverständlich und wird nicht mit Mut assoziiert, wohingegen sie bei der Unterstützung für Fremde überdurchschnittlich couragiert agieren.

## BEISPIEL FÜR MUT

Die aus einer einfachen Bauernfamilie stammende und später heiliggesprochene Jeanne d'Arc war eine bemerkenswert mutige Frau im 15. Jahrhundert. Als junge Frau hatte sie Visionen von Heiligen, die sie motivierten, bei der Befreiung Frankreichs von englischer Herrschaft zu helfen und den sicheren Schutz ihrer Familie und Heimat zu verlassen, um dem französischen König Charles VII. im Krieg zu dienen. Sie führte die französischen Truppen im Hundertjährigen Krieg gegen England an, obwohl sie als Frau mit anfänglichen Widerständen im eigenen Heer kämpfen musste. Mit ihrer Entschlossenheit, Verwegenheit und ihrem Optimismus inspirierte und motivierte sie die Soldaten und schenkte ihnen immer wieder die nötige Zuversicht, um gemeinsam mehrere bedeutende Siege zu erringen. Jeanne d'Arcs Mut, sich für das, woran sie glaubte, einzusetzen, machte sie zu einem Symbol für Mut, Stärke und Tapferkeit.

# IV. WARUM WIR OFTMALS NICHT MUTIG SIND

*„Mut bedeutet nicht, fehlerfrei zu sein,*
*sondern Fehler zu machen*
*und trotzdem weiterzumachen"*
John F. Kennedy

### Bequemlichkeit, Angst und Zweifel –
### warum Mut oft auf der Strecke bleibt

**Von je 100 Befragten nennen folgende Gründe, weshalb viele Bürger nicht mutig sind: Weil …**

| | |
|---|---|
| …sie ihre Komfortzone nicht verlassen wollen | 57 |
| …sie Angst vor den Konsequenzen haben | 53 |
| …sie Angst vor dem Scheitern haben | 53 |
| …sie keine Verantwortung übernehmen wollen | 49 |
| …sie Angst vor Auseinandersetzung haben | 45 |
| …sie nicht genügend Selbstvertrauen haben | 41 |
| …sie negative Erfahrungen gemacht haben | 37 |
| …ein zu großes Sicherheitsbedürfnis vorherrscht | 30 |
| …Mitstreiter oder Verbündete fehlen | 30 |
| …sie es nicht gelernt haben | 30 |
| …es zu viele Regeln gibt | 29 |
| …ihnen Empathie und Mitgefühl fehlen | 20 |
| …die allgemeine Anerkennung fehlt | 19 |
| …es nicht genügend Vorbilder gibt | 19 |

Mutig zu sein, erfordert vor allem Selbstvertrauen, Verantwortungsbereitschaft, Risikobereitschaft und Optimismus. Der jeweiligen Situation entsprechend, ist es zudem wichtig, für seine eigene Überzeugung oder seine Werte einzustehen. Realisiert wird mutiges Verhalten besonders innerhalb der persönlichen Lebenswelt. Was aber hindert viele Bundesbürger daran, diese als positiv empfundene Handlung öfter und auch außerhalb des direkten Umfeldes auszuführen? Sind hierfür äußere Umstände verantwortlich oder doch eher innere Motive?

Fakt ist: Aus Sicht der Bevölkerung lässt sich keine klare Abgrenzung zwischen inneren und äußeren Hemmnissen ziehen. So lassen sich die einzelnen Aspekte zwar grob zwischen den beiden Motiven einordnen, doch bedingen sich diese im Allgemeinen gegenseitig und nehmen Einfluss aufeinander. Ein eindeutig intrinsisches Hemmnis, das zudem am häufigsten genannt wird, ist das Verlassen der eigene Komfortzone. Mut bedeutet Aktivität, Engagement, mögliches Risiko, kann beschwerlich und belastend sein. Als Gegenpole stehen Passivität, Bequemlichkeit und Sicherheit. Eigenschaften, mit denen man es sich im gewohnten Alltag gut gehen lassen kann. Man ist zufrieden, die beruflichen und privaten Herausforderungen zu meistern, und möchte wenig Anstrengung für weitere Aufgaben unternehmen. Man nimmt am politischen und gesellschaftlichen Geschehen Anteil, plant durchaus auch mal ein stärkeres Engagement und träumt von persönlichen Veränderungen und Zielen, doch bleibt es in den meisten Fällen bei einem theoretischen Gedankenspiel des Mutes und des konkreten Angehens und Umsetzens.

**Der Gedanke an Anstrengung und die möglichen Konsequenzen wirkt für viele Bundesbürger zu abschreckend, um mutig zu sein.**

Für zwei von fünf Bürgern zählt zu den inneren Motiven zudem fehlendes Selbstvertrauen sowie für jeden Dritten ein zu starkes Sicherheitsbedürfnis. Wie schon bei der Frage nach den Charaktereigenschaften eines mutigen Menschen zeigt sich auch hier Selbstvertrauen als zentrale Voraussetzung. Ist es nicht vorhanden, können schon mutige Überlegungen – und erst recht mutige Entscheidungen – zu einer großen Herausforderung werden. In Kombination mit einem hohen Bedürfnis nach Sicherheit und einem steten Abwägen von möglichen Risiken wird so ein zuversichtliches Agieren unwahrscheinlich. Das Bedürfnis der Menschen nach Sicherheit ist individuell unterschiedlich und lässt sich zweifellos nicht verallgemeinern. Aber es ist auch immer gesellschaftlich bestimmt, steht in Wechselbeziehung zu der öffentlichen Meinung, zu gesellschaftlichen Strukturen, zu allgemeinen Werten et cetera. Die deutsche Gesellschaft, die oftmals auch als Vollkaskogesellschaft bezeichnet wird, schützt ihre Bürger vor möglichst vielen Unwägbarkeiten, Frühwarnsysteme jeglicher Art minimieren Risiken, Kontrolle und Regeln scheinen Sicherheit zu gewährleisten. Wohl nirgends sonst auf der Welt gibt es so viele Versicherungen, die Schutz vor jedem möglichen Unglück bieten, von Kranken-, Haftpflicht-, Hausrat-, Lebens- und Pflegeversicherung, über eine Berufsunfähigkeits-, Unfall-, Rechtsschutz- und Glasbruchversicherung bis hin zu Handy-, Brillen-, Reisegepäck- oder Tierkrankenversicherung. Sich nicht von diesem Sicherheitsdenken beeinflussen zu lassen und dieses nicht zu verinnerlichen, fällt vielen Bürgern schwer. Somit ist das individuelle Sicherheitsbedürfnis nicht nur ein inneres Hemmnis von Mut, sondern weist auch auf eine gesellschaftliche Problematik hin: eine Kultur, die Risiken und Veränderungen gegenüber eher misstrauisch und ablehnend eingestellt ist.

**Mutiges Handeln führt auch immer zu einer Veränderung des Bestehenden.**

Von einer Mehrheit der Bundesbürger werden zudem Angst vor dem Scheitern und Angst vor Verantwortung als große Hindernisse genannt. Diese beiden genannten Ängste sind nur vordergründig den inneren Motiven zuzuordnen. Aus den Analysen weiterer Forschungs- ergebnisse wird deutlich, dass sie vornehmlich erlernte Verhaltensweisen und Eigenschaften sind und somit eine wechselseitige Beziehung zwischen individuellen und gesellschaftlichen Motiven aufweisen. Die genannte vorherrschende Vollkaskomentalität lässt das Leben als ein allseits abgesichertes Konstrukt erscheinen, welches Fehler oder Scheitern nicht vorsieht. Alles scheint seinen sicheren und geregelten Lauf zu nehmen. Hinzu kommt eine gesell- schaftliche Tendenz der Optimierung und eine mangelnde Fehlerkultur, die wenig Raum für Scheitern oder Risiken vorsieht, die mutigem Verhalten immer innewohnen. In diesem Zusammenhang kann die allgemeine Präferenz von Sicherheit und Erfolg zu einer verinner- lichten Angst vor dem Scheitern führen. Dies wiederum hat einen direkten Einfluss darauf, wie bereitwillig und gern die Bürger Verantwortung übernehmen. Die Vorstellung, im beruf- lichen oder privaten Bereich Eigenverantwortung auszuüben, ist umso negativer besetzt, je offensichtlicher ein mögliches Scheitern von außen als Fehler angesehen wird.

Mutige Entscheidungen werden von den meisten Menschen hauptsächlich im persönlichen Bereich getroffen und entsprechend wird auch nur dort Verantwortung für die Folgen über- nommen. Folglich betrifft die Nennung von Verantwortung als Hindernisgrund für Mut vor allem die berufliche und öffentliche Lebenswelt.

**Es liegt in der öffentlichen Verantwortung, eine Kultur zu fördern, die Ängste vor Ver- antwortung und Scheitern minimiert und Risiken, Fehler und mutige Entscheidungen als etwas Positives integriert und fördert.**

Diese Aussage bestätigt ein weiterer – ebenfalls von einer Mehrheit – genannter Hinder- nisgrund für Mut: die Angst vor den wirtschaftlichen und sozialen Konsequenzen des Handelns. Im wirtschaftlichen Bereich sind hier vordergründig finanzielle Risiken gemeint, wie etwa das benötigte Startkapital, das ungesicherte Einkommen, aufgenommene Schulden oder auch die fehlende Absicherung im Falle eines Scheiterns. Die Befürchtung, nicht genügend monetäre Unterstützung zu bekommen, sowie die Angst vor den Hürden der Kreditwürdigkeit, lässt viele innovative Ideen schon oftmals in der Planungsphase en- den. Verbunden mit einem sehr hohen Arbeitsaufkommen, bürokratischen Regularien sowie äußeren Unsicherheiten (z. B. Inflation, Corona, Ukrainekrieg etc.) schreckt jeder zweite

Bürger vor mutigen Entscheidungen in diesem Bereich zurück. Dieses zeigt sich unter anderem auch in dem seit dem Jahr 2000 zurückgehenden Interesse an beruflicher Selbstständigkeit. Im internationalen Vergleich rangiert das einstige Land der Tüftler und Erfinder als Gründungsstandort mittlerweile weit hinter Ländern wie den USA, Südkorea oder auch Großbritannien, deren ‚TEA-Quote' doppelt so hoch ist. TEA steht für „Total early-stage Entrepreneurial Activity" und zeigt den Prozentanteil von Bürgern, die während der letzten dreieinhalb Jahre ein Unternehmen gegründet haben. Die niedrige Quote in Deutschland lässt sich nicht einfach nur mit fehlendem persönlichen Mut erklären, sondern gründet auch in einer unzureichenden schulischen Gründungsausbildung und strukturellen Hindernissen.

Die Angst vor den möglichen sozialen Folgen sind einerseits mit den wirtschaftlichen Risiken verbunden, die sich aus monetären Unsicherheiten, hoher Arbeitsbelastung, stressanfälliger Arbeitsatmosphäre und reduziertem Sozialleben ergeben. Andererseits benennt fast jeder zweite Bundesbürger auch die Angst vor Auseinandersetzungen und Konflikten.

Mutiges Verhalten bedeutet nicht nur innere Überwindung, sondern ebenso auch eine Auseinandersetzung im persönlichen Umfeld, da dieses meistens direkt oder indirekt betroffen ist. Mut bedeutet Veränderungen oder Unruhe, da sich der Status quo wandelt und sich neue Verhältnisse zusammensetzen. Dabei ist es zweitrangig, um welches mutige Verhalten es geht, sei es nun das Einstehen für Überzeugungen, die Konfrontation mit ungewohnten Entscheidungen, das Einfordern von Bedürfnissen und Erwartungen oder das Äußern von außergewöhnlichen Plänen. In jedem Fall verändern sich dadurch die sozialen Beziehungen, ob auf beruflicher oder privater Ebene. Im positiven Fall wird der Mut als konstruktiv, innovativ, inspirierend oder unerschrocken wahrgenommen, im negativen Fall aber als unruhestiftend, unüberlegt oder vermessen. Die mutig Agierenden geraten oftmals schnell in eine Position der Rechtfertigung.

**In einem vorherrschenden Klima des Sicherheitsdenkens ist es besonders herausfordernd, den Wunsch nach Veränderung zu realisieren und dabei gleichzeitig die sozialen Beziehungen nicht zu belasten.**

Fast jeder dritte Bürger nennt größeren Freiraum als Voraussetzung, um eine mutige Entscheidung zu treffen oder zuversichtlich und engagiert zu agieren. Erneut werden gesellschaftliche Strukturen deutlich, die dem Einzelnen nicht genügend Möglichkeiten bieten, Projekte anzustoßen oder beherzt umzusetzen. Genannt werden in diesem Zusammenhang starre Regularien, Hierarchien oder festgefahrene Muster, die alternative Gedanken oder

Vorhaben schon oftmals in der Ideenphase einschränken oder sogar verhindern. Einge-bunden sind diese in einer Vollkaskogesellschaft, die gegenüber Risiken und Veränderun-gen eher ablehnend eingestellt ist. Dabei sind es gerade Offenheit, Innovationen und das Infragestellen alter Konzepte, die zukunftsweisend für jede Gesellschaft waren und sind. Dieses betrifft nicht nur ökonomische Gestaltungen, sondern reicht in alle Bereiche des Alltags, wie beispielsweise Konzepte der Sharing Economy, der Nachhaltigkeit, der Integration, der Entwicklung von lokalen Schulungsprogrammen, der digitalen Förderung, des nachbarschaftlichen Zusammenlebens und so weiter.

Die Wechselwirkung zwischen gesellschaftlichen, äußeren und inneren Widerständen gegen Mut wird auch im Aspekt der Erfahrungen deutlich. Zwei von fünf Deutschen führen negative Erfahrungen als Hinderungsgrund für ein mutiges Handeln an. Dabei belegen zahlreiche Untersuchungen zu Strategien und Mechanismen, mit denen Menschen Heraus-forderungen bewältigen, wie wichtig positive Erfahrungen sind, um Herausforderungen anzunehmen und innovativ zu agieren. Je öfter Konfliktlösungen als gelungen und konstruk-tiv erlebt wurden, umso zuversichtlicher wird neuen Problemen begegnet. Im Umkehrschluss führen unbefriedigende Lösungen oder Vermeidungsstrategien jedoch zu Frustration, Unmut und Unsicherheit.

**Die Angst vor Misserfolgen sowie negative Erfahrungen führen oftmals dazu, neuen Herausforderungen auszuweichen oder diese als belastend zu empfinden.**

Die negativen Erfahrungen eines mutigen Handelns zeigen sich dabei in unterschiedlicher Form, wie zum Beispiel in einem finanziellen Misserfolg, in sozialen Auseinandersetzungen, im mangelnden Verständnis von anderen, in nachfolgenden Sanktionen oder in fehlender Anerkennung, die so auch von jedem Fünften als wichtiger Hindernisgrund für mutiges Agieren genannt wird. Hier wird deutlich, dass mutiges Handeln immer in einem sozialen Zusammenhang steht und eine positive Rückmeldung, sei sie nun privater oder öffentlicher Natur, diesem förderlich ist. Gerade weil Mut auch Überwindung von Befürchtungen und Bedenken bedeutet, wünschen sich viele eine Wertschätzung, die den Mut auch belohnt.

Fast jeder Dritte nennt die fehlende Lernerfahrung als Hindernisgrund für Mut. Noch stärker als bei der negativen Erfahrung sind hier vor allem gesellschaftliche Gründe von Bedeu-tung. Von der familiären und schulischen Sozialisation ausgehend, über fehlende Möglich-keiten bei der studentischen oder beruflichen Ausbildung, bis hin zum Berufsalltag beklagen gerade Jüngere, dass sie kaum Kenntnisse und Strategien kennengelernt und Chancen erhalten haben, um mutiges Verhalten zu erlernen oder auch auszuprobieren. Dabei bieten sich in diesen Bereichen zahlreiche Optionen an, bietet die familiäre und schulische Lebenswelt doch einen geschützten Rahmen, innerhalb dessen relativ risikoarm bestimmte mutige Verhaltensweisen, wie Zivilcourage und Eigenverantwortung, oder auch kühne Projekte erlernt, initiiert und durchgeführt werden könnten. Derart gewappnet, gestärkt durch positive Rückmeldungen, Erfahrungen und Erfolge, könnten schon Jugendliche lernen, Risiken zu kalkulieren und mögliche Rückschläge oder Misserfolge als Ansporn zu nehmen und eine Kultur zu verinnerlichen, die mutiges Vorgehen belohnt und Fehler und Risiken nicht nur negativ besetzt, sondern vielmehr als Lernprozess und Wissensvorsprung für zukünftige Entscheidungen begreift.

**Sich mutig zu verhalten, selbstbewusst und zuversichtlich zu denken, vollzieht sich in einem interaktiven Lernprozess, in dessen Fokus nicht die Lehrenden stehen, sondern die Lernenden, die im Austausch mit anderen eine aktive Rolle einnehmen.**

Ziel ist es, selbstmotiviert, engagiert und teamorientiert eigene Gedankenwege, Lösungen und Ideen zu entwickeln. In diesem Zusammenhang zeigt sich neben den erwähnten Hemmnissen, wie fehlende positive Erfahrungen und Belohnungen, auch die Bedeutung von mangelnden Vorbildern, sei es im privaten Umfeld (Familie, Freunde, Lehrer, Trainer, Nachbarn etc.) oder auch im öffentlichen Raum (Politiker, Unternehmer, Sportler, Künstler etc.). Vorbilder leisten einen wichtigen Beitrag für die sozial-kognitive Entwicklung des Einzelnen, und dieses nicht nur im Kindesalter, zur Ausbildung der eigenen Identität. Übernehmen zunächst die Eltern als engste Bezugspersonen die Funktion eines Leitbildes, bieten später auch andere Vorbilder eine Orientierung für das eigene Verhalten. Besonders in Situationen, die nicht so geläufig oder mit Unsicherheiten verbunden sind, werden diese nicht einfach nachgeahmt, sondern oftmals auch einer kritischen Reflexion unterworfen, um so das eigene Verhalten besser einordnen zu können.

**Ohne Vorbilder fehlen positive Impulse und Leitbilder, die zeigen, wie sehr es sich lohnt, eigenen Ideen, Idealen oder Träumen zu folgen, wie Widerstände überwunden werden und wie ein Wagnis erfolgreich sein kann.**

Ein weiterer erwähnenswerter Hinderungsgrund ist das Fehlen von Mitstreitern, welcher ebenfalls von jedem dritten Bundesbürger angeführt wird. Dieser Aspekt bildet eine Schnittstelle zwischen der Bedeutung von fehlenden Vorbildern, fehlender Anerkennung und der Angst vor der Verantwortung und dem Scheitern. Es spiegelt sich der Wunsch des Einzelnen wider, Gleichgesinnte zu finden, die eine ähnliche Vorstellung, Idee oder Vision haben und diese ebenfalls mutig und zuversichtlich umsetzen möchten. Die individuelle Scheu vor dem Scheitern oder der Verantwortung lässt sich in der Gemeinschaft sehr viel leichter verteilen und mindern. Auch ist man nicht als Einzelner angreifbar, sondern kann die Konsequenzen des Handelns gemeinsam tragen. Es bedeutet weniger ein Verstecken als ein gemeinschaftliches Beieinanderstehen. Dieses impliziert zudem die gegenseitige Anerkennung, deren Fehlen als Hemmnis für mutiges Verhalten häufig genannt wird. Den Mitstreitern kommt somit die Rolle von Unterstützern zu, die inspirieren und die Zuversicht stärken, wenn Zweifel oder Ängste ob des eigenen Mutes das Handeln erschweren.

## BEISPIEL FÜR MUT

**Die ägyptische Königin Hatschepsut war mutig, weil sie gegen die gängigen Geschlechterrollen und kulturellen Konventionen ihrer Zeit verstieß und als erste Frau das Amt eines ägyptischen Pharaos ausübte. Trotz Widerständen und Bedrohungen aus ihrer Umgebung herrschte sie erfolgreich für mehr als 20 Jahre und führte Ägypten in eine Zeit des Wohlstands und des Fortschritts. Sie förderte den Handel sowie Bauprojekte, unternahm Expeditionen in andere Länder und initiierte Wohlstandsprogramme. Hatschepsut war eine Wegbereiterin für Frauen und inspirierte zukünftige Generationen, ihre Ziele zu verfolgen und ihre Stimme zu erheben.**

> *„Es gibt nur eine Art von Mut,*
> *die wirklich zählt:*
> *der Mut, man selbst zu sein"*
>
> Ernest Hemingway

**Frauen nennen deutlich mehr Hinderungsgründe**

Von je 100 befragten Frauen nennen folgende Gründe,
weshalb viele Bürger nicht mutig sind: Weil ...

Unterschied zu Männern
in Prozentpunkten

| Grund | Wert | Unterschied |
|---|---|---|
| ...sie ihre Komfortzone nicht verlassen wollen | 62 | +10 |
| ...sie Angst vor wirtschaftlichen/sozialen Konsequenzen haben | 57 | +8 |
| ...sie Angst vor dem Scheitern haben | 54 | +3 |
| ...sie keine Verantwortung übernehmen wollen | 51 | +4 |
| ...sie Angst vor Auseinandersetzung haben | 48 | +6 |
| ...sie nicht genügend Selbstvertrauen haben | 41 | +1 |
| ...sie negative Erfahrungen gemacht haben | 41 | +7 |
| ...ein zu großes Sicherheitsbedürfnis vorherrscht | 31 | +1 |
| ...Mitstreiter oder Verbündete fehlen | 29 | −2 |
| ...sie es nicht gelernt haben | 29 | −1 |
| ...es zu viele Regeln gibt | 28 | −1 |
| ...ihnen Empathie und Mitgefühl fehlen | 22 | +4 |
| ...die allgemeine Anerkennung fehlt | 19 | 0 |
| ...es nicht genügend Vorbilder gibt | 18 | −2 |

Zwischen den Geschlechtern herrschen wenige Unterschiede in der Prioritätensetzung. Allerdings nennen Frauen deutlich mehr Hemmnisse fürs Mutigsein. Dieses betrifft vor allem die Aspekte der Bequemlichkeit, der Angst vor Konsequenzen, der negativen Erfahrungen und der Scheu vor Auseinandersetzungen. Durch ihre geschlechtsspezifische Sozialisation haben sie einen anderen Blick auf bestimmte Verhaltensformen, sodass sich einige Unterschiede hinsichtlich ihrer Aussagen auf diese zurückführen lassen. Zudem tragen ihre spezifischen Erfahrungen dazu bei, die Analyse zu erweitern und die jeweiligen Merkmale und ihre Bedeutung differenzierter zu betrachten.

Frauen halten persönliche Bequemlichkeit und den Rückzug in die Komfortzone häufiger als Männer für Faktoren, die mutiges Verhalten beeinträchtigen können. Im positiven Sinne bietet Letztere einen geschützten Raum zur Regeneration und Entspannung. Frei von Zwängen und Anforderungen, fühlt man sich dort sicher, zufrieden und selbstbestimmt. Die Umgebung, die Mitmenschen und das eigene Verhalten sind einem vertraut und vermitteln ein Gefühl der Behaglichkeit. Im negativen Sinne kann diese mit Stillstand und Bequemlichkeit assoziiert werden. Die eigene Komfortzone dient dann nicht mehr als wichtiger Ausgleich zur Aktivität, sondern hat eine Eigendynamik entwickelt, die uns daran hindert, neue Herausforderungen anzunehmen.

**Je mehr man sich daran gewöhnt, unangenehme oder unbekannte Situationen zu vermeiden, desto geringer entwickeln sich Motivation, Neugierde auf Veränderungen und Risikobereitschaft.**

Häufiger als Männer sprechen Frauen den inneren Motiven eine hohe Bedeutung zu. Zum einen greifen sie dabei auf eigene Erlebnisse und Beobachtungen zurück, zum anderen konzentrieren sie sich häufiger auf innere Erklärungen bei Missständen, während Männer öfters äußere Umstände für individuelle Verhaltensweisen verantwortlich machen.

Negative Erfahrungen können mutige Menschen in ihrer Entschlossenheit behindern. So berichten Frauen von zahlreichen negativen Erfahrungen in ihrem Leben, die sie mit einem mutigen Auftreten erlebt haben. Dieses betrifft hauptsächlich die Arbeitswelt. Sie beklagen das Vorhandensein von Vorurteilen in Form von geschlechtsspezifischen Stereotypisierungen. So werden ihnen oftmals mutige Konzepte und Unternehmungen weniger zugetraut, Führungsstärke und Durchsetzungsvermögen abgesprochen und ihre Entschlossenheit und Risikobereitschaft bezweifelt. Da mutiges Verhalten viel Energie, Geduld und Stärke erfordert werden diese zusätzlichen Widerstände als demotivierend und hinderlich angesehen. Weil Frauen eher als Männer Misserfolge mit inneren Motiven in Verbindung setzen, klagen sie darüber, wie sehr negative Erfahrungen sich im Inneren manifestieren, das Selbstbewusstsein mindern und Zweifel an der eigenen Kompetenz nach sich ziehen können.

Im Zusammenhang hiermit steht auch die höhere Zustimmung der Frauen zum Hindernisgrund der Angst vor Konsequenzen, insbesondere bei beruflichen Belangen. Häufiger als Männer sind Frauen von niedrigem Einkommen, fehlendem Zugang zu Ressourcennetzwerken und mangelnder Mentoren-Unterstützung betroffen sowie in höheren Hierarchieebenen unterrepräsentiert. In der Folge haben sie bei mutigen Vorhaben, unkonventionellen Vorschlägen, entschlossenen Forderungen mit strengeren Maßstäben, Missachtung und mehr negativen Folgen zu rechnen – wie beispielsweise Nachteile bei der Karriereentwicklung oder bei Gehaltserhöhungen. Zudem messen Frauen der Furcht vor Konfrontation eine höhere Relevanz als Hindernisgrund zu. Auch hier beziehen sich ihre Aussagen vornehmlich auf den Arbeitssektor und die von ihnen dort gemachten Erfahrungen. So beeinflusst eine immer noch vorhandene geschlechtsspezifische Sozialisation die innere Haltung und Wahrnehmung von Frauen. Dementsprechend neigen viele von ihnen dazu, ein harmonisches und empathisches Miteinander zu präferieren sowie nach Ausgleich und Kooperation zu streben. Entschlossene Auseinandersetzungen, kompromissloses Agieren und mutiges Vorpreschen werden dagegen eher gemieden. In privaten Zusammenhängen, wie etwa bei mutigen Auseinandersetzungen mit Familienmitgliedern, wird diese Angst dagegen eher den Männern zugeschrieben. Auch sie können sich nicht vollständig von gesellschaftlichen Stereotypen und Rollenmustern befreien, wie etwa der Zuschreibung von Kontrolle und Sachlichkeit. So fürchten sie wie Frauen Gefühlsverletzungen und Beziehungsschäden, sind aber oftmals nicht in der Lage, ihre Bedürfnisse und Gefühle zu kommunizieren und meiden emotionale Auseinandersetzungen.

### b. Ältere beanstanden vor allem Bequemlichkeit und fehlendes Verantwortungsbewusstsein

*„Mut bedeutet nicht,*
*die Kraft zu haben, weiterzumachen;*
*Mut bedeutet, weiterzumachen,*
*wenn man keine Kraft hat"*
Theodore Roosevelt

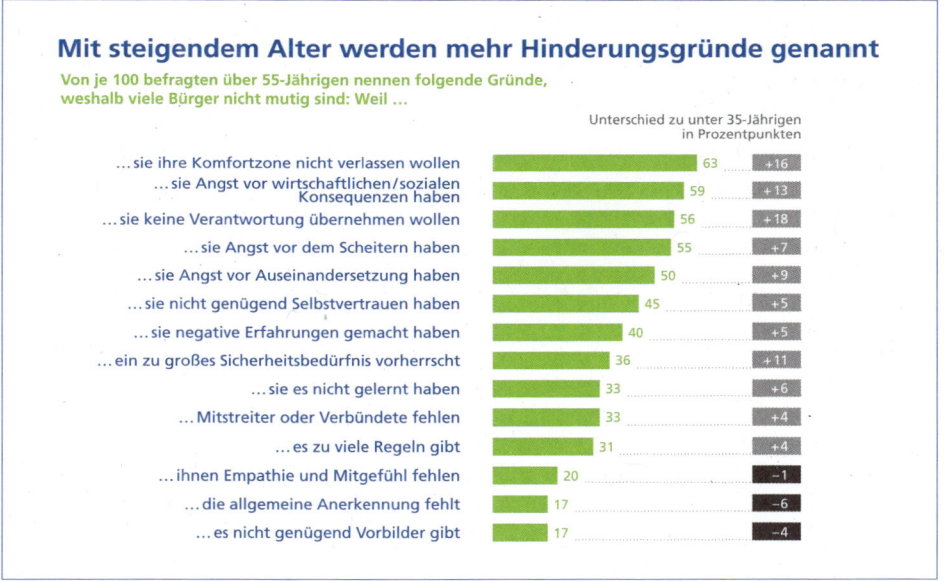

**Mit steigendem Alter werden mehr Hinderungsgründe genannt**

Von je 100 befragten über 55-Jährigen nennen folgende Gründe, weshalb viele Bürger nicht mutig sind: Weil ...

Unterschied zu unter 35-Jährigen in Prozentpunkten

| | | |
|---|---|---|
| ...sie ihre Komfortzone nicht verlassen wollen | 63 | +16 |
| ...sie Angst vor wirtschaftlichen/sozialen Konsequenzen haben | 59 | +13 |
| ...sie keine Verantwortung übernehmen wollen | 56 | +18 |
| ...sie Angst vor dem Scheitern haben | 55 | +7 |
| ...sie Angst vor Auseinandersetzung haben | 50 | +9 |
| ...sie nicht genügend Selbstvertrauen haben | 45 | +5 |
| ...sie negative Erfahrungen gemacht haben | 40 | +5 |
| ...ein zu großes Sicherheitsbedürfnis vorherrscht | 36 | +11 |
| ...sie es nicht gelernt haben | 33 | +6 |
| ...Mitstreiter oder Verbündete fehlen | 33 | +4 |
| ...es zu viele Regeln gibt | 31 | +4 |
| ...ihnen Empathie und Mitgefühl fehlen | 20 | –1 |
| ...die allgemeine Anerkennung fehlt | 17 | –6 |
| ...es nicht genügend Vorbilder gibt | 17 | –4 |

Bei der Frage nach möglichen Hindernissen für Mut betragen die Unterschiede zwischen den Generationen bis zu 20 Prozentpunkte. Dabei erreichen fast ausschließlich die Älteren höhere Werte. Lediglich bei den Merkmalen der fehlenden Vorbilder und Anerkennung stimmen sie etwas unterdurchschnittlich ab. Die höchsten Unterschiede lassen sich bei Gründen feststellen, die der intrinsischen Motivation entspringen.

Laut Aussage vieler Älterer, verharren zahlreiche Bürger zu sehr in ihrer Komfortzone, haben ein übermäßiges Bedürfnis nach Sicherheit und sind nicht bereit, Verantwortung zu übernehmen. Ohne inneren Antrieb und stets auf Sicherheit und Beständigkeit bedacht, steht ihr eigenes Wohlbefinden im Vordergrund und hindert sie daran, sich mutig Herausforderungen zu stellen. Nach Ansicht der Älteren trifft das für ihre eigene Generation jedoch kaum zu. Lediglich das Motiv der Bequemlichkeit gestehen sie sich zum Teil selbst zu, welche jedoch nicht einer fehlenden Motivation entspringt, sondern eher ihrem Alter und nachlassender Energie geschuldet ist.

**Die ältere Generation zieht einen direkten Vergleich zu ihrer eigenen Lebenswelt und vermisst Werte wie Leistungsbereitschaft, Verantwortungsgefühl und Gemeinsinn, vor allem bei den jungen Menschen.**

Rückblickend erinnern sie sich, wie oft sie in ihrem Leben schon Widerständen und Konflikten mit Entschlossenheit begegnet sind, ausdauernd und wagemutig agierten. Dabei verfolgten sie nicht nur ihre eigenen Interessen, sondern handelten in der Verantwortung für die Familie oder die Gemeinschaft. Den Mut vieler Bürger heute sehen sie hauptsächlich in Form von Eigennutz, Risikobereitschaft, Naivität und Leichtsinn. Motive, denen sie eher negativ gegenüberstehen. Erklären lassen sich diese unterschiedlichen Wahrnehmungen zwischen Jung und Alt unter anderem mit einer verklärten Sichtweise der Vergangenheit und der eigenen Geschichte – so glich mancher Wagemut wohl eher einem entschlossenen Auftreten. Zudem vollzieht sich ein Wandel von Werten und Definitionen. So finden viele jüngere Menschen ihre Lebenserfüllung nicht mehr nur in einem leistungsorientierten Arbeitsalltag oder pflichterfüllten Familienleben mit zahlreichen positiven wie negativen Herausforderungen. Sie streben eine Balance zwischen Arbeit und Freizeit an und haben nicht immer den Ehrgeiz für Führungspositionen, Karriere und Familienengagement. Autoritäre Strukturen, die früher im Berufs- und Privatleben weitverbreitet waren und dementsprechend Möglichkeiten des Widerstandes boten, befinden sich heute im Auflösungsprozess, weshalb mutiges Agieren in diesem Zusammenhang wenig erforderlich ist.

Weitere Differenzen zeigen sich bezüglich der Angst, die eher den beruflichen als den persönlichen Bereich umfasst. Ältere Berufstätige vermissen von ihren Kollegen die Bereitschaft, Streitigkeiten auszutragen, für die eigene Überzeugung einzustehen, mutige Vorschläge zu machen oder couragiert Pläne umzusetzen, ohne immer gleich an die Konsequenzen zu denken. Nach ihrer Einschätzung scheuen die meisten sich, sich auf unsicheres Terrain zu wagen, und verstecken sich lieber hinter der schweigenden Mehrheit. Gefangen in ihrem Bestreben nach Sicherheit, wagen sie wenig, fürchten sie doch mögliche berufliche Nachteile. Damit einher geht die Angst vor dem Scheitern und vor Auseinandersetzungen. Diese Wahrnehmung lässt Einblicke in eine vergangene Arbeitswelt zu, die heute in dieser Form kaum mehr existent ist. Dieses betrifft zum einen die schon oben angedeuteten autoritären Strukturen, die mehr Anlass für mutiges Verhalten boten, und zum anderen eine andere Fehlerkultur. So bemängeln viele ältere Bürger die fehlende Fehlerakzeptanz und gleichzeitig vorherrschende Optimierungstendenz. Sie selbst haben dagegen Fehler noch als Lern- und Wachstumschance kennengelernt und entsprechend viele Entscheidungen ohne Sicherheitsnetz getroffen. Zwar empfanden sie das Arbeitsklima nicht immer als harmonisch, oftmals sogar eher als rau, aber eben auch als lebendig, voller Energie und Tatendrang.

**Insgesamt erscheinen die älteren Bundesbürger oftmals entschlossener, motivierter und couragierter als die jüngeren.**

Fehlender Mut liegt für sie vor allem in der individuellen Verantwortung. Dabei vergessen sie zuweilen, wie sehr veränderte Wertevorstellungen, Lebens- und Arbeitsbedingungen auch ein verändertes Verständnis von Mut nach sich ziehen und Mut so neue Formen findet, die sich ihnen nicht immer sofort erschließen.

# IV. WARUM WIR OFTMALS NICHT MUTIG SIND

## c. Ostdeutsche nennen öfter negative Erfahrungen, mangelnde Anerkennung und Angst

*„Mut ist nicht die Abwesenheit von Angst,*
*sondern die Entscheidung,*
*dass etwas anderes wichtiger ist*
*als die Angst"*

Ambrose Redmoon

### Ostdeutsche sehen mehr Hürden für ein mutiges Verhalten

**Von je 100 befragten Ostdeutschen nennen folgende Gründe, weshalb viele Bürger nicht mutig sind: Weil ...**

Unterschied zu Westdeutschen in Prozentpunkten

| Grund | Wert | Unterschied |
|---|---|---|
| ...sie ihre Komfortzone nicht verlassen wollen | 58 | +1 |
| ...sie Angst vor wirtschaftlichen/sozialen Konsequenzen haben | 58 | +6 |
| ...sie Angst vor dem Scheitern haben | 56 | +4 |
| ...sie keine Verantwortung übernehmen wollen | 50 | +2 |
| ...sie Angst vor Auseinandersetzung haben | 46 | +1 |
| ...sie negative Erfahrungen gemacht haben | 44 | +8 |
| ...sie nicht genügend Selbstvertrauen haben | 40 | −1 |
| ...sie es nicht gelernt haben | 33 | +4 |
| ...es zu viele Regeln gibt | 33 | +5 |
| ...Mitstreiter oder Verbündete fehlen | 31 | +1 |
| ...ein zu großes Sicherheitsbedürfnis vorherrscht | 27 | −4 |
| ...die allgemeine Anerkennung fehlt | 25 | +7 |
| ...ihnen Empathie und Mitgefühl fehlen | 21 | +1 |
| ...es nicht genügend Vorbilder gibt | 21 | +2 |

Wenn es darum geht, Hindernisse für mutiges Verhalten zu benennen, sind Ost- und West-deutsche nahezu einer Meinung. Allerdings stimmen mehr Bürger im Osten den jeweiligen Gründen zu. Dieses betrifft insbesondere negative Erfahrungen, fehlende Anerkennung sowie die Angst vor wirtschaftlichen und sozialen Konsequenzen. Dagegen ist ihre Zustimmung zum Hindernisgrund „großes Sicherheitsbedürfnis" weniger stark ausgeprägt.

Auch wenn die Bürger über Hindernisse für die Bevölkerung allgemein sprechen, fließen doch immer ihre eigenen Erfahrungen mit ein. Erfahrungen, die sie mit ihrem persönlichen, sozialen, ökonomischen und historischen Hintergrund gemacht haben und die ihre Wahr-nehmung für die Außenwelt prägten. Sichtweisen auf die Verhaltensweisen von anderen sind somit auch immer ein Spiegel der eigenen Lebenswelt und bieten Erklärungsansätze für Unterschiede bei den Antworten.

Die Nennungen der Ostdeutschen stehen direkt oder indirekt auch ein Vierteljahrhundert nach der Wiedervereinigung noch mit deren ökonomischen und sozialen Folgen in Verbindung. So sehen sie sehr viel stärker als ihre westdeutschen Mitbürger die negativen Erfahrungen als bedeutsame Hürde für Mut.

**Ostdeutsche bemängeln stereotype Vorstellungen und Vorurteile, die zu einer gehemmten – nicht nur finanziellen – Unterstützung für mutige Ideen und Konzepte führen, sowie eine rein negative Sichtweise auf Fehler oder Rückschläge.**

Je öfter diese Erfahrungen gemacht wurden, nicht nur persönlich, sondern auch im Bekannten- oder Freundeskreis, desto stärker sehen sie ein gesellschaftliches Klima der Desillusionierung und des Rückzugs in eine sichere Komfortzone. Laut eigenen Aussagen haben sie selbst vor allem im gesellschaftlichen und beruflichen Umfeld negative Erfahrungen gesammelt, indem ihnen zum Beispiel der Mut abgesprochen und ihnen mit Vorurteilen bezüglich ihrer Motivation, Leistungsbereitschaft und ihres Unternehmergeistes begegnet wurde und zum Teil noch immer wird.

In diesem Zusammenhang bemängeln sie auch die oft sehr eindimensionale Sichtweise auf Mut sowie die Fokussierung auf berufliche Leistung und Erfolg. Im Gegensatz dazu bedeutet Mut für viele Ostdeutsche im Kontext ihrer Familienbiografie die Bereitschaft und Fähigkeit, sich in relativ kurzer Zeit in eine Gesellschaft zu integrieren, die ihren bisherigen Lebenswelten widersprach. So mussten sie wirtschaftliche Veränderungen überwinden, auf soziale Absicherungen verzichten und ganze Lebensentwürfe verwerfen. Dabei haben sie versucht, ihre eigenen Verhaltensweisen und Gewohnheiten nicht völlig aufzugeben und couragiert neue Zukunftspläne zu entwerfen. Ausgehend von diesem mutigen Verhalten bedauern sie stärker als die Westdeutschen, dass die unterschiedlichen Formen von Mut zu wenig beachtet werden, vergangene Leistungen zu wenig gewürdigt und fehlende Anerkennung die Menschen entmutigt. Die positive Resonanz wird dabei nicht nur vom persönlichen Umfeld, sondern auch von gesellschaftlichen Institutionen eingefordert, indem zum Beispiel mutiges Verhalten sichtbarer gemacht wird.

Vor diesem Hintergrund wird auch die überdurchschnittliche Zustimmung der Ostdeutschen zu den Hindernisgründen Angst vor Konsequenzen und Angst vor dem Scheitern klar:

Wo die Familiengeschichten über Generationen erst von Repression und Anpassung und später von Arbeitsplatzverlust und sozialer Unsicherheit beeinflusst wurden, fällt es schwerer, mutige Vorhaben unvoreingenommen und angstfrei anzugehen. Die äußeren Zwänge, materiellen Nachteile und vorhandenen Vorurteile können sich dabei auch im Inneren manifestieren und Unsicherheiten verstärken.

Die geringere Zustimmung zum Aspekt des hohen Sicherheitsbedürfnisses findet seine Begründung ebenfalls in der historischen Biografie vieler Ostdeutscher. Insbesondere die ältere Bevölkerung mit ihrer Sozialisation in der Gesellschaft der DDR entwickelte ein besonderes Improvisationstalent. Sie lernte mit den vorhandenen materiellen Mängeln umzugehen und diese eigenständig und kreativ auszugleichen. Nach der Wende rückten neue Herausforderungen, wie die Suche nach Arbeitsplätzen, Notwendigkeit von Umschulungen oder Anerkennung von Qualifikationen, in den Vordergrund. Die Fähigkeit, mit diesen Veränderungen umzugehen, sowie die gesammelten Erfahrungen schützen sie zwar nicht vor der Angst des Scheiterns oder den weiter reichenden Folgen von mutigem Verhalten, jedoch stärkt es sie in dem Bewusstsein, sich auf die eigenen Strategien der Anpassung und Flexibilität zu verlassen und dem Sicherheitsbedürfnis eine geringere Bedeutung beizumessen als die Westdeutschen.

### d. Geringverdienende sehen negative Erfahrungen und fehlende Empathie, Besserverdienende zu großes Sicherheitsbedürfnis

*„Mut ist wie ein Muskel.*
*Je öfter du ihn benutzt,*
*desto stärker wird er"*

Ruth Gordon

## Gering- und Besserverdienende sehen unterschiedliche Hinderungsgründe

**Von je 100 befragten Besserverdienenden nennen folgende Gründe, weshalb viele Bürger nicht mutig sind: Weil …**

Unterschied zu Geringverdienenden in Prozentpunkten

| Grund | Wert | Unterschied |
|---|---|---|
| …sie ihre Komfortzone nicht verlassen wollen | 64 | +14 |
| …sie Angst vor dem Scheitern haben | 59 | +7 |
| …sie Angst vor wirtschaftlichen/sozialen Konsequenzen haben | 57 | +4 |
| …sie keine Verantwortung übernehmen wollen | 54 | +10 |
| …sie Angst vor Auseinandersetzung haben | 45 | −1 |
| …ein zu großes Sicherheitsbedürfnis vorherrscht | 42 | +5 |
| …sie nicht genügend Selbstvertrauen haben | 41 | +1 |
| …sie negative Erfahrungen gemacht haben | 34 | −9 |
| …sie es nicht gelernt haben | 32 | +2 |
| …es zu viele Regeln gibt | 30 | 0 |
| …Mitstreiter oder Verbündete fehlen | 29 | −2 |
| …ihnen Empathie und Mitgefühl fehlen | 19 | −9 |
| …es nicht genügend Vorbilder gibt | 18 | 0 |
| …die allgemeine Anerkennung fehlt | 17 | −6 |

Interessante Übereinstimmungen werden beim Vergleich des Alters und des Einkommens sichtbar. So nehmen die Besserverdienenden eine fast identische Schwerpunktsetzung wie die ältere Generation vor. Beide stimmen überdurchschnittlich oft den Hindernissen der Bequemlichkeit, der Sicherheit, der fehlenden Verantwortung und der Angst vor dem Scheitern zu. Und beide nehmen dabei für ihre eigene Bezugsgruppe und für sich selbst in Anspruch, sich von diesen Widerständen wenig beeinflussen zu lassen, sondern ordnen sie eher den „anderen" zu.

Während sich die Überlegungen der älteren Menschen vor allem vor dem Hintergrund ihres Alters, ihrer Erfahrungen und ihrer Wertevorstellungen erklären lassen, liegen die Gründe bei den Besserverdienenden hauptsächlich in ihrer monetären Ausgangslage und ihrer beruflichen Position. Dies erklärt auch zum großen Teil die Unterschiede zu den Geringverdienenden. Setzt man die Aussagen der finanziell Wohlsituierten in Zusammenhang mit ihren anderen Angaben, wie etwa zum persönlichen Mut, zeigen sich bestimmte Verhaltensweisen und Denkmuster. Ausgehend von ihren eigenen Erfahrungen sehen sie Herausforderungen nicht als Bedrohung oder Hürde, sondern als einen positiven Anreiz, um das eigene Potenzial voll ausschöpfen zu können und um sich der Außenwelt als eine entschlossene und mutige Person zu präsentieren.

Ihr Denken ist grundsätzlich eher optimistisch, zukunftsorientiert und entschlossen ausgerichtet und Mut zeigt sich bei ihnen hauptsächlich in der Realisierung von beruflichen und persönlichen Veränderungen. Dementsprechend vermissen sie bei ihren Mitbürgern Eigenschaften, die sie selbst als vielversprechend für das eigene Lebensglück wahrnehmen und auch realisieren. In der Folge bemängeln sie überdurchschnittlich oft eine vorhandene Bequemlichkeit, die dazu führt, Risiken aus dem Weg zu gehen und keinen Wagemut zu zeigen.

**Das hohe Sicherheitsdenken fokussiert sich nach Ansicht der Besserverdienenden zu sehr auf negative Konsequenzen und lässt viele Bürger zögerlich und ängstlich agieren, ohne die positiven Folgen von Courage und Veränderungen zu erkennen.**

In diesem Zusammenhang erklärt sich auch ihre Unzufriedenheit hinsichtlich fehlender Verantwortung. Selbst oftmals in leitenden Positionen tätig, ist die Übernahme von beruflicher Verantwortung für sie eine Selbstverständlichkeit oder auch eine reizvolle Herausforderung, der sie sich gerne stellen. Dementsprechend reagieren sie mit Unverständnis auf die mangelnde Bereitschaft hierzu. Dabei unterschätzen sie zuweilen ihre privilegierte Situation und übersehen die mangelnden finanziellen Ressourcen und den fehlenden Zugang zu Informationen und Netzwerken von anderen. So fokussieren sie sich in ihren Aussagen vor allem auf individuelle Hindernisse und vernachlässigen die Bedeutung bestimmter gesellschaftlicher Merkmale, wie etwa geringes Einkommen und geringerer Zugang zu Bildungsressourcen.

Mitbürger mit geringem Einkommen stimmen den oben genannten Gründen aufgrund dieser fehlenden Mittel in einem viel geringeren Maße zu. Überdurchschnittlich oft führen sie dagegen mangelnde Empathie und negative Erfahrungen als Argumente für fehlenden Mut an. Ähnlich wie viele Ostdeutsche und Frauen verbinden sie zudem gescheiterte Versuche des mutigen Handelns mit fehlender Unterstützung, Anerkennung sowie Vorurteilen. Bedingt durch ihre (berufliche) Lebenssituation tun sie sich deutlich schwerer, entschieden und optimistisch neue Pläne zu verfolgen. Wenn sich Optionen ergeben, haben sie vermehrt mit Enttäuschungen und Zurückweisungen zu rechnen. In diesem Zusammenhang weisen sie von allen Personengruppen auch die höchste Zustimmung zum Hindernis der fehlenden Empathie auf. Empathie bedeutet die Fähigkeit, sich in die Gefühle und Perspektiven von anderen Menschen hineinversetzen zu können, deren Bedürfnisse und auch Ängste zu verstehen. Der Mangel an Empathie kann, neben dem zwischenmenschlichen Bereich, auch die Gesellschaft als Ganzes beeinflussen.

**Geringverdienende meinen, dass mutigen Menschen oft nicht genügend Empathie entgegengebracht wird, ihre Entscheidungen und Pläne eher skeptisch und distanziert betrachtet werden und sie daher desillusioniert und enttäuscht werden.**

Dieser Mangel an Einfühlungsvermögen ist auch ein Grund dafür, warum manche Bürger nur auf ihre eigenen Sichtweisen und Interessen fokussiert sind. In der Folge sinkt die Motivation, andere Personen zu unterstützen oder sich für sie einzusetzen. Verbunden mit weiteren Motiven, wie Bequemlichkeit oder Angst vor Risiken, kann so ein gesellschaftliches Klima der Passivität entstehen, in der Zivilcourage als ein nicht notwendiges Wagnis angesehen wird, welches einen persönlich nicht betrifft. Insbesondere Bürger mit einem geringen Einkommen wünschen sich hier eine Stärkung der Empathie und eine mutige und entschlossene Solidarität für den Zusammenhalt der Gesellschaft.

### BEISPIEL FÜR MUT

**Die Ersthelfer und Feuerwehrleute, die nach den Terroranschlägen des 11. Septembers in New York tätig waren, zeigten großen Mut. Sie liefen inmitten der Trümmer und des Chaos in die einstürzenden Gebäude, um Menschen zu retten. Ihr selbstloser Einsatz und ihre Entschlossenheit zu helfen, inmitten einer der größten Katastrophen auf amerikanischem Boden, ist ein Paradebeispiel für den Mut und den Dienst am Nächsten in Gefahrensituationen.**

*„Es gibt keinen Mut ohne Angst,*
*aber wir müssen uns trotzdem trauen"*

Madeleine Albright

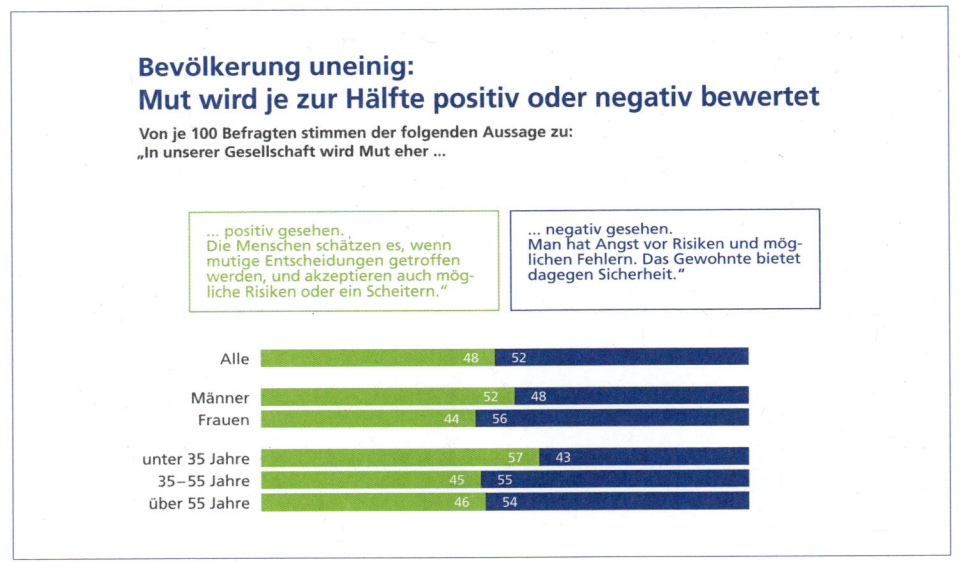

**Bevölkerung uneinig:**
**Mut wird je zur Hälfte positiv oder negativ bewertet**

Von je 100 Befragten stimmen der folgenden Aussage zu:
„In unserer Gesellschaft wird Mut eher ...

... positiv gesehen.
Die Menschen schätzen es, wenn mutige Entscheidungen getroffen werden, und akzeptieren auch mögliche Risiken oder ein Scheitern."

... negativ gesehen.
Man hat Angst vor Risiken und möglichen Fehlern. Das Gewohnte bietet dagegen Sicherheit."

| | positiv | negativ |
|---|---|---|
| Alle | 48 | 52 |
| Männer | 52 | 48 |
| Frauen | 44 | 56 |
| unter 35 Jahre | 57 | 43 |
| 35–55 Jahre | 45 | 55 |
| über 55 Jahre | 46 | 54 |

Wird Mut in der deutschen Gesellschaft positiv oder negativ gesehen? Die Bürger zeigen sich bei dieser Frage gespalten. Wie aus den anderen Fragestellungen ersichtlich wurde, erkennen die Menschen einerseits die positive Bedeutung von mutigen Verhaltensweisen, schätzen Entschlossenheit und Optimismus, glauben an die Bedeutung von Vorbildern und zeigen selbst in unterschiedlichen Situationen ihre Courage. Andererseits benennen sie aber auch zahlreiche Aspekte, die ein solches Verhalten behindern, seien sie nun individueller oder struktureller Natur. Diese reichen von einem mangelnden Selbstbewusstsein über fehlende Freiräume bis hin zu starren institutionellen Regularien. Nur die wenigsten Bürger äußern sich hierbei rein positiv oder rein negativ, sondern weisen eine differenzierte Einschätzung vor. Bei der Fragestellung zur allgemeinen gesellschaftlichen Bewertung von Mut zeigt sich, welche Motive für die Bürger eine größere Bedeutung haben, worin sich ihre jeweilige Wahrnehmung äußert und welche Faktoren diese beeinflussen.

**Gut jeder zweite Bürger ist überzeugt: Mut wird in unserer Gesellschaft eher negativ gesehen.**

Dieses trifft sowohl für den Einzelnen als auch für die öffentlichen und staatlichen Institutionen zu. Hinsichtlich der Institutionen werden besonders die politischen und wirtschaftlichen Bereiche als wenig mutig wahrgenommen. Beide sind von einem Klima gekennzeichnet, welches sich in besonderem Maße der Sicherheit und Stabilität verpflichtet fühlt. Risiken werden hierbei als Bedrohung gesehen, die wahlweise den Status quo, die Zuverlässigkeit, Beständigkeit oder die geregelten Strukturen gefährden. Im Bereich der Wirtschaft wird bei allzu mutigen oder schnellen Konzepten gern auf Begriffe wie „Gefährdung des Wohlstandes" als Gegenargument zurückgegriffen, während die Politik häufig von „Stabilität als oberste Prämisse" spricht, um unsichere Reformen abzulehnen. Es zeigt sich eine auf Sicherheit und Optimierung ausgerichtete Kultur. So müssen in allen Belangen Risikominimierungskonzepte zur Verfügung stehen, alles muss doppelt bedacht werden und das Ergebnis sollte möglichst bereits vorher feststehen. Dadurch werden Fehler vor allem negativ betrachtet, Wagnisse und Unsicherheiten abgelehnt und das Gewohnte als primäres Ziel angestrebt.

Hier weisen die Aussagen auch auf die Bedeutung von Strukturen hin, die das mutige Verhalten von Menschen hemmen. Dieses betrifft zum Beispiel die Diskriminierung von Minderheiten, die ungleiche Verteilung materieller und immaterieller Ressourcen und Geschlechterungleichheit. Stereotypisierungen und Benachteiligungen können den Mut der Betroffenen, sich für ihre Interessen, Ideen oder Pläne einzusetzen, beeinträchtigen und so das allgemeine Klima der Zurückhaltung verstärken.

Überall dort wo die Bürger wenig Bereitschaft für Mut erkennen lassen, werden stattdessen Sicherheit und Gewohnheit umso sichtbarer. Diese äußern sich nicht nur im zurückhaltenden Verhalten der politischen und wirtschaftlichen Führung, sondern auch in zahlreichen Gesetzgebungen, Regularien, Bestimmungen und Versicherungen. Die Bürger fühlen sich umgeben von einem sicheren Rahmen, der sie vor Unwägbarkeiten schützt, ihnen eine Richtung vorgibt und sie in ihrem persönlichen Verhalten hinsichtlich Mut und Entschlossenheit beeinflusst. So kann die strukturelle Absicherung zum Rückzug in die Komfortzone, Bevorzugung von Bequemlichkeit und Vermeidung von Herausforderungen führen. Sichtbar wird dieses Verhalten, wenn das soziale Umfeld sich zunehmend ins Private zurückzieht, ablehnend auf mutige Lebensentwürfe reagiert und Veränderungen als Störung oder Gefahr wahrnimmt. Als besonders bedauerlich empfunden werden hierbei ein zurückhaltendes gesellschaftliches Engagement und fehlende Zivilcourage.

Beeinflusst wird die Wahrnehmung einer auf Sicherheit bedachten Gesellschaft von einer Vielzahl komplexer Zusammenhänge und Aspekte, wie etwa der Persönlichkeit, dem Geschlecht, dem Alter, dem sozialen Umfeld, den individuellen Erfahrungen mit einem mutigen oder sicherheitsbestimmten Verhalten sowie der Prägung durch öffentliche oder private Strukturen und Institutionen (wie z. B. Erziehung, Schule, Medien). Diese Motive befinden sich in einem fortwährenden Austausch, prägen, beeinträchtigen und inspirieren sich gegenseitig. So können oftmals auch keine eindeutigen Ursachen für die jeweilige Wahrnehmung benannt werden, sondern es wird von komplexen wechselseitigen Einflüssen gesprochen, die die eigene Einschätzung und das gesellschaftliche Klima prägen.

Gleiches gilt auch für diejenigen, die eine positive Sichtweise auf den Mut in der deutschen Gesellschaft haben. Sie sprechen von einem optimistischen Klima, mit einer Wertschätzung für mutige Entscheidungen und einer Vielzahl von Möglichkeiten, um individuelle Lebensentwürfe zu realisieren. Sowohl das nähere soziale Umfeld als auch die öffentliche Meinung werden als entschlossen und zuversichtlich bezeichnet. Auch wenn Zögerlichkeit und ein starkes Sicherheitsbedürfnis nicht geleugnet werden, dominiert für sie ein allgemein unerschrockenes Bewusstsein. Im Besonderen wird dieses im persönlichen Lebens- und Berufsumfeld wahrgenommen und weniger innerhalb institutioneller Bereiche, wie etwa der Politik oder den Medien. Im privaten Bereich sprechen die Bürger von zahlreichen Beispielen, bei denen Freunde oder Familienmitglieder selbst mutig agieren oder Wagemut von anderen mit Hochachtung betrachten und unterstützen. Dabei kann es sich zum Beispiel um die Übernahme einer Führungsrolle in einer Gemeindegruppe, das Eintreten für eine gute Sache in den sozialen Medien, ziviles Engagement, Auslandsaufenthalte oder alternative Lebensentwürfe handeln. Diese sind oftmals Gegenstand offener und interessierter Diskussionen und werden in einer Feedbackkultur positiv bewertet. Im Berufssektor wird bei klein- und mittelständischen Unternehmen sowie in allen Formen der Selbstständigkeit ein mutiges Klima wahrgenommen. Vor allem bei Selbstständigen wird eine energiereiche Entschlossenheit, innovative Ideen, der Glaube an sich, die Überwindung von Widerständen oder finanzielle Investitionen genannt.

**Die Bürger sind sich sicher: Die mutige Überzeugung Einzelner wirkt inspirierend und motivierend auf deren Freunde, Familie, Kollegen oder Nachbarn. In der Folge bestärken diese wieder andere und sich gegenseitig in ihrer Zuversicht.**

Durch diese Wechselwirkung profitieren auch zunächst weniger wagemutige Menschen. Zudem kann ein mutiges Agieren in einem Lebensbereich auch einen anderen beeinflussen.

Beispielsweise kann eine berufliche Unerschrockenheit sich auf ein zivilcouragiertes Verhalten übertragen. Hilfreich ist hierbei ein förderndes und unterstützendes soziales Netzwerk. Hierdurch wird eine offene und lernende Gesellschaft gestärkt, in der Vielseitigkeit, Veränderungen, Fehler und Risiken positiv und als Möglichkeit zur Verbesserung gesehen werden.

Ungeachtet der positiven Wahrnehmung von Mut weisen die Aussagen auch auf mögliche Gefahren und Motive hin, die durch allzu mutiges Agieren geschwächt werden könnten. Dieses betrifft zum Beispiel bestimmte Personengruppen, die mehr auf Sicherheit und Stabilität bedacht sind und sich von einem sich stetig veränderten Klima überfordert fühlen. Hier können Ängste verstärkt und der Mut als solcher nur noch mit Leichtsinn, Überheblichkeit und Naivität in Verbindung gebracht werden.

Beim Vergleich der Bildungs- oder Einkommensgruppen lassen sich wie beim Familienstand oder Ost-West-Vergleich nur marginale Unterschiede feststellen. Lediglich beim Geschlecht und Alter sind abweichende Wahrnehmungen nachweisbar. So äußern Frauen eine höhere Zustimmung zu einer negativen Wahrnehmung von Mut in der Gesellschaft als Männer. Dieses kann unter anderem auf die erwähnten strukturellen Hemmnisse zurückgeführt werden. Stärker als Männer werden Frauen mit Rollenzuschreibungen, Vorurteilen und Zurückweisungen konfrontiert, sowohl im beruflichen als auch privaten Bereich. So nehmen sie ihr gesellschaftliches Umfeld starrer und sicherheitsorientierter wahr – stärker auf den Status quo fixiert als offen für Veränderungen. Engagierter als andere setzen Frauen sich zum Beispiel für eine bessere Vereinbarkeit von Beruf und Familie, für flachere Hierarchien oder weniger Geschlechterklischees ein. Ihr Engagement ist jedoch nur begrenzt erfolgreich und verstärkt so die weibliche Wahrnehmung einer wenig mutigen Gesellschaft.

Beim Alter weisen die unter 35-Jährigen eine überdurchschnittliche Zustimmung für die Wahrnehmung einer mutigen Gesellschaft auf. Dieses kann einerseits mit ihren (altersgemäß) fehlenden Erfahrungen erklärt werden, andererseits aber auch mit ihrer größeren Neugier, ihrem stärkeren Idealismus oder ihrer höheren Affinität gegenüber Weiterentwicklungen und Veränderungen. Sie handeln entschlossener, waghalsiger und scheuen weniger die Risiken. Oftmals befinden sie sich sowohl in beruflicher als auch privater Hinsicht noch in einer Orientierungsphase und streben danach, ihre Ideen und Lebensentwürfe auszuprobieren beziehungsweise zu realisieren. Umgeben von Gleichaltrigen erleben sie ihr eigenes Umfeld als energievoll und innovativ, wobei ihre Sicht auf die Außenwelt maßgeblich von der eigenen Einstellung beeinflusst wird. So übertragen die jungen Menschen ihre eigene

Perspektive auch auf die Gesellschaft als Ganzes und nehmen diese entsprechend mutiger wahr als der Rest der Bevölkerung. Dadurch können sie für andere eine wichtige Inspirationsquelle sein, wenn es darum geht, die Gesellschaft eigenverantwortlich mutiger zu gestalten.

### BEISPIEL FÜR MUT

Der Amerikaner James Shaw Jr. liefert ein Beispiel für mutiges Handeln in einer gefährlichen Situation. 2018 wurde er Zeuge eines bewaffneten Angriffs in einem Restaurant in Nashville, bei dem vier Personen getötet wurden. Shaw Jr. handelte wagemutig, indem er dem Täter entgegentrat, diesen entwaffnete und so weitere Tote oder Verletzte verhinderte. Diese Tat zeigt nicht nur seinen Mut, sondern auch seine Entschlossenheit, sich als Einzelner für Unbekannte einzusetzen, auch wenn dieses risikoreich und lebensgefährlich sein kann.

*„Das habe ich noch nie vorher versucht,*
*also bin ich völlig sicher, dass ich es schaffe"*

Pippi Langstrumpf

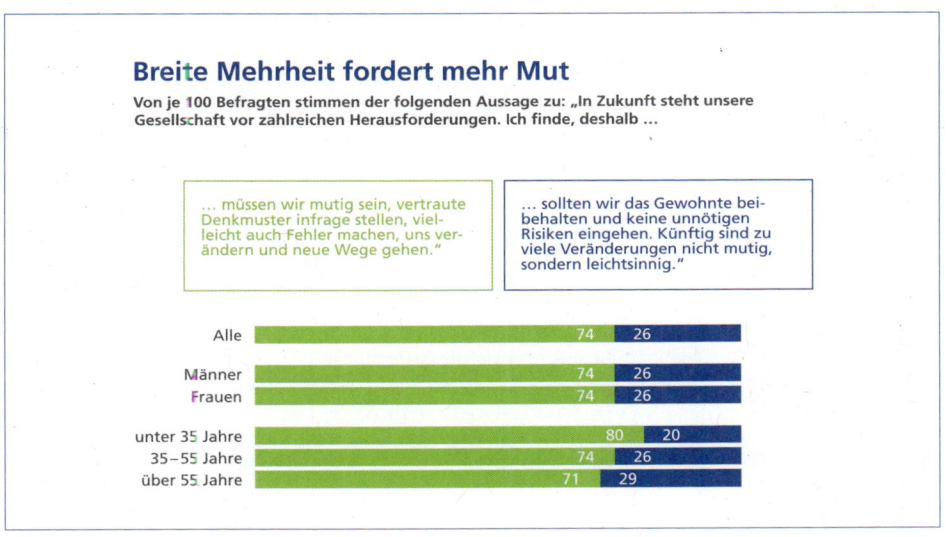

**Breite Mehrheit fordert mehr Mut**

Von je 100 Befragten stimmen der folgenden Aussage zu: „In Zukunft steht unsere Gesellschaft vor zahlreichen Herausforderungen. Ich finde, deshalb ...

... müssen wir mutig sein, vertraute Denkmuster infrage stellen, vielleicht auch Fehler machen, uns verändern und neue Wege gehen."

... sollten wir das Gewohnte beibehalten und keine unnötigen Risiken eingehen. Künftig sind zu viele Veränderungen nicht mutig, sondern leichtsinnig."

| | | |
|---|---|---|
| Alle | 74 | 26 |
| Männer | 74 | 26 |
| Frauen | 74 | 26 |
| unter 35 Jahre | 80 | 20 |
| 35–55 Jahre | 74 | 26 |
| über 55 Jahre | 71 | 29 |

Eine große Mehrheit ist sich einig: Die Herausforderungen der Zukunft lassen sich nur bewältigen, wenn die Gesellschaft bereit ist, alte Denkmuster zu hinterfragen und sich offen für mutige Veränderungen einzusetzen. Die Herausforderungen sind dabei sowohl auf nationaler als auch globaler Ebene zu suchen und werden Deutschland kurzfristig wie auch längerfristig beschäftigen. Hinsichtlich der nationalen Schwerpunkte benennen die Bürger Probleme wie zum Beispiel den oft zitierten Fachkräftemangel, die unsichere Energieversorgung, nötige Reformen des Bildungs- und Gesundheitswesens, die Stadt- beziehungsweise Wohnraumentwicklung, die Integration von Flüchtlingen und Migranten, die zunehmende soziale Spaltung, den demografischen Wandel, den Anstieg des politischen Extremismus, die Digitalisierung oder die schwankende Wettbewerbsfähigkeit und steigende Inflation. Im globalen Zusammenhang werden vor allem die europäische Integration, die internationale Sicherheit, kriegerische Auseinandersetzungen, die Ausbreitung von Pandemien sowie die Folgen der Erderwärmung hervorgehoben. Alle Herausforderungen zeichnen sich zweifellos durch eine hohe Komplexität aus und können nicht isoliert betrachtet werden. Sie alle sind miteinander verbunden und unterliegen ökonomischen, politischen und gesellschaftlichen Entwicklungen und Abhängigkeiten. Daher können diese auch nicht durch einfache politische Maßnahmen oder Gesetzgebungen gelöst werden. Stattdessen ist eine Vielzahl von Maßnahmen und Ansätzen notwendig, um konstruktive und nachhaltige Lösungswege aufzuzeigen. Die meisten Bürger sind sich dieser Komplexität bewusst und erkennen, dass nicht nur strukturelle Hindernisse überwunden werden müssen, sondern alle Bürger gefordert sind, ihr eigenes Denken und Verhalten zu reflektieren. Hier rückt die Bedeutung des Mutes in den Mittelpunkt, da dieser als eine unverzichtbare Voraussetzung angesehen wird, um sich den zukünftigen Herausforderungen zu stellen.

Mut ist für die Bürger in diesem Fall nicht nur eine Charaktereigenschaft unter vielen, sondern eine zentrale Voraussetzung der individuellen und gesellschaftlichen Entwicklung. Mut zeigt sich hierbei in den unterschiedlichsten Formen, umfasst immer den sozialen Austausch mit anderen, betrifft nicht nur den mutig Agierenden, sondern oftmals auch sein soziales Umfeld, die breitere Öffentlichkeit oder sogar die gesamte Gesellschaft. Und immer zieht er eine Veränderung nach sich, schafft neue Konstellationen und Perspektiven.

**Durch zukünftige Herausforderungen werden die Bürger Veränderungen erleben, Modifizierungen annehmen und sich auf neue Verhältnisse einstellen müssen.**

Um diese nicht nur passiv über sich ergehen zu lassen, sondern sie aktiv mitzugestalten, wird der Mut als bedeutsame Eigenschaft gesehen. Auch werden alte Denkmuster nur bedingt in der Lage sein, zukünftige Probleme zu lösen oder überhaupt zu erfassen. Gewohnte Sichtweisen – egal ob vom Einzelnen oder einer Gruppe, egal ob sie nun institutionelle Strukturen oder das soziale Klima betreffen – neigen dazu, Bedenken in den Vordergrund zu stellen und Chancen zu negieren. Im persönlichen Bereich kann dieses deutlich werden, wenn schon früh jugendliches Aufbegehren gegen Autoritäten von den Eltern mit dem Hinweis auf mögliche Sanktionen gebremst wird, Studien- oder Berufswünsche mit dem Risiko von mangelnden Karrierechancen abgewertet oder Auszeiten/Auslandsaufenthalte mit Nachteilen bei der Rentenzahlung missbilligt werden. Später können althergebrachte Einstellungen, wie ein erhöhtes Sicherheitsbedürfnis oder Bequemlichkeit, dazu führen, sich in die gewohnte Komfortzone zurückzuziehen und Wagnisse abzulehnen, egal ob bei privaten oder beruflichen Entscheidungen. In Unternehmen und Institutionen, etwa in Arbeitsprozessen oder bei Handlungen von Entscheidungsträgern, kann die Fokussierung auf Eigennutz, auf festgefahrene Strukturen und starre Traditionen dazu führen, innovative

Ideen, alternative Konzepte oder zukunftsweisende Reformen als Gefahr für den Status quo zu betrachten. Das stete Bedenken von möglichen Risiken, das zaudernde Abwarten, das vorsichtige Rückversichern bieten vordergründig das Bild von Sicherheit und Vernunft, umfassen aber eben auch fehlende Zuversicht, fehlendes Selbstvertrauen und fehlende Visionsfähigkeit. Hinsichtlich der großen Zustimmung zum gesellschaftlichen Mut zeigen sich innerhalb der einzelnen Gruppierungen kaum Differenzen. Lediglich die jüngere Generation zeigt mit 80 Prozent überdurchschnittliche Zustimmung. Wie schon bei anderen Fragestellungen deutlich wurde, zeigen sie sich auch hier offener, neugieriger und risikobereiter. Entsprechend des eigenen Verhaltens wünschen und fordern sie dieses auch stärker von der Gesellschaft. Zudem betreffen und beeinflussen die zukünftigen Herausforderungen, zum Beispiel in der Bildung (mehr Digitalisierung), Arbeit (bessere Vereinbarkeit von Beruf und Familie) oder beim Klimawandel (mehr Nachhaltigkeit) die jungen Menschen im besonderen Maße, weshalb sie sich für neue Wege und Denkweisen aussprechen. In Zusammenhang mit der mehrheitlichen Zustimmung zu mutigen Veränderungen steht auch die Kritik an einer Fehlerkultur, die als zu starr und negativ besetzt empfunden wird. In ihrer sichtbarsten Ausprägung zeigt sie sich im gegenwärtigen Trend zur Optimierung, der scheinbar zielorientiert und effektiv aufgerichtet ist. Wo aber Fehler oder Rückschläge nicht vorgesehen sind, wird Optimierung zum Zwang und hemmt in der Folge mutige Entscheidungen aus Angst vor Misserfolgen. Dieses bestätigt sich auch in der kritischen Sichtweise auf die zunehmende Optimierung von über zwei Dritteln der Bevölkerung.

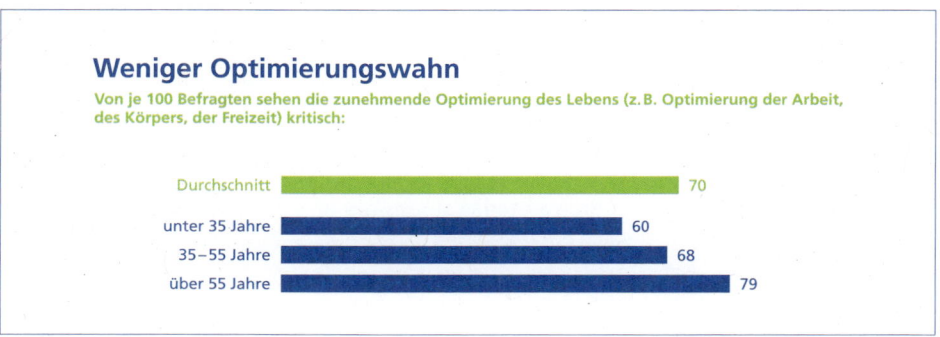

**Weniger Optimierungswahn**

Von je 100 Befragten sehen die zunehmende Optimierung des Lebens (z.B. Optimierung der Arbeit, des Körpers, der Freizeit) kritisch:

| | |
|---|---|
| Durchschnitt | 70 |
| unter 35 Jahre | 60 |
| 35–55 Jahre | 68 |
| über 55 Jahre | 79 |

Der Suchbegriff „Optimiere dein Leben" liefert bei Google etwa 27 Millionen Einträge. Die Themen reichen von Ernährung- und Karriere- über Dating- und Sporttipps bis hin zu Themen wie Zeitmanagement oder Achtsamkeit. Die Optimierung betrifft alle Bereiche der Gesellschaft und geht in ihrer ausgeprägten Form auch mit Risiken einher. Im Bereich der Freizeit kann zum Beispiel die Suche nach den effektivsten Aktivitäten zu einem Gefühl der Überlastung und Erschöpfung führen, verbunden mit fehlender Entspannung und Muße. Hinsichtlich der körperlichen Optimierung sind Tendenzen zur perfekten Fitness und Schönheit kritisch zu hinterfragen, können sie doch zum Verlust der eigenen Körperakzeptanz und einseitigen Schönheitsidealen führen. Im beruflichen Sektor können eine ständige Optimierung und damit verbundene Leistungssteigerung zu verstärkter Konkurrenz, Misstrauen und Neid führen, zu einer erhöhten Burn-out-Gefahr sowie einer schlechteren Vereinbarkeit von Arbeit und Freizeit.

Allen Optimierungstendenzen gemeinsam ist die Gefahr einer Orientierung an fremdbestimmten, äußeren Idealen und Anforderungen, die zu einer Selbstdisziplinierung führt, an deren Ende die innere Unzufriedenheit sowie der Verlust von Diversität und Individualität stehen. Auch besteht das Risiko, sich nicht mehr mutig zu verhalten, da die damit verbundenen Ungewissheiten nicht in einer Nutzen-Risiko-Rechnung optimal kalkuliert werden können. Hinsichtlich der Unterschiede innerhalb der Bevölkerung äußert sich die ältere Generation deutlich kritischer. Sie haben den Großteil ihres Lebens in einer Zeit gelebt, in der der Fokus nicht so stark auf Optimierung und Leistung lag wie gegenwärtig. So wird die Idee einer ständigen Optimierung des Lebens von ihnen als zu oberflächlich und starr empfunden. Aufgrund ihrer Lebenserfahrungen und ihres Alters sind sie zudem Modeerscheinungen und Trends gegenüber weniger anfällig und wissen, das Leben ist nicht immer perfekt oder vorhersehbar. Zum Tragen kommen in ihrer kritischen Einschätzung zudem auch vorhandene Nachteile gegenüber der jüngeren Generation, zum Beispiel hinsichtlich der körperlichen Belastbarkeit oder der Nutzung von technischen Möglichkeiten, die ihnen die Anpassung an die Optimierung erschweren.

Die Jüngeren sind dagegen anfälliger für Gruppenzwänge, Modeerscheinungen sowie Trends und können sich nicht immer den Anforderungen durch die Optimierung entziehen. Dennoch sieht auch die Mehrheit von ihnen die zunehmende Optimierung des Lebens kritisch, wobei sie insbesondere Social-Media-Plattformen für diesen Trend verantwortlich machen, da man sich dort möglichst perfekt zu inszenieren versucht.

**Gerade im Zusammenhang mit Herausforderungen, die das soziale Miteinander der Gesellschaft betreffen, sei es nun im persönlichen oder beruflichen Bereich, wünschen sich Junge wie Alte ein Ende der zunehmenden Optimierung und stattdessen eine konstruktive Fehlerkultur, in der Fehler als Chance des Lernens und der Verbesserung gesehen werden.**

Diese Kultur zeichnet sich durch eine offene Kommunikation, Lernorientierung, Unterstützung und kooperative Lösungsorientierung aus. Vermieden werden sollen dagegen demotivierende Strukturen, einseitige Schuldzuweisungen und Sanktionen.

Für die Bürger trägt ein mutiges gesellschaftliches Klima dazu bei, die eigenen Perspektiven zu erweitern, die Motivation und das Verantwortungsgefühl zu stärken, sich persönlichen Herausforderungen zu stellen und sich mutig mit zukünftigen gesellschaftlichen Anforderungen auseinanderzusetzen. Zudem unterstützt und verpflichtet ein mutiges gesellschaftliches Klima auch die institutionellen Organisationen und die politische sowie wirtschaftliche Führung darin, sich stärker von partikulären Interessen zu lösen, offener zu denken, innovativer zu agieren und mutige Entscheidungen zu treffen. In ihrer wechselseitigen Einflussnahme könnten so alle Bürger die Gesellschaft zuversichtlich und unerschrocken mitgestalten und prägen.

## BEISPIEL FÜR MUT

**Steve Jobs war bereit, für seine Träume und Visionen Risiken einzugehen. Er ließ sich weder von den skeptischen Meinungen anderer beeinflussen noch durch Ablehnung durch die Branche entmutigen. Stattdessen hat er an sich und seine Ideen geglaubt und so die Computerbranche revolutioniert. Mit der Einführung des Apple-Macintosh-Computers, des iPods, des iPads oder des iPhones hat er es geschafft, elektronische Geräte einfach und intuitiv zu gestalten. Jobs hat auch nicht gezögert, das Unternehmen zwischendurch zu verlassen, als es sich in eine Richtung entwickelte, die er für falsch hielt. Seine Entschlossenheit und sein Mut zum Risiko haben ihm geholfen, große Erfolge zu erzielen und einen bleibenden Einfluss in der Technologiebranche zu hinterlassen.**

# VII. FAZIT

> *„Man muss mutig sein,*
> *um glücklich zu sein"*
> Anne Frank

*German Mut* statt *German Angst*, so lautet der Titel dieses Buches. Nach der Auswertung aller Interviews, Daten und Forschungsergebnisse kann dieser Apell nur unterstrichen werden. Der allgemein vorherrschenden Einschätzung, Deutschland sei von einer *German Angst* geprägt, ja teilweise fast gelähmt, können zahlreiche positive und hoffnungsvolle Fakten, Einstellungen und Beispiele entgegengestellt werden. Deutlich geworden sind aber auch die Herausforderungen, Hindernisse und notwendigen Voraussetzungen, die konstruktiv und kreativ angegangen werden sollten.

## KERNERGEBNISSE
**Es gibt ...**
**... überwiegend positive Assoziationen mit dem Begriff „Mut".**
**... einen ausgeprägten Wunsch nach mutigen Vorbildern.**
**... ein entschlossenes Engagement für mutiges Handeln im Familien- und Freundeskreis.**
**... eine starke Beeinträchtigung des Mutes durch Bequemlichkeit und Unsicherheiten.**
**... eine gespaltene Wahrnehmung zur gesellschaftlichen Einstellung gegenüber Mut.**
**... eine Wertschätzung des Mutes für zukünftige Herausforderungen.**

Entgegen der oft zitierten *German Angst* wird das Potenzial von *German Mut* deutlich. Der Begriff „Potenzial", vom lateinischen „potentia", bedeutet so viel wie Macht, Kraft, Leistung, Einfluss, Fähigkeit oder Vermögen und beinhaltet die Option, etwas zu erreichen und vorhandene Möglichkeiten auszuschöpfen, ohne dabei auf Kosten von Gesundheit oder emotionaler Balance den Optimierungstendenzen zu verfallen. Dieses Potenzial zeigt sich in der mutigen Grundhaltung bei der großen Mehrheit der Bürger, die bisher jedoch durch innere und äußere Hemmnisse oftmals in der Praxis nicht zum Tragen kommt. Mut wird mit Personen verbunden, die selbst- und verantwortungsbewusst sind, beherzt für ihre Werte einstehen und bereit sind, innere und äußere Widerstände zu überwinden. Diese Vorstellung deckt sich mit dem Wunsch nach mutigen Vorbildern, von denen die Deutschen sich eine Inspiration für ihre eigene Lebensführung erhoffen. Diese Role Models wünschen sich die Bundesbürger aus dem engeren Familienumfeld oder der eigenen Lebenswelt ebenso wie aus der Politik und dem Feld ihrer Mitbürger allgemein. Von Vorbildern aus diesen Gruppen kann eine starke Signalwirkung für die Gesellschaft ausgehen, in der dann alle Bürger Verantwortung übernehmen und mutig agieren. Allerdings wird diese Sehnsucht in der Realität oft enttäuscht, da keine der genannten Personen oder Gruppen die in sie gesetzten Hoffnungen derzeit erfüllt.

Hinsichtlich eines eigenen couragierten Verhaltens wird dieses vor allem im privaten Bereich, beim Engagement für Familie und Freunde und beim Einstehen für die eigene Überzeugung deutlich. Abgesehen davon lassen die Zahlen und Aussagen insgesamt auf eine eher zurückhaltende idealistische Entschlossenheit in der Praxis schließen. Die Gründe hierfür liegen in individuellen Befindlichkeiten wie auch institutionellen und gesellschaftlichen Strukturen begründet die sich gegenseitig beeinflussen und verstärken. Die Hindernisse reichen von Bequemlichkeit, mangelndem Selbstvertrauen und Verantwortungsbewusstsein über Versagens- und Konfliktängste bis hin zu einschränkenden Strukturen wie zu viele Regularien, zu wenig Anerkennung, eine vorherrschende Fehlerkultur oder ausbleibende Unterstützung. Diese Hemmnisse zeigen sich auch in einem gesellschaftlichen Bewusstsein und Klima, welches von den Bürgern unterschiedlich wahrgenommen wird. Etwa jeweils die Hälfte geht von einer positiven beziehungsweise negativen Bewertung des Mut-Verständnisses in der Gesellschaft aus. Dagegen ist sich die Bevölkerung bei der Bedeutung von Mut für zukünftige nationale und globale Herausforderungen und furchtloses Denken und Handeln weitestgehend einig. Für die große Mehrheit ist Mut ein unabdingbares Attribut für eine konstruktive Gestaltung der Gesellschaft. Besonders die beiden letztgenannten Aussagen zeigen den Widerspruch zwischen der theoretischen Überzeugung und dem Realitätscheck auf. So ist eine große Mehrheit von der positiven und innovativen Kraft des Mutes überzeugt und erkennt die Wichtigkeit von mutigen Vorbildern und die hohe Bedeutung von Mut sowohl für die persönliche Entwicklung als auch für die der Gesellschaft. In der Praxis sehen sie dagegen nur wenig Gelegenheiten für mutiges Verhalten, engagieren sich selbst vornehmlich innerhalb des engen sozialen Umfeldes, klagen über mangelnde furchtlose Vorbilder, sind von ihren Mitbürgern bezüglich eines entschlossenen Vorgehens oftmals enttäuscht und auch die Gesamtgesellschaft wird von vielen als zu sicherheitsorientiert angesehen.

Die Analyse einzelner Bevölkerungsgruppen weist einerseits auf strukturelle Hemmnisse hin, andererseits werden aber auch scheinbare Selbstverständlichkeiten widerlegt. Hindernisse finden sich in den Bereichen Arbeits- und Leitungsstrukturen, materielle Ungleichheit, fehlende Anerkennung und Diskriminierungen wieder. Diese betreffen besonders Geringverdienende, Frauen sowie Ostdeutsche und halten sie davon ab, selbstbewusster und mutiger zu agieren. Aber auch Besserverdienende bemängeln bestimmte berufliche Konstellationen sowie Rahmenbedingungen, die innovative und ungewöhnliche Ideen behindern. Hier zeigen sich für alle Entscheidungsträger vielfältige Möglichkeiten auf, diese

Barrieren und Vorurteile zugunsten größerer Freiräume und Gerechtigkeit zu reduzieren. Die scheinbaren Selbstverständlichkeiten betreffen vor allem die ältere Generation hinsichtlich ihrer Wahrnehmung von Mut und Sicherheit. So wird ihnen oftmals ein höheres Sicherheitsbedürfnis, eine höhere Affinität zum Status quo sowie eine eher ablehnende Haltung zu Neuerungen und Risiken zugesprochen. Diese Einschätzung lässt sich so jedoch nicht bestätigen. Zwar zeigen sich viele Ältere zurückhaltender gegenüber neuen Trends und Entwicklungen, sind weniger risikofreudig und schätzen manche vergangenen Verhältnisse und Verhaltensweisen positiver als aktuelle ein, jedoch bewerten sie Mut insgesamt nicht geringer als andere. Im Gegenteil, aufgrund ihres Alters, ihrer Erfahrungen und ihrer Sozialisation hatten sie öfter in ihrem Leben mit Widerständen zu kämpfen und mussten sich stärker gegen Autoritäten und Traditionen behaupten. Sie haben gelernt, selbstbewusst und optimistisch zu agieren, Verantwortung zu übernehmen und für ihre Überzeugung einzustehen. Auf Grundlage dieser Erfahrungen vermissen sie von ihren Mitbürgern ein beherztes Engagement und Courage und äußern den Vorsatz, sich auch zukünftig selbst mutig zu verhalten.

Die hohe Zustimmung der Bundesbürger zur Notwendigkeit von Mut und Zuversicht für die Bewältigung zukünftiger Herausforderungen wird auch bei der Fragestellung zum eigenen Optimismus deutlich. So wollen in etwa drei Viertel der Bevölkerung in den kommenden zwölf Monaten optimistischer denken. Optimismus kann hierbei als positive Haltung oder Lebenseinstellung definiert werden, die auf zukünftige Ereignisse ausgerichtet ist. Unabhängig von den Inhalten ist man von einer Entwicklung zum Besseren überzeugt. Geprägt wird diese Grundhaltung von der familiären Situation (Erziehung, elterliches Verhalten, häusliche Umgebung, materielle Umstände) sowie weiterer Sozialisationseinflüssen (Schule, Arbeitswelt, Peer-Groups).

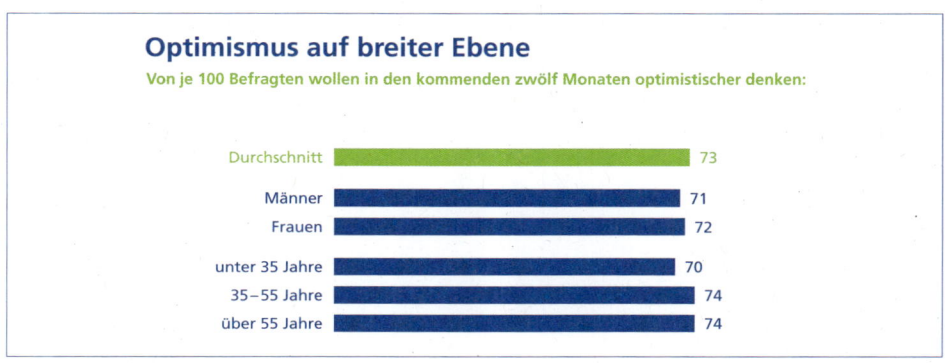

**Optimismus auf breiter Ebene**

Von je 100 Befragten wollen in den kommenden zwölf Monaten optimistischer denken:

| | |
|---|---|
| Durchschnitt | 73 |
| Männer | 71 |
| Frauen | 72 |
| unter 35 Jahre | 70 |
| 35–55 Jahre | 74 |
| über 55 Jahre | 74 |

**Optimismus kann verstärkt, gefördert, behindert und erlernt werden.**

Im privaten Bereich kann Optimismus dazu beitragen, die psychische und emotionale Gesundheit zu stärken und ein Gefühl der Hoffnung und Zuversicht zu entwickeln. Das Positive wird in den Vordergrund gestellt, wohingegen Ablehnungen und Hemmnisse an Bedeutung verlieren. Sowohl im Alltag als auch bei außergewöhnlichen Ereignissen oder in Krisensituationen (Krankheit, Konflikte, Verluste, Misserfolge etc.) hilft positives Denken, Stress zu reduzieren, Rückschläge zu überwinden und sich auf Möglichkeiten und Chancen zu konzentrieren.

Die Bürger äußern das Bestreben, Optimismus stärker verinnerlichen zu wollen und sich weniger auf Hindernisse und Unsicherheiten zu konzentrieren. Dieses betrifft auch den beruflichen und gesellschaftlichen Bereich. Hier nehmen sie sich vor, Widerstände zu überwinden, Herausforderungen anzunehmen und den persönlichen Fokus weniger auf Missstände, Ärgernisse und Probleme zu richten. Konkret werden dabei im Beruf eine Verbesserung des Arbeitsklimas, Karrierebestrebungen und günstigere Arbeitsbedingungen genannt. Auch möchten viele sich intensiver und ernsthafter mit Lebensträumen beschäftigen, vielleicht einmal eine Auszeit nehmen, einen Auslandaufenthalt oder eine längere Urlaubsreise realisieren. Im gesellschaftlichen Zusammenhang möchte sich die große Mehrheit optimistischer gegenüber Herausforderungen zeigen, diese angehen, selbst gestalten und zuversichtlich agieren. Annähernd drei Viertel (72 %) wollen zudem weniger kritisieren und stattdessen toleranter agieren, mehr anerkennen und unterstützen.

Als mögliche Handlungsfelder werden in diesem Zusammenhang die Nachbarschaft oder ein Ehrenamt genannt. Besonders im zwischenmenschlichen Miteinander erhoffen sich die Bürger dadurch eine bessere Gemeinschaft, weniger Egoismus und mehr Zusammenhalt. Dieses weist auch auf eine weitere Auswirkung von Optimismus hin: Optimismus hat nicht nur für das Individuum eine große Bedeutung, sondern verstärkt auch die sozialen Bindungen, Interaktionen und das Gemeinschaftsgefühl. Die einzelnen Mitglieder erfahren und zeigen mehr Interesse, Unterstützung, Motivation und Inspiration. Kurzum: Optimismus ist ansteckend.

**Auch wenn die Bürger unterschiedliche Strategien anwenden, um optimistischer denken und agieren zu können, sie eint der Wunsch nach Optimismus und das Bemühen, mehr Gelegenheiten zu ergreifen, um positive Erfahrungen machen zu können.**

Optimismus kann nicht nur erlernt, sondern durch positives Erleben auch gestärkt und weiterentwickelt werden. Je öfter die Erfahrung gemacht wird, dass eine positive Einstellung dabei helfen kann, Ziele zu erreichen, desto mehr steigert sich das Selbstwertgefühl und neue Herausforderungen werden zuversichtlicher angenommen. Die Bürger möchten ihre soziale Lebenswelt erweitern, um Inspiration und Motivation von anderen zu erhalten. Sie erhoffen sich ein Unterstützungssystem über den Freundes- und Familienkreis hinaus. Dieses können zum Beispiel Gleichgesinnte mit gemeinsamen Interessen, Vereinsmitglieder, Nachbarn, aber auch Fremde sein, die ihnen ein Vorbild an Motivation und Zuversicht bieten und die sie selbst auch mit ihrem Optimismus ermuntern können. Entsprechend wünschen sich beispielsweise neun von zehn Bundesbürgern (89 %) eine Nachbarschaft, in der man sich gegenseitig hilft und die sich auch in schwierigen Situationen optimistisch zeigt. Fast alle Bürger wollen ihre gedanklichen Perspektiven erweitern, indem sie gegenteilige Überzeugungen oder Lebensentwürfe nicht verurteilen, sondern auch als Möglichkeit zur Reflexion annehmen und positive Aspekte hierin erkennen. Die Bedeutung der Reflexion wird auch im Zusammenhang mit der Öffentlichkeit und den Medien sichtbar. So bedauern es viele Bürger, wie sehr ihre eigene Wahrnehmung von den Medien beeinflusst wird, die ihren Fokus häufig auf eine eher negative Berichterstattung legen.

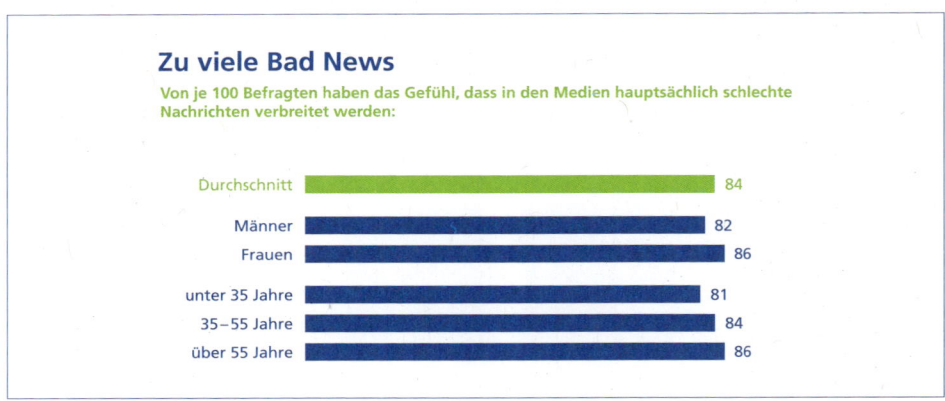

So sind aktuell mehr als acht von zehn Bundesbürgern davon überzeugt, in den Nachrichten überwiegend negative Schlagzeilen zu sehen, zu hören oder zu lesen. Innerhalb der Bevölkerung herrscht dabei weitestgehend Einigkeit und das Geschlecht, der Wohnort, das Einkommen, der Bildungshintergrund oder das Alter spielen kaum eine Rolle.

„Only bad news are good news" ist ein bekannter Satz aus der Medienbranche. Schlechte Neuigkeiten verkaufen sich dieser Annahme nach besser als gute und erreichen häufig schneller die Aufmerksamkeit der Bevölkerung. Der Inhalt der Nachrichten ist dabei nicht entscheidend und kann von wirtschaftlichen Abschwüngen über Naturkatastrophen bis hin zu persönlichen Tragödien oder Verfehlungen reichen. Auch wenn so manche schlechte Nachricht durchaus positive Auswirkungen haben kann (z. B. als Warnung dienend oder zur Anregung von Maßnahmen, um eine Verbesserung zu erreichen), so gehen Bad News fast immer mit negativen Folgen einher. Eine der gravierendsten ist der emotionale Tribut, den sie bei vielen Bürgern fordern können. Wenn sich die meisten Berichte um Kriege, Rezessionen, Klimakatastrophen, politische Verfehlungen, Skandale oder Spaltungen drehen, entsteht oftmals ein Gefühl der Angst und der Hoffnungslosigkeit. Auch können zu viele schlechte Nachrichten den Vertrauensverlust in Politiker und Institutionen verstärken und eine resignative Abwehrhaltung fördern. Diese Sichtweise erschwert es, Probleme auf konstruktive Weise anzugehen.

**Die Bürger möchten keine geschönten Nachrichten, doch vermissen sie Informationen, Reportagen, Berichte und Erzählungen, die von zuversichtlichen Entwicklungen, nachhaltigen Erfolgen, optimistischen Konzepten oder Praktiken sprechen.**

Neben den Medien üben auch andere Parameter einen Einfluss auf eine optimistische oder pessimistische Grundhaltung aus, wie schwierige Lebensverhältnisse (z. B. materielle Mängel, Arbeitslosigkeit), strukturelle Ungleichheit (z. B. Diskriminierung) und instabile wirtschaftliche oder politische Verhältnisse. So ist der Vorsatz zu mehr individuellem Optimismus auch vor dem Hintergrund der gesellschaftlichen Herausforderungen der vergangenen Jahre (Pandemie, Ukrainekrieg oder Inflation) zu sehen.

Fortschritte in der Wissenschaft und Technologie, wirtschaftliche Entwicklungen und Trends, politische Entscheidungen und demografische Entwicklungen sind treibende Kräfte für Veränderungen in der Gesellschaft. Aber die tatsächliche Umsetzung liegt aber auch bei jedem Einzelnen, indem er mit Mut und Zuversicht das gesellschaftliche Klima mitgestaltet. Mut ist dabei nicht nur eine Eigenschaft, sondern zeigt sich in den unterschiedlichsten Facetten: So bezieht sich *moralischer Mut* auf die Fähigkeit, für Überzeugungen und Werte einzustehen, auch wenn diese nicht populär sind. *Emotionaler Mut* wird sichtbar, wenn man Verletzungen oder Verluste überwindet. Beim *physischen Mut* begibt man sich in gefährliche Situationen, um sich selbst oder andere zu schützen, während *kreativer Mut* beim Verfolgen innovativer Ideen zum Tragen kommt. *Selbstreflexiver Mut* bezieht sich auf die Fähigkeit, Fehler zu machen, zu akzeptieren und daraus zu lernen. *Kultureller Mut* hinterfragt Werte und Normen. *Intellektueller Mut* scheut sich nicht vor neuen Ideen und Reflexion, auch wenn sie dem bisherigen Wissen widersprechen, und *sozialer Mut* kommt in zwischenmenschlichen Situationen zum Vorschein, wenn er Interaktionen initiiert und sich für die Rechte anderer einsetzt.

Zweifellos gibt es keine einfache Antwort darauf, was notwendig ist, damit die deutsche Gesellschaft mutiger wird. Jedoch zeigen sich zahlreiche Maßnahmen und Möglichkeiten, die helfen können, den Mut innerhalb einer Gesellschaft zu fördern und das vorhandene Potenzial zu stärken.

1. Erziehung und Bildung: Beide gehören ohne Frage zu den wirksamsten Instrumenten zur Förderung von Mut. Schon früh können das Selbstbewusstsein und die soziale Intelligenz in Familien und Kindergärten gestärkt werden. Später sollte in der Schule kritisches Denken gefördert werden, um so die Perspektiven der Schüler zu erweitern und sie zu couragierten eigenverantwortlichen Projekten zu ermutigen. Universitäten und Hochschulen könnten zudem Mut als eine der Schlüsselkompetenzen in ihre Curricula aufnehmen.

2. Ermutigung zu offenem Dialog und Diskussion: Die Möglichkeit und die Förderung eines offenen Dialogs können dem Einzelnen helfen, seine Ängste und Sorgen mitzuteilen, diese zu überwinden, anderen Perspektiven, Denk- und Verhaltensweisen zu begegnen und eigene Vorurteile zu hinterfragen.

3. Förderung von Solidarität und gesellschaftlichem Engagement: Unterstützung und Anerkennung von gemeinnützigen Projekten, Ehrenamt und Freiwilligenarbeit, die Menschen dazu ermutigen, sich für die Gemeinschaft einzusetzen und andere zu unterstützen. Ein Schwerpunkt könnte hierbei auf der Ansprache von jungen Menschen liegen, denen man vermehrt Freiräume und Entscheidungsmöglichkeiten zur Verfügung stellt, um ihre Zukunft aktiv gestalten zu können.

4. Mehr Medienkompetenz und Good News: Nur mit ausreichender Medienkompetenz ist man in der Lage, die erhaltenen Informationen und deren Entstehung einzuordnen und kritisch zu hinterfragen. Hierdurch reduziert sich des Weiteren die Angst vor der scheinbaren Manipulation durch die Medien. Darüber hinaus ist eine stärkere Sichtbarmachung von positiven Nachrichten zu empfehlen, um eine allgemeine zuversichtliche Grundhaltung zu stärken.

5. Förderung der politischen Partizipation: Die Ermutigung zur aktiven Gestaltung der Gesellschaft, sei es durch Wahlen, auf Online-Plattformen, in Bürgerforen oder durch Mitgliedschaften in politischen Organisationen oder NGOs, kann dazu beitragen, die Eigenverantwortung des Einzelnen zu stärken und Gefühle der Hilflosigkeit und Ohnmacht abzubauen. Bürger müssen die Gewissheit haben, dass ihre Meinungen und Bedürfnisse Gehör finden und sie an Entscheidungen beteiligt werden.

6. Förderung von Unternehmertum und Innovation: Einrichtung von Förderprogrammen und Ressourcen, die Unternehmer und Innovatoren unterstützen, neue und mutige Ideen und Geschäftsmodelle zu entwickeln.

7. Schaffung von offenen Arbeitsbedingungen: Entwicklung von Programmen und Maßnahmen, die Unternehmen und Arbeitgeber ermutigen, attraktive und fördernde Entfaltungsmöglichkeiten für ihre Angestellten zu schaffen und diesen dadurch mehr Raum für mutige Ideen und selbstverantwortliches Arbeiten zu bieten.

8. Führungsrolle: Eine entschlossene, zuversichtliche und inspirierende Führung, sei sie politisch, wirtschaftlich, wissenschaftlich, gesellschaftlich oder medial, kann dazu beitragen, dass eine Gesellschaft mutiger handelt. Erforderlich hierfür sind eine offene Kommunikation, authentisches Auftreten und klare Formulierungen von Überzeugungen, Visionen und Zielen, die sowohl motivieren als auch nachvollzogen werden können.

9. Fehlerkultur: Förderung einer Kultur, die sich durch Offenheit, Lernorientierung, Verantwortung und Optimismus auszeichnet und Fehler nicht als Versagen sieht, sondern als wichtige Möglichkeit für Wachstum.

10. Positive Vorbilder: Vermehrte Auszeichnung von mutigen Menschen, Projekten, Konzepten, Ideen, um ihnen die gebührende Anerkennung zu geben und dem Wunsch der Bürger nach positiven Vorbildern nachzukommen.

**Die Realisierung eines jeden dieser Vorschläge erfordert Anstrengung, Verantwortungsbewusstsein und die Bereitschaft, Widerstände zu überwinden. Kurzum: SIE ERFORDERT MUT.**

## MEHR MUT

Christiane Goetz-Weimer
Wolfram Weimer

# CHRISTIANE GOETZ-WEIMER, WOLFRAM WEIMER

Verleger der WEIMER MEDIA GROUP

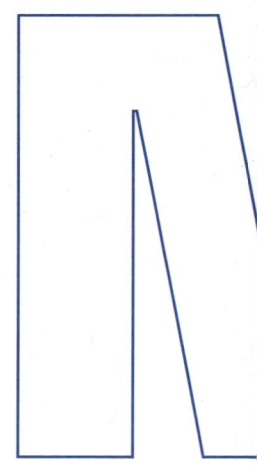

Der Philosoph Sören Kierkegaard machte die deutsche Angst 1844 zur Weltvokabel. Martin Heidegger und Karl Jaspers polierten sie existentialistisch auf. Weltkriege, Ideologien und Diktaturen wurden mit der German Angst in Verbindung gebracht, jenem vermeintlichen Charakterzug einer Nation, die durch ihre geografische Mittellage von Ur-Ängsten geprägt und getrieben sei. „Wie Hypochonder befürchten die Deutschen immer das Schlimmste", diagnostiziert der Historiker Frank Biess, dessen Buch „Republik der Angst" die deutschen Traumata beleuchtet. Womöglich fühlen sich „letzte Generationen" hierzulande wohler als anderswo. Jedenfalls hat es die deutsche Vokabel „Angst" doch tatsächlich ins Oxford Dictionary geschafft.

Und doch spaziert die Vokabel von der „German Angst" zuweilen wie Falschgeld durchs Land. Weil „made in Germany" unser Bild in der Welt noch viel mehr bestimmt hat. Denn Deutschland ist zugleich von jeder Menge Tatkraft und Zuversicht geprägt. Das Land der Dichter, Denker, Erfinder und Ingenieure wäre nicht so erfolgreich, wenn es nur ängstlich wäre. Ist Deutschland womöglich eher durch Mut als durch Angst richtiger charakterisiert?

Wir haben uns auf die Spurensuche begeben. Bei mehr als vierzig Vordenkern aus unterschiedlichen Disziplinen, aus Wissenschaft und Wirtschaft, aus Politik und Publizistik. Eben bei jenen, die unseren Ludwig-Erhard-Gipfel jedes Jahr am Tegernsee so vorwärtstreibend mit ihren kreativen Gedanken und Taten aufladen. Denn natürlich ist machen wie wollen, nur krasser.

# TUT

## mehr
## MUT

Wie also steht es wirklich um die German Angst? Was macht Mut? Was verhindert Mut in Deutschland? Wie ermutigen die Multiplikatoren und Menschen mit Definitions- und Gestaltungsmacht sich und andere, etwas zu wagen? Die Antworten zu diesen Fragen sind in diesem Buch versammelt. Sie sind klug, nachdenklich und vordenkend zugleich. Zuweilen überraschend und kontraintuitiv. Immer geprägt von „MOVE" – Mut, Optimismus, Vertrauen und Engagement. Am Ende entsteht ein Panoptikum neuen Muts. Das Buch zeigt, dass German Angst nicht einmal die halbe Kulturgeschichte erzählt. Die andere Hälfte beginnt hier.

*Wir wünschen nachdenkliche Inspiration und Lesespaß bei der Beschäftigung mit unseren Vordenkern.*

*Ihre*
Christiane Goetz-Weimer und Wolfram Weimer

# 03

## 44 INTERVIEWS

# ILSE AIGNER

Präsidentin
des Bayerischen Landtags, MdL

## Wie sehen Sie das Verhältnis zwischen der German Angst und der Notwendigkeit von Veränderungen, um aktuelle und zukünftige gesellschaftliche Herausforderungen zu bewältigen?

Ich finde die Tatsache, dass so oft über German Angst geredet wird, beängstigend. Wer tut das eigentlich und warum? Ich kenne mehrheitlich Menschen, aber auch Unternehmen, die das Gegenteil von ängstlich sind: Die klare, mutige Strategien haben für die Zukunft und Krisen durchaus als Chancen sehen – genau das ist doch die richtige Einstellung! Sicher: Es sind etwas viele Krisen auf einmal, die wir zu bewältigen haben oder hatten. Erst zwei Jahre Pandemie, dann der russische Angriffskrieg gegen die Ukraine. Und über allem steht der Klimawandel – auch eine Krise, vielleicht sogar unsere größte Herausforderung. Den Menschen wird viel zugemutet, ein andauernder Krisenmodus macht mürbe und viele haben große Probleme, da wieder herauszufinden. Aber genau das müssen wir: nach vorn schauen. Denn wir müssen uns damit abfinden, dass Veränderungen, Herausforderungen und auch Krisen normal sein werden. Die Welt ist nicht mehr wie früher. Wir befanden uns in Deutschland jahrzehntelang in einer Komfortzone, die uns geradezu passiv machte: eine stabile Demokratie, andauernder Wohlstand, soziale Gerechtigkeit, Frieden in Europa. Jetzt müssen wir aktiv darum kämpfen – denn wir wissen: Das Erreichte ist nicht selbstverständlich.

## Welche gesellschaftlichen Entwicklungen oder Bewegungen machen Ihnen Mut für die Zukunft?

Allein dass Deutschland so gut aus der Pandemie gekommen ist, macht mir Mut. Das haben andere Länder bei Weitem nicht so gut gemeistert. Mir macht Mut, dass sich junge Menschen wieder für Politik interessieren und sich engagieren – auch wenn das Themenspektrum manchmal noch sehr eng gefasst ist. Ich finde auch, dass wir in Sachen Gleichberechtigung große Fortschritte gemacht haben, auch wenn der Weg noch nicht zu Ende ist. Wir haben in der Krise erkannt, dass wirtschaftliche Abhängigkeiten fatal sind – viele Unternehmen stellen sich breiter auf und überdenken mutig ihre bisherigen Strategien. Mir macht Mut, dass unsere transatlantische Verteidigungsallianz wiederbelebt und gestärkt wurde und allen klar ist, dass dauerhafter Frieden nur durch Verteidigungsfähigkeit erreicht werden kann. Und mir macht Mut, wenn sich weiterhin so viele Menschen – in Bayern sind es besonders viele – ehrenamtlich engagieren. Denn das Ehrenamt ist eine Stütze unserer Gesellschaft.

### Worin sehen Sie die größten Hindernisse in unserer Gesellschaft, zuversichtlicher und mutiger zu denken und zu handeln?

Ich habe leider oft den Eindruck, dass nicht immer die richtigen Prioritäten gesetzt werden und wir oft den zweiten Schritt vor dem ersten machen. Dass wir aus einer Stimmung heraus handeln und dabei zu kurz denken. Und dass wir uns ideologisch oft im Weg stehen, wenn die Menschen pragmatische Lösungen erwarten. Damit meine ich konkret auch die Debatte um unsere Energiesicherheit. Der Fukushima-Schock hat zu einem vorzeitigen Ausstieg aus der Atomenergie geführt. Nun stellt sich aber heraus, dass wir diese Brückentechnologie durchaus etwas länger gebraucht hätten, anstatt auf russisches Gas zu setzen. Ideologische Scheuklappen verhindern derzeit längere Laufzeiten unserer AKWs. Ich sehe diese ideologische Unbeweglichkeit oft als das größte Hindernis, um mutiger zu sein.

### Wie ermutigen Sie andere und sich selbst, etwas zu wagen?

Indem ich als Landtagspräsidentin darum werbe, sich zu engagieren: aktiv zu werden für unsere Demokratie oder sich ehrenamtlich in der Mitte der Gesellschaft einzusetzen. Indem ich Mut mache und sage: keine Angst vor Veränderungen! Indem ich aber auch sage: Was gut ist und sich bewährt hat, das sollte erhalten bleiben und gepflegt werden. Manchmal braucht es auch Mut, um Werte zu bewahren und vor schnelllebigem Zeitgeist zu schützen.

# HUBERT AIWANGER

Stellvertretender Bayerischer Ministerpräsident,
Staatsminister für Wirtschaft,
Landesentwicklung und Energie, MdL

### Wie sehen Sie das Verhältnis zwischen der German Angst und der Notwendigkeit von Veränderungen, um aktuelle und zukünftige gesellschaftliche Herausforderungen zu bewältigen?

Das, was gerne als German Angst bezeichnet wird, hat nicht nur Schlechtes. Eine gesunde Portion Vorsicht und kritisches Hinterfragen tragen wesentlich dazu bei, Dinge zu durchdenken, sich der eigenen Stärken bewusst zu werden und klug zu handeln. Nur so haben wir es geschafft, zur Hightech-Nation aufzusteigen, und können heute auf wichtigen Zukunftsfeldern an der Weltspitze mitspielen.

Aber klar ist auch: Die German Angst darf uns nicht lähmen. Denn gerade angesichts der vielen Herausforderungen, die wir im globalen Wettbewerb meistern müssen, können wir uns kein zu zögerliches und unentschlossenes Handeln erlauben. Grundsätzlich bin ich allerdings überzeugt, dass wir uns trotz der zahlreichen enormen Herausforderungen, vor denen wir zweifelsohne stehen, einen gewissen Grundoptimismus nicht nehmen lassen dürfen.

### Welche gesellschaftlichen Entwicklungen oder Bewegungen machen Ihnen Mut für die Zukunft?

Es sind vor allem drei Punkte, die mich angesichts der Herausforderungen und Entwicklungen in Bayern, Deutschland und der Welt zuversichtlich stimmen.

Erstens hat nicht zuletzt die Energiekrise zu einem spürbaren Bewusstseinswandel in unserem Land geführt. Sie hat sowohl den Bürgerinnen und Bürgern als auch den Unternehmen und allen politischen Akteuren klargemacht, dass Veränderungen unausweichlich sind. Und so bekommen auch wichtige Zukunftsthemen endlich den nötigen Schwung. Beispiel Wasserstoff: Durch die hohen Energiepreise und die Gefahr einer Gasmangellage arbeiten viele Betriebe mit Unterstützung der Politik nun erstmals ganz konkret an der Umstellung auf die $H_2$-Technologie.

Zweitens haben wir in Bayern und Deutschland mutige und innovative Unternehmen, die den technologischen Wandel aktiv mitgestalten. Ich denke hier auch ganz besonders an die vielen dynamischen Start-ups, die sich als echte Innovationstreiber erweisen. Sie entwickeln nicht nur Lösungen für effizienten Klimaschutz und Digitalisierung, sondern auch die Exportschlager von morgen.

Und drittens können wir mit gut ausgebildeten Fachkräften im nationalen wie internationalen Vergleich punkten. Neben unseren Hochschulen und Universitäten ist dabei vor allem die berufliche Bildung ein großes Plus im weltweiten Wettbewerb. Dieses Modell ist absolut zukunftsfest und die Ausbildungsbereitschaft der Betriebe trotz Krise erfreulicherweise weiter groß.

## Worin sehen Sie die größten Hindernisse in unserer Gesellschaft, zuversichtlicher und mutiger zu denken und zu handeln?

Leider vertraut die Politik auf Bundes- und europäischer Ebene viel zu wenig auf die Innovationskraft des Marktes. Dabei ist sie der stärkste Fortschrittstreiber. So wird häufig zu dirigistischen Ansätzen gegriffen – auf Kosten der Technologieoffenheit. Bestes Beispiel ist das Verbot des Verbrennungsmotors ab 2035, das Effizienzsteigerungsmaßnahmen und dem Einsatz von E-Fuels von vorneherein eine Absage erteilt.

Statt solcher planwirtschaftlicher Ansätze brauchen wir aktivierende Impulse, vor allem auch für junge Start-ups. Noch immer ist es für sie in Deutschland relativ schwer, ausreichend Kapital zur Finanzierung ihrer Unternehmensideen zu akquirieren. In Bayern haben wir daher nicht nur einen Start-up-Fonds aufgelegt, sondern diesen auch um einen Scale-up-Fonds ergänzt, der Gründerinnen und Gründer bei der Skalierung ihres Geschäfts gezielt unterstützt.

## Wie ermutigen Sie andere und sich selbst, etwas zu wagen?

Ermutigend ist der Blick auf das, was wir alles schon geschafft haben. Unser Land ist nach dem Ende des Zweiten Weltkriegs zu einer der führenden Wirtschaftsnationen der Welt aufgestiegen und hat diese Position über Jahrzehnte gegen viele Widrigkeiten verteidigt, zuletzt etwa gegen die Auswirkungen der Coronapandemie. Das war aber nur möglich mit Vertrauen in die eigenen Fähigkeiten, einer gewissen Risikobereitschaft, mit Offenheit für Neues und einer zuversichtlichen Grundeinstellung. Unsere zahlreichen kleinen und mittelständischen Unternehmen, die vielen erfolgreichen Start-ups, aber auch die bei uns im Freistaat beheimateten Global Player stehen als bestes Beispiel für die hohe Innovationskraft sowie unternehmerische Weitsicht. Ich bin mir deshalb sicher, dass wir mit diesem Geist auch die Herausforderungen der Zukunft erfolgreich meistern werden.

# BURKHARD BALZ

Vorstandsmitglied
der Deutschen Bundesbank

Wie sehen Sie das Verhältnis zwischen der German Angst und
der Notwendigkeit von Veränderungen, um aktuelle und zukünftige
gesellschaftliche Herausforderungen zu bewältigen?

Ich mag den Begriff German Angst nicht, weil er eine generelle Panik und Ohnmacht in
Deutschland andeutet. Die Bewältigung der Coronakrise und aktuell der Energiekrise infolge des russischen Krieges gegen die Ukraine zeigt ein anderes Bild. Ich sehe einen breiten
politischen Diskurs, in dem Risiken sorgsam abgewogen und geeignete Maßnahmen ge-
funden werden. Mit Blick auf die großen globalen Herausforderungen wie Klimawandel,
Demografie und Digitalisierung könnte Deutschland durchaus eine stärkere europäische und
internationale Führungsrolle übernehmen.

Welche gesellschaftlichen Entwicklungen oder Bewegungen
machen Ihnen Mut für die Zukunft?

Tatsächlich macht es mir Mut, wie wir als Gesellschaft auf aktuelle Herausforderungen durch
Krisen reagieren. In der Coronapandemie haben wir beispielsweise sowohl die dramatische
Gesundheitskrise als auch die Folgen des in seinem Tempo beispiellosen Einbruchs der Welt-

wirtschaft bewältigt. Besonders beeindruckend fand ich vor diesem Hintergrund, wie schnell sich Wirtschaft, Politik und Gesellschaft auf die neuen Gegebenheiten eingestellt haben. Um nur ein Beispiel zu nennen: Als zuständiges Vorstandsmitglied für den Zahlungsverkehr in der Bundesbank habe ich erlebt, wie Kartenzahlungen und das kontaktlose Bezahlen mit der Karte in kurzer Zeit wesentlich an Bedeutung gewonnen haben. Eine solche Innovationskraft wird uns auch durch künftige Herausforderungen tragen.

### Worin sehen Sie die größten Hindernisse in unserer Gesellschaft, zuversichtlicher und mutiger zu denken und zu handeln?

Die größten Hindernisse sind meiner Ansicht nach zu bürokratische Prozesse und eine vielfach immer noch vorherrschende Kirchturmpolitik. Neue Ansätze, zukunftsorientierte Lösungen und vielversprechende Projekte scheitern oft an einer zu starren Regulierung oder benötigen zu viel Zeit für ihre Umsetzung in der Abstimmung zwischen Bund, Ländern und Kommunen.

### Wie ermutigen Sie andere und sich selbst, etwas zu wagen?

In diesem Punkt halte ich es ganz mit Albert Einstein, der einmal gesagt hat: „Probleme kann man niemals mit derselben Denkweise lösen, durch die sie entstanden sind." Auch das zunächst unmöglich Erscheinende lässt sich erreichen. Dazu müssen wir aber öfter „out of the box" denken und neue Wege gehen, auch wenn nicht jeder Weg zum Erfolg führt.

# ELKE
# BENNING-ROHNKE

Advisor, Aufsichtsrätin und Beirätin
der Benning & Company GmbH

**Wie sehen Sie das Verhältnis zwischen der German Angst und
der Notwendigkeit von Veränderungen, um aktuelle und zukünftige
gesellschaftliche Herausforderungen zu bewältigen?**

Dazu ein kurzer geschichtlicher Exkurs: Einst verstand sich das Kaiserreich China als Zentrum der Welt, umgeben von barbarischen Völkern. Selbst das prosperierende Europa wurde als randständig betrachtet. Dieses überschätzte Selbstverständnis führte dazu, dass das „Reich der Mitte" die industrielle Revolution verschlief. China wurde zum Armenhaus.

Die Vergangenheit sollte uns eine Warnung sein. Heute laufen wir in Deutschland Gefahr, den Anschluss zu verpassen. Wir brüsten uns mit unserer wirtschaftlichen Stärke, gefallen uns als Exportweltmeister und glauben, dass diese Position unantastbar ist. Vor ihrer ersten Wiederwahl als Bundeskanzlerin sagte Angela Merkel auf einer privaten Veranstaltung, bei der ich anwesend war: „Den Deutschen sind keine Reformen zuzumuten. Deshalb mache ich auch keine." Mit Blick auf ihre Wiederwahl mag diese Vorgehensweise für sie die richtige gewesen sein. Für unser Land ist die Haltung fatal: Wir sind in vielen zukunftsweisenden Bereichen rückständig aufgestellt. Die Politik der letzten Jahre hat versäumt, die Bevölkerung aus einer Position der Stärke für Veränderungen zu öffnen und Debatten anzustoßen, wie wir uns in einer pluralistischen Welt mit neuen Aufsteigern positionieren müssen. Die aktuellen Krisen haben den Handlungsdruck verschärft. Angesichts eines latenten Abstiegsgefühls nehmen in weiten Teilen der Gesellschaft Verlustängste, Empörung und Erschöpfung zu. Die Parteien wiederum beschwichtigen und verschieben notwendige Reformen. Milliarden werden investiert, um wirtschaftliche Konsequenzen abzufedern und das Gefühl einer Wohlstandsgesellschaft zu bewahren. Wahrheiten werden kaschiert, Ressourcen nicht zukunftsgerichtet allokiert. Es ist nicht die German Angst, die uns im Wege steht. Vielmehr das kurzfristige parteipolitische Taktieren um vermeintliches Wählerwohlwollen.

### Welche gesellschaftlichen Entwicklungen oder Bewegungen machen Ihnen Mut für die Zukunft?

Mit der Generation Z starten junge, gut ausgebildete Digital Natives in die Arbeitswelt, die mehr „Spiel in den freien Raum" zulassen. Ein Mindset, das sich hoffentlich auf die Innovationskraft und die Attraktivität des Wirtschaftsstandorts Deutschland auswirken wird. Darüber hinaus gilt heute bei vielen jungen Menschen das Credo: Kooperation statt Konkurrenz. Daraus erhoffe ich mir nicht nur eine Qualitätssteigerung unseres Outputs, sondern auch eine Stärkung des gesellschaftlichen Miteinanders. Und zu guter Letzt haben wir eine gut integrierte zweite Generation von Migranten. Viele sind verantwortungsvolle Gestalter und hoch motiviert, unsere Gesellschaft zu bereichern.

### Worin sehen Sie die größten Hindernisse in unserer Gesellschaft, zuversichtlicher und mutiger zu denken und zu handeln?

Wir befinden uns an einem Scheideweg. Davor verschließen aber noch zu viele Menschen die Augen. Ein „Weiter so!" fühlt sich bequemer an. Wenn wir jedoch auch zukünftig unsere demokratischen Werte in diese pluralistische Welt hinaustragen wollen, müssen wir unsere Wettbewerbsfähigkeit stärken. Das geht mit tiefgreifenden Veränderungen und Investitionen einher. In der Konsequenz brauchen wir an diesem Scheideweg kompetente Politiker, die faktenbasiert und mit Weitsicht neue Rahmenbedingungen für unsere Zukunftsfähigkeit schaffen.

### Wie ermutigen Sie andere und sich selbst, etwas zu wagen?

Jeden Tag bewege ich mich aus meiner Komfortzone. Jeden Tag empfehle ich eine gute Frau aus meinem Netzwerk. Jeden Tag versuche ich, ein Role Model zu sein.

# MARCUS BERRET

Senior Partner, Global Managing Director
bei Roland Berger

**Wie sehen Sie das Verhältnis zwischen der German Angst und der Notwendigkeit von Veränderungen, um aktuelle und zukünftige gesellschaftliche Herausforderungen zu bewältigen?**

Angst darf weder politische noch unternehmerische Entscheidungen leiten, denn aus Angst entsteht keine Innovation. Aus meiner Sicht hat Deutschland allerdings weniger ein Angst- als ein Bequemlichkeitsproblem: Wir verharren in unserer Komfortzone, weil es uns als Gesellschaft in den letzten Jahrzehnten sehr gut ging und sich ein Urvertrauen aufgebaut hat, dass schon alles gut gehen wird. Statt den Status quo zu bewahren, müssen wir jetzt Risiken in Kauf nehmen, Entscheidungen auch ohne „Airbag" treffen – nur so setzen wir die Transformation in Gang, die unsere globale Wettbewerbsfähigkeit langfristig erhält.

**Welche gesellschaftlichen Entwicklungen oder Bewegungen machen Ihnen Mut für die Zukunft?**

Mut machen mir insbesondere das Engagement der jüngeren Generation und der exponentielle technologische Fortschritt. Oftmals wird jungen Erwachsenen fehlende Leistungsbereitschaft und politisches Desinteresse vorgeworfen. Dabei sind vor allem sie es, die scheinbare Gewissheiten hinterfragen und Wandel anstoßen. Fridays for Future haben erreicht, dass auch abstrakte Themen wie die Klimakrise in der Mitte der Gesellschaft kritischer diskutiert werden. Technologische Errungenschaften der letzten Jahre haben nicht nur die rasante Impfstoffentwicklung in der Coronapandemie ermöglicht, sie werden uns beispielsweise auch dabei helfen, unsere Energieabhängigkeit drastisch zu reduzieren.

Ein Blick in die Vergangenheit beweist, dass weitreichende Reformen durchaus erfolgreich sein können: Wurde Deutschland Anfang der 2000er noch als „kranker Mann Europas" betitelt, hat die umstrittene Agenda 2010 uns zur stärksten Volkswirtschaft Europas gemacht.

## Worin sehen Sie die größten Hindernisse in unserer Gesellschaft, zuversichtlicher und mutiger zu denken und zu handeln?

Der demografische Wandel ist ein nicht zu unterschätzender Faktor, wenn es um die deutsche „Beharrungskultur" geht. Das Interesse und die höhere Risikoaversion der älteren Generationen werden in politischen Entscheidungen überproportional widergespiegelt. Doch Veränderung erfordert Mut – das gilt auch mit Blick auf die deutsche Wirtschaft, die sich radikal transformieren muss.
Wir brauchen die Einsicht, dass etablierte Geschäftsmodelle teilweise an ihre Grenzen stoßen, und müssen für ein Investitionsumfeld sorgen, in dem Unternehmen mutige Entscheidungen treffen können. Denn: Deutschland hat in den letzten Jahren deutlich unterinvestiert und wird im weltweiten Wettbewerb zunehmend abgehängt. Damit Deutschland attraktiver Wirtschaftsstandort bleibt, braucht es einen breit angelegten Strukturwandel, den öffentlicher und privater Sektor gemeinsam stemmen müssen.

## Wie ermutigen Sie andere und sich selbst, etwas zu wagen?

Um als Gesellschaft voranzukommen, brauchen wir ein positives Zukunftsbild. Statt uns zu fragen, was schiefgehen kann, müssen wir die Chancen erkennen, die im Wandel liegen, und seine Potenziale nutzen. Oftmals führen neue Ideen zum Erfolg, die so noch in keinem Management-Handbuch stehen. Deswegen schauen wir mit unseren Kunden auch regelmäßig über den Tellerrand der eigenen Branche hinaus. Grundsätzlich gilt: Zum Unternehmertum gehört seit jeher ein gewisses Wagnis und in der heutigen Zeit, in der multiple Krisen die Unsicherheit verstärken, müssen wir lernen, diese anzunehmen und resilienter zu wirtschaften.

# MARKUS DUESMANN

Vorsitzender des Vorstands der AUDI AG,
Mitglied des Vorstands
des Volkswagen Konzerns

**Wie sehen Sie das Verhältnis zwischen der German Angst und der Notwendigkeit von Veränderungen, um aktuelle und zukünftige gesellschaftliche Herausforderungen zu bewältigen?**

Klar ist: Veränderungsbereitschaft und Anpassungsgeschwindigkeit sind angesichts der multiplen Krisen wichtiger denn je. Wir müssen flexibel auf die aktuellen und zukünftigen Herausforderungen reagieren und bereit sein, in einem unsicheren Umfeld schnelle Entscheidungen zu treffen. Auch vor dem Hintergrund protektionistischer Tendenzen in Nordamerika und China ist aktuell der wohl schlechteste Zeitpunkt, zögerlich zu sein. Deutschland und Europa müssen unbürokratischer und entschlossener handeln. Dabei sollten wir die eigenen Interessen klar formulieren, ohne aber selbst eine Entkopplung zu fördern. Gleichzeitig bin ich überzeugt, dass das grundsätzliche Bedürfnis nach einer sicheren Zukunft für uns ein zusätzlicher Ansporn sein kann, uns langfristig widerstandsfähiger aufzustellen und eine eigenständige europäische Position im globalen Wettbewerb zu entwickeln.

**Welche gesellschaftlichen Entwicklungen oder Bewegungen machen Ihnen Mut für die Zukunft?**

Die große Solidarität der Menschen in der Coronapandemie und auch im Ukrainekrieg hat mich sehr beeindruckt. Der Zusammenhalt in unserer Gesellschaft ist eine unserer großen Stärken. Eine Spaltung sollten wir um jeden Preis verhindern. Denn um die Herausforderungen der Zukunft zu meistern, ist es wichtig, dass alle gemeinsam daran arbeiten.

## Worin sehen Sie die größten Hindernisse in unserer Gesellschaft, zuversichtlicher und mutiger zu denken und zu handeln?

**W**ir brauchen mehr Vertrauen. Vertrauen in uns und unsere Qualitäten. Der Begriff der German Angst ist glücklicherweise nicht das Erste und Einzige, wofür Deutschland in der Welt bekannt ist. Da denke ich eher an „made in Germany" als internationales Gütesiegel für Qualität. Diesen hohen Anspruch an uns selbst sollten wir nicht aufgeben. Gleichzeitig darf uns der Hang zur Perfektion nicht davon abhalten, neue Dinge anzupacken – auch wenn wir nicht sicher wissen, ob sie am Ende exzellent sein werden.

## Wie ermutigen Sie andere und sich selbst, etwas zu wagen?

**I**ndem ich in erster Linie auf die Chancen blicke. Und es bietet sich gerade jetzt die Chance, uns mit nachhaltigen technischen Innovationen „made in Germany" international zu behaupten. Diese sollten wir jetzt schnell ergreifen. Beispielsweise das Verbrenner-Aus ab 2035, das die EU beschlossen hat, ist dafür ein wichtiger Schritt, schafft Planungssicherheit für die Industrie und setzt die richtigen Reize, unsere Innovationskraft zu beweisen.

# KIRSTEN FEHRS

Bischöfin im Sprengel Hamburg und Lübeck
der Nordkirche

## Wie sehen Sie das Verhältnis zwischen der German Angst und der Notwendigkeit von Veränderungen, um aktuelle und zukünftige gesellschaftliche Herausforderungen zu bewältigen?

**Z**unächst erscheint es mir wichtig, der Angst in der aktuellen Situation eine Berechtigung einzuräumen. Es hat noch nie eine Zeit gegeben, die ich erlebt habe, in der Menschen in diesem Maße Angst hatten, und zwar vor konkreten Bedrohungen: Krieg in Europa, Klimawandel, Coronakrise, Demokratiemüdigkeit, Existenzangst, weil kein Geld für Heizung und Brot übrig bleibt, Rohstoffe fehlen, der Umsatz einbricht. Das ist meines Erachtens kein Phänomen einer typisch deutschen Befindlichkeit, sondern der zutiefst verunsichernden Gefährdungslage geschuldet.

Entscheidend ist aber, wie wir uns zu dieser Angst verhalten. Verharren wir in ihr, oder finden wir einen Ausweg der Hoffnung. Vielleicht geht es nicht zuerst um die Bewältigungsstrategien, sondern um eine Haltung, die unsere Herzen, unsere Resilienz stärkt. Und mit der wir in den Blick nehmen, was wir den Bedrohungen entgegenzusetzen haben, trotz allem. Die Schönheit der Menschlichkeit zum Beispiel, die Leid, Not und Schmerz nicht übersieht, sondern empathisch einbezieht. Die Schönheit des Wortes, das sich für andere einsetzt. Die Schönheit von Musik, Theater, Ballett, die uns die Kostbarkeit des Lebens vor Augen führen. Wenn wir von der Schönheit geprägte starke Herzen haben, können wir zuversichtlich und zukunftsfähig handeln.

## Welche gesellschaftlichen Entwicklungen oder Bewegungen machen Ihnen Mut für die Zukunft?

**M**ir macht die Vielfalt der kleinen Schritte Mut. Menschen, die einfach anpacken, pragmatisch und unerhört mitfühlend. Nicht stehen zu bleiben bei den niederschmetternden Einsichten, Prognosen und Bilanzen unserer Kriegs- und Krisenzeit, sondern hoffend handeln. Ganz konkret vor Ort, im eigenen beruflichen, familiären, nachbarschaftlichen Kontext leisten so viele menschenfreundlichen mitfühlenden Friedensdienst: bei den Tafeln, in Kitas und Krankenhäusern, im Quartier, mit Geflüchteten, in kulturellen Initiativen, als Nachbarschafts- und Obdachlosenhilfe und, und, und! Dass es für so viele nicht nur um die persönliche Wohlstands- und Wachstumsprognose geht, sondern um Gemeinschaft, gutes Miteinander, soziale und ökologische Transformation, das erfüllt mich mit Hoffnung.

## Worin sehen Sie die größten Hindernisse in unserer Gesellschaft, zuversichtlicher und mutiger zu denken und zu handeln?

Unsere Kultur des Perfektionismus, manchmal auch der Besserwisserei steht uns oft im Weg. Wir denken und planen zu lange und verlieren das Handeln aus dem Blick. Mit Kompromissen tun wir uns schwer und desavouieren uns lieber gegenseitig in Debatten um die hundertprozentigen Lösungen. Das gilt auch für die Kirche. Unsere großen, sehr gut organisierten Institutionen haben lange für Aufschwung, Wohlstand und Sicherheit gesorgt. Sie sind darüber aber auch unbeweglich und behäbig geworden. Es wäre schön, wenn wir zu einem dynamischen lebendigen Miteinander finden, in dem mehr Menschen zuerst fragen, was sie für die Gesellschaft tun können, und sich nicht darin einrichten, sich darüber zu empören, was die Verantwortlichen falsch machen.

## Wie ermutigen Sie andere und sich selbst, etwas zu wagen?

Als Christenmenschen haben wir das Glück, uns nicht nur auf uns selbst verlassen zu müssen. Wir glauben an eine Kraft außerhalb von uns selbst: die dynamische Geistkraft Gottes, inspiratio. Ich erlebe es tatsächlich, dass sie wirksam ist als Veränderungsimpuls, der der Angst vorm Handeln entschieden Lebenslust entgegensetzt. Es geht dann um aktives Hinhören und Handeln. Gib mir ein hörendes Herz, heißt es bei König Salomo in der Bibel. Ein hörendes Herz, das ist wagemutig. Eine wunderbare Leitlinie, auch ein Leitungsprinzip. Dazu in Meditation und Stille zu den Quellen zu finden, zu dem, was Gott in mich gelegt hat, ist die beste Ermutigung, um in die Welt zu gehen und hoffend – inspiriert eben – zu handeln. Dann muss nicht alles gelingen, aber das, was ich tue, ergibt Herz und Sinn, für mich selbst und die anderen.

# ISABEL FROMMELT-GOTTSCHALD

Botschafterin des Fürstentums Liechtenstein

**Wie sehen Sie das Verhältnis zwischen der German Angst und der Notwendigkeit von Veränderungen, um aktuelle und zukünftige gesellschaftliche Herausforderungen zu bewältigen?**

Die German Angst als Charakterisierung einer ganzen Nation kann ich so nicht erkennen. Eher gab oder gibt es in Teilen der Bevölkerung eine Grundstimmung, die sich vermutlich genauer beschreiben lässt mit einer Mischung aus Zögerlichkeit, Zukunftsängsten und einem Sicherheitsbedürfnis, die sich auch mit den erlebten Katastrophen der ersten Hälfte des 20. Jahrhunderts begründen lässt. Aus solchen werden immer Lehren gezogen, die prägend sind für Jahre oder Jahrzehnte. Aber auch in anderen Ländern mit mehr oder weniger Kriegserfahrung gibt es solche Ängste. In der Politik sind eine gewisse Zurückhaltung und der Wunsch nach Risikovermeidung durchaus auch positiv zu werten. Staaten, die sich so verhalten, sind oft besonders bemüht und erfolgreich, bei unterschiedlichen Positionen gemeinsame Ergebnisse zu erzielen. Die ängstliche Grundstimmung wird durch die verschiedenen Krisen der letzten Jahre und ganz besonders durch den Angriffskrieg auf die Ukraine natürlich geschürt. Über allem schweben die Fragen, ob es noch schlimmer kommt und wie lange dieser Zustand der Unsicherheit andauert. Die Nachkriegsordnung, wie wir sie kannten, gibt es nicht mehr – eine neue ist noch nicht erkennbar. Ich denke, darin liegt für Deutschland eine große Chance, mit all den Facetten, die die Zeitenwende mit sich bringt. Deutschland sollte diese nutzen, sich aktiv und mutig zu engagieren. Denn aus globaler Perspektive betrachtet, ist Deutschland nach wie vor ein Vorzeigeland mit enormen Errungenschaften in wirtschaftlicher, politischer und kultureller Hinsicht. In der neuen sicherheitspolitischen Ordnung kann Deutschland eine wichtige Führungsrolle einnehmen, aufgrund seiner Bedeutung und Größe in Europa, seiner geografischen Lage, seiner transatlantischen Nähe und Nähe zum Osten und insbesondere auch aufgrund seiner historischen Erfahrung. Deutschland hat außerdem eine hervorragende Ausgangslage, auch in der Klimawende eine Leader-Rolle zu übernehmen. Das ist langfristige Risikovermeidung und Wohlstandsgarantie.

## Welche gesellschaftlichen Entwicklungen oder Bewegungen machen Ihnen Mut für die Zukunft?

Wir streben alle eine gute Zukunft an, der wir zuversichtlich entgegenblicken. Doch dies erfordert Engagement, manchmal Verzicht und den Mut, Durststrecken durchzustehen. Ich bin überzeugt von unseren westlichen Werten der Demokratie und Rechtsstaatlichkeit, sodass es keine Alternative dafür gibt, sich dafür einzusetzen und alle Handlungsspielräume zu nutzen. Mut macht mir unsere ausgeprägte Zivilgesellschaft, eine Fridays-for-Future-Bewegung, die bereit ist, sich auch gegen Widerstand für Themen einzusetzen, oder die kreative Start-up-Szene in Deutschland.

## Worin sehen Sie die größten Hindernisse in unserer Gesellschaft, zuversichtlicher und mutiger zu denken und zu handeln?

Eines der wesentlichen Hindernisse ist, dass wir in Wohlstandsgesellschaften leben, in denen es seit dem Ende des Zweiten Weltkrieges immer „aufwärts" ging. Zumindest gibt es das vorherrschende Gefühl, dass die letzten Jahrzehnte immer einhergingen mit: Mehr Wachstum, finanziellen Ressourcen und Mobilität; fast alle Weltregionen sind erreichbar und die Welt kann (medial) nach Hause geholt werden. Im Ergebnis scheinen wir unendliche Möglichkeiten zu haben. Das hat aus meiner Sicht auch zu einer Bequemlichkeit geführt. Nun haben uns aber gerade die Pandemie und die sich verschärfende Klimakrise gezeigt, wie abhängig dieser Lebensstandard von unseren Vernetzungen ist und dass wir viele Krisen nicht von uns fernhalten können. Bei vielen führt dies zu einer Sorge um den Wohlstand, zusammen mit einem Kontrollverlust angesichts der Entwicklungen, auf die wir gefühlt kaum Einfluss nehmen können. In dieser Situation kann die Politik wichtige Impulse und Anreize zu Risikofreude und Veränderungs- und Gestaltungsbereitschaft geben.

## Wie ermutigen Sie andere und sich selbst, etwas zu wagen?

Bei Vorhaben, die Mut erfordern, stelle ich mir vor, welche Chancen diese bieten und was möglicherweise schiefläuft. Oft hilft mir, die Situation zu visualisieren und zu „erfühlen". Meine Erfahrung ist, dass sich mutige Schritte meist lohnen.

# ANGELIKA GIFFORD

Vice President EMEA at Meta
& Supervisory Board Member

**Wie sehen Sie das Verhältnis zwischen der German Angst und der Notwendigkeit von Veränderungen, um aktuelle und zukünftige gesellschaftliche Herausforderungen zu bewältigen?**

Die Antwort liegt in der Digitalisierung: Digitale Technologien transformieren mittlerweile alle Lebensbereiche. Angesichts dieser tiefgreifenden Veränderungen sollten wir in Deutschland und Europa bei der Gestaltung und Anwendung dieser Technologien mitbestimmen – zumal in Europa bereits weltweite Standards bei der Regulierung der digitalen Welt gesetzt werden. Die Voraussetzung dafür ist, dass wir unsere Zurückhaltung bei Investitionen in die Digitalisierung überwinden: Insbesondere der Mittelstand könnte hier noch mehr Maßnahmen ergreifen. Wenn wir mit anderen Ländern mithalten möchten, müssten die Investitionen nach aktuellen Berechnungen von aktuell 18 Milliarden Euro auf 35 bis 50 Milliarden Euro im Jahr steigen.

**Welche gesellschaftlichen Entwicklungen oder Bewegungen machen Ihnen Mut für die Zukunft?**

Ich finde es beeindruckend, dass wir selbstbewusst sind, wenn es darum geht, die Potenziale digitaler Technologien auszuschöpfen. Die Digitalisierung steht ganz oben auf den Aufgabenzetteln der Führungskräfte eines Landes. Die Gespräche, die ich im Rahmen des Buches „Deutschlands digitale Dekade" geführt habe, bestätigen eindeutig, dass wir hierzulande kein Erkenntnisproblem mehr haben. Jetzt geht es an die Umsetzung: pilotieren, iterieren und skalieren.

So zeigt beispielsweise die Entwicklung des KI-Sektors in Deutschland deutlich, wie man vor Ort Innovation gestalten und vorantreiben kann. Auch die Bundesregierung unterstützt mit der Nationalen KI-Strategie schon heute KI made in Germany. Bis zum Jahr 2025 sind Investitionen von fünf Milliarden Euro geplant. Ich bin sehr optimistisch, dass das gelingen wird.

## Worin sehen Sie die größten Hindernisse in unserer Gesellschaft, zuversichtlicher und mutiger zu denken und zu handeln?

Wir müssen noch mehr in die nächste Generation und ihre Interessen investieren. Bei der digitalen Bildung landet Deutschland unter den 32 OECD-Ländern nur auf Platz 18. Katrin Suder beschreibt in ihrem Beitrag in „Deutschlands digitale Dekade" treffend, dass Schulen Kinder schon früh an Themen wie Daten und Technologien heranführen sollten. Dazu brauchen wir natürlich auch eine zeitgemäße digitale Infrastruktur, die immer noch in 33 Prozent aller deutschen Schulen fehlt. Auch bei Diversität und Gleichstellung müssen wir aufholen. Im EU-Gleichstellungsindex belegt Deutschland lediglich den elften Platz. Doch es geht hierbei nicht um das Abschneiden in internationalen Rankings. Vielfalt und Inklusion sind essenziell für eine zukunftsfähige Entwicklung, Innovation und Geschäftserfolg.

## Wie ermutigen Sie andere und sich selbst, etwas zu wagen?

Als Führungskraft ist meine Strategie: eine Vertrauenskultur schaffen. Es geht darum, Menschen eine Aufgabe zu geben und ihnen die Freiheit zu lassen, „einfach mal zu machen". Durch die Förderung einer Fehlerkultur, bei der Fehler als Chance zum Lernen betrachtet werden, kann man Menschen zu noch größeren Leistungen motivieren und ihnen Mut machen, Neues zu wagen.

# GREG HANDS

Minister without Portfolio at the Cabinet Office,
Chairman of the Conservative Party, MP (UK)

**Wie sehen Sie das Verhältnis zwischen der German Angst und der Notwendigkeit von Veränderungen, um aktuelle und zukünftige gesellschaftliche Herausforderungen zu bewältigen?**

Meine ersten Eindrücke von Deutschland stammen aus meiner Jugendzeit, da ich in den Jahren 1978 bis 1984 in der Schule Deutsch gelernt habe und dann nach dem Abitur immer wieder einige Zeit zwischen 1985 und 1988 in Deutschland verbracht habe, genauer im damaligen Westberlin, wo ich im Sommerbad Kreuzberg unweit der Wilhelmstraße (und anderen geschichtsträchtigen Symbolen) einen Job hatte.

Zur gleichen Zeit studierte ich an der Universität von Cambridge Geschichte, hauptsächlich deutsche und mitteleuropäische Geschichte. Eines der ersten Bücher, das ich während meines Geschichtsstudiums bearbeitete, war, kurz nach seiner Veröffentlichung, „Nach Hitler. Der schwierige Umgang mit unserer Geschichte" von Martin Broszat. Durch dieses Buch habe ich damals als 20-jähriger Student erstmals vom Konzept der „Vergangenheitsbewältigung" erfahren und verstanden, dass Deutschland einen einzigartigen Umgang mit seiner Vergangenheit hat.

Für Besucher ist dies im ganzen Land immer wieder sichtbar und stellt den tiefsinnigen Hintergrund der deutschen Gesellschaft der letzten 80 Jahre zur Schau. Diese „Vergangenheitsbewältigung" muss Deutschland hoch angerechnet werden und kann überwiegend als erfolgreich bezeichnet werden. Nun gilt Deutschland als Beispiel für andere Länder, die dunkle Kapitel in ihrer Geschichte haben. Davon bin ich 40 Jahre nach meinen ersten Erfahrungen tief überzeugt. Gegenwärtig, aus der Perspektive internationaler Partner, muss Deutschland, als viertmächtigste Wirtschaftsmacht der Welt und mit Westeuropas größter Bevölkerung, eine noch größere Schlüsselrolle auf der internationalen Bühne spielen.

## Welche gesellschaftlichen Entwicklungen oder Bewegungen machen Ihnen Mut für die Zukunft?

Bisweilen wird Deutschlands Beitrag zum Ukrainekrieg kritisiert. Ich persönlich hingegen bin von der deutschen Leistung beeindruckt, zum Beispiel angesichts des sensiblen Themas, dass deutsche Panzer in der Nähe des Dnjepr im Einsatz sein könnten. Das Verhältnis zu Russland ist auch, laut Broszat, ein Teil des „schwierigen Umgangs mit Deutschlands Geschichte". Meines Erachtens hat Deutschland viel an die Ukraine geliefert und wir arbeiten eng zusammen.

Die deutsche Reaktion auf die Energiekrise ist ebenfalls imponierend. Wer hätte gedacht, dass ein Politiker wie Robert Habeck den Bau von Flüssiggasterminals innerhalb eines Jahres nach der russischen Invasion in Auftrag geben würde? Ich kann mich noch gut an den Machtkampf innerhalb der Grünen Partei zwischen den Fundis und den Realos in den 1980ern erinnern – das war während meiner Abiturzeit! Vielleicht ist Herr Habeck jetzt „Realo in Chief"!

Historisch – und von außen – betrachtet, bewegte sich Deutschland immer etwas langsam und im Konsens. Während sich dies nun doch etwas geändert zu haben scheint, wünsche ich mir dennoch einen etwas positiveren Zugang zur Kernenergie.

## Worin sehen Sie die größten Hindernisse in unserer Gesellschaft, zuversichtlicher und mutiger zu denken und zu handeln?

Ich hatte immer das Gefühl, dass es in Deutschland einer intensiveren inneren Debatte bedarf. Konsens ist gut, zugleich sind jedoch Umdenken und Hinterfragen nicht unangebracht. Es scheint mir, dass Deutsche meist sehr gut gebildet sind. Nur ist die Bildung oft sehr kongruent. Kontroversen und Vielfältigkeit verbessern sowohl den Entscheidungsprozess als letztlich auch die Ergebnisse.

## Wie ermutigen Sie andere und sich selbst, etwas zu wagen?

In meiner elfjährigen Ministerlaufbahn habe ich erfahren, dass es recht einfach ist, sich der Regierungslinie zu fügen. Um den Job besser auszuführen, ist es allerdings ratsam, für sich selbst zu denken und den Konsens zu hinterfragen. Die Welt verändert sich ständig und politische Denker und Entscheider müssen sich dem anpassen – so wie es Deutschland im letzten Jahr getan hat.

Persönlich sehe ich mich oft als Brückenbauer zwischen Großbritannien und Deutschland, und ich möchte andere ermutigen, ebenfalls an einer Vertiefung des deutsch-britischen Verhältnisses zu arbeiten.

# STEFAN HARTUNG

Vorsitzender der Geschäftsführung
der Robert Bosch GmbH

**Wie sehen Sie das Verhältnis zwischen der German Angst und der Notwendigkeit von Veränderungen, um aktuelle und zukünftige gesellschaftliche Herausforderungen zu bewältigen?**

Deutschland ist heute ein weltoffenes, global vernetztes und glücklicherweise auch diskursfreudiges Land. Ein lebendiger Austausch möglichst ohne Denkverbote und Vorurteile ist die beste Grundlage für eine Gesellschaft, die sich zukunftssicher aufstellen will. Natürlich gibt es in einem konsensorientierten Gemeinwesen dabei manchmal vielleicht etwas zu zaghaft geführte Debatten oder Beschlüsse, die von einigen als übervorsichtig oder halbherzig wahrgenommen werden. Aber: Die immer wieder beschworene German Angst kann ich aktuell nicht erkennen, ebenso wenig wie einen zu großen Einfluss durch Schwarzseher oder Bedenkenträger. Das könnten wir uns auch gar nicht erlauben: Wir müssen auf vielen Feldern schneller werden, sei es bei der Digitalisierung, nachhaltigen Energien oder auch in der Bildung. Dafür braucht es Mut, internationale Zusammenarbeit und möglichst freie Fahrt für den großen Drang nach Verbesserung, den so viele Menschen in sich tragen.

**Welche gesellschaftlichen Entwicklungen oder Bewegungen machen Ihnen Mut für die Zukunft?**

Paradoxerweise hat uns gerade das Zusammentreffen mehrerer heftiger Krisen in aller Klarheit gezeigt, dass Wegducken keine Lösung ist. Nicht die Resignation wächst vielerorts in Deutschland und in Europa, sondern die Resilienz. Der Krieg in der Ukraine hat gezeigt, wie geschlossen, pragmatisch, konsequent und dennoch ausgewogen viele Länder angesichts außerordentlicher Herausforderungen agieren können. Das sind ermutigende Zeichen. Wir bei Bosch sind davon überzeugt, dass Technologie einer der entscheidenden Schlüssel im Kampf gegen Klimawandel und Energieknappheit sein wird. Und damit stehen wir nicht allein, wie die Ergebnisse unseres jüngsten Bosch Tech Compass bestätigen: Zwei von drei Deutschen stimmen der Einschätzung zu, dass technologischer Fortschritt die Welt zu einem besseren Ort macht, deutlich mehr als noch vor einem Jahr. Die Tendenz stimmt also.

### Worin sehen Sie die größten Hindernisse in unserer Gesellschaft, zuversichtlicher und mutiger zu denken und zu handeln?

Mut und Zuversicht entstehen bekanntlich nur selten im Klein-Klein von Tagespolitik und Tagesgeschäft, sondern dann, wenn eine Gesellschaft auf möglichst breiter Basis eine klare Vorstellung von einer positiven Zukunft entwickelt. Insofern sollten wir über den unmittelbar anstehenden Aufgaben nicht vergessen, auch eine Strategie für das nächste Jahrzehnt zu entwickeln. Als entschiedener Optimist würde ich mir wünschen, dass wir dabei die Chancen ebenso leidenschaftlich und offen erörtern wie die Bedenken. Ideologische Vorbehalte oder der Ruf nach Sonderwegen bringen uns nicht weiter. Die großen Herausforderungen wie etwa den Klimawandel meistern wir nicht im Alleingang, sondern nur als globale Gemeinschaft.

### Wie ermutigen Sie andere und sich selbst, etwas zu wagen?

Im Großen und Ganzen gesehen, ist das Leben für viele Menschen heute besser als vor 50 oder 100 Jahren. Und ich bin überzeugt, dass dieser Trend anhalten wird – allerdings nicht ohne unser aller Zutun. Die Zukunft ist gestaltbarer, als viele denken, zumal es an ambitionierten Visionen nicht fehlt. Nur ein Beispiel: Bosch entwickelt derzeit den Fertigungsprozess für MEMS, also mikroelektromechanische Systeme, entscheidend weiter. In unserer Chipfabrik in Dresden wollen wir als eines der ersten Unternehmen MEMS-Sensoren auch auf 300-Millimeter-Wafern fertigen – ein wichtiger Schritt, der die europäische Halbleiterbranche noch wettbewerbsfähiger machen wird. In anderen Industrien gibt es jede Menge ähnlich ehrgeizige Ziele – in der Summe zeigen sie immer in eine Richtung: nach vorne. Und das macht Mut.

# ANGELIKA HUBER-STRASSER

Regionalvorständin Süd
der KPMG AG

**Wie sehen Sie das Verhältnis zwischen der German Angst und der Notwendigkeit von Veränderungen, um aktuelle und zukünftige gesellschaftliche Herausforderungen zu bewältigen?**

German Angst ist ein Begriff, der die deutsche Zögerlichkeit mit dem Blick von Außen auf die Deutschen beschreibt. Was man aber nicht vergessen darf: Bei der Zögerlichkeit ist auch ein wesentlicher Anteil von deutscher Gründlichkeit und „wir machen es richtig und gut" dabei. Dieser Perfektionismus war ein Baustein unserer Wirtschaft und unseres wirtschaftlichen Erfolgs in der Vergangenheit. In diesen Zeiten des dynamischen Wandels ist aber auch Mut gefragt, nicht im Alten zu verharren, sondern die neuen Technologien und Möglichkeiten zu nutzen, um eine bessere Welt zu erschaffen.

**Welche gesellschaftlichen Entwicklungen oder Bewegungen machen Ihnen Mut für die Zukunft?**

Mut macht mir das breite gesellschaftliche Engagement der Deutschen: So viele Menschen, egal ob alt oder jung, sind in Vereinen, in NGOs, in sozialen und karitativen Einrichtungen oder für den Umweltschutz – einfach für eine bessere Welt – engagiert.

### Worin sehen Sie die größten Hindernisse in unserer Gesellschaft, zuversichtlicher und mutiger zu denken und zu handeln?

Das größte Hindernis sehe ich im schwindenden Vertrauen in die Gesellschaft und der mangelnden Toleranz, das Anderssein auszuhalten. Menschen, die Vertrauen in sich selbst, den anderen und die Gesellschaft und auch die Gemeinschaft haben, können mutig und zuversichtlich handeln. Und wir brauchen Führungskräfte, die genau über diese Fähigkeiten verfügen.

### Wie ermutigen Sie andere und sich selbst, etwas zu wagen?

Die Ermutigung sollte immer sein: sich selbst zu verändern! Ein junger Mann hat mal eine weise Frau gefragt: „Wie kann ich die Welt verändern?" Und sie sagte: „Auch ich wollte die Welt verändern, als ich so alt war wie du. Ich habe versucht, die Welt zu verändern, aber die Welt war so groß, und ich habe es nicht geschafft. Dann versuchte ich, mein Land zu verändern, aber auch das hat nicht geklappt. Anschließend wollte ich meine Stadt verändern, aber auch das misslang. So beschloss ich, meine Familie zu verändern, aber auch damit hatte ich keinen Erfolg. Ich erkannte, dass das Einzige, was ich ändern konnte, ich selbst war. Hätte ich mich verändert, hätte ich die Familie verändert. Die Familie hätte die Stadt verändert und die Stadt hätte das Land und das Land hätte die Welt verändern können." Veränderungen müssen immer bei einem selbst beginnen, und dazu bedarf es der Reflexion und des Mutes, es zu tun.

# MICHAEL KÄFER

Vorstand der Käfer AG

**Wie sehen Sie das Verhältnis zwischen der German Angst und der Notwendigkeit von Veränderungen, um aktuelle und zukünftige gesellschaftliche Herausforderungen zu bewältigen?**

Zwei Dinge vorweg: Ich bin kein ängstlicher Mensch, im Gegenteil. Manchmal gehen meine Begeisterungsfähigkeit und meine Impulsivität mit mir eher durch. Damit bin ich auch nicht allein, wie ich aus meinem beruflichen und privaten Umfeld weiß. Daher halte ich es für falsch, den Deutschen generell den Charakterzug der German Angst zu attestieren, damit macht man es sich zu einfach. Auf der anderen Seite ist eine gewisse negative Sicht auf die Dinge eine Stärke, da wir dazu neigen, Probleme zu lösen, statt sie auszusitzen.

Aber ich muss auch feststellen, dass sich Politik und Gesellschaft hierzulande schwertun mit Veränderungen am Status quo. Neue Ideen – in welchem Bereich auch immer – bergen immer gewisse Risiken, nicht alles klappt auf Anhieb. Doch als Unternehmer weiß ich, dass nichts schädlicher für das Geschäft ist als Stillstand, der aus Zögerlichkeit oder aus dem Wunsch heraus, es allen rechtmachen zu wollen, entsteht. Jeder wünscht sich eine Zukunft in Wohlstand und Sicherheit, und die bekommt man nicht durch Abwarten. Eine vernünftige Balance zwischen Abwägung und Risiko ist daher unabdingbar, aber ich sehe uns da trotz aller Kritik auf einem guten Weg.

**Welche gesellschaftlichen Entwicklungen oder Bewegungen machen Ihnen Mut für die Zukunft?**

Ich habe den Eindruck, dass Hilfsbereitschaft und soziales Engagement trotz oder vielleicht gerade wegen der derzeit schwierigen Rahmenbedingungen wieder zunehmen. Achtsamkeit ist auch ein Trend, den ich im Umgang mit anderen und mit der Umwelt sehr positiv finde. Mit der Generation Z beginnen zudem junge Menschen gesellschaftliche Verantwortung zu übernehmen, denen Nachhaltigkeit, Diversität, Toleranz und Freiheit besonders wichtige Werte sind. Diese Generation – auch wenn sie ebenfalls schon von Zukunftssorgen und Ängsten geplagt wird – werden Politiker, Arbeitgeber und Verbände durch ihre Argumente und ihr Handeln überzeugen müssen.

### Worin sehen Sie die größten Hindernisse in unserer Gesellschaft, zuversichtlicher und mutiger zu denken und zu handeln?

Wir brauchen mehr Vordenker, die motivieren und über die positiven Aspekte in den Veränderungen sprechen. Wir müssen uns vor Augen halten, wie gut es uns im Vergleich zu vielen anderen Ländern geht und dass wir so viele Chancen haben, die wir aber auch ergreifen müssen. Doch wo man auch hinhört: überall Bedenkenträger, die auf jedem neuen Weg nur die Stolpersteine sehen. In den Medien enthält gefühlt jede zweite Überschrift „warnen", „befürchten" oder andere negativ besetzte Begriffe, weil sich anscheinend mit Alarmismus die meisten Klicks generieren lassen. Wir sollten uns nicht hochschaukeln und uns so gegenseitig blockieren – die Geschichte zeigt doch, dass Krisen oft deutlich glimpflicher verlaufen, als von den Warnern prophezeit wurde, und dass es danach auch immer weitergegangen ist. Wir sollten viel mehr Vertrauen in unsere Resilienz und unsere Stärke haben und dies an andere weitergeben.

### Wie ermutigen Sie andere und sich selbst, etwas zu wagen?

Wie heißt es so schön: Wer nicht wagt, der nicht gewinnt. Ich habe als Unternehmer in meinem Leben schon einige Niederlagen einstecken müssen, konnte aber auf der anderen Seite deutlich mehr Siege einfahren. Auf das richtige Verhältnis kommt es an, und Erfolg spornt unheimlich an. Ich versuche, andere durch positives Denken und Handeln sowie durch Vorleben zu motivieren. Das Leben macht einfach so viel mehr Spaß ohne diffuse Angst und ständige Bedenken.

# GEORG KELL

Vorsitzender des Vorstands
der Arabesque Group

**Wie sehen Sie das Verhältnis zwischen der German Angst und der Notwendigkeit von Veränderungen, um aktuelle und zukünftige gesellschaftliche Herausforderungen zu bewältigen?**

Die deutsche Angst – zu verstehen als die Tendenz, ängstlich und düster zu sein – besitzt eine politische und eine wirtschaftliche Kehrseite. Sie ist hilfreich, um den politischen Extremismus in Schach zu halten, aus Angst, die Fehler der Vergangenheit zu wiederholen. Sie ist aber gleichzeitig eine gewaltige Bremse für Innovation und Unternehmertum. Während in anderen Kulturen unternehmerisches Scheitern als Ehrenzeichen und Grund dafür gesehen wird, sich noch mehr anzustrengen, wird es in Deutschland als soziales Stigma betrachtet und hemmt Risikobereitschaft und Kreativität. Außerdem führt die kollektive Angst zu kostspieliger Überregulierung und irrationalen Entscheidungen. Zu den Beispielen aus jüngster Zeit zählen der Beschluss, Atomkraftwerke mit hohem Standard abzuschalten, während man mit Atomkraft erzeugten Strom aus Nachbarländern importiert, oder das Verbot des „Fracking" von Gas aus heimischen Quellen zu niedrigen Kosten mit niedrigen Emissionen und Risiken, während das teure Gas mit hohem Emissionsgehalt aus anderen Ländern importiert wird.

**Welche gesellschaftlichen Entwicklungen oder Bewegungen machen Ihnen Mut für die Zukunft?**

Drei Trends sind besonders auffällig: Zum einen haben die Deutschen einen ausgeprägten Sinn für soziale Fairness und Integration, was eine wichtige Grundlage für eine breit angelegte Erneuerung ist. Zum anderen gibt es einen großen Fundus an wissenschaftlichem und technischem Fachwissen, und es gibt zahlreiche Fachleute, die stolz auf ihre Arbeit sind und die ihre Tätigkeit gerne verbessern. Zum Dritten haben die Deutschen gegenüber dem Rest der Welt (mit Ausnahme einiger anderer europäischer Länder) einen großen Vorsprung darin zu verstehen, dass es sich beim Klimawandel um eine systemverändernde Kraft handelt. Dies sind die Grundlagen, auf denen eine von Erfolg gekrönte Verjüngung der deutschen Wirtschaft erreicht werden kann. Sollte dies gelingen, kann Deutschland zu einem Wegweiser in die Zukunft werden.

## Worin sehen Sie die größten Hindernisse in unserer Gesellschaft, zuversichtlicher und mutiger zu denken und zu handeln?

**W**ie es scheint, werden hohe Einkommen und ein hoher Lebensstandard in der deutschen Politik und in der öffentlichen Meinung als eine Selbstverständlichkeit betrachtet. Wie die Wettbewerbsfähigkeit in Zukunft gesichert werden kann, wird weder ausreichend verstanden noch diskutiert, da sie von den scheinbar endlosen Debatten über Ansprüche und die Verteilung des in der Vergangenheit erwirtschafteten Wohlstands überschattet wird. Dies könnte sich als fatal erweisen. Wir Deutsche sind heute mehr auf die Verwaltung der Vergangenheit fixiert als auf Investitionen in die Zukunft. Denn Erfolg lässt einen träge werden und führt zu einer Anspruchsmentalität. Auch in der weltberühmten deutschen Bürokratie und Überregulierung spiegelt sich dieses systemische Problem wider. Das gegenwärtige System ist ganz offensichtlich nicht darauf ausgelegt, Erneuerung und Wandel zu unterstützen, sondern eher auf die Verteidigung des Status quo.

## Wie ermutigen Sie andere und sich selbst, etwas zu wagen?

**N**ach beinahe drei Jahrzehnten, in denen ich mit den Vereinten Nationen neue globale Netzwerke aufgebaut habe, bin ich nun begeistert, Arabesque zu unterstützen. Das Technologieunternehmen hat sich zum Ziel gesetzt, das Finanzwesen mithilfe von KI und Nachhaltigkeit zu verändern. Ich blicke immer in die Zukunft und bemühe mich, Gelegenheiten zu entdecken. Bei der Umsetzung finde ich es motivierend, in „Potenzialen" zu denken und Wege zu erkunden, diese durch Erzählungen und Ermutigung zu aktivieren. Die Menschen haben häufig großartige Fähigkeiten, aber es fehlt ihnen an Selbstvertrauen und Willenskraft. Ich empfinde es als sehr motivierend und lohnend, anderen dabei zu helfen, ihr gesamtes Potenzial zu erschließen. Häufig sage ich jungen Menschen, dass eine der bedeutendsten Entscheidungen, die wir im Leben haben, in der Kritik dessen besteht, was andere tun – was zwar einfach, aber auch billig ist – oder darin, etwas aufzubauen, selbst oder mit anderen, auf das wir stolz sein können. Streben Sie danach, ein „Homo ludens" anstelle eines Zynikers zu sein!

# LARS KLINGBEIL

Bundesvorsitzender der SPD, MdB

Wie sehen Sie das Verhältnis zwischen der German Angst und
der Notwendigkeit von Veränderungen, um aktuelle und zukünftige
gesellschaftliche Herausforderungen zu bewältigen?

Transformation und Wandel sind keine höheren Mächte, denen wir ausgeliefert sind. Es sind Prozesse, auf die wir einen starken Einfluss haben. Wir brauchen also keine Angst vor ihnen zu haben, wir brauchen Zuversicht, um sie zu gestalten.
Klar ist: Es liegen viele Veränderungen vor uns. Ich möchte, dass wir darin die Chancen sehen, dass wir aus den Veränderungen Verbesserungen machen. Das kommende Jahrzehnt bietet ein enormes ökonomisches Potenzial. Wir können Deutschland in Europa als Technologieführer, als Innovations- und Industriestandort langfristig sichern und stärken, Standards setzen und Arbeitsplätze schaffen. Die Entscheidungen darüber werden heute getroffen und ich bin froh, dass eine starke SPD über die Weichenstellungen für morgen mit entscheidet.

Welche gesellschaftlichen Entwicklungen oder Bewegungen
machen Ihnen Mut für die Zukunft?

Nach dem dritten Jahr mit vielfältigen Herausforderungen stellen wir fest, dass die Menschen in Deutschland stark sind und dass wir gut in der Lage sind, uns aus Krisen herauszukämpfen. Das stimmt mich grundsätzlich sehr optimistisch.

Besonderen Mut machen mir die große Hilfsbereitschaft etwa gegenüber Geflüchteten und der starke gesellschaftliche Zusammenhalt – trotz der Spaltungsversuche von politischen Akteuren wie der AfD. Die Menschen in diesem Land haben sehr viel Kraft und wollen zusammenstehen – darauf können wir stolz sein. Und darauf können wir aufbauen.

### Worin sehen Sie die größten Hindernisse in unserer Gesellschaft, zuversichtlicher und mutiger zu denken und zu handeln?

Ich glaube, dass wir uns als Gesellschaft insgesamt selbstbewusster aufstellen können, mit Blick auf das, was wir gemeinsam erreichen können. Als Politik haben wir die Verantwortung, alle Bürgerinnen und Bürger mitzunehmen, ihnen im Wandel Sicherheit zu geben. Das ist auch eine Frage des Respekts vor persönlichen Lebensleistungen und Lebenswegen. Wer sich heute abgehängt fühlt, dem fehlt oft die Zuversicht für morgen. Daher darf Transformationspolitik keine abstrakte Chancenerzählung bleiben. Die Aufgabe von Politik ist, deutlich zu machen: Wir arbeiten Tag für Tag daran, Perspektiven zu sichern und neue zu schaffen – und zwar für alle. Wir stärken den gesellschaftlichen Zusammenhalt, denn er ist die Grundlage für Fortschritt. Dann können wir mutig unsere gemeinsame Zukunft gestalten. Das ist auch ein Kernversprechen der Sozialdemokratie: eine sich verändernde Gesellschaft zusammenzuhalten.

### Wie ermutigen Sie andere und sich selbst, etwas zu wagen?

Mut ist auch immer eine Frage von Zutrauen. Die Sozialdemokratie war schon immer eine Kraft für mutigen Fortschritt, weil sie die Stärken in uns allen sieht und den politischen Anspruch formuliert, Menschen etwas zuzutrauen. Dieses Zutrauen entwickeln wir auch hinsichtlich konkreter Lösungen – sei es beim Bürgergeld, in den Fragen moderner Einwanderungspolitik oder mehr internationaler Verantwortung Deutschlands in der Welt. Wir sind gerade auf einem sehr guten Weg zu einer Gesellschaft, die sich positiven Wandel zutraut. Das ermutigt mich.

# JULIA KLÖCKNER

MdB, wirtschaftspolitische Sprecherin der
Unionsfraktion, Bundesministerin a. D.

**Wie sehen Sie das Verhältnis zwischen der German Angst und
der Notwendigkeit von Veränderungen, um aktuelle und zukünftige
gesellschaftliche Herausforderungen zu bewältigen?**

Angst ist in der Regel kein guter Ratgeber, um kluge Entscheidungen zu treffen. Angst
lähmt, und Angst macht unfrei. Aber ich verbinde mit Deutschland nicht primär Angst. Es
gibt nicht nur die sprichwörtliche German Angst, sondern auch die deutsche Qualitätsarbeit,
die deutsche Genauigkeit und Verlässlichkeit. Made in Germany wurde einst erfunden von
den Briten, um Waren aus unserem Land zu kennzeichnen als mindere Qualität. Daraus
geworden ist aber ein weltweit anerkanntes Qualitätssiegel. Solidität, Erfindungsreichtum,
Verlässlichkeit und Wettbewerbslust – auch das macht unser Land aus. Was wir für die kommenden Herausforderungen brauchen? Kein Klein-Klein. Großes und mutiges Denken, zum
Beispiel für eine Staatsreform, für eine gewisse Entrümpelung von Vorschriften, Auflagen,
Zuständigkeiten, Bürokratie. Da heißt auch: Risiken eingehen. Der Staat kann weder alles
absichern noch alles kompensieren.

## Welche gesellschaftlichen Entwicklungen oder Bewegungen machen Ihnen Mut für die Zukunft?

Unternehmertum und Erfindungsreichtum und die Gründerszene der jungen Generation.

## Worin sehen Sie die größten Hindernisse in unserer Gesellschaft, zuversichtlicher und mutiger zu denken und zu handeln?

Verlustängste sind ein großes Hindernis. Wir leben in Deutschland im Durchschnitt auf einem hohen Niveau, zum Beispiel mit Blick auf staatliche Leistungen und Aufgaben. Das kann eine Fokussierung auf die Individualisierung statt auf den Gemeinsinn haben, was wiederum den notwendigen Veränderungswillen hemmt. Einmal erreichte Standards, zum Beispiel bei Verdienst, Arbeitsrecht, staatlichen Leistungen, will man nicht aufgeben – auch wenn Steuereinnahmen sinken, die Staatsverschuldung steigt, die Wirtschaft schwächelt oder die Sozialsysteme überlastet sind. Statt offen für Reformen zu sein, werden Politiker und Parteien gerne abgestraft, die diese Reformnotwendigkeit konkretisieren.

## Wie ermutigen Sie andere und sich selbst, etwas zu wagen?

Mit Optimismus, mit guten Beispielen, wo Wagen sich gelohnt hat.

# ANNEGRET KRAMP-KARRENBAUER

Bundesministerin der Verteidigung a. D.

## Wie sehen Sie das Verhältnis zwischen der German Angst und der Notwendigkeit von Veränderungen, um aktuelle und zukünftige gesellschaftliche Herausforderungen zu bewältigen?

In den vergangenen zwei Jahrzehnten hat sich die Welt verändert. Die Anschläge vom 11. September 2001 auf das World Trade Center, die Wirtschafts- und Finanzkrise, die Flüchtlingskrise, die Coronakrise und der russische Krieg gegen die Ukraine haben unseren Alltag bestimmt. Langfristig verändern die Klimakrise, neue Technologien und der Aufstieg Chinas die Welt noch grundlegender. Diese Herausforderungen machen Angst. Das ist normal. Die Angst darf allerdings nicht größer sein als die Herausforderung selbst. Und sie muss es auch nicht, denn natürlich gibt es auch Entwicklungen, die Hoffnung machen. Die EU ist an der Wirtschafts- und Finanzkrise nicht zerbrochen. In der Pandemie gab es große internationale Solidarität. Die Ukraine ist nicht gefallen. Im Gegenteil. Unsere Wirtschaft hat sich trotz steigender Energiepreise und Inflation robust gezeigt. Es gibt also Gründe genug, um mutig zu sein.

## Welche gesellschaftlichen Entwicklungen oder Bewegungen machen Ihnen Mut für die Zukunft?

Unsere Vergangenheit und die Menschen in Deutschland. Nach dem Ende der NS-Diktatur lagen wir in Trümmern, im wahrsten und umfassendsten Sinne des Wortes. Der Mut von Millionen Menschen und Politikern wie Konrad Adenauer, Robert Schumann und Charles de Gaulle hat den Wiederaufbau und den Bau eines vereinten Europas geschafft. Der Mut der Demonstranten und Demonstrantinnen in der DDR, der Mut von Helmut Kohl, den Mantel der Geschichte zu ergreifen, hat uns die Wiedervereinigung geschenkt. Immer wenn es um große Herausforderungen ging, hat Deutschland die „Mutprobe" bestanden.

Im „Kleinen Hobbit" von J. R. R. Tolkien sagt der Zauberer Gandalf: „Ich finde, es sind die kleinen Dinge, alltägliche Taten von gewöhnlichen Leuten, die die Dunkelheit auf Abstand halten." Viele ganz gewöhnliche Menschen halten in unserem Land die Dunkelheit auf Abstand. Sie arbeiten, engagieren sich und stellen sich den Herausforderungen. Solange es von ihnen mehr gibt als Bedenkenträger, sind wir auf dem richtigen Weg.

## Worin sehen Sie die größten Hindernisse in unserer Gesellschaft, zuversichtlicher und mutiger zu denken und zu handeln?

Max Frisch hat gesagt: „Krise ist immer ein produktiver Zustand. Man muss ihr nur den Beigeschmack der Katastrophe nehmen." Eine solche Haltung ist nicht einfach einzunehmen. Jeder und jede kennt das aus dem eigenen Leben. Wenn etwas passiert, was unser gewohntes Leben drastisch verändert, trauern wir um das Verlorengegangene, sind wütend über die aufgezwungen Veränderungen, halten krampfhaft an der Vergangenheit fest. Alles mehr als menschlich. Aber wir wissen auch, dass es dabei nicht bleiben kann. Dass wir weitermachen müssen, so schwer es uns auch fallen mag. Das ist in der Politik nicht anders. Wenn wir in Deutschland in jeder Entwicklung zuerst und ausschließlich die Katastrophe sehen und nicht die Chance, bleiben wir in unserer Entwicklung stehen.

## Wie ermutigen Sie andere und sich selbst, etwas zu wagen?

Ich versuche mit gutem Beispiel voranzugehen. Mein Mantra dabei: Wenn die Gelegenheit da ist, ergreife sie. Tue es, auch wenn es risikoreich ist. Frage dich, was das Schlimmste ist, was dir passieren kann. Wenn du bereit bist, damit zu leben, brauchst du dich vor nichts zu fürchten.

# RICARDA LANG

Bundesvorsitzende von Bündnis 90/Die Grünen, MdB

**Wie sehen Sie das Verhältnis zwischen der German Angst und der Notwendigkeit von Veränderungen, um aktuelle und zukünftige gesellschaftliche Herausforderungen zu bewältigen?**

Ich finde den Begriff German Angst hier fehl am Platze. In der Krise gibt es Menschen, die sich berechtigte Sorgen machen, ob sie ihre Rechnungen noch bezahlen können, ob das Geld zum Leben reicht. Das nehme ich sehr ernst. Wir müssen da als Politik Antworten geben und das tun wir auch. Mit Blick auf die zukünftigen gesellschaftlichen Herausforderungen allerdings braucht es Mut und Innovationskraft. Wir haben in den letzten 16 Jahren erlebt, wie der Ausbau der Erneuerbaren stagnierte, wie die Solarbranche hier verlor und in China boomte, wie in Bayern der Ausbau der Stromnetze verschlafen wurde. Das hat mit German Angst nichts zu tun, sondern mit Scheuklappen und fehlender politischer Vorsorge. Die Ampel hat im ersten Jahr bereits viele wichtige Weichen gestellt, das ist ja auch etwas, was viele Unternehmerinnen und Unternehmer honorieren. Jetzt braucht es Entschlossenheit in der gesamten Gesellschaft, in Bund, Ländern und Kommunen. Auch Unternehmen müssen gemeinsam handeln, damit die Transformation gelingt. Die Wirtschaft der Zukunft ist klimaneutral, erneuerbare Energien sind ein Job-Motor. Nur wenn wir hier vorangehen, wird Deutschland als Wirtschaftsnation erfolgreich bleiben können.

**Welche gesellschaftlichen Entwicklungen oder Bewegungen machen Ihnen Mut für die Zukunft?**

Mir macht die anhaltende gegenseitige Solidarität, die unser Land trotz multipler Krisen immer wieder zusammenhält, Mut für die Zukunft. Und natürlich habe ich eine ganze Liste von Bewegungen im Kopf: In Deutschland und auch international schätze ich natürlich weiterhin die Arbeit von Fridays for Future. Sie motivieren regelmäßig Tausende junge Menschen auf der ganzen Welt, friedlich für den Klimaschutz zu demonstrieren. Aber auch der unglaubliche Mut der Frauen, der Menschen im Iran, die täglich ihr Leben riskieren, um sich und ihren Kindern eine bessere Zukunft zu ermöglichen, ist absolut wichtig.

### Worin sehen Sie die größten Hindernisse in unserer Gesellschaft, zuversichtlicher und mutiger zu denken und zu handeln?

Ein großes Thema ist Gerechtigkeit. Das fängt ja schon im Bildungssystem an, aber hört da längst nicht auf. Und gerade bei jungen Menschen erlebe ich aktuell ein großes Hadern angesichts sich überlagernder Krisen und globaler Ungleichheit. Politik und Wirtschaft müssen gemeinsam zeigen, dass es besser geht. Ich glaube, Wachstum und Gerechtigkeit schließen sich genauso wenig aus wie Wachstum und Nachhaltigkeit – entscheidend ist, was wächst, und vor allem, wie es verteilt wird. Aber das heißt auch: Wir müssen dafür sorgen, dass Zukunftstechnologien wie erneuerbare Energien oder grüner Stahl wachsen können – und nicht die fossilen.

### Wie ermutigen Sie andere und sich selbst, etwas zu wagen?

Wandel ist möglich, wenn wir zusammenarbeiten: uns gegenseitig ermutigen und inspirieren, voneinander lernen, Kompromisse finden. Letztlich ist Regierungsarbeit genau das: Ideen zu äußern, andere zu überzeugen, sie gemeinsam zu verbessern, Konsens zu finden und sie schließlich in die Tat umzusetzen. Ich persönlich finde auch immer wieder Ermutigung beim Lesen. Einer meiner liebsten Autoren, James Baldwin, schrieb in den 1960er-Jahren: „Not everything that is faced can be changed, but nothing can be changed until it is faced." Daran halte ich mich.

# CHRISTIAN LINDNER

Bundesminister der Finanzen, MdB,
Bundesvorsitzender der FDP

**Wie sehen Sie das Verhältnis zwischen der German Angst und der Notwendigkeit von Veränderungen, um aktuelle und zukünftige gesellschaftliche Herausforderungen zu bewältigen?**

Im Jahr 2015 leiteten wir Freie Demokraten unseren innerparteilichen Erneuerungsprozess ein. Unser Leitsatz war: German Mut statt German Angst. German Angst hat damals wie heute die Menschen in unserem Land kleingehalten, unsere Handlungsfähigkeit und Entschlossenheit gelähmt. German Mut dagegen stärkt die Menschen, fördert Gestaltungsfreude und verhindert die Flucht in eine lähmende Angststarre.

Dieser Leitgedanke lässt sich zweifelsfrei auf die gegenwärtigen und zukünftigen Herausforderungen übertragen, vor denen unsere Gesellschaft steht. Die zu durchlaufenden ökologischen, ökonomischen, infrastrukturellen und sicherheitspolitischen Transformationsprozesse sind erforderlich. Während German Angst in der Vergangenheit dazu geführt hat, dass Veränderungen politisch versäumt wurden, braucht es heute umso mehr die Tugenden des German Mutes: Der den Blick nach vorne richtet, diese Herausforderungen erkennt und Reformehrgeiz verkörpert. Und die gute Nachricht ist: Wenn ein Land sich selbst im Weg steht, dann kann es sich auch selbst den Weg frei geben!

## Welche gesellschaftlichen Entwicklungen oder Bewegungen machen Ihnen Mut für die Zukunft?

Mich beeindruckt, in welchem Umfang die Menschen und Unternehmen in unserem Land in Anbetracht der Folgewirkungen des russischen Angriffskriegs Widerstands- und Innovationsfähigkeit bewiesen haben. Kolportierte Szenarien über den industriellen Kollaps unseres Landes sind nicht eingetroffen. Viele Betriebe sind dabei ohne Staatshilfen ausgekommen, haben ihren Energieverbrauch erkennbar reduziert, Prozesse angepasst und dabei wesentlich zur Stabilisierung Deutschlands und Europas beigetragen.

## Worin sehen Sie die größten Hindernisse in unserer Gesellschaft, zuversichtlicher und mutiger zu denken und zu handeln?

In unserem Land gab es lange eine Zufriedenheit mit dem Status quo. Beharrlich hielt man an den Erfolgen der Vergangenheit fest. So wurde die Chance verpasst, wichtige Vorhaben zur Modernisierung des Landes anzustoßen. Somit bedarf es einer neuen Handlungsentschlossenheit und eines ausgeprägten Wunsches nach Veränderungen. Mich stimmt zuversichtlich, dass dieser Wille bereits in weiten Teilen des Landes zu spüren ist.

## Wie ermutigen Sie andere und sich selbst, etwas zu wagen?

Auf der Grundlage meiner eigenen Erfahrungen versuche ich, anderen Mut zu machen: Wagt etwas, probiert es, auch wenn ihr scheitert. Und wenn ihr scheitert, lernen wir alle etwas daraus. Für mich ist das ein großes Thema: Risiken einzugehen und im Falle des Scheiterns neue Chancen zu geben.

# CARSTEN LINNEMANN

Stellvertretender Bundesvorsitzender CDU, MdB

Wie sehen Sie das Verhältnis zwischen der German Angst und der Notwendigkeit von Veränderungen, um aktuelle und zukünftige gesellschaftliche Herausforderungen zu bewältigen?

Uns ist in Deutschland die „Einfach mal machen"-Mentalität abhandengekommen. Statt mutig neue Wege zu probieren, verstecken wir uns aus Angst, vielleicht einen Fehler begehen zu können, hinter Paragrafen. Dabei hat die Pandemie doch gezeigt, was alles möglich ist, wenn man nur will. Ich wünsche mir deshalb, dass Deutschland zu einem Land der Experimentierräume wird. Warum testen wir neue Ideen nicht in Pilotregionen, in denen Vorschriften für eine gewisse Zeit aufgehoben werden? Anschließend wird analysiert, was gut lief und was nicht. Was floppt, wird gestoppt, was gut läuft, wird auf ganz Deutschland ausgerollt. Damit würden wir den vielen Bedenkenträgern und „Es geht nicht, weil …"-Sagern in Deutschland ein Stoppschild vorsetzen.

Welche gesellschaftlichen Entwicklungen oder Bewegungen machen Ihnen Mut für die Zukunft?

Laut einer Jugendstudie der Bertelsmann-Stiftung aus dem August 2022 wollen 80 Prozent der Jugendlichen die Zukunft aktiv gestalten und mehr Verantwortung übernehmen. Drei von fünf Jugendlichen blicken der Studie zufolge mit Zuversicht in die eigene berufliche Zukunft. Auch Mut zum Gründen eines eigenen Unternehmens ist bei vielen jungen Menschen vorhanden. Darüber hinaus stimmt mich die Spenden- und Hilfsbereitschaft sehr positiv, die in Deutschland trotz Inflation und Energiekrise ungebrochen hoch ist.

## Worin sehen Sie die größten Hindernisse in unserer Gesellschaft, zuversichtlicher und mutiger zu denken und zu handeln?

Ein großes Hindernis für mehr Mut ist nach meiner Einschätzung die mangelnde Fehlerkultur in unserer Gesellschaft. Wir müssen die lähmende Angst überwinden, wir könnten an unseren Fehlern scheitern. Selbstverständlich streben wir alle nach Erfolg. Aber die Angst vor dem Scheitern darf doch nicht dazu führen, dass wir Dinge erst gar nicht probieren. Wir müssen daher Fehler mehr als Chancen begreifen, weil sie uns helfen dazuzulernen. Dazu gehört, dass wir anderen nicht mit Häme begegnen, die den Mut hatten, etwas zu probieren. Wir müssen insgesamt auf mehr Freiheit und Eigenverantwortung der Bürger setzen. Denn wo sich eine hohe Staatsgläubigkeit oder gar eine Vollkaskomentalität breitmacht, werden Mut, Eigeninitiative und Unternehmergeist abgewürgt, können keine Innovationen entstehen.

## Wie ermutigen Sie andere und sich selbst, etwas zu wagen?

Ich habe kürzlich ein Buch veröffentlicht mit dem Titel „,Die ticken doch nicht richtig!': Warum Politik neu denken muss". Darin fordere ich einen Mentalitätswandel in Deutschland, mehr Mut, mehr „einfach mal machen" und rufe dazu auf, dass wir unsere Komfortzonen verlassen und echte Strukturreformen anpacken – auch wenn es hier und da wehtun wird. Nur so werden wir die Zukunft gewinnen.

Dementsprechend habe ich auch meinen neuen Podcast „Einfach mal machen" genannt. Einmal im Monat hole ich mir spannende Gäste an den Tisch, die meinen Optimismus teilen und das Land verändern wollen. Auch via Instagram präsentiere ich in Live-Interviews spannende Vorbilder, die etwas gewagt haben und voller Tatendrang sind.

Wir dürfen jedoch nicht nur die Leistungsträger in den Blick nehmen, sondern müssen vor allem die Schwächeren der Gesellschaft ermutigen. Ich habe deshalb vor mehr als zehn Jahren eine Stiftung gegründet, die Stiftung LEBENSlauf. Wir haben uns zum Ziel gesetzt, Jugendlichen, die am Rande der Gesellschaft stehen, eine Perspektive zu geben. In einem jeweils neunmonatigen Projekt vermitteln wir den Teilnehmern Freude an Bewegung, Spiel und Sport. Durch das Sportprojekt schenken wir ihnen ein neues Selbstwertgefühl und zeigen, dass sich Mut und Fleiß langfristig auszahlen.

# JOCHEN MAAS

Geschäftsführer Forschung & Entwicklung
der Sanofi-Aventis Deutschland GmbH

**Wie sehen Sie das Verhältnis zwischen der German Angst und der Notwendigkeit von Veränderungen, um aktuelle und zukünftige gesellschaftliche Herausforderungen zu bewältigen?**

In Deutschland ist das Glas bezüglich neuer Technologien fast immer halb leer, während es in anderen Ländern halb voll ist. Daraus resultiert oft ein innovationsbremsender Technologie-Skeptizismus. Historische Beispiele sind die Debatten über die Atomkraft oder die grüne Gentechnik, aktuelle Beispiele sind die Verwendung von Gesundheitsdaten für die Forschung, die personalisierte Medizin oder auch die Gentherapie. Dabei ist nur in den seltensten Fällen eine Technologie per se angsteinflößend oder gar gefährlich, sondern immer nur die Menschen, die diese falsch anwenden. Wir sollten uns der Tatsache bewusst sein, dass wir nur mit neuen und innovativen Technologien die großen gesellschaftlichen Herausforderungen zu bewältigen in der Lage sein werden, aber nicht gegen diese. Das betrifft nicht nur die Medizin, sondern auch viele andere der aktuell kritischen Themen wie die Klimaforschung, die Biodiversitätsforschung, die Untersuchung der Migrationsströme und -hintergründe und vieles mehr. Um all diese Aufgaben bewältigen zu können, brauchen wir einen breiten gesellschaftlichen Konsens, denn nur mit dem können wir die German Angst letztendlich minimieren. Dazu bedarf es einer umfassenden Kommunikation mit der Unterstützung von Wissenschaftlern, Theologen, Ethikern, Journalisten, Politikern und vielen anderen Gruppen mehr.

### Welche gesellschaftlichen Entwicklungen oder Bewegungen machen Ihnen Mut für die Zukunft?

Es macht Mut, dass die Menschen rasch umdenken können, vor allem in Krisenzeiten. So hat die Pandemie vielen gezeigt, wie wichtig und lebensrettend die Gentechnik sein kann: Wir hätten bis heute ohne diese Technologie keinen einzigen Impfstoff. Auch die Erkenntnis, dass es Situationen geben kann, in denen der Gesundheitsschutz über dem Datenschutz steht, hat durch den Vergleich der Covid-Todeszahlen in Ländern mit guter Infektions-kettennachverfolgung gegenüber Ländern mit schlechter einen Auftrieb erfahren. Bleibt aber die Frage: Warum brauchen wir für solche Erkenntnisse eigentlich eine Krise?

### Worin sehen Sie die größten Hindernisse in unserer Gesellschaft, zuversichtlicher und mutiger zu denken und zu handeln?

Wir sind es spätestens seit der Aufklärung gewohnt, Dinge kritisch zu hinterfragen und zu versuchen, Prozesse immer erst ganz zu Ende zu denken, bevor wir sie überhaupt starten. Diese Attitude ist absolut zu begrüßen, hat uns gesellschaftlich und auch wissenschaftlich weit gebracht und weltweit viel Anerkennung eingetragen. Manchmal wäre es vielleicht aber auch besser, den Mut zu haben, Dinge zu starten und „unterwegs" zu korrigieren und nicht von Anfang an den gesamten Prozess detailliert bis zum Ende festzulegen.

### Wie ermutigen Sie andere und sich selbst, etwas zu wagen?

Mut, Offenheit, Ehrlichkeit und Transparenz sind Conditiones sine qua non. Mit diesen Grundeigenschaften dann zunächst die Chancen neuer Ansätze auszuleuchten – ohne allerdings deren Risiken zu vernachlässigen – und nicht mit den Risiken zu beginnen und sich erst am Ende den Chancen zu widmen, würde uns insgesamt optimistischer stimmen und mit mehr Zuversicht in die Zukunft blicken lassen. Gesellschaften wie die amerikanische machen uns das vor.

# ROBERT MAYR

Vorstandsvorsitzender
der DATEV eG

**Wie sehen Sie das Verhältnis zwischen der German Angst und
der Notwendigkeit von Veränderungen, um aktuelle und zukünftige
gesellschaftliche Herausforderungen zu bewältigen?**

Auch wenn das Schlagwort so griffig ist: Die viel zitierte Angst ist nur die Spitze des Eisbergs. Schon die im sprichwörtlichen „deutschen Wesen" angelegte Vorsichtigkeit ist in einer Situation problematisch, in der Veränderungsbereitschaft unumgänglich ist. Es geht um die allgemeinen Einstellungen, das Mindset der Gesellschaft, die bremsend auf den Fortschritt wirken. In Deutschland testen wir eine Erfindung lieber einmal mehr, als die Gefahr einzugehen, mit der Idee zu scheitern. Aber digitale Produkte funktionieren anders: Sie sind nie endgültig fertig, werden quasi „live" weiterentwickelt. Mit Absicherungsmentalität ist das schwer vereinbar. Deshalb müssen wir viel stärker auf die Chancen als auf die Risiken schauen und Menschen mit Ideen fördern, ihnen Strukturen schaffen, die auch ein Scheitern akzeptieren.

**Welche gesellschaftlichen Entwicklungen oder Bewegungen
machen Ihnen Mut für die Zukunft?**

Da ist für mich ganz klar die digitale Transformation ein Favorit. In der Pandemie haben wir einen Digitalisierungsschub erlebt, und auch jetzt geht es weiter voran – wenn auch nicht immer mit spektakulären Projekten. Ein Beispiel: Die Zahl der Unternehmen, von denen die buchführungsrelevanten Belege digitalisiert bei uns in der DATEV-Cloud gespeichert sind, hat kürzlich die Millionenmarke überschritten. Warum finde ich das spannend: Die Belegdigitalisierung ist die unabdingbare Basis für weitere Digitalisierungsschritte in den kaufmännischen Prozessen. Darin steckt großes Potenzial für Effizienzgewinne, bis hin zur komplett automatisierten Weiterverarbeitung dieser Daten in den einzelnen Prozessschritten. Das hilft, unsere Unternehmen schneller und schlagkräftiger zu machen.

## Worin sehen Sie die größten Hindernisse in unserer Gesellschaft, zuversichtlicher und mutiger zu denken und zu handeln?

Gemessen am Ziel, Innovation und Fortschritt in Deutschland zu fördern, haben wir eindeutig zu viel staatliche Regulierung. Wir müssen das Unternehmertum stärken und bürokratische Hürden beseitigen. Selbstständigkeit muss sich lohnen, damit aus kreativen Ideen starke Unternehmungen werden können, die innovative Produkte und Dienstleistungen hervorbringen. Ein großes Hindernis dabei ist sicher unser tradiertes „Preußisches Verwaltungssystem". Die Digitalisierung und der Übergang in eine datengetriebene Wirtschaft brauchen ein digitales Mindset. Aus Datenströmen soll Mehrwert für alle entstehen, statt dass einzelne Behörden Datensilos verwalten, die keinen volkswirtschaftlichen Nutzen stiften. Doch in der Verwaltung bedeutet Digitalisierung leider vielfach immer noch die simple digitale Abbildung papierbasierter Prozesse. Damit können Bürger und Wirtschaft viele Effizienzpotenziale nicht heben, sobald sie auf die Verwaltung angewiesen sind.

## Wie ermutigen Sie andere und sich selbst, etwas zu wagen?

Für mich geht es in erster Linie darum, offen für Neues zu bleiben, Gelegenheiten zu erkennen und dann zu ergreifen – beispielsweise mit dem Ziel, Mehrwert für die Kunden zu schaffen. Diese Geisteshaltung, dieses Mindset fördere ich auch bewusst in meinem Umfeld. Es muss akzeptiert und normal sein, ausgetretene Pfade zu verlassen, in anderen Bahnen zu denken und sich mit anderen auszutauschen. Dinge auszuprobieren, zu scheitern, zu lernen, nicht aufzugeben, bis eine Problemstellung gelöst ist. Dazu gehört natürlich auch eine Fehlerkultur, die keine Schuldzuweisungen kennt.

# FRIEDRICH MERZ

Vorsitzender der CDU Deutschlands, MdB

## Wie sehen Sie das Verhältnis zwischen der German Angst und der Notwendigkeit von Veränderungen, um aktuelle und zukünftige gesellschaftliche Herausforderungen zu bewältigen?

Wir Deutschen haben mitunter regelrecht Spaß daran, uns selbst Angst zu machen. Es gibt eine verbreitete Neigung, sich selbstquälerisch mit der Zukunft auseinanderzusetzen. Zum massiven Problem wird German Angst, wenn sie auf höchster politischer Ebene ihre Anhänger hat. Dafür liefern uns die Bundesregierung und Bundeskanzler Olaf Scholz immer wieder Beispiele. Die Scholz-Regierung zögert und zaudert, wo Zupacken geboten ist. Politisches Personal muss Vorbild sein. Und das heißt: Je größer die Herausforderungen, umso größer muss unser Glaube daran sein, sie zu bewältigen. Denn Zukunft kann nur mit Zuversicht und Zutrauen in die eigenen Fähigkeiten gestaltet werden.

## Welche gesellschaftlichen Entwicklungen oder Bewegungen machen Ihnen Mut für die Zukunft?

Seit dem 24. Februar 2022 sind wir Zeugen des russischen Angriffskriegs gegen die Ukraine. Wir sind Zeugen, wie Wladimir Putin versucht, ein ganzes Volk auszulöschen. Aber wir sind auch Zeugen, wie sich die ukrainische Nation diesem Terror heldenhaft entgegenstellt. Ja, die Ukraine kämpft auch für unsere Freiheit. Und es ist, wie die estnische Premierminis-

terin Kaja Kallas gesagt hat: „Energie mag teurer werden, aber Freiheit ist unbezahlbar."
Vielen Menschen wird wieder bewusst, was Freiheit bedeutet und welchen Wert sie hat.
Und diesen Geist der Freiheit, diese Geisteshaltung, das brauchen wir in vielen anderen
Bereichen auch. Die Probleme unserer Zeit sind lösbar, diese Botschaft sollten wir entwickeln.

## Worin sehen Sie die größten Hindernisse in unserer Gesellschaft, zuversichtlicher und mutiger zu denken und zu handeln?

Die Politik hat hier eine Verantwortung, der sie aus meiner Sicht nicht immer gerecht wird.
Sie begnügt sich zu oft mit der Beschreibung dessen, was ohnehin passiert, oder versucht,
mit dem Zeitgeist Schritt zu halten. Anspruch der Politik muss es sein, den Zeitgeist zu prägen und Vorstellungen zu formulieren, die über den Tag hinausreichen. Demut ist wichtig,
aber Mut darf deshalb nicht unter den Tisch fallen. „Wohlstand für alle" – dieses Versprechen von Ludwig Erhard war nicht Zeitgeist, ganz im Gegenteil. Es war ein mutiger Blick
in eine Zukunft, die den allermeisten Deutschen unerreichbar erschien, so kurz nach dem
Zweiten Weltkrieg. Wir müssen wieder dahin kommen, groß und mutig zu denken.

## Wie ermutigen Sie andere und sich selbst, etwas zu wagen?

Wer etwas wagt, begibt sich in Verantwortung. Aber Verantwortung zu übernehmen – in
einer Partei, in einem Unternehmen, für das Land und seine Menschen –, hat in den allermeisten Fällen etwas ungemein Erfüllendes. Und ich halte es mit Karl Popper: „Optimismus
ist Pflicht."

# FRANK ULRICH MONTGOMERY

Vorstandsvorsitzender Weltärztebund

**Wie sehen Sie das Verhältnis zwischen der German Angst und der Notwendigkeit von Veränderungen, um aktuelle und zukünftige gesellschaftliche Herausforderungen zu bewältigen?**

Deutschland kommt mir vor wie ein gelähmter Riese. Die deutschen Zwerge haben Gulliver Deutschland am Boden festgeschnürt. Dabei bräuchten wir nichts dringender als Aufbruch und Innovation, Perspektive und Zukunftsfreude. Wir müssen den kleinkarierten Streit ums letzte Detail vermeiden lernen. Wir müssen handeln und nicht nur (zer)reden. Wir müssen wieder lernen, vernünftigen „Gebrauch" zu regeln, und aufhören, aus Angst vor „Missbrauch" jeden Fortschritt zu verhindern.

**Welche gesellschaftlichen Entwicklungen oder Bewegungen machen Ihnen Mut für die Zukunft?**

Unsere Chance liegt in den jungen Menschen in diesem Land. Selbstbewusst, innovativ, kämpferisch – das ist unsere Zukunft. Fridays for future sind so eine Bewegung. Noch nie haben sich so viele so junge Menschen politisch engagiert. Wir müssen wieder von der

Gerontokratie zu einer Vertretung der Zukunftsinteressen kommen. Meine Generation (in Politik und Gesellschaft) muss aufhören, dauernd an sich selbst zu denken, und viel mehr dafür tun, dass wir unseren Nachfolgern eine Welt mit lösbaren Problemen hinterlassen.

## Worin sehen Sie die größten Hindernisse in unserer Gesellschaft, zuversichtlicher und mutiger zu denken und zu handeln?

Irgendwie ist der große Zusammenhalt unserer Gesellschaft weitgehend verloren gegangen. Statt konzertierter Aktion, statt Gemeinsamkeit regiert das Ich vor dem Wir. Der gesellschaftlichen Vereinzelung folgt der individuelle Egoismus – und daraus wird eine thematische Isolation, bei der der Blick über den Tellerrand, das Interesse für den anderen und das andere Thema auf der Strecke bleiben. Politik ist zu einem Interessenspiel weitgehend verkommen. Es fehlen die großen Entwürfe, es fehlen auch die großen Persönlichkeiten. Ja, wir haben eine Zeitenwende. Aber warum musste uns die von außen oktroyiert werden? Nicht wir haben die Zeiten gewendet, sondern uns wurde die Wende notgedrungen aufgezwungen.

## Wie ermutigen Sie andere und sich selbst, etwas zu wagen?

Offenheit, Transparenz, Toleranz und Wahrheit sind die einzig vernünftigen Triebfedern für gesellschaftliche Veränderungen. Damit wird man die Vernünftigen schon motivieren können, sich zu engagieren. Aber Fake News müssen auch erkannt, benannt und ausgemerzt werden. Wer zweifelt, wer unsicher oder verwirrt ist, kann nicht optimistisch, zukunftsorientiert und vorwärtsgewandt handeln.

# HILDEGARD MÜLLER

Präsidentin
des Verbandes der Automobilindustrie

Wie sehen Sie das Verhältnis zwischen der German Angst und
der Notwendigkeit von Veränderungen, um aktuelle und zukünftige
gesellschaftliche Herausforderungen zu bewältigen?

Wir in Deutschland müssen alte Denkmuster hinter uns lassen, um heute und in Zukunft
die großen Herausforderungen erfolgreich zu bewältigen. Eine German Angst wird uns genauso wenig weiterbringen wie einfach so weiterzumachen wie bisher. Während wir noch
zaudern und zögern, wird in anderen Teilen der Welt kreativ an der Zukunft gearbeitet. Ich
denke hier insbesondere an die Herausforderungen, vor die uns der Klimawandel stellt.

Aber natürlich sehen wir auch bei anderen Themen, dass es bei uns oft nicht schnell genug
geht. Zum Beispiel muss eine der Konsequenzen aus Russlands brutalem Angriffskrieg auf
die Ukraine sein, noch intensiver auf die internationale Zusammenarbeit mit zuverlässigen
Partnern zu setzen. Wir müssen unsere Handelspartnerschaften jetzt diversifizieren, wir
brauchen jetzt neue Energie- und Rohstoffpartnerschaften. Auch bei der Digitalisierung
und den Infrastrukturvorhaben dürfen wir nicht länger zögerlich agieren, sondern müssen
schnell die richtigen Rahmenbedingungen schaffen, damit neue Vorhaben rasch umgesetzt
werden können.

### Welche gesellschaftlichen Entwicklungen oder Bewegungen machen Ihnen Mut für die Zukunft?

Es ist vor allem die innovative Entwicklung der deutschen Industrie, die mir Mut für die Zukunft macht. Die Unternehmen aus den verschiedensten Bereichen zeigen derzeit, dass sie einen beispiellosen Transformationsprozess gestalten. Alle wollen ihren Beitrag zum Klimaschutz leisten und stellen die Produktion um. Das sehen wir bei uns in der Automobilindustrie, aber auch in unzähligen anderen Branchen. Die Unternehmen gehen hier mit einem unfassbaren Engagement voran, das seinesgleichen sucht. Wenn der Staat die Rahmenbedingungen so setzen würde, dass diese Kraft entfesselt würde und die Unternehmen nicht mit immer strikteren Regulierungen konfrontiert würden, hätte ich keine Sorgen um die Zukunft.

### Worin sehen Sie die größten Hindernisse in unserer Gesellschaft, zuversichtlicher und mutiger zu denken und zu handeln?

Der Reformdruck in unserem Land ist enorm. Die Steuer-, Abgaben- und Umlagenlast ist zu hoch – für die Bürgerinnen und Bürger, aber auch für die Unternehmen. Die Bezugsquellen von Energie und Rohstoffen sind zu wenig divers. Und alles ist zu analog. Das wissen wir schon länger. Doch passiert ist bislang viel zu wenig. Es fehlen vor allem die Geschwindigkeit und oft auch der Wille, neue Wege zu gehen und altes Denken hinter sich zu lassen. Hier müssen wir in Deutschland – und in Europa! – besser, mutiger werden. Sonst werden wir im internationalen Standortwettbewerb von mutigeren und entschlosseneren Ländern abgehängt.

### Wie ermutigen Sie andere und sich selbst, etwas zu wagen?

Ich bin überzeugt, dass man sich immer wieder selbst in Situationen begeben sollte, bei denen man aus der eigenen Komfortzone tritt. Das sage ich auch meinen Mitarbeiterinnen und Mitarbeitern immer wieder. In neuen Situationen lernen wir etwas dazu und unsere Persönlichkeit wächst dabei. Wir dürfen nicht in einem Zustand der persönlichen Lethargie verharren, sondern müssen uns immer wieder aufs Neue selbst herausfordern.

# ANGELIKA NIEBLER

Mitglied des Europäischen Parlaments,
Vorsitzende der CSU-Europagruppe

## Wie sehen Sie das Verhältnis zwischen der German Angst und der Notwendigkeit von Veränderungen, um aktuelle und zukünftige gesellschaftliche Herausforderungen zu bewältigen?

German Angst? In den Unternehmen sehe ich viel Bereitschaft zu Veränderungen, zu Innovationen, zu der Lust, immer wieder neu zu denken und Neues auszuprobieren. Von German Angst nehme ich gerade in der Wirtschaft wenig wahr, vielmehr die Sorge vor einer überbordenden Regulatorik und Rahmenbedingungen, die extrem innovationsfeindlich sind.

Große Sorgen bereiten mir dagegen Technologiefeindlichkeit und eine Politik, die die Illusion nährt, der Staat könne den Menschen alle Sorgen abnehmen. Natürlich muss in Krisensituationen gerade den Menschen geholfen und müssen die Betriebe unterstützt werden, die auf staatliche Unterstützung angewiesen sind. Maßstab sollte aber stets die soziale Marktwirtschaft sein, die Eigenverantwortung einfordert mit sozialer Absicherung. Politik muss Mut machen, Ziele geben, Visionen aufzeigen und das Vertrauen in die eigenen Fähigkeiten stärken. Wenn das Mindset stimmt, dann können wir auch gesellschaftliche Herausforderungen wie die demografische Entwicklung besser bewältigen.

## Welche gesellschaftlichen Entwicklungen oder Bewegungen machen Ihnen Mut für die Zukunft?

In der Pandemie haben wir zusammengehalten, die vor dem russischen Angriffskrieg zu uns geflohenen Ukrainerinnen und Ukrainer wurden in vielen Familien aufgenommen, viele Menschen pflegen ihre Angehörigen zu Hause, engagieren sich in Vereinen, helfen ehrenamtlich anderen Menschen oder engagieren sich für mehr Klimaschutz. Es gibt so viele

Bürgerinnen und Bürger, die sich für andere oder eine gute Sache einsetzen, das macht Mut. Mut machen auch Wissenschaftler wie Ugur Sahin und Özlem Türeci, die den Impfstoff gegen Corona entwickelt haben. All dies zeigt doch eindrucksvoll, wozu wir als Gesellschaft, als Staat, als Wirtschaft in der Lage sind, wenn es darauf ankommt. Es waren die Wissenschaftler, viele Mitarbeiterinnen und Mitarbeiter, die alles gegeben haben, um eine Antwort auf das gefährliche Virus zu finden. Das ist auch der beste Beleg, warum die soziale Marktwirtschaft gerade in Zeiten der Umbrüche das erfolgreichste Gesellschaftsmodell ist. Ludwig Erhard hat schon 1957 gesagt: „Das mir vorschwebende Ideal beruht auf der Stärke, dass der Einzelne sagen kann: Ich will mich aus eigener Kraft bewähren, ich will das Risiko des Lebens selbst tragen, will für mein Schicksal selbst verantwortlich sein. Sorge du, Staat, dafür, dass ich dazu in der Lage bin."
Diese Leitideen waren die Ursache für die vielen Wohlstandsjahre, die wir in Deutschland erlebt haben. Wenn wir uns wieder stärker auf die Grundprinzipien der sozialen Marktwirtschaft besinnen, dann habe ich keinen Zweifel, dass wir die multiplen Krisen der Gegenwart erfolgreich bewältigen werden.

## Worin sehen Sie die größten Hindernisse in unserer Gesellschaft, zuversichtlicher und mutiger zu denken und zu handeln?

Wir haben uns einen großen Wohlstand erarbeitet und haben nun Angst, dieser könnte ob all der Veränderungen verloren gehen. Das Erreichte zu verteidigen, ist eine verständliche Reaktion. Nur verteidigen ist aber zu wenig. Wenn der Wohlstand erhalten bleiben soll, muss sich vieles verändern. Stillstand ist Rückschritt. Es liegt auch an der Politik, Mut zu machen, Zukunftschancen zu geben, besonders in Krisen. Die Menschen müssen wissen, dass ihre Sorgen ernst genommen werden. Sie erwarten zu Recht ehrliche Antworten.

## Wie ermutigen Sie andere und sich selbst, etwas zu wagen?

Da kann ich mir selbst und anderen immer nur sagen: Raus aus der Komfortzone! Man muss sich selbst etwas zutrauen und man darf keine Angst davor haben, auch einmal zu scheitern. Ich ermutige andere gerne darin, etwas Neues auszuprobieren und zu wagen. Das können Anstöße zum Handeln, zum Überwinden persönlicher Hemmschwellen oder zum Durchhalten in schwierigen Situationen sein. Jeder macht Fehler, Hauptsache ist doch, daraus zu lernen. Nur mit Mut gewinnen wir die Zukunft.

# FRANK NIEHAGE

CEO der flatexDEGIRO AG

**Wie sehen Sie das Verhältnis zwischen der German Angst und der Notwendigkeit von Veränderungen, um aktuelle und zukünftige gesellschaftliche Herausforderungen zu bewältigen?**

Angst ist nie ein guter Ratgeber für Veränderungen. Wir müssen aber an vielen Stellen überholte Verhaltensmuster dringend über Bord werfen, um unseren gesellschaftlichen Wohlstand zu sichern. Das betrifft jeden Einzelnen von uns. Ohne eine private Altersvorsorge wird beispielsweise für die meisten von uns ein finanziell abgesicherter Ruhestand kaum mehr möglich sein. Die Einführung der staatlichen Aktienrente ist hier ein positives Signal. Um die German Angst vor langfristigen Anlagen am Kapitalmarkt aber nachhaltig zu überwinden, braucht es auch direkte Incentivierungen aller Privathaushalte seitens der Politik. Andere Länder wie Frankreich, Schweden oder Großbritannien sind da schon viel weiter.

**Welche gesellschaftlichen Entwicklungen oder Bewegungen machen Ihnen Mut für die Zukunft?**

Bildung. Finanzbildung im Speziellen. Nur wer Kapitalmärkte versteht, kann erfolgreich Vermögen aufbauen. Dazu kooperieren wir seit Jahren mit der Frankfurt School of Finance & Management und haben 2016 den ersten „FinTech-Bachelor" ins Leben gerufen. Und mit unserer Dokumentation „Die Kunst des Investierens" haben wir schon weit über eine Million Zuschauer erreicht. Auch dass wir mittlerweile in Deutschland erkannt haben, dass ob der geopolitischen Lage eine verteidigungsfähige Armee erstrebenswert ist, und wir dafür bereit sind, 100 Milliarden Euro zusätzlich aufzuwenden, halte ich für richtig.

## Worin sehen Sie die größten Hindernisse in unserer Gesellschaft, zuversichtlicher und mutiger zu denken und zu handeln?

Der Volksmund sagt: Not macht erfinderisch. Da ist sicher was dran. In Deutschland sind wir seit zwei, drei Generationen in der glücklichen Lage, keine Not mehr zu kennen. So erfreulich das gesellschaftlich ist, so haben uns „Wirtschaftswunder" und „Qualität made in Germany" über die Jahre träge werden lassen. An vielen Stellen wird Bestandsschutz größer geschrieben, als ein unternehmerisches Risiko einzugehen. Falsche Anreizsysteme tun ihr Übriges. Nehmen Sie den Bankbereich: Als Vorstand hafte ich persönlich für zehn Jahre, das ist doppelt so lange wie bei Nichtbanken. Gleichzeitig begrenzt die Institutsvergütungsverordnung die erfolgsabhängige Vergütung auf die Höhe des jährlichen Festgehalts. Für einen Bankenvorstand bedeutet das: höheres Risiko, bei geringerer Chance. Dass die deutsche Finanzbranche so nicht zum innovativen Vorreiter wird, sondern stattdessen international immer weiter abfällt, ist wenig überraschend.

## Wie ermutigen Sie andere und sich selbst, etwas zu wagen?

Mut muss belohnt werden. Darum ist „unternehmerisches Handeln" für alle Mitarbeitenden bei flatexDEGIRO auch nicht nur eine Floskel, sondern gelebter Alltag. Auch dank eines Mitarbeiterprogramms partizipieren heute etwa die Hälfte unserer 1.300 Mitarbeitenden als Aktionäre von flatexDEGIRO direkt am wirtschaftlichen Erfolg, den wir uns gemeinsam durch mutige Entscheidungen erarbeitet haben und der uns in wenigen Jahren vom deutschen Nischenanbieter zu Europas führendem Onlinebroker gemacht hat.

# SUSANNE PORSCHE

Deutsche Filmproduzentin
und Investorin

**Wie sehen Sie das Verhältnis zwischen der German Angst und
der Notwendigkeit von Veränderungen, um aktuelle und zukünftige
gesellschaftliche Herausforderungen zu bewältigen?**

German Angst ist meines Erachtens Folge des Wunsches, stets perfekt zu sein, nicht zu
versagen, nicht Ziel von Kritik zu werden und nicht angreifbar zu sein. Die Furcht vor dem
Scheitern zeigt sich im öffentlichen wie im privaten Bereich. Sie fördert einerseits Bedacht-
samkeit, Augenmaß, Fleiß, Zuverlässigkeit sowie ein Bewusstsein für die Wichtigkeit von
Regeln und Ordnung. Andererseits kann die Furcht vor dem Scheitern positive Entwicklungen behindern oder gar beschränken. Wichtig ist es zu verstehen, dass Hinfallen keine
Schande ist, sondern es ein Fehler ist, nach dem Fall nicht wieder aufzustehen. Denn wer
einmal hingefallen und wieder aufgestanden ist, spürt und verdient den Respekt der Gemeinschaft. In dieser Hinsicht können wir von den Amerikanern viel lernen. Wir sind auf
einem guten Weg, weil wir vor dem Hintergrund des Scheiterns zum Beispiel von Start-ups
gelernt haben, dass wir durchaus die Möglichkeit haben, gesellschaftliche, wirtschaftliche
und politische Herausforderungen zu bestehen.

## Welche gesellschaftlichen Entwicklungen oder Bewegungen machen Ihnen Mut für die Zukunft?

Mut für die Zukunft macht mir, dass wir trotz aller Widrigkeiten und Herausforderungen eine großartige, weltweit beachtete und bewährte Ausbildungs- und Bildungskultur haben, die Elite fördert, Kreativität anstößt und Zukunftschancen eröffnet. Das ist ein hohes Gut, das bewahrt werden muss und das nicht durch Einsparungen oder Neiddiskussionen gefährdet werden darf.

## Worin sehen Sie die größten Hindernisse in unserer Gesellschaft, zuversichtlicher und mutiger zu denken und zu handeln?

Das größte Hindernis in unserer Gesellschaft ist, dass wir nur selten auf unsere Politiker stolz sein können. Die zuvor beschriebene hohe Ausbildungs- und Bildungskultur trifft man bei Politikern eher selten an. Politiker ohne eine abgeschlossene Ausbildung und/oder ohne praktische Berufserfahrung wollen ihren Wählern vorgeben, wie es geht. Das kommt bei vielen Menschen nicht an. Politiker schauen auf ihre Wiederwahl und trauen sich nicht, langfristige Perspektiven zu entwickeln. Ihnen fehlt der Mut, für Entscheidungen geradezustehen – aus Angst, nicht wiedergewählt zu werden.

## Wie ermutigen Sie andere und sich selbst, etwas zu wagen?

Wir müssen die junge Generation begleiten, ihnen Werte vermitteln, diese vorleben und sie an unserem Erfahrungsschatz teilhaben lassen. Wir sollten sie in die Lage versetzen, mutig zu sein, nach einem Scheitern wiederaufzustehen, an sich und ihre Ziele zu glauben und zu erkennen, dass es wichtig ist, das selbst gesetzte Ziel stets im Auge zu behalten, auch wenn der Weg dorthin nicht frei von Hindernissen und Herausforderungen sein wird. Meine Lebenserfahrung hat mich gelehrt, dass jede Niederlage mich stärker werden ließ und mich ein Stück weitergebracht hat.

# KATHERINA REICHE

Vorsitzende des Vorstands
der Westenergie AG

**Wie sehen Sie das Verhältnis zwischen der German Angst und der Notwendigkeit von Veränderungen, um aktuelle und zukünftige gesellschaftliche Herausforderungen zu bewältigen?**

So verständlich die Sehnsucht nach Frieden und Sicherheit auch ist: Gerade in Zeiten multipler Krisen brauchen wir Mut und Vertrauen in unsere eigenen Kräfte. Ludwig Erhard glaubte zutiefst an die soziale Marktwirtschaft und ihre Grundpfeiler: Freiheit und Verantwortung, Markt und Wettbewerb. Diesen Glauben gilt es heute mehr denn je zu stärken, denn die Prinzipien sind weiterhin gültig. Erhard wollte, dass jeder Einzelne sagen kann: Ich will mich aus eigener Kraft bewähren und für mein Schicksal selbst verantwortlich sein. Doch dafür braucht es keine Angst – sondern Mut.

**Welche gesellschaftlichen Entwicklungen oder Bewegungen machen Ihnen Mut für die Zukunft?**

Selten zuvor wurde öffentlich so viel über die Zukunft der Energieversorgung diskutiert. Das sehe ich als große Chance, denn ich glaube fest an den menschlichen Erfindergeist. Und tatsächlich gibt es in vielen Bereichen der Energieerzeugung und -versorgung beeindruckende Fortschritte: Batterien werden immer leistungsfähiger, Kerosin und Pkw-Kraftstoff lassen sich synthetisch herstellen, die bislang fossilen Erdgasnetze können zu 100 Prozent Wasserstoff statt Erdgas transportieren. Und der Bau des Flüssiggasterminals in Wilhelmshaven zeigt: Ist der Druck erst groß genug, kann Deutschland nicht nur gründlich, sondern auch schnell. Das macht mir Mut.

### Worin sehen Sie die größten Hindernisse in unserer Gesellschaft, zuversichtlicher und mutiger zu denken und zu handeln?

Im Sinne Ludwig Erhards dürfen wir nicht auf dirigistische, staatliche Lösungen setzen, sondern müssen auf das Zusammenspiel der Marktkräfte im Wettbewerb vertrauen. Erhard hatte ein positives Menschenbild: Er glaubte an Kreativität, Verantwortungsbereitschaft und Pioniergeist. Und er war optimistisch, dass freier Wettbewerb Fortschritt ermöglicht. Insofern sollten wir die Krise als Chance begreifen, Altes zu überwinden und Neues zu wagen.

### Wie ermutigen Sie andere und sich selbst, etwas zu wagen?

Mut erfordert, dass wir unsere Komfortzone verlassen. Im ersten Schritt kann es helfen, die eigenen Ängste zu analysieren. Wovor fürchten wir uns, was kann schlimmstenfalls passieren? Wer das weiß, verschafft sich Erleichterung, reduziert die Angst und schöpft neuen Mut. Im zweiten Schritt sollte man sich bewusst machen: Jede neue Idee erntete zunächst Widerstand, jede Veränderung stößt auf Zweifel. Ohne Mut gibt es keinen Fortschritt, egal ob ökonomisch oder gesellschaftlich. Wer wagt, muss nicht immer gewinnen. Aber wer nichts wagt, hat schon verloren.

# HAGEN RICKMANN

Geschäftsführer Geschäftskunden
der Telekom Deutschland GmbH

**Wie sehen Sie das Verhältnis zwischen der German Angst und der Notwendigkeit von Veränderungen, um aktuelle und zukünftige gesellschaftliche Herausforderungen zu bewältigen?**

Das hängt davon ab, wie man German Angst definiert. Ich denke, dass unsere Angst zwei Facetten hat: Die eine Facette ist Zukunftsangst – sie steht Veränderungen nicht entgegen. Im Gegenteil: Sie kann uns sogar zu Veränderungen antreiben, denn bei unsicheren Zukunftsaussichten macht man nicht einfach weiter wie bisher. Die andere Facette ist eine gewisse Verzagtheit, und das ist im Hinblick auf Veränderungen natürlich alles andere als vorteilhaft. Wir sollten lernen, dieser Facette Herr zu werden. In einer Zeit, in der vieles in der Welt neu verteilt wird, ist diese Verzagtheit fehl am Platz. Deutschland ist ein Technologieland; wir legen großen Wert auf Qualität. Ganz wichtig ist, unser Augenmerk künftig noch stärker auf Innovation zu legen.

**Welche gesellschaftlichen Entwicklungen oder Bewegungen machen Ihnen Mut für die Zukunft?**

Mir macht die heutige Jugend Mut. Dass der Begriff „die Jugend von heute" eher negativ konnotiert ist, kann ich nicht nachvollziehen. Die junge Generation ist in vielerlei Hinsicht umtriebiger als die Generation vor ihr. Sie ist reflektierter, selbstkritischer – und sie hat keine Scheu, das, was ihr von der älteren Generation vorgelebt wird, zu hinterfragen. Wenn ich beispielsweise mit meinen Kindern über Klimaschutz gesprochen habe, traue ich mich danach kaum noch, ein Taxi zu nehmen. Spaß beiseite: Es stimmt mich zuversichtlich, dass sich kommende Generationen aktiv für einen Wandel einsetzen.

## Worin sehen Sie die größten Hindernisse in unserer Gesellschaft, zuversichtlicher und mutiger zu denken und zu handeln?

Wir sind traditionell prozessverliebt und perfektionistisch. Offen, agil und bereit sein, auch mal ein Scheitern in Kauf zu nehmen? Eher selten. Wenn wir unseren Zwang überwinden könnten, alles Erdenkliche im Vorfeld berücksichtigen zu wollen, wäre bereits viel gewonnen. Es ist ja nicht so, dass wir keine mutigen Ideen hätten. Wir stecken jedoch mehr Arbeit in das Finden von „Aber"-Einwänden als in die pragmatische Umsetzung dieser Ideen.

## Wie ermutigen Sie andere und sich selbst, etwas zu wagen?

Indem ich mich an Vorbildern orientiere oder auf diese verweise. In Deutschland gelten rund 1.500 Unternehmen als Hidden Champions – also als Betriebe, die in der breiten Öffentlichkeit zwar wenig bekannt, aber Weltmarktführer ihrer Branche sind. Diesen Status haben sie, weil sie Mut gezeigt haben. Sie haben entweder neue Produkte, Technologien oder Services erfunden und an den Start gebracht oder Trends frühzeitig erfasst und für den Mittelstand übersetzt. Sich mit ihnen zu befassen, ist unheimlich inspirierend. Das sage ich auch unseren Kunden. Im Übrigen sind die Voraussetzungen dafür, etwas zu wagen, in Deutschland viel besser, als man gemeinhin denkt: Es gibt hier mehr Förderprogramme als in den meisten anderen Ländern Europas. Nicht von ungefähr gilt Deutschland als Top-2-Land für Start-ups auf dem Kontinent – lediglich in Großbritannien fließt noch mehr Risikokapital in junge Unternehmen.

# SARNA RÖSER

Bundesvorsitzende des Wirtschaftsverbandes
DIE JUNGEN UNTERNEHMER

**Wie sehen Sie das Verhältnis zwischen der German Angst und der Notwendigkeit von Veränderungen, um aktuelle und zukünftige gesellschaftliche Herausforderungen zu bewältigen?**

Aus der Hirnforschung wissen wir, dass noch aus den Zeiten von Höhlenbewohnern und Säbelzahntigern die Vorsicht bei Veränderungen zehnmal stärker in uns wirkt als die Vorfreude auf bessere Zeiten. Trotzdem haben wir es geschafft, aus der Steinzeit auszubrechen. Aus Sicht unserer jungen Generation sind auch jetzt wieder Veränderungen ein Muss! Dafür braucht es Mut, und den haben wir trotz der uns nachgesagten German Angst immer wieder bewiesen. An vielen Stellen haben wir uns einen Namen als Land der Erfinder, Qualitätslieferer und Innovatoren gemacht. Die Zahl an innovativen Weltmarktführern im deutschen Mittelstand ist der beste Beleg dafür. Und trotzdem gibt es Handlungsbedarf!
Mit gesellschaftlichen Herausforderungen sind wir durch Pandemie, Inflation und die Energiekrise schon geübter als noch vor einigen Jahren. Unsere Resilienz wurde weiter gestärkt – und wir alle haben gelernt, dass die soziale Marktwirtschaft ein Erfolgsmodell ist, aber auch, dass unsere Wirtschaft fragiler ist, als die meisten dachten. Wohlstand ist keine Selbstverständlichkeit, sondern muss erarbeitet werden. Dazu müssen alle anpacken – jeder wo er kann. Der Staat sollte dafür Brücken bauen, sodass jeder Einzelne seinen Weg gehen und seine Geschichte schreiben kann. Bildungsangebote und Standortbedingungen müssen dafür aber rasant verbessert werden, um dem German Mut eine nachhaltige Startrampe zu bieten.

**Welche gesellschaftlichen Entwicklungen oder Bewegungen machen Ihnen Mut für die Zukunft?**

Durch Globalisierung und Vernetzung weitet sich der Blick für Neues und Veränderungen überall auf der Welt. Gerade junge Menschen in Deutschland wollen dabei eine führende

Rolle spielen. Das zeigen die vielen zukunftsträchtigen Start-up-Gründungen in den letzten Jahren. Großer Standortvorteil in Deutschland sind dafür die gewachsenen Strukturen vieler Familienunternehmen. Sie sind groß geworden, weil sie innovativ sind; sie zeigen, wie neue Ideen in einen nachhaltigen Geschäftserfolg verwandelt werden können.

Doch mehr denn je locken ausländische Standorte mit vielfach besseren Rahmenbedingungen. Damit Unternehmen bei Marktveränderungen gut aufgestellt sind, brauchen sie Gestaltungsspielraum und gute Bedingungen für Investitionen in Forschung und Entwicklung. Hier gilt es anzusetzen und Deutschland im Standortwettbewerb wieder besser aufzustellen – und für den Wettbewerb zu wappnen.

## Worin sehen Sie die größten Hindernisse in unserer Gesellschaft, zuversichtlicher und mutiger zu denken und zu handeln?

Der ungestoppte Ausbau des Sozialstaats hat seine Wurzeln in der German Angst. Mit jeder Wahl werden mehr Wählergruppen bedient und gegen große finanzielle Versprechen Stimmen gesichert. Indem jeder in jeder Lebenslage aufgefangen und gut gepolstert durch jede Krise gebracht wird, nötigt der Staat den mündigen Bürger in die Abhängigkeit unseres Staates. In der Konsequenz wächst der Glaube daran, dass der Staat es schon irgendwie richten wird. Das kann er aber nur, wenn Steuergeld hierzulande erwirtschaftet wird und nicht der Erfindungs- und Innovationswille und damit letztendlich auch die Selbstverwirklichung vieler durch immer größere Staatseingriffe gehemmt werden. Mein Appell: Krise sollte immer auch als Chance und nicht nur als Anlass für immer größere staatliche Zuwendungen begriffen werden. Stattdessen braucht es in die Zukunft gerichtete Maßnahmen, vor allem mehr Bildung in den Bereichen Wirtschaft und Digitales, endlich Bürokratieabbau und ein Verständnis dafür, dass Politiker und Beamte keinesfalls besser als die Unternehmen wissen, welche Technologien sich künftig bei den Bürgern durchsetzen können.

## Wie ermutigen Sie andere und sich selbst, etwas zu wagen?

Nach meiner Erfahrung spielen Positivbeispiele, Vorbilder und ein „Informationswerkzeugkoffer" die größte Rolle. Viele junge Menschen haben tolle Ideen und wissen nur noch nicht, wohin damit. Unsere Verantwortung ist, mutigen jungen Menschen zu zeigen, was alles geht. Deswegen sind mir der Austausch in Verbänden wie Die jungen Unternehmer, gute Öffentlichkeitsarbeit und der Dialog mit der Politik so wichtig. Der Wille zu gestalten und Veränderung voranzutreiben, ist schon der erste Schritt. Es liegt aber auch in der Verantwortung unserer Politik, dass eine Umsetzung darauf folgen kann.

# ANDREAS RÜTER

Geschäftsführer und Local Market Leader
von AlixPartners Deutschland

### Wie sehen Sie das Verhältnis zwischen der German Angst und der Notwendigkeit von Veränderungen, um aktuelle und zukünftige gesellschaftliche Herausforderungen zu bewältigen?

Die German Angst, deren Ursprung wahrscheinlich in den zutiefst verunsichernden Erfahrungen in der ersten Hälfte des 20. Jahrhunderts liegt, ist für den Umgang mit Krisen und deren Bewältigung nicht hilfreich. Deutsche sehen das Ausmaß einer Krise kollektiv in der Regel deutlich schlimmer, als es dann im Rückblick gewesen ist.

Dies ist kontraproduktiv für die Bewältigung von Herausforderungen. Zwar ist die deutsche Wirtschaft aus Krisen wie der Ölkrise in den 1970er Jahren, dem Platzen der Dotcom Blase oder der Finanzkrise immer gestärkt hervorgegangen – man fragt sich aber: Muss es immer erst eine Krise geben als Katalysator für notwendige Veränderung? Und ist die Polykrise jetzt Druck genug, Kräfte zu einen, Ideologien hinten anzustellen, die German-Angst-Bremse zu lösen – und den Schalter für Veränderungen umzulegen?

„Geht nicht, gibt's nicht." Man wünscht sich die Besinnung auf deutsche Tugenden. Auf Ingenieurskunst und Innovationskraft, Mut und Zuversicht – um jetzt die Herausforderungen von geopolitischem Wandel und Klimazielen im Einklang mit wirtschaftlichem Erfolg anzugehen. Dabei mittelfristig zu denken, anstatt alles kurzfristig und mit Ad-hoc-Einzelmaßnahmen umzusetzen.

### Welche gesellschaftlichen Entwicklungen oder Bewegungen machen Ihnen Mut für die Zukunft?

Die Stabilität des Arbeitsmarktes und der ungebrochene unternehmerische Mut im Mittelstand. Die deutsche Gesellschaft verfügt aufgrund ihrer Finanzkraft und ihrer im Kern sehr stabilen politischen und staatlichen Systeme über ein hohes Maß an Resilienz – vorausgesetzt es gelingt, den öffentlichen Diskurs in einem vernunftgeleiteten, sachlichen Rahmen zu halten.

Wenn selbst auf Restrukturierungs- oder Investoren-Konferenzen Konformität mit Umweltstandards und nicht nur Rentabilitätskriterien diskutiert werden, ist das ermutigend. Wenn wir auf unsere Innovationskraft setzen, werden wir die Klimakrise nicht nur meistern, sondern in Zukunft auch profitieren.

Eine politisch aktive und sensibilisierte junge Generation, die den Mut hat, grundlegende Prioritäten der Lebensplanung neu zu denken und die Bereitschaft, den Status quo infrage zu stellen, kann positive Effekte auslösen.

## Worin sehen Sie die größten Hindernisse in unserer Gesellschaft, zuversichtlicher und mutiger zu denken und zu handeln?

Zunehmende „Verbotspolitik" und Regulation: Überbordende Bürokratie und Regulierung sind ein limitierender Faktor.

Der Hang zur Perfektion: Es gibt zu viele Hürden, um eine gute Idee schnell und effizient in ein marktrelevantes Produkt und Unternehmen zu überführen.

Gesunde Diskussions- und Streitkultur: Die Presse hatte früher stets eine Funktion, die Diskurskultur hochzuhalten. Die heutige Medienlandschaft, insbesondere mit Einfluss der sozialen Medien und teilweise gezielter Manipulation trägt zur Frontenbildung bei und ist unproduktiv für die gesellschaftliche Entwicklung.

Gleichmacherei: Die Verdammung von Eliten und der Versuch, sich auf den kleinsten gemeinsamen Nenner zu fokussieren, sind einer innovativen und fortschrittlichen Industrie und Gesellschaft nicht dienlich.

## Wie ermutigen Sie andere und sich selbst, etwas zu wagen?

Gemeinsam Neues angehen und vorantreiben. Freiraum lassen, motivieren, positiv aufladen. Verstärkt über die Chancen und nicht nur über die Risiken sprechen. Eine offene Grundhaltung gegenüber Neuem erzeugen und bei Rückschlägen Mut zusprechen. Und nie zu vergessen: Gute Freunde, Partner, Vertraute an der Seite haben.

# SONJA SCHWETJE

Chefredakteurin von ntv

Wie sehen Sie das Verhältnis zwischen der German Angst und der Notwendigkeit von Veränderungen, um aktuelle und zukünftige gesellschaftliche Herausforderungen zu bewältigen?

Veränderungen rufen nicht nur bei Mitarbeitenden in Unternehmen, sondern auch bei Bürgern eines Landes häufig Unsicherheiten und Widerstände hervor. Je komplexer die Krisen und je größer die Herausforderungen sind, desto stärker die Beharrungskräfte. Insbesondere nach einer langen Phase von Stabilität und Wohlstandswachstum ist es daher erklärbar, dass viele Menschen sich an diese Phase klammern und besonders kritisch auf Veränderungsprozesse, erst recht disruptiver Art, blicken. Wie in einer Organisation ist hier eine intensive Kommunikationsbegleitung entscheidend für das Gelingen des Umbruchs. Das ist in einem Land mit rund 83 Millionen Bürgern nicht einfach. Doch neben einer ganzheitlichen Zukunftsstrategie, die dann auf einzelne Bereiche heruntergebrochen wird, braucht es auch die passende Kommunikationsstrategie.

Welche gesellschaftlichen Entwicklungen oder Bewegungen machen Ihnen Mut für die Zukunft?

Ich beobachte ein hohes Maß an Energie und Gestaltungswillen in Teilen der Gesellschaft. Es gibt viel mehr Menschen, die bereit zum Aufbruch sind, als die, die versuchen, Bestehendes um jeden Preis zu bewahren. Die richtige Mischung zu finden, ist ein Balanceakt. Bestimmte Werte und Fähigkeiten haben das Fundament für den Erfolg der deutschen Wirtschaft gelegt. Sie können helfen, uns in die nächste Stufe der Transformation zu bringen. Gleichzeitig muss man sich von einigen früheren Erfolgsfaktoren trennen, weil sie in einer digitalisierten Welt eher bremsen.

## Worin sehen Sie die größten Hindernisse in unserer Gesellschaft, zuversichtlicher und mutiger zu denken und zu handeln?

Die Flut an Informationen, die Gleichzeitigkeit von Krisen und die schier unlösbaren globalen und lokalen Herausforderungen unserer Zeit überfordern viele Menschen und lösen ein Gefühl der Hilflosigkeit aus. Es ist menschlich völlig nachvollziehbar, dass das lähmend wirken kann. Wenn dann noch einzelne Ereignisse hinzukommen, die auf Fehlfunktionen beziehungsweise Versagen von Verwaltung oder öffentlichen Institutionen zurückzuführen sind, verlieren manche den Glauben daran, dass unsere Gesellschaft die richtigen Rahmenbedingungen bietet, um gute Ideen umzusetzen. Ein Beispiel ist die Pannenwahl zum Berliner Abgeordnetenhaus 2021, die nun wiederholt werden muss.

## Wie ermutigen Sie andere und sich selbst, etwas zu wagen?

Kommunikation und Reflexion spielen in allen Bereichen der Veränderung eine entscheidende Rolle. Wir müssen uns immer wieder verdeutlichen, wo unser Handlungsspielraum ist, und uns fragen, ob wir ihn wirklich ausnutzen. Häufig ist er größer als gedacht. Und es hilft, sich immer wieder vor Augen zu halten, dass die Lösung für ein komplexes Problem nicht in einem einzigen Schritt erfolgen kann, sondern durch viele zielführende Teillösungen, zu denen jeder und jede Einzelne beitragen kann.

# RAINER SESSNER

Geschäftsführer
von Bayern Innovativ

**Wie sehen Sie das Verhältnis zwischen der German Angst und der Notwendigkeit von Veränderungen, um aktuelle und zukünftige gesellschaftliche Herausforderungen zu bewältigen?**

Ich halte den Begriff German Angst für ein stereotypes Vorurteil. Es impliziert, dass die deutsche Wirtschaft per se ängstlich agiere. Wir erleben bei Bayern Innovativ im täglichen Austausch mit bayerischen Unternehmen aber oft genug das Gegenteil, nämlich eine große Bereitschaft zur Veränderung. Deshalb bin ich der Überzeugung, dass die negative Stimmung in der Berichterstattung einen viel größeren Raum einnimmt, als ihr zukommen sollte.
Wir müssen uns vor Augen halten, wie innovativ und leistungsfähig unsere Wirtschaft ist – insbesondere der Mittelstand. Und genau das brauchen wir, um für die Zukunft gerüstet zu sein. Veränderung ist der Schlüssel zur Bewältigung aktueller und zukünftiger gesellschaftlicher Herausforderungen. Gleichzeitig müssen wir uns darüber im Klaren sein, dass eine funktionierende soziale und nachhaltige Marktwirtschaft weiter einer Leistungsgesellschaft bedarf.

**Welche gesellschaftlichen Entwicklungen oder Bewegungen machen Ihnen Mut für die Zukunft?**

Die Geschichte zeigt, dass die Menschheit aus nahezu jeder Krise gestärkt hervorgegangen ist. Das macht mir Mut. Insofern kann die aktuelle Zeit ein wichtiger Schritt sein. Der Preis, den viele Menschen dafür zahlen müssen, ist jedoch viel zu hoch – sei es durch Krieg, Trockenheit, Überschwemmungen oder andere Katastrophen.

Positiv stimmen mich unsere Kunden bei Bayern Innovativ. Die meisten haben die Notwendigkeit zur Veränderung realisiert und erkennen deren Chancen. Unsicherheit herrscht eher über das Wie. Vor allem kleine und mittlere Firmen brauchen Impulse und Unterstützung. Und die leisten wir mit Wissen um Zukunftstechnologien sowie -trends und indem wir die richtigen Werkzeuge oder sogar Partner an die Hand geben. Und das branchenübergreifend.

### Worin sehen Sie die größten Hindernisse in unserer Gesellschaft, zuversichtlicher und mutiger zu denken und zu handeln?

Eine gesättigte Öffentlichkeit, die keine Lust (mehr) hat, sich zu ändern, und deshalb Veränderungen blockiert, ist ein großes Hindernis. Wenn wir uns schon von vorneherein einschränken, indem wir beispielsweise neue Technologien nicht nutzen, werden wir keine positive Zukunft gestalten. Außerdem ist stellenweise ein Rechts- und Verwaltungssystem entstanden, das eine freie, soziale Marktwirtschaft behindert. Es befeuert das teils verschobene Verhältnis aus Anspruch, Leistung und der Bereitschaft, gesellschaftliche Verantwortung zu übernehmen. Die Frage ist, was ist Henne und was Ei.

### Wie ermutigen Sie andere und sich selbst, etwas zu wagen?

Das ist seit 27 Jahren unsere DNA – etwas, das wir mit großer Leidenschaft tun. Wir unterstützen bayerische Firmen, sich neu aufzustellen und Veränderungen zu meistern – sei es mit neuen Technologien oder Geschäftsmodellen. Dabei sind Netzwerke und Wissenstransfer wichtiger denn je. Ich bin überzeugt, dass Wirtschaft, Wissenschaft und Forschung in Zukunft noch intensiver zusammenarbeiten müssen und werden. Ein perfekter Ausgangsort ist unser Thinknet Bayern. Es ist mit über 75.000 Kontakten das größte Netzwerk des Freistaats und verknüpft Wirtschaft, Wissenschaft und Politik mit Branchen-, Technologie- und Partnernetzwerken.

# MARGRET SUCKALE

Mitglied des Aufsichtsrats
der Infineon Technologies AG

**Wie sehen Sie das Verhältnis zwischen der German Angst und der Notwendigkeit von Veränderungen, um aktuelle und zukünftige gesellschaftliche Herausforderungen zu bewältigen?**

Den Deutschen wird in der Tat nachgesagt, besonders ängstlich zu sein, und da ist sicher auch was dran. An Bedenkenträgern mangelt es uns jedenfalls erkennbar nicht im Land. Ich will damit die großen Herausforderungen, die vor uns liegen, gar nicht kleinreden. Im Gegenteil: Krieg, Pandemie, Inflation, Gasknappheit – all das bereitet allergrößte Sorgen. Aber es kommt darauf an, wie man mit diesen enormen Herausforderungen bestmöglich umgeht. Angst ist der denkbar schlechteste Ratgeber. Wir brauchen mehr Selbstvertrauen in die eigenen Stärken, verbunden mit dem Willen, notwendige Veränderungen gemeinsam anzugehen. Andere Länder machen auch komplexe Dinge mit mehr Leichtigkeit. In den USA steht der „Pursuit of Happiness" sogar in der Unabhängigkeitserklärung. Ich wünsche mir auch für Deutschland viel mehr positive Energie.

**Welche gesellschaftlichen Entwicklungen oder Bewegungen machen Ihnen Mut für die Zukunft?**

Die Realität schlägt glücklicherweise regelmäßig die vielen pessimistischen Vorhersagen. Anders als von so manchem Experten prognostiziert, sind die Gasspeicher in diesem Winter gefüllt, die ersten LNG-Terminals sind in Rekordzeit errichtet worden. Die Industrieproduktion ist bei Weitem nicht so zurückgefallen wie befürchtet. Auch der Arbeitsmarkt zeigt bisher keine Schwäche, im Gegenteil. Das sind alles wirklich positive Signale. Und dann schaue ich auf die anhaltend hohe Innovationsfähigkeit der deutschen Unternehmen. Um das Know-how unserer Naturwissenschaftler und Ingenieure beneiden uns zu Recht viele. Unsere Wissenschaftler machen die große Transformation in so vielen Bereichen überhaupt erst möglich.

### Worin sehen Sie die größten Hindernisse in unserer Gesellschaft, zuversichtlicher und mutiger zu denken und zu handeln?

Das Land der Dichter und Denker zu sein, ist ja per se nichts Schlechtes. Aber wir sind viel zu kompliziert geworden, oft auch selbstzufrieden, wollen alles regulieren und leisten uns eine enorme Bürokratie. Bauvorhaben zum Beispiel dauern viel zu lange. Auch die Digitalisierung der Verwaltung müsste viel schneller erfolgen. Viele gute Ideen scheitern bei uns häufig an der Umsetzung. Das muss nicht sein. Das sollten wir ändern. Weniger „Wenn und Aber" und mehr „Einfach machen" sollten dabei die Devise sein.

### Wie ermutigen Sie andere und sich selbst, etwas zu wagen?

In Diskussionen konzentriere ich mich mehr denn je auf die Stärken der deutschen Wirtschaft: gut ausgebildete Mitarbeiter:innen, der Erfindergeist deutscher Techniker und Ingenieure, großartige Unternehmen mit guten Arbeitsbedingungen und eine ständig wachsende Szene interessanter Start-ups. Internationale Kapitalgeber investieren zunehmend in deutsche Gründungen, und die Anzahl der Unicorns in Deutschland wächst. Der Mut und die Begeisterung der jungen Gründer:innen sind wirklich bemerkenswert und ein Beispiel dafür, dass nur gewinnt, wer auch wagt.
Ich bin eine optimistische Realistin. Meine Devise lautet: „Was ist, ist!" Daher versuche ich keine Zeit mit dem Beklagen von Situationen zu verlieren, die nicht zu ändern sind, sondern mich darauf zu fokussieren, wo wir den Hebel ansetzen und etwas verbessern können.

# HORST M. TELTSCHIK

Honorarprofessor
der Technischen Universität München

Wie sehen Sie das Verhältnis zwischen der German Angst und
der Notwendigkeit von Veränderungen, um aktuelle und zukünftige
gesellschaftliche Herausforderungen zu bewältigen?

Der Begriff German Angst ist gegenwärtig vor allem in den angelsächsischen Medien populär. Mit einer gewissen Schadenfreude wird damit die Hilflosigkeit der deutschen Politik charakterisiert, überzeugende und vor allem unmissverständliche Entscheidungen über militärische Hilfeleistungen für die Ukraine zu treffen.

Tatsächlich entstehen Ängste, wenn offensichtliche Probleme wie der Krieg in der Ukraine oder zunehmende Umweltkatastrophen oder Pandemien und anderes mehr über die Massenmedien oder individuell erfahrbar werden und gleichzeitig die Verantwortlichen in Politik und Gesellschaft keine nachvollziehbaren Antworten oder gar Entscheidungen aufweisen können. Vielen wäre geholfen, so meine Erfahrung in Politik und Wirtschaft, wenn man ihnen die Ursachen und die Komplexität der Probleme verständlich erklären würde, um aufzuzeigen, dass es keine schnellen und einfachen Antworten geben kann. Wenn ich etwas verstehe, kann ich mich auch individuell besser darauf einstellen.

### Welche gesellschaftlichen Entwicklungen oder Bewegungen machen Ihnen Mut für die Zukunft?

Mut für die Zukunft – das ist zuallererst eine Anfrage an jeden Einzelnen. Heute sind Wissen und Informationen in Sekundenschnelle weltweit verfügbar und damit positiv wie negativ nutzbar. Das hat beispielsweise der Arabische Frühling gezeigt oder die anhaltenden Proteste der jungen Menschen im Iran, aber auch die der Klimaaktivisten oder die Aufmärsche von Rechtsradikalen in Teilen Ostdeutschlands. Mut für die Zukunft macht die Tatsache, dass es immer schwieriger wird, geschlossene Gesellschaften aufrechtzuerhalten und Menschenrechtsverletzungen zu verbergen.

### Worin sehen Sie die größten Hindernisse in unserer Gesellschaft, zuversichtlicher und mutiger zu denken und zu handeln?

Jammern ist einfacher, als darüber nachzudenken, wie Probleme lösbar wären, und selbst dabei anzupacken. Letzteres setzt aber Wissen voraus. Wer vermittelt es und wie? Sind Eltern, Schulen, Vereine, Medien willens und fähig, Wissen und Eigenverantwortung zu vermitteln? Führt individuelles Scheitern zum Ausschluss aus einer Gemeinschaft oder zu hilfreicher Solidarität und Ermutigung, Neues zu wagen?

### Wie ermutigen Sie andere und sich selbst, etwas zu wagen?

Intellektuelle Neugierde wecken, um sich notwendiges Wissen anzueignen. Selbstvertrauen wecken und fördern. Erfolge würdigen, Niederlagen analysieren und zu neuen Lösungsversuchen ermutigen.
Die Losung muss lauten: Never give up!

# FRANK THELEN

Europäischer Seriengründer,
Technologie-Investor und TV-Persönlichkeit

## Wie sehen Sie das Verhältnis zwischen der German Angst und der Notwendigkeit von Veränderungen, um aktuelle und zukünftige gesellschaftliche Herausforderungen zu bewältigen?

Veränderungen sind immer schmerzhaft und besonders in Deutschland haben wir das Problem, dass es uns aufgrund unserer starken Vergangenheit heute noch gut geht. Wir sind in eine Art Wohlstandsschlaf verfallen und müssen jetzt dringend erkennen, dass wir von unserer Substanz leben. Wir sehen Probleme, aber keine Chancen, dabei sind die großen Herausforderungen unserer Zeit gleichzeitig auch die größte Chance, Deutschland und Europa neu zu erfinden. Dazu gehört auch, eine neue Fehlerkultur zu etablieren und so die German Angst abzulegen. Viele deutsche Unternehmen bringen keine Innovationen hervor, weil ihre Mitarbeiter sich nicht trauen, neue Ideen und Visionen zu verfolgen. Es fehlt die nötige Incentivierung, auch mal von bestehenden Prozessen abzuweichen. Mit „das haben wir schon immer so gemacht" kommen wir nicht weiter. Wovor wir wirklich Angst haben sollten: Wenn wir so weitermachen wie bisher, werden wir schon bald nicht mehr auf Augenhöhe mit den Weltmächten USA und China verhandeln können. Wir brauchen German Mut statt German Angst.

## Welche gesellschaftlichen Entwicklungen oder Bewegungen machen Ihnen Mut für die Zukunft?

Wir haben herausragende Universitäten und weltweit führende Forschung. Unsere Hidden Champions sind noch stark und es gibt das Phänomen der globalen Nischenmarktführer im Mittelstand nur hier. Was wir jetzt brauchen, sind NextGen-Champions, die in die Fußstapfen von Ferdinand Porsche und Robert Bosch treten. Ich darf mit Freigeist einige der Hoffnungsträger unterstützen: mit Lilium Aviation kommt einer der führenden Player im EVTOL-Taxi-Markt aus Deutschland und Kraftblock hat einen Energiespeicher entwickelt, der schon bald unsere Industrie dekarbonisieren und langfristig den Umstieg auf erneuerbare Energien ermöglichen kann. Es braucht aber auch die richtigen Impulse aus der Politik – hier würde ich mir wünschen, dass politische Entscheidungen zukünftig mehr auf Erkenntnissen der Wissenschaft und den Gesetzen der Natur basieren. Der Klimawandel ist eine der größten Herausforderungen der Menschheit, es gibt technische Lösungen, aber wir fahren unsere Kohlekraftwerke hoch.

### Worin sehen Sie die größten Hindernisse in unserer Gesellschaft, zuversichtlicher und mutiger zu denken und zu handeln?

Wir haben in Deutschland keine Heldenkultur. Im Silicon Valley sieht das anders aus: ein Elon Musk oder Jeff Bezos werden dort, auch wenn sie teilweise kontroverse Entscheidungen treffen und ihre Unternehmen sehr progressiv führen, für ihre Erfolge gefeiert. Ob man jede ihrer Entscheidungen deshalb gut finden muss, sei mal dahingestellt. Aber das positive Momentum im Silicon Valley lebt nicht zuletzt davon, dass Gründer dort deutlich mehr Support finden – sei es von Investoren oder den Medien.

### Wie ermutigen Sie andere und sich selbst, etwas zu wagen?

Ich bin im Laufe meines Lebens oft gescheitert und habe gelernt, immer wieder aufzustehen. Auch jetzt gerade erlebe ich durch den Tech-Sell-off viele Herausforderungen. Darüber spreche ich auch ganz offen in meinen Büchern und Auftritten. Ich hoffe, mein Lebensweg kann andere dazu inspirieren, große Ideen zu verfolgen und dafür auch mal Risiken einzugehen. Auch in meinen Unternehmen lebe ich eine gesunde Fehlerkultur. Mein Team arbeitet eigenverantwortlich, mit flachen Hierarchien und auf Augenhöhe. Mich begeistert die Chance mehr als der mögliche Fehltritt.

# ANGELA TITZRATH

Vorstandsvorsitzende
der Hamburger Hafen und Logistik AG

## Wie sehen Sie das Verhältnis zwischen der German Angst und der Notwendigkeit von Veränderungen, um aktuelle und zukünftige gesellschaftliche Herausforderungen zu bewältigen?

Wir Deutschen sind kein Volk der Angsthasen. Wir sind konsensorientiert und überlegt vorsichtig in unserem Tun. Dieses Bemühen um Maß und Mitte stabilisiert gleichzeitig unser demokratisches Gemeinwesen. Gründlichkeit vor Schnelligkeit ist häufig besser, als unkalkulierbare Risiken einzugehen. Dies ist sicherlich ein deutscher Wesenszug, der manchmal als German Angst interpretiert wird. Wir verfügen durchaus über die Fähigkeiten und Möglichkeiten, den Wandel voranzutreiben, insbesondere wenn es wirklich darauf ankommt, fokussiert und klar zu handeln. Es ist bemerkenswert, in welcher Geschwindigkeit beispielsweise der Impfstoff gegen Covid entwickelt und produziert wurde. Auch wie wir letztlich die Coronapandemie bewältigt haben, zeigt: Wir können notwendige Herausforderungen meistern.

## Welche gesellschaftlichen Entwicklungen oder Bewegungen machen Ihnen Mut für die Zukunft?

Mut ist die positive Energie, die wir benötigen, um die großen Herausforderungen, vor denen die Menschheit steht, zu bestehen. Ob Klimawandel, Auswirkungen der demografischen Entwicklung, die Folgen einer wachsenden Weltbevölkerung hinsichtlich Ernährung und Energieversorgung oder der Ressourcenverbrauch durch die Industriestaaten – es bedarf mutiger und verantwortungsvoller Entscheidungen in der Politik genauso wie in der Wirtschaft. Dass es eine Bewegung wie Fridays for Future geschafft hat, das Bewusstsein für ein höheres Tempo beim Klimaschutz zu schärfen, stimmt zuversichtlich. Auch die große Zahl an herausragenden wissenschaftlichen Leistungen auf dem Gebiet der Medizin und der Gesundheitsvorsorge beweist, dass wir Menschen selbst die stärkste Bewegung sind, um eine lebensfähige Zukunft zu schaffen.

## Worin sehen Sie die größten Hindernisse in unserer Gesellschaft, zuversichtlicher und mutiger zu denken und zu handeln?

Unsere Haltung ist entscheidend und ermöglicht oder verhindert mutiges Handeln. Wir haben von der Globalisierung profitiert, weil Produkte „Made in Germany" weltweit gefragt sind. Erfolgreich zu bleiben, ist jedoch eine kontinuierliche Aufgabe. Wir haben in den vergangenen Jahren die Arbeiten daran nicht mehr mit der Leidenschaft und Entschiedenheit vorangetrieben, wie es angesichts der globalen Veränderungen seit Ende der 1990er-Jahre notwendig gewesen wäre. Zu beobachten ist vielmehr ein verhängnisvolles Missverhältnis zwischen der Bereitschaft, eigenverantwortlich zu handeln, und einer inzwischen weitverbreiteten Ansicht, der Staat werde das schon alles regeln, insbesondere in Krisenzeiten. Wir können dankbar sein, dass durch staatliche Leistungen viele Menschen unterstützt werden können und das soziale Netz so engmaschig ist, dass niemand so schnell ins „Bergfreie" fällt, wie es im Ruhrgebiet heißt. Es gibt aber eine Kehrseite …

Die Fülle an Verordnungen und die vielen Möglichkeiten des juristischen Einspruchs bremsen Eigeninitiative und Selbstengagement. Dies gilt es auszubalancieren, denn das Entscheidungs- und Handlungstempo im globalen Wettbewerb um Lösungen ist weiterhin hoch. Ein bedenkliches Ergebnis ist beispielsweise Deutschlands Rückstand bei der Digitalisierung von Verwaltung und Infrastruktur. Auch der Zustand von Schulen und Hochschuleinrichtungen sowie die Qualität der Bildung müssen alarmieren. Als Land ohne Rohstoffe sind Investitionen in die Köpfe der Menschen unsere größte Chance, auch künftig zu den führenden Industrienationen zu zählen.

## Wie ermutigen Sie andere und sich selbst, etwas zu wagen?

Ich bin ein Kind des Ruhrgebiets. Ich habe miterlebt, wie sich diese Region verändert hat. Das war nicht immer eine Erfolgsstory, die sich auf dem Reißbrett planen lässt. Bei Rückschlägen heißt es: Ärmel hochkrempeln und weiter geht's. Diese Einstellung hat mich geprägt. Deshalb bestärke ich jeden, der etwas Neues wagen will. Ins Risiko gehen heißt auch dazuzulernen. Wichtig ist es, Freiräume zu schaffen, wo Neues jenseits von etablierten Prozessen ausprobiert werden kann. Ich habe großes Vertrauen in die Fähigkeit des Menschen, neue Wege zu gehen und mit Mut ins Tun zu kommen. Es ist unsere Haltung, die den Unterschied macht, denn wenn vieles ungewiss ist, dann ist auch vieles möglich.

# JOHAN VANDERMEULEN

Chief Transformation Officer, BAT plc
Aufsichtsratsvorsitzender,
BAT Germany Gruppe

**Wie sehen Sie das Verhältnis zwischen der German Angst und der Notwendigkeit von Veränderungen, um aktuelle und zukünftige gesellschaftliche Herausforderungen zu bewältigen?**

Seit einigen Jahren habe ich das Privileg, Aufsichtsratsvorsitzender von BAT Germany sein zu dürfen. Denke ich als Ingenieur an Deutschland, dann denke ich nicht nur an das Land der Dichter und Denker, sondern vor allem auch an das Land der Erfinder. Veränderungen können der Anlass für Erfindungen sein. Genauso können Erfindungen aber auch der Motor für Veränderungen sein. In einer von Ungewissheit und unablässigem Wandel gekennzeichneten Zeit sollten wir als Gesellschaft mutig und optimistisch innovative, nachhaltige Lösungen für unsere Zukunft gestalten. Mit unserem Unternehmen und unserem gesellschaftlichen Engagement, vor allem mit unserer Stiftung für Zukunftsfragen, widmen wir uns verantwortungsbewusst der Zukunft. Wir geben positive Impulse, um als Wegweiser und Weichensteller bereits heute auf das Morgen vorzubereiten.

**Welche gesellschaftlichen Entwicklungen oder Bewegungen machen Ihnen Mut für die Zukunft?**

Wir möchten bei BAT eine Kultur schaffen, die uns darin unterstützt, als Unternehmen erfolgreich zu sein und einen Beitrag für die Gesellschaft zu leisten. Die treibende Kraft dafür ist unser Ethos. Ein Ethos, das auf den ständigen Wandel reagiert und eine Lernkultur verkörpert, die sich der fortlaufenden Verbesserung verschrieben hat: bold, fast, empowered, responsible und diverse. Diese Werte nehme ich auch mehr und mehr in der Gesellschaft wahr. Mut, Optimismus, Solidarität, Eigenverantwortung sowie die Bereitschaft, das eigene Verhalten zum Wohle einer nachhaltigen Lebensweise zu hinterfragen.

### Worin sehen Sie die größten Hindernisse in unserer Gesellschaft, zuversichtlicher und mutiger zu denken und zu handeln?

Vom deutschen Dramatiker und Lyriker Friedrich Hebbel stammt das Zitat „Es gehört oft mehr Mut dazu, seine Meinung zu ändern, als ihr treu zu bleiben". Mutig zu denken und zu handeln, erfordert Offenheit. Offenheit im Sinne einer Bereitschaft, Veränderungen und Neues zuzulassen sowie bei Bedarf umzudenken. BAT hat einen klaren Unternehmenszweck definiert: eine bessere Zukunft, A Better Tomorrow™, aufzubauen, indem die gesundheitlichen Folgen des Geschäfts minimiert werden. Der Unternehmenszweck fußt auf dem Prinzip der Risikoreduzierung. Erwachsene Verbraucher sollten eine Wahl haben und in der Lage sein, eine informierte Entscheidung zu treffen. Ein Umfeld zu schaffen, das die durch das Rauchen verursachten Schäden klar benennt und gleichzeitig ganzheitlich und konsequent erkennt, wo echte Vorteile für die öffentliche Gesundheit erzielt werden können, erfordert die Bereitschaft, unsere Industrie als Teil der Lösung zu akzeptieren. Wenn das gelingt, bin ich davon überzeugt, dass wir die öffentliche Gesundheit verbessern können, indem wir durch das Konzept der Risikoreduzierung Schadensbegrenzung betreiben.

### Wie ermutigen Sie andere und sich selbst, etwas zu wagen?

Gestalten zu können, ist ein Privileg, aber auch eine Verantwortung. Diese Verantwortung wahrzunehmen, groß zu denken, innovativ zu sein, abweichende Standpunkte wertzuschätzen, sich gegenseitig zu fordern und zu fördern, Erfahrungen auszutauschen, sich selbst zu hinterfragen sowie mit Integrität zu handeln, bildet ein Rahmenwerk, das Wagnisse belohnt. So wird ermöglicht, dass am Ende nicht nur Ergebnisse stehen, sondern auch sinnhaft gehandelt wurde. Oder um es mit dem griechischen Philosophen Demokrit zu sagen: „Mut steht am Anfang des Handelns, Glück am Ende."

# MATTHIAS VOELKEL

CEO der Guppe Börse Stuttgart

**Wie sehen Sie das Verhältnis zwischen der German Angst und der Notwendigkeit von Veränderungen, um aktuelle und zukünftige gesellschaftliche Herausforderungen zu bewältigen?**

In unserer komplexen, volatilen Welt bestehen wir nur, wenn wir uns verändern. Gestalten statt Reagieren. Damit tun wir uns in Deutschland leider seit Jahren schwer. German Angst ist kein guter Ratgeber. Ich will aber nicht schwarzmalen. In Deutschland gibt es nach wie vor viele Macher und Unternehmer, die unaufgeregt das Richtige tun, wegweisende Innovationen hervorbringen und die Probleme unserer Zeit angehen. Dieses Land hat das Potenzial, sich politisch als wertegeleitete, aber nicht moralisierende Führungsmacht zu positionieren und sich ökonomisch und technologisch wieder an die Spitze zu setzen. Wenn wir dieses Potenzial heben und nicht länger hinnehmen, dass in vielen Bereichen auch German Mediokrität gedeiht, dann bin ich optimistisch. Die aktuelle Krise bietet uns die großartige Chance, uns neu zu erfinden.

**Welche gesellschaftlichen Entwicklungen oder Bewegungen machen Ihnen Mut für die Zukunft?**

Zum einen das Engagement und die Solidarität der Menschen in diesem Land. Ich denke zum Beispiel an die bewundernswerte Wiederaufbauleistung der Bewohner im Ahrtal nach der schrecklichen Katastrophe und die beeindruckende landesweite Solidaritätswelle. Zum anderen die Dynamik der Gründerszene. Nehmen wir das Ökosystem Digital Finance, das wir als Gruppe Börse Stuttgart europaweit mitgestalten: Kreative Gründer mit neuen Ideen treffen auf etablierte Unternehmen. Hier geschieht Digitalisierung, sodass sie nicht nur die Finanzmärkte, sondern auch unser tägliches Leben verbessern. Es macht mir Mut, so viel Energie für positive Veränderungen zu sehen.

### Worin sehen Sie die größten Hindernisse in unserer Gesellschaft, zuversichtlicher und mutiger zu denken und zu handeln?

Ich sehe den aufkommenden Etatismus und das stetige Wachsen staatlicher und quasi-staatlicher Strukturen als Hindernis. Wir brauchen nicht mehr Bürokratie, sondern smarte Regulierung. Ein weiteres Hindernis ist der Hang zum Dreiklang „Mahnen, Warnen, Besserwissen", dem einige deutsche Meinungsführer verhaftet sind. Nachdenken ist wichtig, keine Frage. Aber es ist ebenso wichtig, ein Gespür dafür zu entwickeln, wann es an der Zeit ist, Dinge auszuprobieren. Nach Moore's Law gibt es alle zwei Jahre einen exponentiellen Wachstumssprung der digitalen Leistungsfähigkeit. Hier dürfen wir die USA und China nicht weiter enteilen lassen. Auch ist unsere teils nabelschauende Selbstzufriedenheit ein Hindernis. Wir sollten uns fragen, ob unsere politische Grundausrichtung wirklich funktioniert. Bei der Energie- und Verteidigungspolitik erfolgt dies nach dem Schock des russischen Angriffskriegs gegen die Ukraine nun erfreulicherweise allmählich. Lassen Sie uns einen Schritt zurücktreten: Welches ambitionierte Land würde sich in politischen Grundsatzfragen wirklich an unserem Weg orientieren? Ich meine: nicht eines. Das sollte uns zu denken geben.

### Wie ermutigen Sie andere und sich selbst, etwas zu wagen?

Ich persönlich bin von Natur aus neugierig – Gestaltung erfüllt. Ich brauche also weniger Ermutigung. Andere ermutige ich, indem ich versuche, eine begeisternde Zukunftsvision zu zeichnen. Eines ist klar: Wer nichts wagt, dessen Zukunft wird von anderen bestimmt. Von denen, die etwas wagen. Unser Anspruch muss es sein, zur letzteren Gruppe zu gehören.

# FRANK WALTHES

Vorstandsvorsitzender
der Versicherungskammer Bayern

Wie sehen Sie das Verhältnis zwischen der German Angst und
der Notwendigkeit von Veränderungen, um aktuelle und zukünftige
gesellschaftliche Herausforderungen zu bewältigen?

Angst hat für mich ganz grundsätzlich zunächst etwas Positives, etwas Hilfreiches. Denken
Sie beispielsweise an Lampenfieber, als einer Ausprägung von Angst. Wenn man sich davon
nicht lähmen lässt und es als etwas Gutes, ja Normales annimmt, führt es dazu, dass man
sich besonders gut vorbereitet und viel konzentrierter an die Sache herangeht.
Die German Angst ist ja oft wenig fassbar, unkonkret, nebulös. Und doch hat sie sich zwi-
schenzeitlich gar international einen Namen gemacht, wenngleich wir wissen, dass sich die
meisten Befürchtungen der Deutschen in den vergangenen rund 70 Jahren nicht bewahr-
heitet haben. Vielfach ist German Angst eine historische Chimäre im kollektiven Gedächtnis
aller Deutschen und sie zeigt sich nicht selten im Attentismus, einer von Opportunismus
geprägten, abwartenden Haltung. Das empfinde ich als gefährlich. Gemeinschaftlich sollten
wir diese Angst zur Mobilisierung unserer (Abwehr-) Kräfte nutzen, initiativ werden und
den wirtschaftlichen und sozialen Zusammenhalt stärken. Zur Überwindung der Angst und
zur Bewältigung der Zustände, die diese Angst auslösen. Oft sind es Verlustängste, zumeist
Ängste vor Wohlstandseinbußen. Ich bin überzeugt, das wird nicht geschehen, da wir heute
eingebettet sind in vielerlei Bündnisse, wie EU oder NATO, und damit auf entsprechende
Solidarität und Unterstützung vertrauen dürfen.

### Welche gesellschaftlichen Entwicklungen oder Bewegungen machen Ihnen Mut für die Zukunft?

Wir haben im Zuge des russischen Angriffskriegs auf die Ukraine große Solidaritätsbekundungen in Europa erlebt. Die europäische Union steht zu den Rechtsstaatsprinzipien und handelt im Großen und Ganzen nach diesen. Ich sehe einen wirtschaftlichen und sozialen Zusammenhalt der freiheitlich-demokratischen Kräfte. Das sollte uns allen Mut machen und uns weiter in unserer Willenskraft bestärken, den Diskurs zu suchen und eine Einigung in der Wahl der Mittel gegen die zahlreichen Folgen der russischen Aggression zu finden.

### Worin sehen Sie die größten Hindernisse in unserer Gesellschaft, zuversichtlicher und mutiger zu denken und zu handeln?

Ich darf Nelson Mandela mit seinem Satz „Es scheint immer unmöglich, bis es erreicht ist" zitieren. Für wichtig bei uns halte ich die Bereitschaft und die Fähigkeit, soziale Grenzen zu überwinden und den Wert beziehungsweise das hohe Gut der Chancengleichheit zu erkennen. Hier sehe ich einen bedeutenden Hebel, wenn wir es schaffen, allen Bürgern Zukunftsperspektiven aufzuzeigen, unabhängig von ihrer sozialen Herkunft. Das setzt eine noch deutlich höhere Solidarität bei uns voraus, als wir sie heute kennen. Und ein weiterer Aspekt, den ich für eine stetige Weiterentwicklung unserer Gesellschaft für alternativlos halte, ist eine stärkere Diversität in allen Funktionen und Hierarchien. Wir brauchen diese Vielfalt, denn Menschen mit unterschiedlichen Erfahrungen, unterschiedlicher Herkunft und interkulturellen Kontakten bestärken sich gegenseitig deutlich mehr als homogene Zusammensetzungen. Es geht um interdisziplinäres, crossfunktionales und hierarchieübergreifendes Denken und Handeln.

### Wie ermutigen Sie andere und sich selbst, etwas zu wagen?

Zur Ermutigung kann ich nur Psalm 23 empfehlen.

# FALCO WEIDEMEYER

Head of EY-Parthenon EMEIA,
Global Head of Turnaround & Restructuring

Wie sehen Sie das Verhältnis zwischen der German Angst und
der Notwendigkeit von Veränderungen, um aktuelle und zukünftige
gesellschaftliche Herausforderungen zu bewältigen?

Es stimmt, die Deutschen sind oft nicht bekannt für Ihren Optimismus. Wir befragen alle
sechs Monate CEOs, was sie aktuell beschäftigt – und 98% der CEOs in Deutschland gaben
zuletzt an, dass sie mit einem Abschwung im Jahr 2023 rechnen, 57 Prozent sogar mit einem
starken Abschwung. Ich habe die German Angst allerdings nie als echte Ängstlichkeit gesehen, eher als tendenziell konservative Grundhaltung, gewissermaßen als Pfadabhängigkeit.
In diesem Bedürfnis nach Orientierung und in der Konsequenz, mit der Werte und Ziele verfolgt werden, kann auch eine Chance liegen. Denn eine Ergänzung des unternehmerischen
Zielsystems um ökologische, soziale und geopolitische Aspekte wird nötig sein – und die
folgende Transformation nicht einfach.

Die Beharrlichkeit, die eine hohe erste Hürde erzeugt, kann dann genau die Stärke sein, die
Unternehmen auf ihrem Weg nach vorn benötigen. Und auch die Zahlen zeigen: Zukunfts-
investitionen stehen weiterhin weit oben auf der Agenda deutscher CEOs. Jeder zweite
Befragte sagt, dass die Fortsetzung der digitalen und technologischen Transformation hohe
Priorität habe.

## Welche gesellschaftlichen Entwicklungen oder Bewegungen machen Ihnen Mut für die Zukunft?

Zwei Dinge – erstens die Tatsache, dass die großen sozialen und ökologischen Herausforderungen im „Mainstream" der politischen, gesellschaftlichen und wirtschaftlichen Diskussion angekommen sind, und zweitens die Relevanz, die diese Themen für die jüngere Generation haben. So entsteht ein „Push" und „Pull", das dazu führt, dass die Themen aus dem wirtschaftlichen, politischen und gesellschaftlichen Diskurs nicht wegzudenken sind.

## Worin sehen Sie die größten Hindernisse in unserer Gesellschaft, zuversichtlicher und mutiger zu denken und zu handeln?

In einer Gesellschaft, die eher nach Erleichterung statt nach Erlösung und eher nach Gemeinwohl statt nach Gemeinsamkeit strebt, ist unser lieb gewonnener Wohlstand die größte Hürde. In seiner jetzigen Form wird er sich womöglich nicht einfach weiter steigern lassen. Hier kann eine Neubestimmung nötig werden. Vielleicht ist das wirtschaftliche Wachstum etwas geringer, dafür sind aber der ökologische und soziale Ausgleich größer. Das hat Implikationen für Unternehmen und Individuen gleichermaßen – das Zielsystem der Unternehmen ergänzt finanzielle Ziele um soziale und ökologische; der ganz persönliche Begriff von Wohlstand oder Reichtum erweitert sich ebenfalls. Das ändert nichts an temporären Einbußen und Wachstumsdellen, aber es hilft, sie anders einzuordnen.

## Wie ermutigen Sie andere und sich selbst, etwas zu wagen?

Zunächst mit einer logischen Kette – wenn wir einmal unterstellen, dass die ökologischen- und sozialen Handlungsbedarfe existenziell sind und nicht einfach verschwinden, werden die Konsumenten und Märkte das eher früher als später integrieren – und dann wird es eine unternehmerische Notwendigkeit. Jedenfalls wenn man weiter Unternehmen finanzieren, Kunden begeistern und Mitarbeiter inspirieren will. Darüber hinaus mit der Tatsache, dass zwar die Transformation nur geschafft werden kann, wenn Konsumenten, die Regulatorik und Unternehmen gemeinsam umdenken, dass aber den Unternehmen eine besondere gestalterische Verantwortung zukommt. Und schließlich als Vater zweier Söhne – ich würde mir ungern vorwerfen lassen, Jahrzehnte auf Führung und Management von beratenen Unternehmen Einfluss genommen zu haben, ohne Impulse zu setzen.

# VOLKER WISSING

Bundesminister für Digitales und Verkehr, MdB

## Wie sehen Sie das Verhältnis zwischen der German Angst und der Notwendigkeit von Veränderungen, um aktuelle und zukünftige gesellschaftliche Herausforderungen zu bewältigen?

Es klafft eine Lücke zwischen dem, was wir uns vornehmen, und dem, was wir bereit sind, in unserem Leben zu verändern. Unsere Gesellschaft setzt sich extrem große Ziele. Wenn es aber in die konkrete Umsetzung geht, neigen viele dazu, darum zu kämpfen, dass alles so bleibt wie es ist. Daran müssen wir arbeiten. Denn ein grundlegender Wandel zum Beispiel hin zu klimaneutraler Mobilität bedeutet sehr weitreichende Veränderungen. Wir müssen uns daher als Gesellschaft ehrlich machen und klarstellen: Was können wir schaffen – und wo übernehmen wir uns? Wir müssen die Dinge so steuern, dass wir Veränderungen in dem Maße vorantreiben, wie die Gesellschaft bereit ist, sie zu tragen. Ansonsten laufen wir Gefahr, den Zusammenhalt innerhalb der Gesellschaft zu verlieren. Das wäre fatal. Wir alle sind aufeinander angewiesen.

## Welche gesellschaftlichen Entwicklungen oder Bewegungen machen Ihnen Mut für die Zukunft?

Unsere junge Generation macht mir Mut. Es gibt nichts Schlimmeres für eine Gesellschaft als eine orientierungslose Jugend. Wir aber haben eine, die weiß, was sie will, die politisch ist, sich einbringt – und auch eigene Wertvorstellungen entwickelt. Das ist eine Riesenchance